THE PRACTICE OF QUALITATIVE RESEARCH

Dedicated with love to Sarah Alexandra,
Julia Ariel, and Madeline Claire

THE PRACTICE OF QUALITATIVE RESEARCH

SHARLENE NAGY HESSE-BIBER
BOSTON COLLEGE

PATRICIA LEAVY
STONEHILL COLLEGE

SAGE Publications
Thousand Oaks ■ London ■ New Delhi

For information:

Sage Publications, Inc.
2455 Teller Road
Thousand Oaks, California 91320
E-mail: order@sagepub.com

Sage Publications Ltd.
1 Oliver's Yard
55 City Road
London EC1Y 1SP
United Kingdom

Sage Publications India Pvt. Ltd.
B-42, Panchsheel Enclave
Post Box 4109
New Delhi 110 017 India

Printed in the United States of America

Library of Congress Cataloging-in-Publication Data

Hesse-Biber, Sharlene Nagy.
The practice of qualitative research / Sharlene Nagy Hesse-Biber, Patricia Leavy.
    p. cm.
Includes bibliographical references and index.
ISBN 0-7619-2826-X (cloth) — ISBN 0-7619-2827-8 (pbk.)
    1. Social sciences—Research. 2. Qualitative research.
I. Leavy, Patricia, 1975- II. Title.
H62.H478 2006
001.4′2—dc22   2005008591

This book is printed on acid-free paper.

05   06   07   08   09   8   7   6   5   4   3   2   1

Acquisitions Editor:	Lisa Cuevas Shaw
Editorial Assistant:	Karen Wong
Production Editor:	Diane S. Foster
Copy Editor:	Peter McCurdy
Typesetter:	C&M Digitals, (P) Ltd.
Proofreader:	Joyce Li
Indexer:	Molly Hall
Cover Designer:	Ravi Balasuriya

CONTENTS

ACKNOWLEDGMENTS

In the work toward this book, we appreciate the help of a number of people who supported the endeavor. Thank you to the many scholars who let us "behind-the-scenes" with them and shared their personal stories about the qualitative research process. We are deeply grateful to our students at Boston College and Stonehill College, particularly those in our qualitative research methods courses, for their inspiration and support. We want to acknowledge the research assistance we received from so many. Thanks to Stonehill graduates Laura Kelly and Lauren Cucci for their help with the "suggested websites" sections of this book. We are grateful to Stonehill graduate Lauren Sardi for her help in conducting a literature review for the chapters on oral history and content analysis and contacting scholars for our Behind-the-Scenes sections in this book. We would particularly like to express a heartfelt thank-you and our deep gratitude to Stonehill students Paul Sacco and Laura MacFee for their unfailing support during all aspects of putting this book together. Paul and Laura, we thank you for your help conducting literature reviews, formatting, proofing, and so much more, including your good nature and humor. We are also grateful for the support we have received from the staff and administration of Stonehill College. In particular, thank you to Bonnie Troupe and Kathy Conroy for running the Summer Undergraduate Research Experience Program (SURE) through which we were able to obtain first-rate student research assistance for two years. Thank you to Katie Conboy, Vice President of Academic Affairs, and Karen Talentino, Dean of Faculty, for supporting this project and helping us with small grants and project equipment. Thank you to Stonehill College IT experts Gary Hammon and Glenn Everett who helped with the technical aspects of this project, such as creating charts and graphics. We want to especially thank Stephen Vedder, media specialist at Boston College, for his assistance with the graphic images. Sharlene Nagy Hesse-Biber is especially grateful to her family for their patience, love, and understanding during all phases of the preparation of this book. Sharlene dedicates this work to her exceptional daughters, Sarah Alexandra and Julia Ariel. Sharlene wants to thank her husband, Michael Peter Biber, M.D., for his support and encouragement.

Patricia Leavy is deeply grateful to her family and friends for their help, support, patience, inspiration, and humor during the preparation of this book. To DGR, Patricia says thank you. Patricia dedicates this work to her remarkable daughter Madeline Claire who makes each day special and reminds her that "marvelous things can happen." We are also grateful to our friend C. Deborah Laughton for her help with the book proposal. We want to acknowledge the enthusiastic support, encouragement and advice we received from the staff at SAGE Publications. In particular we extend a spirited thank-you to Alison Mudditt, Lisa Cuevas Shaw, Karen Wong, Peter McCurdy, and Margot Beth Crouppen.

The contributions of the following reviewers are gratefully acknowledged:

Kimberly Gregson	Park School of Communication, Ithaca College
Kathy Charmaz	Sonoma State University
Karen Kaminski, Ph.D.	Colorado State University
Monica Nandan	Missouri Western State College
Louis V. Paradise, Ph.D.	University of New Orleans

● CREDITS

The graphics in this book are Microsoft clipart and have been used in accord with their terms of use.

PREFACE

Qualitative research is not something that can simply be learned through written explanations alone. As all qualitative research practitioners and professors know, there is much more to understanding the practice of qualitative research than can be gleaned from a laundry list of methods. Qualitative research is a complex process that intimately links epistemology, theory, and method. In order to make this book user-friendly for students and scholars alike, and to get inside the practice of qualitative inquiry, we have included several distinct features in this book.

Inspired by Erving Goffman's creative concepts of "front stage" and "back stage," we began to realize that the information available in many research methods books represents the "front stage" of the research process. In other words, most research methods books present definitions of key terms and concepts followed by descriptions of research methods and models for how to design a research project. What this kind of approach fails to get at is the complexity of the *practice* of social research. What guides a researcher's topic selection? How do epistemological beliefs and theoretical commitments come to bear on the research process? What values, issues, and motivations do researchers bring to their projects? How do ethics play out in practice? What are the emotional aspects of a research project *really like?* Why do some researchers select particular methods and how do those methods enable their research? In an attempt to get at some of these issues, we have conducted in person, e-mail, and telephone interviews with a diverse range of well-respected researchers and scholars. The material they have given us, which many wrote as a short piece, is included throughout the book in what we call "Behind-the-Scenes" boxes. These boxes offer a glimpse behind the curtain of qualitative research—a window into the researcher's vantage point.

In addition to Behind-the-Scenes segments with scholars, we have also included the following material:

- *Suggested websites* so that students and scholars can continue to research topics of interest, looking at up-to-date work in the field.
- *Discussion questions* created and tested by undergraduate students, aimed at generating further thinking about key issues, group discussions, and practice work with the various methods and methodologies reviewed.
- *Glossary of terms* that will help to solidify student learning of key concepts contained within each chapter.
- *In-depth examples* carried through each chapter, such as our staple example of studying body image from a variety of theoretical frameworks and with various research methods, so that students and scholars alike can see how different approaches to a particular topic allow a researcher to ask certain questions and gain particular kinds of insights.

We strongly believe that learning needs to engage each reader on multiple levels as they enter into a new area of study and it is hoped that this book will especially promote the adventurous spirit that is contained within each researcher. We provide a journey through our book that challenges your intellect, draws on your multiple emotions, expands your technical and creative skills, as well as uplifting your understanding of the nature of social reality. Let the journey begin!

PART I

THE QUALITATIVE PARADIGM

CHAPTER 1

THE CRAFT OF QUALITATIVE RESEARCH

A Holistic Approach

Imagine an epidemic is sweeping the globe, but this epidemic is like none ever seen before. The disease causing this epidemic has devastating physical consequences, and, unlike many other diseases, it includes a period often referred to as "living dying." Sadly, there is no cure for this debilitating illness, and the mortality rate is increasing to such an extent that some populations are losing significant numbers of people. Without a cure, the outlook is bleak. But well beyond the devastating transmission and mortality rates of the disease is what really makes it unlike other diseases: the social meanings and stigma attached to infection, which vary across cultures. Beyond the social repercussions of the illness is a series of educational, health, and economic realities not associated with epidemics such as cancer that accompany this often long-term illness. Moreover, even family structures are altered by this disease, as roles are reversed, and young people are the ones getting sick, and seniors and sometimes children must care for the dying. And this is just the tip of the iceberg. Of course we all know that we don't have to "imagine" such an epidemic, we have one: human immunodeficiency virus/acquired immunodeficiency syndrome (HIV/AIDS), from which no group is immune.

Now imagine how desperately researchers from across disciplines (the social sciences, healthcare, education, and communications) would want to build knowledge about the disease and its various facets, including its social dimension and effective prevention and intervention strategies. For example, the medical community has acquired enough knowledge about the disease and its transmission that we now understand it to be a preventable illness. But how is this knowledge communicated differently to different groups in a global context? Moreover, despite the preventable nature of the illness, we are faced with a global epidemic. This raises a host of questions, such as: why do some people engage in risky sexual behavior, how does sexual identity shape sexual decision making, how does social context (education, geography, sexism, heterosexism) impact people's intimate relationships and their sexuality? Why doesn't sexually transmitted disease (STD) education in the United States seem to work? These are just a few of the questions that arise in trying to understand the HIV/AIDS epidemic. There are many other research questions that emerge when considering the *experience* of HIV/AIDS, from both a physical and social perspective. For example, what does it feel like to test positive, how does a positive diagnosis shape personal and sexual relationships as well as identity, what is the daily experience of a positive diagnosis in terms of the social stigma attached to the disease? There is also the *experience* of caring for a loved one with HIV/AIDS, which varies cross-culturally and often involves a restructuring of the family, financial challenges, and so forth.

The preceding represents just some of the questions researchers confront surrounding this social issue. These kinds of questions can only be asked and answered by working through the qualitative window into knowledge construction. These questions begin with words like "why," "how," and "what." They require gaining complex knowledge directly from people with certain attributes or life experiences—knowledge about their experience and the contexts influencing their relations to others, behavioral choices, and attitudes. These are the kinds of questions that can be answered by qualitative approaches to research. By the time we return to this example in the concluding chapter, we hope that you will see how integral qualitative research is to our knowledge about HIV/AIDS and many other important issues.

● INTRODUCTION

Many research books present a series of "methods"—techniques for gathering data. While this is an important component of the research process, the appropriate selection of research methods cannot be divorced from a researcher's theoretical concerns as well as his or her conception of knowledge building. Accordingly, this book is different from most other books about research methods in that we begin with an in-depth discussion of the knowledge-building process—*holistically.* That is to say, we first discuss all aspects of the knowledge-building process, of which method is one part. To talk about particular methods before talking about the assumptions about what is knowable, who is a knower, and how we come to know would be to put the cart before the horse. So, in this vein, in Part I we move into a discussion of the two major approaches to knowledge construction, then into a discussion of research design, including method selection, and end with a review of ethics and research. Additionally, while qualitative research methods vary greatly, what the perspectives covered in this text have in common is that they challenge positivistic views of knowledge building. Part II is devoted to an examination of particular methods.

Qualitative research is an exciting interdisciplinary landscape rich with perspectives on knowledge construction and enabled by a multitude of techniques available for generating knowledge. Qualitative practice offers a range of epistemological, theoretical, and methodological possibilities. With attention to the holistic nature of knowledge building, qualitative research is truly unique in content, focus, and form. When we say that the craft of qualitative research involves a *holistic* approach, we mean that the practice of qualitative research is reflexive and *process driven,* ultimately producing culturally situated and theory-enmeshed knowledge through an ongoing interplay between theory and methods, researcher and researched. Specifically, qualitative research differs from research models that focus on the creation of knowledge in a contained and event-oriented manner. As we will show, the holistic nature of the research process, the interplay between different phases of it, from topic selection to write-up, makes qualitative research a unique and important perspective and practice. Moreover, qualitative research produces both exploratory and highly descriptive knowledge while deemphasizing the solely causal models and explanations that have historically dominated the research process.

More than a concept or a series of techniques that can simply be employed, qualitative research is an intellectual, creative, and rigorous craft that the practitioner not only learns but also develops. In order to understand what qualitative researchers do and the craft of this practice, we must first be able to distinguish qualitative research as a particular and distinct terrain. In order to do so we must compare and contrast the qualitative approach with its quantitative counterpart. While there are many theoretical and practical differences *within* the field of qualitative research, for the time being we assume the qualitative and quantitative approaches to be two different general points of view—two unique groundings, two different ways of asking questions, two particular ways of thinking. Juxtaposing these conceptualizations of knowledge building also reveals a historical push-pull relationship between the qualitative and quantitative groundings. This back-and-forth struggle remains a dynamic component in researchers' decision-making practices. By distinguishing between the qualitative and quantitative approaches, we will also begin to home in on the distinct contributions of qualitative research specifically related to our conceptions of knowledge and its creation. As we will show, the qualitative approach offers a whole new way of thinking about social reality.

In order to illuminate the difference between qualitative and quantitative research, an illustrative example may be helpful. After setting up an in-depth example, we will break down the differences in the quantitative and qualitative approaches, revealing the key assumptions and choices embedded within the example and how they reflect a historical struggle between seemingly disparate ways of knowing.

● QUALITATIVE AND QUANTITATIVE APPROACHES TO THE STUDY OF BODY IMAGE

Quantitative research is often privileged as "hard" science. A quantitative researcher relies on numbers, rates, and percentages typically presented in a table, grid, or chart in order to communicate meaning (Hesse-Biber & Leavy, 2004, p. 1). For illustrative purposes, let's use body image as our research subject. A quantitative researcher might approach the study of body image and body dissatisfaction by constructing a survey consisting of multiple-choice questions, each with a finite number of possible responses (the Likert-type scale is often used). The survey, a quantitative instrument, would then be distributed to a preselected sample of respondents for completion. The researcher's process is dependent on identifying a set of factors that "get at," or measure, body image dissatisfaction and then constructing survey questions that elicit data on each identified body dissatisfaction indicator. The quantitative researcher might then display the survey data in the form of statistics on a chart or graph. The researcher's interpretation is based on successfully identifying a set of variables that contribute to people's body satisfaction.

For example, Banfield and McCabe sought to better define the term *body image* and obtain data on the particular dimensions of body image (2002, p. 373). In accord with their goals, they constructed two surveys designed to measure the four factors previously hypothesized to constitute body image (p. 373). Based on their literature review they identified (1) perception, (2) affect, (3) cognition, and (4) behavior as the four key dimensions of body image and their subsequent analysis was dependent on asking questions aimed at accessing data about each of these four dimensions. The questions were compiled from 10 body image instruments that have been deemed valid (p. 375). The scale was closed-ended and relied on a Likert-type scale where respondents had five possible response choices. Banfield and McCabe presented the resulting data in several statistical tables.

A qualitative researcher would approach the topic of body image in very different ways. For example, a qualitative researcher might be interested in conducting in-depth interviews with college-aged women in order to better understand how they experience body image and the ways that their own body image identity has been shaped and now continues to shape their lives. In this circumstance, the researcher would ask a series of open-ended questions about the interviewees's self-image, such as how their self-image has developed, what *they view* as the significant cultural factors and social relationships that impact their body image, the locations and manifestations of pressures regarding physical appearance, their behavioral and emotional strategies for dealing with their body perception, and what *they view* as the fundamental factors in their own lives related to positive and negative body perceptions. In order to understand the meaning that the women attach to body image within their lived experiences, the researcher's point of origin *is* the perspective of the women being studied. In other words, the researcher seeks descriptive data from the research participants—they are the origin of the data and also to a large extent influence where the emphasis will be placed during data collection.

A qualitative researcher interested in studying how women of various racial, ethnic, and social class backgrounds interpret body image and what they define as the key factors in their own relationships with their body identity and their social environment might consider conducting focus group interviews in order to explore the topic. As a part of a larger qualitatively driven body image study we have used focus groups and other qualitative interview methods in order to gain descriptive data on body image from the perspective of different groups, including female college students. Hesse-Biber (1995–1999) conducted one such focus group interview with local female college students in order to understand their body image issues and related aspirations, both in terms of their looks and the rest of their lives. After learning that being "beautiful/pretty" was important to several participants, she asked an open-ended follow-up question in order to gain greater understanding of what the respondents meant: "So what does it mean, do you think, to look pretty?" One participant, who must remain anonymous, responded as follows:

> Yeah, when the final comes down to the whole point of my issue with eating, I think is that (A) I want to look like I'm so affected by glamour

magazines and *Vogue*, and all that, because that's a line of work I want to get into. I'm looking at all these beautiful women. They're thin. I want to be just as beautiful. I want to be just as thin. Because that is what guys like.

And I want guys to be attracted to me. And my final affirmation of how pretty I am, and how thin, and what a great body I have, is when guys look at me and what guys think. (Hesse-Biber, 1995–1999, p. 14)

As you can see, this data is detailed and guided by the respondent's own interpretation and what she felt to be meaningful. A qualitative researcher might interpret this data by looking for themes grounded in the respondent's words. This qualitative approach to interpretation requires the researcher to tend to the text and spend time with the respondent's words in order to construct a critical theme that is derived from the perspective of the respondent. Qualitative researchers are concerned with text and words as opposed to numbers. Thus, qualitative researchers build and analyze themes embedded within transcripts they have helped create such as, in the case of our focus group, data or preexisting texts. This is because qualitative researchers are after *meaning*. The development of themes and thematic categories is a way qualitative researchers try to extract meaning from their data. Researchers think of these themes as "codes"—a concept which we will discuss in detail later. In terms of the transcript excerpt, the response, later coded as "wants to be beautiful" and "values thinness" (which are themes), reflects the respondent's aspirations for weight and appearance as related to other assumptions, beliefs, and aspirations—she relates being "pretty" and thin to her career and romantic/relational desires. This data then has a depth of social meaning. This descriptive data, derived from the participant's viewpoint, contextualizes the participant's feelings about beauty/thinness in relation to her other aspirations. So, the qualitative approach produces meaning that does not result from the quantitative surveys.

The data yielded by focus groups, such as in the preceding example, could stand alone or could help shape intensive interview or oral history questions conducted on a one-on-one basis, both of which generate highly descriptive data and lead to understanding/meaning in a process-orientated way. A multimethod qualitative design like that yields both exploratory and descriptive data on the way personal body image is experienced and interpreted by those living with one. And, as we will discuss in more detail later in the book, the two research methods in this example don't merely augment each other but also interact with and influence each other.

A qualitative researcher interested in examining the relationship between race and body image issues might conduct focus groups or in-depth interviews in order to access data about body image from the viewpoint of the research participants. This is particularly important when studying the relationship between race and body image, because data on body image disturbance has traditionally been derived from white (middle and upper-class) samples, resulting in a presumption that white middle and upper-class females are the most vulnerable to poor body image and related issues such as eating disorders. If we imposed previously validated questionnaires on our research, the assumption that ethnic and racial minorities are protected from body image disturbance might be inaccurately reified. This is because those measurement instruments may ask questions that are indicators for the kinds of body image issues white girls and women have and may not ascertain the specific body image issues faced by women of other racial and ethnic groups. This was illustrated in focus groups conducted by Hesse-Biber in which she found that young black girls had a range of different body image concerns than their white counterparts. Specifically, the black girls had many issues pertaining to their hair rather than the desire for thinness that usually plagues white girls (Hesse-Biber, Leavy, & Yaiser, 2004).

The quantitative researcher can also examine body dissatisfaction differences in terms of race and ethnicity; however, this dimension of their design would be based solely on stratifying their sample (the survey respondents) in terms of racial identification, which could be done by ascertaining general demographic information with the questionnaire. Molloy and Herzberger (1998) wanted to know how women's body perception differs based on race and ethnicity. They hypothesized that black American women would be more satisfied with their physical appearance than white American women. In this vein, they surveyed 114 women from two community colleges and stratified their sample based on race, resulting in 45 black and 69 white respondents. The results supported their hypothesis that black women exhibited less body disturbance (of the kinds measured) than their white counterparts. Other examples of studies using survey data stratified on the basis of race, ethnicity, and gender, from which statistical data results, include: Abrams and Cook Stormer, 2002; Chamorro and Flores-Ortiz, 2000; Chandler, Abood, Lee, Cleveland, & Daly, 1994; Falconer and Neville, 2000; Nielsen, 2000. We caution you to be wary of the assumption that non-white women are somehow protected from eating disorders and body dissatisfaction, as some scholars indicate that women of color may in fact be more vulnerable to body disturbance (Thompson, 1996). Likewise, since the majority of research on body image has been conducted on white samples, it is quite possible that new instruments are needed in order to understand how women of color experience body image and body disturbance. It may not be adequate to add women of color to these preexisting models—exploratory qualitative research may produce important insights into this as well. The following list shows, in a general way, the steps a qualitative researcher might follow as compared with a quantitative researcher.

Qualitative Model	Quantitative Model
1. Topical Area	1. Formulate a Research Question
2. Analyze Subset of Data	2. Develop a Hypothesis
3. Generate Codes (Literal to Abstract)	3. Define Variables
4. Reanalyze Data; Analyze Additional Data	4. Construct Measurement Instrument
5. Memo Notes	5. Coding
6. Analyze Additional Data	6. Sampling (Random Sampling)
7. Refine Codes; Generate Meta-Codes	7. Reliability and Validity Checks
8. Analyze Additional Data	8. Statistical Check (if necessary)
9. Embodied Interpretation	9. Calculate Results
10. Representation	10. Represent Results (typically on charts or graphs)

When determining if your research project will engage with a quantitative or qualitative design (or a combination of the two), you must first ask:

- What is the primary research question?
- What part of social reality do I want to get at?

If you are interested in predicting and controlling numbers (those that indicate how many or how much) and/or the relationships between variables and any intervening factors (such as race), a quantitative design will yield the kind of data you are looking for. In other words, a quantitative approach is suited to answering the research questions as you have framed them. A quantitative approach answers what you want to know and what you think you can know. For example, a researcher interested in predicting whether, and to what degree, gender is a good indicator of eating disorder vulnerability, would ask: to what degree does gender predict eating disorder susceptibility? As we saw from the quantitative studies of body image, quantitative approaches are useful for identifying potential causal relationships, such as the link between gender and body image disturbance, while accounting for mediating factors such as race, ethnicity, sexuality, and social class (if these dimensions are built into the research design). The nature of these relationships, and the social conditions from which these patterns flow, as well as individual agency and experience, may remain unknown in a solely quantitative study, however.

The comparative example of studying body image from a qualitative versus quantitative approach illustrates that qualitative research is about understanding social meaning while quantitative research focuses on patterns and predictability.

> Most quantitative data techniques are data condensers. They condense data in order to see the big picture. . . . Qualitative methods, by contrast, are best understood as data enhancers. When data are enhanced, it is possible to see key aspects of cases more clearly. (Charles Ragin, 1994, p. 92, as quoted by Neuman, 1997, pp. 14–15)

In other words, quantitative research produces a *quantity* of data—generalizability—whereas qualitative researchers are after *depth* in their data and analysis rather than quantity. An overall difference between qualitative and quantitative research is already evidenced, so now we return to our illustrative body image research example in order to explore the assumptions, beliefs, and practices brought to bear by each approach. This discussion is situated in a historical discussion of positivism, the concept of objectivity, and the interrelated development of qualitative inquiry. In other words, we explain how the body image research example shown from the quantitative and qualitative viewpoints actually reflects large-scale struggles over, and transformations within, the knowledge-building process.

● POSITIVISM, OBJECTIVITY, AND THE
RESEARCH NEXUS: THE QUALITATIVE
AND QUANTITATIVE APPROACHES

The positivist view of social reality has historically dominated knowledge construction, and positivism is the epistemological basis of the quantitative paradigm—it was long seen as the only credible approach to inquiry, with its objective reliance on the "scientific method." We will look at epistemology more generally and then address positivism and alternative models that have developed in opposition to the tenets of positivist epistemology.

Epistemology

Both the qualitative and quantitative approaches are infused with *epistemology* (Hesse-Biber & Leavy, 2004, p. 2). An e*pistemology* is "a theory of knowledge" (Harding, 1987, p. 3). Drawing on the work of Crotty (1998), Creswell elaborates on the preceding definition and says an epistemology is "a theory of knowledge embedded in a theoretical perspective" (2003, p. 4) which informs all aspects of the research process. In other words, an epistemology is a philosophical belief system about who can be a knower and what can be known (Harding, 1987; Guba & Lincoln, 1998; Hesse-Biber & Leavy, 2004). Beyond asking who can be a knower and what can be known, epistemology addresses how knowledge is created: an epistemological position lays the foundation for the knowledge-building process. The conscious and unconscious questions, assumptions, and beliefs that the researcher brings to the research endeavor serve as the initial basis for an epistemological position. Actions within the research process are, like all human endeavors, influenced by previously held attitudes. We research what we believe to be knowable and in ways that we believe will be effective—both of which are reflections of our epistemological position.

For example, what the researcher assumes to be true or relevant about body image, what she or he assumes can be known, and what she or he wants to know about body image, are the foundation of an epistemology. Molloy and Herzberger believed there was a direct relationship between race and body disturbance vulnerability. This assumption, which developed into a hypothesis, guided all aspects of their research, including topic selection and question formulation. Likewise, Hesse-Biber assumed that women attach multiple meanings to their body-related goals and feelings which can best be understood from their own vantage point, and this impacted all phases of her body image study. The researcher's epistemological position will impact every aspect of the research process, including topic selection, question formulation, method selection, theoretical backdrop, and methodology. Some of the specific choices influenced include:

- Who will be included in the study of body image (gender, age, racial/ ethnic diversity, sexual orientation, socioeconomic status)?
- What aspect of body image are we trying to explain (sociocultural, economic, psychological, medical, behavioral, attitudinal, perceptual)?
- How will we attempt to get at the lived experiences related to our topic, and how will we make sense of and communicate the resulting knowledge?

If we are trying to measure causal relationships between demographic factors such as gender and race and the prevalence of eating disorders, we are asking a quantitative question which already bears several assumptions regarding the nature of social reality.

Positivist Epistemology and Objectivity

The epistemology through which quantitative practice developed as the model of "science" is important to understand. Positivist science holds several basic beliefs about the nature of knowledge, which together form *positivist epistemology,* the cornerstone of the quantitative paradigm. Positivism holds that there is a knowable reality that exists independent of the research process. The social world, similar to the natural world, is governed by rules, which result in patterns. Accordingly, causal relationships between variables exist and can even be identified, proven, and explained. Thus, patterned social reality is predictable and can potentially be controlled. This describes the nature of social reality from the positivist perspective. The quantitative approach to the study of body image can be understood as a manifestation of these assumptions: there is a knowable, predictable reality that exists "out there" constituted by clear causal relationships, such as patterned and predictable relationships between gender and race and multiple dimensions of eating disorder vulnerability identified as existing regardless of the research process and subsequently "tested" in our earlier example. So far we have been describing the nature of social reality according to positivism, but we must go further to also examine assumptions about *the relationship between that reality and the researcher who aims to explain it.*

Positivism places the researcher and the researched, or knower and what is knowable, on different planes within the research process. The researcher and the researched, or subject and object, are conceptualized in a dichotomous model. Not only is there a rigid division between the subject and the object, but the division is also a *hierarchical* division in which the researcher is privileged as the knower. This is particularly important in the social sciences, where data is largely derived from human subjects who, under this framework, become viewed as objects for research processes: they are acted on by others—the knowers. For example, the surveys used to gather data in our quantitative example were given to human subjects who, in the positivist worldview, are transformed into knowable objects of inquiry.

The quantitative study of body image described in our survey-driven research example can be understood as a manifestation of positivism and its employment of the term "objectivity." This is evidenced by the assumptions that (1) a knowable reality exists independent of the research process, such as causal links between gender and race and body dissatisfaction, and (2) the division between the subject and object is a necessary part of the discovery of knowledge, as seen by the researcher constructing and then uniformly distributing questionnaires to research participants. Positivism has a particular view of "objectivity," which is infused into the research process during all phases of it, whether on conscious or subconscious levels. Positivist epistemology assumes that there is an objective reality "out there" which can be explained by objective value-free researchers through the use of objective replicable methods. In other words, reality is objective and can be empirically studied/tested by value-neutral researchers. Researchers, like respondents, are then easily replaced for the purposes of replicating research. The researcher is assumed to be unbiased, emotionless, and nonpolitical during knowledge construction. This conception of knowledge, particularly the implications of this kind of reliance on objectivity, has generated resistance from the research community from the outset, culminating in the growing field of qualitative research.

Alternative Ideas About the Nature of Social Reality

Early on, the *hermeneutic tradition,* more commonly referred to as the *interpretive perspective,* developed as a direct challenge to positivist epistemology and its interpretation/application of objectivity. The interpretive epistemology is based on the interpretation of interactions and the social meaning that people assign to their interactions (Nielsen, 1990, p. 7). This perspective epistemologically believes that social meaning is created during interaction. The implication is that different social actors may in fact understand social reality differently, producing different meanings and analyses. Moreover, this perspective on knowledge building is based on observational and interactional ways of knowing. Research of this kind involves the building of relationships between the researcher and research participants, who are collaborators in the research process. Reciprocal relationships between subjective participants (both the researcher and the researched) were not always considered a part of interpretive practice. Schutz (1967; Schult & Luckmann, 1974) pioneered the interpretive perspective, and, while he legitimized the idea that human action could not be understood devoid of the meaning attached to it, he nonetheless endorsed a positivist subject–object split by urging researchers to "bracket" their subjectivity while engaged in research (Nielsen, 1990, p. 8). Feminists as well as critical theorists, as we discuss in more detail later, challenged this notion of "bracketing" and developed new models of knowledge building based on subjectivity, reciprocity, and process.

The hermeneutic perspective combats the positivist notion of objectivity in several ways, each of which reflects a different conception of knowledge construction. Social reality is not conceived of as "out there" waiting to be discovered and measured, but rather it is relational and subjective, produced during the research process. The researcher is not assumed to be value-neutral and "objective" but rather an active participant, along with the research subjects, in the building of descriptive, exploratory, and explanatory knowledge. Likewise, the value of the research is not based on whether it is replicable, but rather on how it adds to our substantive knowledge on a particular subject. The interpretive tradition developed in opposition to the assumptions of positivism and continues to offer strong resistance against positivist conceptions of the research endeavor. This is an example of how there has always been resistance to positivism and the quantitative approach it fuels based on epistemological grounds. Research conducted from the interpretive perspective produces qualitative results in the form seen in the body image focus group data. The problem for researchers who do not subscribe to positivist assumptions is that their research is often devalued. The data produced by the quantitative study of body image was generalizable and replicable and claimed to identify key causal relationships between sociocultural factors and body dissatisfaction vulnerability. This data is often popularly referred to as "hard" and "scientific," giving it a sense of legitimacy within research and academic communities. The descriptive data yielded from the qualitative focus groups would typically be characterized as "soft" and therefore less "scientific." Likewise the quantitative data is assumed to be "generalizable" to larger populations and thus "representative." By contrast, qualitative data such as that seen from our focus group transcripts is often referred to as "representational" or "constructed," which implies it is less scientific and therefore less rigorous and less important. These stereotypical hierarchical ways of thinking about qualitative research in relation to quantitative research should be recognized and avoided. The longstanding bias which favors positivism over other ways of knowing, and its implications for qualitative researchers, will become clearer when we look at methods of data collection. For now let's look at the qualitative approach in terms of its epistemological options.

Qualitative knowledge is produced from a variety of rich perspectives on social reality. While they share attentiveness to interpretation, they also focus on different aspects of social reality, such as women's perspectives, conflict, popular culture, and so on. For example, feminist perspectives often focus on the social, cultural, and economic status of women locally and globally. Postmodern perspectives are frequently applied to the qualitative study of popular culture and mass media, while those working from critical perspectives are likely to focus on the micropolitics of power in a variety of politically charged contexts. We will discuss these perspectives in more detail later in this chapter, but for now it is important to understand that the qualitative approach is enriched by multiple traditions beyond the umbrella interpretive approach. These traditions include positivism, postpositivism, interpretive, phenomenology, ethnomethodology, feminist, postmodern, poststructural, postcolonial, critical, and standpoint. Qualitative research is an exciting and unique terrain in part *because* it is characterized by a diverse range of epistemological positions and thus asks many kinds of social scientific questions, both questions previously addressed in other ways and those not asked before, and it asks old questions in new and complex ways. As seen by the body image focus group transcripts, qualitative research allows for "thick descriptions" of social life (Geertz, 1973) compared to the generalizable but often flat data produced by quantitative surveys. As we saw by comparing positivism to the interpretive perspective, not only does epistemology address assumptions about the nature of knowledge and the knower, but it also addresses assumptions about the relationship *between* the knower and what can be known, or put differently, the researcher and subject of the research (Guba & Lincoln, 1998, p. 201). When deciding whether your body image study will use a qualitative approach, you must give serious weight to what the nature of the relationship will be between the researcher and the research participants within the study. Will the relationship be based on a hierarchical division between researcher and researched, as prescribed by positivism, or will it be based on a reciprocal relationship built through rapport, such as is prescribed by the interpretive tradition, or will it take some other configuration? An analysis of positivism and its alternatives shows that these choices are not made arbitrarily but rather they are intimately linked to belief systems about how human beings produce knowledge through varied degrees and forms of interaction—this guiding belief system is the bedrock of an epistemology.

Epistemology and Theory

As Creswell explains (2003), an epistemology is embedded within a *theoretical perspective.* We could also say that an epistemology is tied to or intimately linked to a theory, or, that epistemological beliefs are enacted through a theoretical frame. In general terms, theory is an account of social reality or some component of it that extends further than what has been empirically investigated, such as body image dissatisfaction (Hesse-Biber & Leavy, 2004, p. 3). Social theory is always a part of the research process. Theory is particularly important in the practice of qualitative research because generating, building, and refining theory is one of its prime goals. The empirical data collected during a specific study can be generalized to larger social phenomena through the building of social theory. Qualitative researchers do not just use theory, they also create it. Our focus group data on body image is an example of how thematic coding and analysis can lead to theory creation. In that instance, after extracting themes from the transcript, we had several themes that seemed to relate to a larger theme concerning aspirations and body image. It was there that theory developed, as we used our empirical data to derive larger statements about the relationships between a range of personal aspirations and body disturbance vulnerability.

Researchers apply theory throughout the research process, and their theoretical perspective is linked with their epistemological beliefs. Research, in a general sense, can be conducted using a deductive or inductive approach. Whether a project relies on deductive or inductive logic is directly linked to how theory is conceived of and used in it, and whether new theory is generated. *Deductive approaches* are typically used in positivist quantitative research and involve testing theory.

> In *quantitative* studies, one uses theory deductively and places it toward the beginning of the plan for a study. With the objective of testing or verifying a theory rather than developing it, the researcher advances a theory, collects data to test it, and reflects on the confirmation or disconfirmation of the theory by the results. The theory becomes a framework for the entire study, an organizing model for the data collection procedure. . . . The researcher tests or verifies a theory by examining hypotheses or questions derived from the theory. (Creswell, 2003, pp. 125–126)

This is very different from the inductive approaches to research that are typically used by qualitative researchers. Qualitative researchers are interested in generating theory. With this in mind, qualitative researchers often rely on *inductive models* where the theory develops directly out of the data. One such model often used by interpretive and feminist researchers (though not exclusively or uniformly) is grounded theory. While we discuss this in more detail later in the book when we consider approaches to analysis and writing, under this approach theory develops directly out of the empirical data. In other words, by using the narratives produced in interviewing, ethnography, or texts (in the case of content analysis), qualitative researchers who use inductive approaches use the empirical data to develop larger theories about social life that emerge from the people who experience the aspect of social reality being studied. These issues will be fleshed out later. However, for now it is important to understand the key difference between testing and generating theory or deductive versus inductive ways of knowing, as these basic research models have multiple implications for the nature of knowledge itself. The relationship between theory and epistemology is perhaps best illustrated through a research example.

For example, if we were to study the relationship between patriarchal capitalist culture and body disturbance among girls and women, we might employ a radical feminist theoretical perspective. This theoretical framework involves a critique of patriarchy as the source of physical and other forms of "violence" against girls and women—including patriarchal beauty standards (Ritzer, 2000, p. 462). In other words, this theoretical perspective assumes a general relationship between women's oppression and contemporary beauty standards that reflect and are otherwise tied to patriarchal capitalist interests (Hesse-Biber, 1996). A feminist epistemological position would likely be guiding and shaping the employment of this radical feminist theoretical frame. This means that we bring certain assumptions to bear on the project, including the notion that it is possible to know the relationship between macro patriarchal practices and body image disturbance as experienced on both macro and micro levels of analysis. Furthermore, we assume that women can be knowers, women's concerns can be the locus of analysis, and social reality is already mediated by patriarchal and capitalist ways of seeing the world, which must be brought to light and diffused. This becomes clearer in Chapter 2 when we discuss "paradigms" or "worldviews."

Methods as Research Tools

When people talk about research, the focus is very often on methods of data collection; however, *research methods* are intimately linked to epistemology and theory. Qualitative researchers have been at the fore-front of explicitly acknowledging and engaging with the link between method and theory, as opposed to disavowing it. Methods are the tools that researchers use in order to gather data. These techniques for learning about social reality allow us to gather data using individuals, groups, and multimedia texts as our sources. Sandra Harding defines research methods in the following way:

> A research method is a technique for . . . gathering evidence. One could reasonably argue that all evidence-gathering techniques fall into one of the three categories: listening to (or interrogation) informants, observing behavior, or examining historical traces and records. (1987, p. 2)

Qualitative researchers often use one or more of the following methods (though this is not an exclusive list): ethnography, in-depth interviewing, oral history, autoethnography, focus group interviewing, case study, discourse analysis, and content analysis. As you can see, qualitative researchers employ a diverse range of methods, making the possible research topics and questions as vast as our imaginations. The quantitative approach lends itself to a different set of research methods, which are typically experiments, surveys/questionnaires, evaluation, content analysis, and statistical analysis. Since the quantitative approach is based on positivist assumptions (though researchers of other epistemological positions, including feminism, also use quantitative designs), methods of measurement are appropriate to this epistemological and theoretical belief system, which guides method selection and implementation. Accordingly, these are the methods that allow for hypothesis testing and ultimately produce quantitative numerical results. Some researchers might label qualitative and quantitative methods in stereotypical ways. Thinking back to our body image research comparison, the quantifiable data produced from the surveys might be called scientific, reliable, representative, valid, and objective. The descriptive focus group data might likewise be called soft, relational, situated, partial, and subjective. As you can see, all of these adjectives make qualitative methods seem less important than quantitative methods. The long-standing hierarchy that has been created which places quantitative research above qualitative research is often based on the research methods used and the kind of data they generate. Quantitative instruments of measurement are simply assumed to be rigorous, and accordingly, data resulting from their use takes on the presumption of *validity*. Open-ended and thematic qualitative methods of interview, observation, and content analysis are dichotomously assumed to lack validity in their pursuit of depth and authenticity. It is important to bear in mind that our concept of "validity" developed in direct relation to positivist science, which serves as the yardstick by which validity is measured. Qualitative approaches have problematized our very conceptions of legitimacy, though a long-standing hierarchy remains an issue. The privileging of positivism has created tremendous pressure for researchers to conform to the more accepted traditional research model. Researchers seeking funding may find out quickly that positivist quantitative research is more often funded, funded at higher amounts, and more likely to be published in top-tier peer-reviewed journals than qualitative research. These material realities are then coupled with how a qualitative researcher's work is regarded within their academic institution and among peers in the discipline. Together, these mechanisms of privileging quantitative research and rewarding researchers who conform to the validated model create very real pressure-infused environments in which qualitative researchers must operate. Our discussion of validity will continue in Chapter 2.

Although multiple methods may be used for a variety of reasons, qualitative researchers dealing with the external pressures that encourage quantitative research may use *multimethod approaches* as a way of combining qualitative and quantitative methods. For example, Madeline Altabe (1998) combined quantitative and qualitative approaches in order to study the relationship between ethnic diversity and body image disturbance. If a researcher is using qualitative methods for *triangulation* or *confirmation,* often the quantitative data will become privileged if there is a discrepancy between the quantitative and qualitative results and they appear to be incongruent. Having said this, qualitative research is distinct in that it often uses multiple methods within the context of one research project to ask and answer complex research questions. In addition to combining qualitative and quantitative techniques, multiple method designs may gain qualitative data in various forms. It is important to bear in mind that multimethod designs, in their best execution, do not simply rely on more than one method of data collection for the sake of yielding "more data" per se. When multiple methods are used, the methods interact with each other and inform the research process as a whole. Qualitative researchers who are engaged in a holistic approach to knowledge building are particularly cognizant of this. Additionally, multimethod designs help us to frame new research questions that would not otherwise be possible. Likewise, multimethod projects help us to ask questions previously posed in new and often more far-reaching ways. Some multimethod designs may even constitute the development of an emergent method.

Methodology: A Bridge Between Theory and Method

Epistemology, theory, and method web to create what we refer to as *the research nexus;* however, theory and method together also have a unique

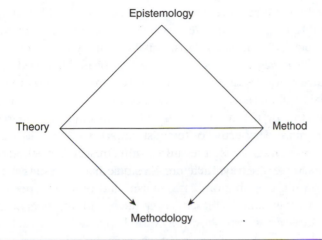

Figure 1.1   Methodology: A Bridge Between Theory and Method

and important relationship within the research process. It is in *methodology* that theory and method come together in order to create a guide to, and through, research design, from question formulation through analysis and representation. Harding explains that a methodology is a theory of how research does or should proceed (1987, p. 3). Methodology is the bridge that brings theory and method, perspective and tool, together. It is important to remember that this is a bridge that the researcher travels throughout the research process. In other words, methodology fuses theory and method, serving as a strategic but malleable guide throughout the research experience. In terms of malleability, methodology can be altered during research to the extent the researcher's epistemological beliefs allow for modification. A researcher's conception of subjectivity and objectivity within the research process is likely to influence whether or not they will be open to revising their methodology once data gathering has begun.

Feminist scholar Ingrid Botting (2000) conducted a study on domestic servants from the 1920s and 1930s who migrated to a mill town in Newfoundland for work. She twice modified her project based on the accessibility of data as well as her early findings, which prompted a reconfiguration. Botting's experience illustrates how important reflexivity is in the research process as well as the holistic and process-driven nature of qualitative inquiry (her study combined oral histories and census data). Through a rigorous process of reflection, Botting was able to "listen to the data," as we say, and follow it so that, in the end, like many feminist qualitative researchers, she was able to create a research design where the data was best able to "speak."

While there are research methods that generally yield qualitative data, such as oral history, in-depth interviewing, and ethnography, many research methods, such as content analysis, can be employed in both qualitative and quantitative ways. And as our discussion of multimethod approaches showed, qualitative researchers often use research methods that generate quantitative data. Moreover, theoretical perspectives are neither qualitative nor quantitative by nature, as evidenced by quantitative researchers who employ a feminist perspective or feminist empiricists who follow a positivist orientation. Feminists utilize the full range of research methods available, including surveys, which typically produce quantitative results. We will now elaborate on the contributions of feminism and other perspectives to the richness, diversity, and increased acceptance and practice of qualitative research. Moreover, we will show how varied approaches to qualitative practice all uniquely conceptualize research as a holistic process and have expanded our ideas about knowledge building.

● HOLISTIC CONCEPTIONS OF KNOWLEDGE BUILDING: QUALITATIVE PERSPECTIVES

So far we have been discussing qualitative research under the umbrella of an interpretive tradition and only alluding to and referencing variations in qualitative practice. While qualitative research is generally conducted from an inductive approach and aims at extracting social meaning, understanding social processes, and generating theory, there are many perspectives from which qualitative research is conducted. These perspectives and approaches vary tremendously, offering social scholars a range of ways to engage in qualitative research as well as diverse ways to think about knowledge and its production.

Postpositivism

Typically, qualitative research is associated with interpretive, feminist, and critical perspectives and not the positivist and postpositivist perspectives from which quantitative researchers operate; however, there are instances of researchers working from positivist and postpositivist approaches in qualitative practice. We have already discussed the tenets of positivism, so now we will briefly discuss postpositivism as an atypical approach for qualitative researchers.

Postpositivism is very similar to positivism, the difference being that, when studying social reality, postpositivism recognizes that researchers cannot be absolutely positive about their knowledge claims (Creswell, 2003, p. 7). Getting away from the positivist idea of *proving* causal relationships that constitute the social world, postpositivists *build evidence* to support a pre-existing theory. In other words, relying on deductive logic and hypothesis testing, just like positivists, postpositivists attempt to create evidence that will confirm or refute a theory, though not in absolute terms. In sum, postpositivism assumes that there is an objective reality "out there" constituted by testable cause and effect relationships. Social reality thus exists independent of the researcher and research project. Relying on deductive logic, these researchers engage in measurement and hypothesis testing in order to create evidence in support of, or against, an existing theory. You can see, given the assumptions about reality and knowledge construction, that this perspective is more congruent with quantitative analysis; however, some qualitative researchers may also choose to work from this kind of theoretical framework.

Qualitative researchers generally work from under the interpretive umbrella (a term we are using loosely), although this does not mean researchers follow the hermeneutic tradition per se. As we have already discussed the interpretive tradition, we will now talk about other major theoretical perspectives that fall under a more interpretive framework and tend to examine the social world as socially constructed. In particular, we will discuss the contributions of ethnomethodology, phenomenology, feminism, and critical theoretical perspectives to the domain of qualitative research. These approaches have significantly contributed not only to qualitative research but also to our conceptions of social reality, knowledge, and knowledge production. These are far-reaching highly expansive theoretical and epistemological positions with many variations within them. Therefore, as an introduction to these approaches, we will speak primarily in general terms. Please bear in mind that the use of generalizations means that a lot of nuance, difference, and tension within these perspectives will be left out of our discussion. For a more in-depth discussion of these topics, please refer to our book *A Feminist Research Primer* (2004).

Phenomenology

Phenomenology has its roots in the 18th century, partly as a critique of positivism. Phenomenologists were critical of the natural sciences for assuming an "objective" reality independent of individual consciousness. Phenomenology is closely associated with European philosophy in the early 1900s, most notably the works of German philosopher Edmund Husserl (Husserl, 1913 [in German], translated in 1931; see also Heidegger, 1982) and French phenomenologist Merleau-Ponty (1996). Husserl was interested in human consciousness as the way to understand social reality, particularly how one "thinks" about experience. In other words, *how consciousness is experienced.* For Husserl, consciousness is always "intentional," that is, it is directed at some phenomenon. To understand how consciousness operates enables us to capture how individuals create an understanding of social life. Husserl was especially interested in how individuals consciously experience experience. How is it that we become aware of experiences? Alfred Schutz (1967), a colleague of Husserl, brought the phenomenological perspective to American sociology. He was particularly interested in how individuals process experience in their everyday lives. Phenomenology is not only a philosophy but also a research method for capturing the lived experiences of individuals. Phenomenologists are interested in such questions as:

- How do individuals experience dying? (Kubler-Ross, 1969)
- How does one experience depression? (Karp, 1997)
- How does one experience divorce? (Kohler-Riessman, 1987)

For the phenomenologist, there is no "one reality" to how each of these events is experienced. Experience is perceived along a variety of dimensions: How the experience is lived in time and space and vis-à-vis our relationship to others as well as to bodily experience. Phenomenologists use a variety of methods, including observation, in-depth interviewing, and examining written accounts of experiences found in materials such as diaries. The type of question that might come up in an interview situation regarding one of the experiences listed above would be:

- Can you tell me what it is like to live with depression (impending death, divorce)?

In sum, phenomenology is a theoretical perspective aimed at generating knowledge about how people experience things.

Ethnomethodology

Ethnomethodology draws on the phenomenological perspective and is related to phenomenology in that both focus on the process whereby individuals understand and give a sense of order to the world in which they live. Ethnomethodologists are particularly interested in how meaning is negotiated in a social context through the process of interaction with others. Ethnomethodology was popularized as a perspective in the field of sociology in the 1960s through the work of Harold Garfinkel (1967). Ethnomethodologists ask such questions as:

- How do people go about making sense of their everyday lives?
- What are the specific strategies, especially those that appear to be commonsensical, that individuals use to go about the meaning-makingprocess?

To the ethnomethodologist, social life itself is created and recreated based on the micro understanding individuals bring to their everyday "social contexts." Ethnomethodologists utilize a range of methods to go about capturing this process of meaning making that can range from observing individuals in natural settings as they go about their daily rounds, to participant observations, to interviews. Ethnomethodologists are especially interested in how individuals engaged in interaction talk about their experiences, asking:

- How is meaning created in the everyday conversations individuals have with each other?

As you can see, this theoretical tradition lends itself to qualitative methods of inquiry. In other words, the main theoretical tenets of ethnomethodology are congruent with the methods of observation and interview that dominate qualitative practice.

FEMINIST THEORETICAL PERSPECTIVES ●

Feminist perspectives developed as a way to address the concerns and life experiences of women and girls, who, due to widespread androcentric bias, had long been excluded from knowledge construction both as researchers and research subjects. The history of correcting male-centered bias in the research process, and thus including women in social scientific research, is important and interesting; however, it is peripheral to the focus of this text. The minuscule version is that eventually women were included in the research process, though the research process *itself* remained unchallenged. Over time, researchers working from a feminist standpoint came to realize that adding women to preexisting frameworks, such as positivism, replicated traditional knowledge production, only now with women—at least numerically—included (for an in-depth discussion of this topic, please see our book *A Feminist Research Primer*). This is where our conversation about feminism and qualitative research merges with the historical progression.

Many feminists began to question the nature of knowledge construction *itself*, invariably realizing that new substantive concerns and related research questions (women-centered) necessitated new ways of thinking about and engaging in research. In this vein, some feminists began to challenge the main epistemological assumptions on which positivism rests. These initial challenges led to an unraveling of the dominant paradigm and multiple subsequent *transformations* in what is considered knowable and how we come to know.

In general terms, feminism challenges the *dichotomous thinking* that dominates positivism and then provides alternative ways of thinking about social reality and, correspondingly, the research process. Feminists critique the subject–object split as a false dualism that is inherently flawed, artificial, and ultimately undesirable. The feminist critique of the subject–object split has its roots in earlier feminist efforts to expose and correct the exclusion of women from research in the social and natural sciences. Halpin (1989) importantly links traditional scientific objectivity to a general process of "othering," in which women, people of color, and sexual minorities have been deemed "other" and as a result treated as inferior to the traditional white heterosexual male scientist. This process has resulted in systematic "scientific oppression" (Halpin, 1989). A key dimension to this historical routinized exclusion/distortion has been the placing of the researcher on a higher plane than the research participants because the researcher is conceptualized as the knowing party (Sprague & Zimmerman, 1993). Feminism itself has emerged from this historical struggle and seeks to create contextualized and partial truths and avoid the absolutes that have historically oppressed women and other marginalized peoples. In other words, feminists generally reject the positivist and postpositivist "view from nowhere" assumed by traditional scientific "objectivity" in favor of creating a "view from somewhere" (Sprague & Kobrynowicz, 1999)—that is, an engaged view.

This is not to imply that feminists do not grapple with complex issues related to objectivity within the research process. In fact, feminism has not simply called into question our assumptions about "objectivity" but has offered exciting new ways to think about it, adding greatly to research perspectives and practices. Many researchers aim not at abandoning objectivity but rather at transforming it into "feminist objectivity" (Bhavani, 1993; Haraway, 1991; Harding, 1993).

Feminist objectivity means quite simply *situated knowledges*. (Haraway, 1988, p. 581)

This means that feminists seek to engage with pure objectivity, while simultaneously acknowledging its impossibility, based on the fact that all research is conducted within a social context.

> Feminist objectivity is about limited location and situated knowledge, not about transcendence and splitting the subject and object. It allows us to become answerable for what we learn to see. (Haraway, 1988, p. 583)

Dismantling a dichotomous view of objectivity and subjectivity, feminist objectivity places the two in a dialectical relationship lived throughout the entire research process (Hesse-Biber, Howling, Leavy, & Lovejoy, 2004). Sandra Harding (1993) has been at the forefront of this discussion.

Harding's position is that it is not the positivist notion of objectivity that is problematic, but rather the limited application of "objectivity" within the actual research process. This is a prime example of the kind of holistic thinking that we believe characterizes and distinguishes qualitative research. Harding coined the term "strong objectivity" as a means of urging researchers to apply objectivity and reflexivity *throughout* the research process. By *reflexivity* we mean the ongoing questioning of one's place and power relations within the research process. Historically, Harding explains, objectivity (whether inherently flawed itself or not) has only been applied to *the context of justification*. This refers to a justification, provided by the researcher, as to *how* research subjects were sampled or selected, methods were employed, measurement tools were validated, and so forth, but not *why*. By using objectivity *strongly*, Harding advocates the rigorous application of objectivity and critical reflexivity during the *context of discovery* as well. This means that when we select our topic, create our initial research questions, construct our design, and move through data collection, analysis, and representation, we must not disavow the subjectivity (emotions, politics, and standpoint) that we each bring to bear on our research, but rather own it, disclose it, and critically engage with it. Harding's significant contribution to our understanding of objectivity–subjectivity throughout the research process is meant to serve as one example of variation and contribution within the larger intellectual exchange about objectivity that is a part of feminism.

Linked to the more general feminist rejection of the subject–object split that we were discussing is the feminist critique of the rational–emotional division, which, like the subject–object split, is a fundamental component of positivism and even of later postpositivist frameworks. Again, not only is the rational–emotional split artificial, but it is also undesirable to many researchers. This may be particularly true for feminists who have a commitment to improving the life chances of women and girls both locally and globally. In other words, feminists are centrally concerned with social justice, and as a result, social activism, changes in social policy, and other politically imbued aspirations impact their work during all phases of the process (from topic selection to final representation). As Alison Jaggar (1989) and Sprague and Zimmerman (1993) explain, emotions often serve as the impetus for a research project. This was true in the case of our research on girls and body image, which developed out of our political and scholarly commitment to women's issues and our personal experiences with female students who live in a cultural pressure cooker. Likewise, in the case of qualitative research such as ethnography, reciprocal emotional relationships may be an important and necessary data source (Bailey, 1996). In this same vein, Patricia Hill-Collins (1990) advocates a multifaceted "ethic of caring" for the engaged researcher. The necessarily political nature of feminist research, as well as any research centrally concerned with hearing the voices of those silenced, othered, and marginalized by the dominant social order, such as the work done by queer theorists and those working from multicultural frames, makes the concept of "value-free" or "value-neutral" research irrelevant on all levels. And so new social concerns not only call into question the legitimacy of the dominant epistemological position but also expose a need for new ways of thinking about knowledge and the research process. Given this general and abridged feminist critique of positivism and postpositivism, the reasons for the use of qualitative research methods as primary or supplemental methods by large numbers of feminist researchers is clear. Generally speaking, the assumptions within and kinds of questions answerable with qualitative methods of inquiry are congruent with the feminist principles held by many. Specifically, qualitative methods of interview and observation necessitate reciprocal relationships where researchers and research participants are placed on the same plane in the research process. Likewise, qualitative methods require the researcher to be deeply engaged with the data in order to extract meaning, understand process, and modify the project as appropriate (if they are willing to do so). For example, in the case of our body image focus group data, during the process of data collection it became clear to the interviewer (Hesse-Biber) that the black girls had different issues of central importance to them than the white respondents interviewed earlier. By being critically engaged with the emerging data, she was able to get at what was important in the lives of her respondents. Qualitative research methods lend themselves to this kind of reflexive engagement because they yield exploratory, descriptive, and process-oriented data instead of attempting to prove or corroborate hypothesized causal relationships. Qualitative methods ask not only "what is it?" but, more importantly, "explain it to me—how, why, what's the process, what's the significance?" These questions are answered through holistic and reflexive engagement on all levels. Having said all of this, there are numerous differences within the feminist paradigm. While a broad discussion of these positions is available in our feminist companion to this text, for now we will briefly discuss *feminist standpoint epistemology* as one feminist perspective from which many qualitative researchers work.

FEMINIST STANDPOINT EPISTEMOLOGY ●

Derived from Hegel's master–slave dialectic, and Karl Marx's subsequent scholarship, Dorothy Smith (1974) and Nancy Hartsock (1983) pioneered feminist standpoint epistemology. In essence, *standpoint epistemology* (which has evolved into a methodology as well) is based on the assumption that in a hierarchically structured social world, different "standpoints" are necessarily produced. For example, the United States has a long history of involvement in genocide and slavery and continued racial inequality. This constitutes an environment that is hierarchically structured along economic, social, and political lines based on the construct of race and/or ethnicity. In such a context people have different visions of the world based on the racial categorization that they embody and their corresponding space in the social structure, which, as implied, is hierarchical and thus differentiated.

Feminist standpoint theorists have primarily focused on the position that women occupy within a social context characterized by a patriarchal sex–gender system. Women and men occupy different social positions (even more complicated by race, class, and sexuality) that produce different life experiences, differential access to the economic, cultural, and political reward system, and thus, ultimately different standpoints. Some standpoint theorists argue that women's vision is not only different but in fact more complete and less distorted because they occupy a position of oppression in which they must come to understand their own social position as well as that of the dominant group (Hartsock, 1983; Jaggar, 1989).

Drawing on Marx's class analysis, Hartsock explains that the differential material (economic and work) conditions under which men and women live produce radically different standpoints. In such a situation, not only do men and women have different viewpoints but quite literally different experiences in the private and public spheres, which provide substantive research material for scholars as well as a new way of approaching research.

> Women's work in every society differs systematically from men's. I intend to pursue the suggestion that this division of labor is the first and in some societies the only division of labor, and moreover, that it is central to the organization of social labor more generally. On the basis of an account of the sexual division of labor, one should be able to begin to explore the oppositions and differences between women's and men's activity and their consequences for epistemology. (Hartsock, 1983, p. 154)

By looking at the conditions under which differential standpoints are produced, such as the division of labor in both the public and private spheres, it becomes clear that standpoint is an achievement—you earn it through your life experiences. We earn our unique and engaged vision through our material and symbolic realities.

Patricia Hill-Collins (1990) has added immeasurably to our understanding of standpoint as an epistemology and critical methodology by introducing the idea of an *Afrocentric feminist epistemology* that begins with the unique standpoint of black women. In essence, Hill-Collins explains that we live in a "matrix of domination" where race and gender are overdetermined in relation to each other, producing a unique standpoint fostered by these "interlocking systems of oppression." By accessing the different standpoints within our social world, researchers are able to ask and answer new questions and challenge and even resist former conceptions of truth and ways of knowing.

> Alternative knowledge claims in and of themselves are rarely threatening to conventional knowledge. Such claims are routinely ignored, discredited, or simply absorbed and marginalized in existing paradigms. Much more threatening is the challenge that alternative epistemologies offer to the basic process used by the powerful to legitimate their knowledge claims. If the epistemology used to validate knowledge comes into question, then all prior knowledge claims validated under the dominant model become suspect. An alternative epistemology challenges all certified knowledge and opens up the question of whether what has been taken to be true can stand the test of alternative ways of validating truth. The existence of a self-defined Black women's standpoint using an Afrocentric feminist epistemology calls into question the content of what currently passes as truth and simultaneously challenges the process of arriving at that truth. (Hill-Collins, 1990, pp. 205–206)

And so we can see that standpoint epistemology provides a new way of thinking about both social reality itself and the way we can approach studying that reality. Likewise, feminism is a particular standpoint that is earned through politically engaged practice, making the practice of feminist research itself an achievement.

Critical Perspectives

Like feminist perspectives, *critical approaches* to knowledge construction are numerous, with many variations in epistemology, theory, substantive concerns, and methodological designs that inform qualitative research. Having said this, we will provide a brief and very general overview of some of the key issues and beliefs that critical theorists bring to knowledge construction. These perspectives are revisited and elaborated on in Chapter 8, where we discuss unobtrusive methods.

Critical theorists reject the main tenets of positivism and explain that the assumptions within positivism and the historical practice of this epistemological position have maintained radically unequal power relations. They are particularly wary of notions of absolute Truth and base their concerns on the historical inequities produced by this rigid view of knowledge. The traditional scientific process ultimately creates knowledge that is used to maintain (justify, fortify, reconstruct) the status quo in which all those forced to the peripheries of the social system (women, people of color, sexual minorities, and the lower socioeconomic classes) are continually oppressed through the reproduction of the hierarchical dominant ideology. Critical theory seeks to reflexively step outside of the dominant ideology (insofar as possible) in order to create a space for resistive, counterhegemonic, knowledge production that destabilizes the oppressive material and symbolic relations of dominance. Critical theorists seek to access "subjugated knowledges" and often examine the "micro-politics of power" (Foucault, 1976). There are many variations under the larger umbrella of critical theory. *Postmodernism* has developed into one of the main epistemological traditions within the broader umbrella category and is now practiced widely. We will now break down some of the tenets of critical scholarship, focusing primarily on postmodern epistemology (though many of the scholars we mention have been categorized in different ways—as poststructuralists and deconstructionists, for example).

Postmodern and related theories focus on the prominence of dominant ideology and the discourses of power that normalize this ideology to the maintenance of a dominant world order—locally, nationally, and globally. In particular, the discursive logic that accompanies the postmodern capitalist system is investigated. Frederic Jameson, who has contributed immeasurably to the development of postmodern theory, explains that we must examine the "cultural logic of late capitalism" (also called postmodernity) which is both a moment and a discourse (Jameson, 1991). Antonio Gramsci (1929) explains that people partly consent to their own oppression through the internalization of dominant ideology. In other words, hegemonic authority is maintained because, as Foucault (1976) would say, our ideas become the chains that bind us best. Being social creatures, our ideas are not simply created in our minds, but are rather a part of a larger social and political context with its own materiality. The project of critical scholarship thus becomes accessing the voices of the oppressed and their unique knowledges, which Foucault labels *subjugated knowledges,* in order to transform power relations. Since all knowledge is produced within shifting fields of power

(Foucault, 1976), research must be historically engaged (Bhavani, 1993). One method of pursuing this politicized intellectual project is *critical deconstruction*. During a discussion of the oppression of women within the symbolic and material realms, critical feminist scholar Luce Irigaray posits deconstruction as follows:

> It is surely not a matter of interpreting the operation of a discourse while remaining *within* the same type of utterance as the one that guarantees discursive coherence . . . the issue is not one of elaborating a new theory . . . but of *jamming the theoretical machinery itself*, of suspending its pretension to the production of a truth and of a meaning that are excessively univocal. (Irigaray, 1985, italics added)

As you can see, critical theory is concerned with creating transformational tension within the social system itself, rather than producing knowledge that feeds the system. In this vein, critical scholar Jacques Derrida (1966), who was at the forefront of changing how researchers think about knowledge and its production, urges a method of critical deconstruction where what has been marginalized through social historical processes is transformed into the locus of investigation (this is elaborated in Chapter 8). Postmodern research is thus a process of decentering in order to create situated knowledges that challenge dominant ideology. This is necessarily an *engaged* process. Pierre Bourdieu (1992) puts forward "reflexive sociology" as a necessary epistemological and practical part of the research process.[1]

> For me, sociology ought to be meta but *always vis-à-vis itself*. It must use its own instruments to find out what it is and what it is doing, to try to know better where it stands. (Bourdieu & Wacquant, 1992, p. 191)

Researchers use many terms to signify the importance of reflexivity in postmodern practice, including *power-reflexive* (Haraway, 1991) and *power-sensitive* (Pfohl, 1992). Bhavani (1993) touches on a similar theme by explaining that it is not enough merely to recognize the "micro-politics of the research situation," we must also analyze them (p. 74).

Postmodern scholars are often criticized for being too "relative" because they reject the idea of "objective" reality and assert that all knowledge is produced within socially and historically specific power relations, making it socially constructed and thus partial (Nielsen, 1990, p. 9). Let's analyze this critique in order to demonstrate one of the key points of critical theory itself. In fact, this often repeated "relativist" criticism of critical scholarship, and more specifically postmodern theory, *must* itself be analyzed from a critical perspective in order to be understood. This is because postmodernism is not broken down from within its own philosophical positioning, but rather based on the conventional deductive logic of positivism. The foundation of the critique is therefore curious. It is a situation whereby postmodern research is being judged by the tenets of positivist conceptions of science—objectivity, reliability, generalizability, validity. These categories of scientific judgment, however, have been *destabilized* by postmodern principles, and thus a postmodern researcher would argue that the assumptions that have historically created and reified those standards of measurement have come to take a place of prominence out of a power-imbued and distorted process. The critique is distorted and irrelevant because the foundation on which the critique is based remains the product of dominant ideology—which is what postmodern theory seeks to challenge, resist, and transform.

Additionally, many positivist, postpositivist, interpretive, and feminist estimations of postmodern knowledge production go on to assert that not only does this stance produce unreliable relative truths, but that in its attempt to create partial truths (which of course postmodernists argue all truths are even if they are not disclosed as such), postmodern theory has created an array of disconnected "truths." Generally speaking, this criticism is problematic because postmodern researchers aim at creating embodied truths that are not disconnected from the historical material realities that produced them. In this way, while postmodern research is often thought of as antithetical to empiricism, knowledge produced from a postmodern approach is quite grounded in ongoing historical processes and the power–knowledge relations in which it is enmeshed.

GETTING BACKSTAGE: THEORY, METHOD, ● AND EPISTEMOLOGY IN PRACTICE

The purpose of this chapter has been to introduce you to the field of qualitative research. In order to differentiate qualitative practice as a unique and fruitful terrain, we have compared it to its quantitative counterpart using real-world research examples about the study of body image. Likewise, in the latter portion of the chapter we have introduced, in broad terms, some of the main epistemological and theoretical approaches qualitative researchers employ. Theories and methods can be employed in many different ways, so our position is that what really distinguishes qualitative research as a unique perspective on knowledge building is that it is a *holistic* and *engaged* process. We hope that you are starting to see why. In the next chapter we discuss some of the issues that begin to emerge during research design, including how a qualitative researcher selects a topic and then begins to think about creating a methodological design that fits their research questions. This discussion is situated within an exploration of "paradigms" or "worldviews."

In the following chapters we also hope that you will begin to see how multifaceted and complex the actual practice of qualitative research is. In this vein, we have included "Behind-the-Scenes" boxes in each of the following chapters. These sections contain material we have solicited from respected scholars in the field of qualitative research. These sections are meant to introduce you to the practice of social research—what it is *really* like to work with particular methods and methodologies from the point of view of researchers. Rarely do we get to see some of the complexity in conducting research unless we are actively engaged in the process ourselves. Through these behind-the-scenes glimpses into various phases of the research endeavor, you will be introduced to the inner workings of how scholars put a project together. In this chapter we have discussed the link between method, methodology, and epistemology. But what is the connection between these aspects of research in actual practice? As qualitative research has dismantled the notion of the "view from nowhere" and replaced it with a "view from somewhere," how does a researcher's standpoint impact various aspects of their research? By going behind the curtain of the research project, we will be able to get into the researcher's standpoint (so to speak) as they enter their research project. We will be introduced to the range of issues, motivations, and values brought to bear on their research. This backstage view will help link the *theory of qualitative research* with the *actual practice of social research,* ultimately providing a more holistic view of the qualitative endeavor.

● GLOSSARY

Afrocentric Feminist Epistemology: Patricia Hill-Collins (1990) has added immeasurably to our understanding of standpoint as an epistemology and critical methodology by introducing the idea of an *Afrocentric feminist epistemology* that takes the premise of standpoint epistemology and begins with the unique standpoint of black women.

Context of Discovery: This refers to the construction of a research topic and research questions and how we design and implement research projects. According to Sandra Harding (1993), when we select our topic, create our initial research questions, construct our design, and move through data collection, analysis, and representation, we must not disavow the subjectivity (emotions, politics, and standpoint) that we each bring to bear on our research, but rather own it, disclose it, and critically engage with it.

Context of Justification: This refers to a justification, provided by the researcher, as to how research subjects were sampled or selected, methods were employed, measurement tools were validated, and so forth, but not *why* (which is accounted for in the context of discovery).

Critical Approach: Critical theory seeks to reflexively step outside of the dominant ideology (insofar as possible) in order to create a space for resistive, counterhegemonic knowledge production that destabilizes oppressive material and symbolic relations of dominance. Critical theorists seek to access "subjugated knowledges" and often examine the "micro-politics of power" (Foucault, 1976).

Critical Deconstruction: Since all knowledge is produced within shifting fields of power (Foucault, 1976), research must be historically engaged (Bhavani, 1993). One method of pursuing this politicized intellectual project is critical deconstruction, an approach developed by Jacques Derrida (1966).

Deductive Approach: Typically used in positivist quantitative research, deductive approaches begin with a hypothesis which is then tested.

Epistemology: A theory of knowledge; "a theory of knowledge embedded in a theoretical perspective" (Creswell, 2003, p. 4) which informs all aspects of the research process. In other words, an epistemology is a philosophical belief system about who can be a knower and what can be known (Guba & Lincoln, 1998; Harding, 1987; Hesse-Biber & Leavy, 2004). Beyond asking who can be a knower and what can be known, epistemology addresses how knowledge is created: an epistemological position lays the foundation for the knowledge-building process. The conscious and unconscious questions, assumptions, and beliefs that the researcher brings to the research endeavor serve as the initial basis for an epistemological position.

Ethnomethodology: Ethnomethodology draws on the phenomenological perspective and is related to phenomenology in that both focus on the process whereby individuals understand and give a sense of order to the world in which they live. Ethnomethodologists are particularly interested in how meaning is negotiated in a social context through the process of interaction with others. Ethnomethodology was popularized as a perspective in the field of sociology in the 1960s through the work of Harold Garfinkel (1967). Ethnomethodologists ask such questions as: (1) How do people go about making sense of their every day lives? (2) What are the specific strategies, especially those that appear to be commonsensical, that individuals use to go about the meaning-making process? To the ethnomethodologist, social life itself is created and recreated based on the micro understanding individuals bring to their everyday "social contexts." Ethnomethodologists utilize a range of methods to go about capturing this process of meaning making that include observing individuals in natural settings as they go about their daily rounds, participant observations, and interviews.

Feminist Perspectives: Feminist perspectives developed as a way to address the concerns and life experiences of women and girls, who, due to widespread androcentric (sexist) bias, had long been excluded from knowledge construction both as researchers and research subjects.

Feminist Standpoint Epistemology: Standpoint epistemology is based on knowing a society from within. This means that groups differentially located in the society will have different experiences and thus earn a unique perspective. Feminist standpoint theorists have primarily focused on the position that women occupy within a social context characterized by a patriarchal sex-gender system.

Hermeneutic Tradition: *See* Interpretive Perspective.

Hierarchical: Division in the relationship between the researcher and the researched in which the researcher is privileged as the knower.

Holistic: The practice of qualitative research is reflexive and process-driven, ultimately producing culturally situated and theory-enmeshed knowledge through an ongoing interplay between theory and methods, researcher and researched. By *holistic* we mean that researchers must continually be cognizant of the relationship between epistemology, theory, and methods and look at research as a process.

Inductive Model: A model in which theory develops directly out of the data; one such model often used by interpretive and feminist researchers (though not exclusively or uniformly) is grounded theory.

Interpretive Perspective: This perspective developed as a direct challenge to positivist epistemology and its interpretation/application of objectivity. The interpretive epistemology is based on the interpretation of interactions and the social meaning that people assign to their interactions (Nielsen, 1990, p. 7). This perspective epistemologically believes that social meaning is created during interaction and people's interpretations of interactions. The implication is that different social actors may in fact understand social reality differently, producing different meanings and analyses. Research of this kind involves the building of relationships between the researcher and research participants who are collaborators in the research process.

Methodology: It is in methodology that theory and method come together in order to create a guide to, and through, research design, from question formulation through analysis and representation. Harding explains that a methodology is a theory of how research does or should ensue (1987, p. 3). Methodology is the bridge that brings theory and method, perspective and tool, together. It is important to remember that this is a bridge that the researcher travels throughout the entire research process. In other words, methodology fuses theory and method, serving as a strategic but malleable guide throughout the research experience.

Multimethod Approach: This is when a researcher uses more than one method in a research project. Researchers can combine qualitative methods or use qualitative and quantitative methods in conjunction with one another. Ideally, the methods should speak to the research question and to each other.

Phenomenology: Phenomenology has its roots in the 18th century, partly as a critique of positivism. Phenomenologists were critical of the natural sciences for assuming an "objective" reality independent of individual consciousness. Phenomenology is not only a philosophy, but also a research method for capturing the lived experiences of individuals. Phenomenologists are interested in such questions as (1) How do individuals experience dying? (Kubler-Ross, 1969); (2) How does one experience depression? (Karp, 1997); (3) How does one experience divorce? (Kohler-Riessman, 1987). For the phenomenologist there is no "one reality" to how each of these events is experienced. Experience is perceived along a variety of dimensions—how the experience is lived in time, in space, vis-à-vis our relationships to others as well as as a bodily experience. Phenomenologists use a variety of methods, including observation, in-depth interviewing, and looking at written accounts of people's experiences in materials such as diaries.

Postmodernism: Postmodern and related theories focus on the prominence of dominant ideology and the discourses of power that normalize this ideology to the maintenance of a dominant world order—locally, nationally, and globally. Postmodernism argues that we have moved beyond modernity into a postmodern era characterized by a focus on reproductive technologies. This new epoch requires new approaches to knowledge construction.

Postpositivism: Postpositivism is very similar to positivism—the difference being that in the study of social reality, postpositivism recognizes that researchers cannot be absolutely positive about their knowledge claims (Creswell, 2003, p. 7). Getting away from the positivist idea of *proving* causal relationships that constitute the social world, postpositivists *build evidence* to support a preexisting theory. In other words, relying on deductive logic and hypothesis testing, just as positivists do, postpositivists attempt to create evidence that will confirm or refute a theory, though not in absolute terms.

Positivist Epistemology: Positivism holds that there is a knowable reality that exists independent of the research process, and it can be discovered and tested through objective means and a neutral researcher.

Reflexivity: The ongoing questioning of one's place and power relations within the research process.

Research Methods: Methods are the tools that researchers use in order to gather data. A research method is a technique for gathering evidence. One could reasonably argue that all evidence-gathering techniques fall into one of the three categories: listening to (or interrogation of) informants, observing behavior, or examining historical traces and records (Harding, 1987, p. 2). Qualitative researchers often use one or more of the following methods (though this is not an exhaustive list): ethnography, in-depth interviewing, oral history, autoethnography, focus group interviewing, case study, discourse analysis, and content analysis.

Research Nexus: The "webbing" together of epistemology, theory, and method.

Situated Knowledges: Often produced by feminists who reject the idea of provable truths, situated knowledges are partial truths that are located in particular contexts.

Standpoint Epistemology: This is based on the assumption that in a hierarchically structured social world, different "standpoints" are necessarily produced. By accessing the different standpoints within our social world, researchers are able to ask and answer new questions and challenge and even resist former conceptions of truth and ways of knowing. In a hierarchical social order our standpoints are earned viewpoints.

Theoretical Perspective: An epistemology is embedded within a theoretical perspective, meaning that an epistemology is tied to or intimately linked to a theory, or that epistemological beliefs are enacted through a theoretical frame.

Triangulation: The use of three research methods.

Validity: Researchers working within the qualitative paradigm conceptualize validity differently than traditional positivist conceptions of the term. Generally speaking, validity is one of the issues researchers address as they make a case or argument for the knowledge they have produced. In other words, that the knowledge produced reflects some aspect of the social world and/or is compelling.

DISCUSSION QUESTIONS ●

1. What does it mean to conceptualize the research process holistically? How does this perspective impact the production of knowledge?

2. Qualitative researchers seek meaning; what does approaching a topic with the goal of generating meaning do to the process, the interpretation, and the final result?

3. In what ways does the researcher's epistemological position influence the methods used?

4. How does the hierarchical division produced by the positivism of researcher–researched (subject/object) impact the research process?

5. Discuss objectivity and subjectivity and their importance in the research process. How do different theoretical and epistemological perspectives conceptualize objectivity and subjectivity?

6. What is the research nexus and how does it impact knowledge building?

7. How can reflexivity enrich one's data and the interpretative process?

SUGGESTED WEBSITES ●

Forum: Qualitative Social Research

http://www.qualitative-research.net/fqs/fqs-eng.htm

FQS is a peer-reviewed multilingual online journal for qualitative research. The main aim of *FQS* is to promote discussion and cooperation among qualitative researchers from different countries and social science disciplines.

Association for Qualitative Research

http://www.latrobe.edu.au/aqr/

This site is useful because, although the most recent month's publication is not free on the website, all previous publications are. Students can access full texts.

Qualitative Research Consultants Association

http://www.qrca.org/

This website is for a nonprofit organization whose mission is promoting excellence in qualitative research. Site is useful for those who are interested in becoming part of an organization dealing with qualitative research.

The Association for Qualitative Research

http://www.aqrp.co.uk/

Anyone who is interested in qualitative research is welcome to join this association. Founded in the early 1980s, AQR is a recognized and respected organization in the marketing services arena.

The Qualitative Research Report

http://www.nova.edu/ssss/QR/qualres.html
http://www.nova.edu/ssss/QR/web.html

Leading online qualitative research journal with many additional sources about qualitative research.

The National Organization for Women

http://www.now.org/

This is an up-to-date website containing information about feminist research as well as feminist issues. It has an up-to-date link to current events dealing with feminism as well as legislative updates.

The Feminist Majority Foundation (Research Center)

http://www.feminist.org/research/1_public.html

This website contains a plethora of information dealing with women's issues and, in particular, feminist research. It has links to current research, women's studies programs, feminist journals, feminist Internet search utilities, women research centers, and feminist magazines.

The Feminist Institute for Studies on Law and Society

http://www.sfu.ca/~fisls/engines.htm

This website has a link focusing specifically on feminist research as well as a broader subject guide. It also contains links to feminist journals and papers, along with a list of feminist search engines.

Sociological Research Online

http://www.socresonline.org.uk/2/3/3.html

This is a link to a specific journal article about feminist research and the authors' experience with feminist research. Miller talks about such things as the power in the search process, power in the research relationship, as well as personal experiences with feminist research. Methodologies and feminist epistemologies are also discussed.

NOTE ●

1. He was writing specifically about sociology; however, we believe he would extend his position out to include all social scientific research, if not all research itself.

REFERENCES ●

Abrams, L., & Cook Stormer, C. (2002). Sociocultural variations in the body image perceptions of urban adolescent females. *Journal of Youth and Adolescence, 31*(6), 443–451.

Altabe, M. (1998). Ethnicity and body image: Quantitative and qualitative analysis. *International Journal of Eating Disorders, 23,* 153–159.

Bailey, C. (1996). *A guide to field research.* Thousand Oaks, CA: Pine Forge Press.

Banfield, S., & McCabe, M. (2002). An evaluation of the construct of body image. *Adolescence, 37*(146), 373–394.

Bhavani, K. (1993). Tracing the contours: Feminist research and feminist objectivity. *Women's Studies International Forum, 16*(2), 95–104.

Botting, I. (2000). Understanding domestic service through oral history and the census: The case of Grand Falls, Newfoundland. *Feminist Qualitative Research, 28*(1, 2), 99–120.

Bourdieu, P. (1992). *The logic of practice.* Stanford, CA: Stanford University Press.

Bourdieu, P., & Wacquant, L. (1992). *An invitation to reflexive sociology.* Chicago: University of Chicago Press.

Chamorro, R., & Flores-Ortiz, Y. (2000). Acculturation and disordered eating patterns among Mexican American women. *The International Journal of Eating Disorders, 28*(1), 125–129.

Chandler, S., Abood, D., Lee, D., Cleveland, M., & Daly, J. (1994). Pathogenic eating attitudes and behaviors and body dissatisfaction differences among black and white college students. *Eating Disorders: The Journal of Treatment and Prevention, 2,* 319–328.

Creswell, J. W. (2003). *Research design: Qualitative, quantitative, and mixed methods approaches* (2nd ed.). Thousand Oaks, CA: Sage.

Crotty, M. (1998). *The foundations of social research: Meaning and perspective in the research process.* London: Sage.

Derrida, J. (1966). The decentering event in social thought. In A. Bass (Trans.), *Writing the difference* (pp. 278–282). Chicago: University of Chicago Press.

Falconer, J., & Neville, H. (2000). African American college women's body image: An examination of body mass, African self-consciousness, and skin color satisfaction. *Psychology of Women Quarterly, 24,* 236–243.

Foucault, M. (1976). Power as knowledge. In R. Hurley (Trans.), *The history of sexuality, vol. 1: An introduction* (pp. 92–102). New York: Vintage Books.

Garfinkel, H. (1967). *Studies in ethnomethodology.* Englewood Cliffs, NJ: Prentice Hall.

Geertz, C. (1973). *The interpretations of cultures.* New York: Basic Books.

Gramsci, A. (1929). Intellectuals and hegemony. *Selections from the Prison Notebooks.* New York: International Publishers Co.

Guba, E., & Lincoln, Y. (1998). Competing paradigms in qualitative research. In N. Denzin & Y. Lincoln (Eds.), *The landscape of qualitative research: Theories and issues* (pp. 195–220). Thousand Oaks, CA: Sage.

Halpin, Z. (1989). Scientific objectivity and the concept of "The Other." *Women's Studies International Forum, 12*(3), 285–294.

Haraway, D. (1991). *Simians, cyborgs, and women: The reinvention of nature.* New York: Routledge.

Haraway, D. (1988). Situated knowledges: The science question in feminism and the privilege of partial perspective. *Feminist Studies, 14*(13), 575–599.

Harding, S. (1993). Rethinking standpoint epistemology: What is "strong objectivity?" In L. Alcoff & E. Potter (Eds.), *Feminist epistemologies* (pp. 49–82). New York: Routledge.

Harding, S. (1987). *Feminism and methodology.* Bloomington: Indiana University Press.

Hartsock, N. (1983). The feminist standpoint: Developing the ground for a specifically feminist historical materialism. In S. Harding & M. Hintikka (Eds.), *Discovering reality* (pp. 283–305). Dordrecht, The Netherlands: Reidel.

Heidegger, M. (1982). The Craft of Qualitative Research. In A. Hofstadter (Trans.), *The basic problems of phenomenology.* Bloomington: Indiana University Press. From the German original of 1975. The text of a lecture course in 1927.

Heidegger, M. (1962). The Craft of Qualitative Research. In J. Macquarrie & E. Robinson (Trans.), *Being and time.* New York: Harper & Row. From the German original of 1927.

Hesse-Biber, S. (1995–1999) Body Image Focus Group transcript (including aspiration codes).

Hesse-Biber, S. (1996). *Am I thin enough yet: The cult of thinness and the commercialization of identity.* New York: Oxford University Press.

Hesse-Biber, S., Howling, S. A., Leavy, P., & Lovejoy, M. (2004). Racial identity and the development image issues among African American adolescent girls. *The Qualitative Report, 9*(1), 49–79.

Hesse-Biber, S., & Leavy, P. (Eds.). (2004). *Approaches to qualitative research: A reader on theory and practice.* New York: Oxford University Press.

Hesse-Biber, S., Leavy, P., & Yaiser, M. (2004). Feminist approaches to research as a process: Reconceptualizing epistemology, methodology, and method. In S. Hesse-Biber & M. Yaiser (Eds.), *Feminist perspectives on social research* (pp. 3–26). New York: Oxford University Press.

Hill-Collins, P. (1990). Black feminist thought in the matrix of domination. *Black feminist thought: Knowledge, consciousness, and the politics of empowerment.* London: HarperCollins.

Husserl, E. (1963). The Craft of Qualitative Research. In W. R. Boyce Gibson (Trans.), *Ideas: A general introduction to pure phenomenology.* New York: Collier Books. From the German original of 1913, originally titled *Ideas pertaining to a pure phenomenology and to a phenomenological philosophy.*

Husserl, E. (1931). The Craft of Qualitative Research. In W. R. Boyce Gibson (Trans.), *Ideas: General introduction to pure phenomenology.* New York: Macmillan.

Irigaray, L. (1985). *This sex which is not one.* Ithaca, NY: Cornell University Press.

Jaggar, A. (1989). Love and knowledge: Emotion in feminist epistemology. *Inquiry, 32,* 151–172.

Jameson, F. (1991). *Postmodernism, or, the cultural logic of late capitalism.* Durham, NC: Duke University Press.

Karp, D. (1997). *Speaking of sadness: Depression, disconnection, and the meaning of illness.* New York: Oxford University Press.

Kohler-Riessman, C. (1987). When gender is not enough: Women interviewing women. *Gender and Society, 1,* 172–207.

Kubler-Ross, E. (1969). *On death and dying.* New York: Macmillan.

Merleau-Ponty, M. (1996). The Craft of Qualitative Research. In C. Smith (Trans.), *Phenomenology of perception.* London and New York: Routledge. Taken from the French original published in 1945.

Molloy, B., & Herzberger, S. (1998). Body image and self-esteem: A comparison of African-American and Caucasian women. *Sex Roles: A Journal of Research, 38*(7–8), 631–644.

Neuman, W. L. (1997). *Social research methods: Qualitative and quantitative approaches* (3rd Ed.). Boston: Allyn & Bacon.

Nielsen, L. (2000). Black undergraduate and white undergraduate eating disorders and related attitudes. *College Student Journal, 34*(3), 353.

Nielsen, J. (1990). *Feminist research methods.* Boulder, CO: Westview.

Pfohl, S. (1992). *Death at the parasite cafe.* New York: St. Martin's Press.

Ragin, C. (1994). *Constructing social research.* Thousand Oaks, CA: Pine Forge Press.

Ritzer, G. (2000). *Sociological theory* (5th Ed.). New York: McGraw-Hill.

Schutz, A. (1967). *The phenomenology of the social world* (G. Walsh & F. Lehnert, Trans.). Evanston, IL: Northwestern University Press.

Schutz, A., & Luckmann, T. (1974). The Craft of Qualitative Research. In R. M. Zaner & H. T. Engelhardt (Trans.), *The structures of the life-world: Volume 1.* London: Heinemann.

Smith, D. (1974). Knowing a society from within: A woman's standpoint. In *The conceptual practices of power: A feminist sociology of knowledge* (pp. 21–24). Boston: Northeastern University Press.

Sprague, J., & Kobrynowicz, D. (1999). A feminist epistemology. In J. Saltzman Chafetz (Ed.), *Handbook of the sociology of gender* (pp. 25–44). New York: Kluwer Academic/Plenum.

Sprague, J., & Zimmerman, M. (1993). Overcoming dualisms: A feminist agenda for sociological method. In P. England (Ed.), *Theory on gender/feminism on theory* (pp. 255–279). New York: Aldine DeGruyter.

Thompson, B. (1996). Multiracial feminist theorizing about eating problems: Refusing to rank oppressions. *Eating Disorders, 4*(2), 104–114.

CHAPTER 2

THE RESEARCH PROCESS

PARADIGMS: WINDOWS INTO THE REALITY ●

Sociologist Joseph Diaz is a "classical" ethnographer trained in the positivist tradition. This tradition provides him with a ready-made "window" into how he approaches a research project. He wants to conduct a modern ethnography of a plasma-buying clinic located on the Las Vegas Strip. He begins his research project by noting:

> I intended to write a colorful, but "classical" ethnography where I find causes, effects, and decipher the hidden codes of the plasma donors and workers. I think I owe this default approach to inquiry to my training as a quantitative methodologist, which teaches, within the positivist perspective, that there is a knowable reality. (Diaz, 1999, p. 1)

What Diaz soon finds out, much to his dismay, is that this window into the social world wasn't working for him:

> In the early data gathering phase of this study, I had to admit that the "plasma experience" appeared neither homogeneous nor easily modeled as a finite and discrete set of causes and effects. When I noticed that my notes, thoughts, experiences, beliefs, and observations regarding my plasma-donating experiences were often contradictory with each other, I realized that my approach needed to be changed. In short, I sought to find a "Truth" which I soon realized does not exist in human interaction and experience. . . . I tried, therefore to employ the approach that seemed

most appropriate to this confusing, and often self-contradictory practice of selling plasma: The Postmodern Ethnography. (Diaz, 1999, pp. 1–2)

The reality of events unfolding in the plasma clinic instead was highly "subjective," filled with contradiction, and Diaz soon finds himself playing a crucial role in the data gathering and interpretation of that world. As a participant observer he uncovers a series of "tales" of plasma donor experiences, including his own:

> . . . in this study I accept the post modern notion that an author can never be truly objective . . . nor can the descriptions events, people, places, and situations be entirely "true," concretely factual, or objectively representative. . . . Instead of attempting to remove myself (the author) from the study and pretend that my assumptions and interpretations of given events are correct and irrefutable, as one might in a "classical ethnography," I will instead make my presence in the study explicit and will respond to occurrences and evoke emotions and thoughts rather than try to define a given event or situation. (Diaz, 1999, p. 2)

Diaz started out his research project with a set of *philosophical assumptions* concerning the nature of the social world. These assumptions may often go unstated and unexamined, but they are crucial underpinnings to the research enterprise and help shape its process. The philosophical "substructure" of a research enterprise guides us and our interpretation of reality regarding some core metaphysical issues:

- What is the *nature* of social reality?
- What is the nature of the individual? (our concept of social reality/humanity or *ontology*)?
- How is knowledge constructed?
- Who can be a knower?
- What can be known? (our view of *epistemology*)?

How we answer these questions, in turn, affects how we engage *methodologically* (theoretically) with the concrete social world as well as the types of *methods* we consider appropriate for a research project.

Joseph Diaz is trained as a classical ethnographer working in the *quantitative* tradition. He is a positivist and as such he views the social world as ordered, knowable, and objective. As reviewed in Chapter 1, a *qualitatively* oriented researcher, on the other hand, possesses a different orientation and employs an "interpretative approach" to reality in which the goal is to understand and explore the nature of social life. Instead of "testing and controlling" events, as we first saw Joseph Diaz do as he applied "causes and effects" in order to comprehend the reality of the plasma donor clinic, a qualitative analyst asks questions such as:

- What meanings do individuals give to the nature of reality?
- How can we understand the variety of meanings individuals impart to the plasma donor experience?

Not all qualitative researchers approach their craft with exactly the same window into the social world. Instead, they come from a multitude of paradigmatic traditions. The *"traditional"* research paradigm Joseph Diaz started out with has its origins in the beginning of the 1900s and continues to operate to the present day. While we associate this paradigm with a *quantitative* approach to research, there are qualitative researchers whose research gains insights from this approach:

> The positivist and postpositivist traditions linger like long shadows over the qualitative research project. Historically, qualitative research was defined within the positivist paradigm, where qualitative researchers attempted to do good positivist research with less rigorous methods and procedures. Some mid-20th century qualitative researchers (e.g., Becker, Geer, Hughes, & Strauss, 1961) reported participant observation findings in terms of quasi-statistics. As recently as 1998, Strauss and Corbin, two leaders of grounded theory approach to qualitative research, attempted to modify the usual canons of good (positivist) science to fit their own post-positivist concept of rigorous research. (Denzin & Lincoln, 2000, p. 9)

A positivistic perspective looks at the concrete social reality as something "out there" waiting to be described and explained or at least approximated (postpositivist). In order to do so, the researchers should be "objective" in their interpretation of that reality; that is, not allow their values or attitudes or feelings to enter into the research process, by holding them in abeyance or "bracketing" these attitudes and values. The researched is often objectified as a research object. Classical ethnographers studying a community are most likely to treat villagers as "foreigners" or "the other" and to construct a story from the field that is thought to be an "objective" account of events in the field. Denzin and Lincoln (1998a) note that these accounts are often more like "tales" from the field that often reflect a given ethnographer's attitudes, beliefs, and values (p. 14).

Returning home with his data, the Lone Ethnographer wrote up an objective account of the culture he studied. These accounts were structured by the norms of classical ethnography. This sacred bundle of terms (Rosaldo, 1989, p. 31) organized ethnographic texts in terms of four beliefs and commitments: a commitment to objectivism, a complicity with imperialism, a belief in monumentalism (the ethnography would create a museum like picture of the culture studied), and a belief in timelessness (what was studied never changed). This model of the researcher, who could also write complex, dense theories about what was studied, holds to the present day. (Denzin & Lincoln, 1998a, p. 14)

This traditional model has been rejected by a new generation of qualitative researchers who hold very different philosophical views on the nature of the social world. Denzin and Lincoln (1998a) note the importance of three "interpretative paradigms" in qualitative research: *constructivist-interpretive, critical* (Marxist, emancipatory), and *feminist.* Neuman (2003) also cites three types of qualitative paradigms that he terms *positivism, interpretive,* and *critical* (p. 83). Each of these paradigmatic approaches to research makes certain assumptions concerning the nature of reality and the individual (ontology), the type of theory (methodology) they employ, what can be known, and what constitutes knowledge (epistemology).

If I take a *constructivist* or *interpretative* approach to research I would assume a reality that is subjective and consists of stories or meanings produced or constructed by individuals within their "natural" settings. Constructivists in particular assert that there is no "objective" social reality, "out there" waiting to be found out. Miller and Crabtree (1999) note that interpretavists:

> . . . trace their roots back to phenomenology (Schutz, 1967) and hermeneutics (Heidegger, 1927/1962). This tradition also recognizes the importance of the subjective human creation of meaning but doesn't reject outright some notion of objectivity. Pluralism, not relativism, is stressed, with focus on the circular dynamic tension of subject and object. (p. 10) ·

A *critical paradigm* deals with how power, control, and ideology dominate our understanding of reality. The focus of research revolves around how *power* dynamics generate a given set of meanings (ideologies) about individuals' social reality and lived experiences. An example of work from this paradigm comes from *postmodernist* research, which questions the very foundation of what one means by "reality." A postmodernist examines how social life is produced and privileged by those in power. The goal of knowledge building is to "emancipate" and to expose social injustice. Some variations on this paradigm are said to include Marxist, feminist, ethnic, cultural, and queer studies. Denzin and Lincoln pose a separate paradigm for these variations which they term a *materialist-realist ontology* (Denzin and Lincoln, 2000, p. 21). Reality is viewed as "representational" rather than "real" or "the truth."

Paradigms or worldviews are neither right nor wrong; one way of seeing is another way of not seeing. But paradigms are powerful ways of looking at reality, and they provide windows into information about the social world and often frame the particular questions we seek to answer.

THE RESEARCH QUESTION

We often think of qualitative questions involving an "inductive" approach, which focuses on describing (the "What" questions) or generating theories or ideas about a given social phenomenon. The researcher asks open-ended questions such as:

- What is happening here?
- How do individuals make sense of their lived experiences?

Research aims would be exploratory and descriptive: to discover, explain, and generate ideas/theories about the phenomenon under investigation; to understand and explain social patterns (the "How" questions). As Gubrium and Holstein (1997) note, there is a distinction between the "What" and "How" questions in qualitative research, and this can differentiate the types of qualitative paradigms described above.

> The commanding focus of much qualitative research is on questions such as *what* is happening, *what* are people doing, and *what* does it mean to them? The what questions address the content of meaning as articulated through social interaction and as mediated by culture. The resulting research mandate is to describe reality in terms of what it naturally is. (Gubrium & Holstein, 1997, p. 14)

The "What" questions focus on individuals and social settings, "looking for the meanings that exist in, emerge from, and are consequential for, those settings" (Gubrium & Holstein, 1997, p. 14).

The "How" questions in qualitative research are different. They often set aside meaning and are interested in how meaning is constructed by respondents within a given setting:

> . . . *how* questions typically emphasize the production of meaning. Research orients to the everyday practices through which the meaningful realities of everyday life are constituted and sustained. The guiding question is *how are the realities of everyday life accomplished?* (Gubrium & Holstein, 1997, p. 14)

Does this mean that qualitative research questions do not tackle the "Why?" of social reality? Providing explanations about the social world is approached with some skepticism. Qualitative researchers do not usually make generalizations about the wider social system. "Why" questions usually are the province of quantitative researchers. When qualitative researchers entertain "Why" questions, they search "closer to home for answers":

> . . . to identify distant conditions can risk giving short shrift to the fine points of, and ways in which, everyday realities are lived and represented. It also opens qualitative inquiry to the possibility that everyday life might be portrayed as a mere reproduction of the so-called broader realities. This is not to suggest that . . . studies should reject macrolevel explanations, only that the risk of eclipsing the common threads of qualitative inquiry for totalized explanation lurks threateningly in the background. (Gubrium & Holstein, 1997, p. 196)

In pursuing a *quantitative* question, a more *deductive* approach is used; asking questions that serve to describe, explain, and even predict events in the social reality. Questions focus on quantifiable factors:

- How many?
- How much?
- How often?

Returning to our body image example: *What is the association between gender and eating disorders among college students?* Deductive questions often presuppose some "testing" of the relationship between two or more "variables." The idea is to create a statement that is testable in the form of *propositions* (statements) about the relationship between two or more variables, one that is independent (assumed to be the cause) and the other dependent (assumed to be the effect or outcome). So in the above example we would state the following:

- What is the relationship between gender (independent variable) and eating disorders (dependent variable) among college students?

DERIVING RESEARCH QUESTIONS ●

- How do researchers formulate questions?
- What is a good research question?
- How does one get research ideas?

Qualitative research problems derive from many different arenas. As we mentioned earlier, underlying any research problem is a set of *philosophical assumptions* about a given researcher's notion of reality. But beyond this general standpoint regarding the social reality, questions very often will arise from personal experience and can also come from a particular issue in the research literature on a topic.

Sociologist Diane Vaughan's research on intimate relationships in her book *Uncoupling: Turning Points in Intimate Relationships* (1990) provides one such example. Vaughan's research questions concerning the ending of intimate relationships involves asking a series of questions she derived from her personal experience as well as from the research literature:

> How do relationships end? Why does one partner suddenly become discontented with the other—and why is the onset of that discontent not so sudden after all? What signals do partners send each other to indicate their doubts? Why do those signals so often go unnoticed? How do people who saw themselves as part of a couple come to terms, not just with absence and abandonment, but with a new, single identity? (Vaughan, 1990, back cover of book)

The issue of "uncoupling," as she terms this phenomenon, grew out of Vaughan's personal experience with separation and divorce and her reflecting back on these life changes:

> I was married for twenty years. As I reflected on the relationship after our separation, the marriage seemed to have been coming slowly apart for the last ten. Certainly we had our good times, but I could retrospectively pick out turning points—moments when the relationship changed, times when the distance between us increased. These turning points did not hinge around arguments or the typical emotional catastrophes that beset any relationship. Instead, they appeared to be related to changes in each of our social worlds. For example, I started

college because I realized I was never going to have the steady companionship of my partner and needed something of my own to do. This step, innocently taken, changed me—and us. . . . Although we personally experienced the ending of the relationship as chaotic and disruptive, its demise took on a kind of social rhythm. That an experience could be orderly and disorderly at the same time was counterintuitive. Perhaps this orderliness was because ours was a long marriage and thus its ending extended over a long period, giving the appearance of an orderly dissolution. Perhaps it was a natural reflection of my occupation then: a graduate student in sociology, being trained to look for order. (Vaughan, 1990, p. 3)

Her research questions also arose from a particular article she reviewed in research literature on married life. An article on the marriage process caught her interest and described for her the "*reversal*" of the process she was experiencing in her own marriage:

During this same period, I came across an article describing marriage as a process in which two individuals renegotiate who they are with respect to each other and the world around them. They restructure their lives around each other. They create common friends, belongings, memories, and a common future. They redefine themselves as a couple in their own eyes and in the eyes of others, who respond to the coupled identity they are creating. . . . These ideas immediately captured my interest, for what appeared to have happened as my own relationship deteriorated was reversal of this process: we slowly and over time began redefining ourselves as separate people. Rather than an abrupt ending, ours appeared to have been a gradual transition. Long before we physically separated, we had been separating socially, developing separate friends, experiences, and futures. . . . In order to answer the questions raised by my own experience and future stimulated by my reading, I began interviewing people about how their relationships ended. (Vaughan, 1990, pp. 2–3)

There may also be certain *economic* and *time* constraints placed on a researcher in considering the topic for a research project. James A. Banks' decision to study how black Americans are portrayed in textbooks partly came about because of economic and time constraints and practical issues of access to research subjects in completing his Ph.D. thesis:

My first idea for a Ph.D. research project was to study the effects of an experimental training program on the attitudes and beliefs of teachers in urban schools. I had to abandon this idea for several reasons. First, it was necessary that I complete my study within a one-year period, and it was unlikely that I would have been able to design and implement the kind of study I had in mind within those limitations. Second, I needed the cooperation of a large urban school district and numerous teachers to conduct the study, and the initial response I received from one large city school district convinced me that it was unwilling to cooperate with me in implementing the study. Third, the study would have been quite expensive to conduct, and I did not have the funds to finance this type of research project. Although I was disappointed because I was unable to implement my "ideal" study, I did not despair. I realized that although the classroom teacher is the most important factor in the child's learning environment, there are other variables that influence student mastery of content and acquisition of attitudes. Of these other variables, the textbook was perhaps the most important. (Banks, 1976, pp. 383–384)

A researcher may pursue a particular topic and setting because there is funding available to study that topic. There may be granting agencies, public (e.g., government) and private (e.g., foundations), who are dispensing funds to study specific societal issues. Such was the case with Stella Jones' (1976a) dissertation study on geographic mobility. She was interested in the topic of adult socialization. Focusing on the extensive literature in this area, Jones narrowed down her topic to issues dealing with the "status passages" of adults, that is, how they cope/adjust to new major life changes as they progress through their life cycle (Jones, 1976a, p. 316). She became more interested in "the effects status passage has upon the adult personality, and this interest gradually was more narrowly defined as I considered the adult female and her traditional wife-mother role" (Jones, 1976b, p. 328). The specific research problem and setting she selected for her research were dictated by the type of research population she could obtain access to as well as the funding she could receive to carry out her research interests:

. . . the sociology department in which my husband has a position . . . began planning a symposium on the effects of geographical mobility upon the wife-mother. This symposium was to be funded by a major van line. It occurred to me . . . that I might generate some input for this occasion. I assumed that being female would be helpful to my cause. The symposium format called for the presentation of original research . . . this format meant that I would need to develop a research design, get funding from the van line and gain acceptance as part of the symposium. . . . The van line was most receptive to the research proposal. The relative ease of access to funding and a mailing list was a complete surprise to me given the understanding I had of how difficult it can be to gain access into organizations to do research. (Jones, 1976b, pp. 328–329)

Standard research practice advises that the selection of a research problem should determine the type of research method employed within the study. In some cases, however, preference for a given method may serve to dictate the problem to be studied. Anthony N. Doob and Alan E. Gross (1976) were interested in understanding the psychological phenomenon of "frustration." However they wanted to study this topic using an "unobtrusive" method, whereby research subjects would not know they were being studied. Their method served to guide the specific type of research question they arrived at to study their topic. They note their dilemma:

Most social science research looks as if it were planned in a straightforward, logical fashion. Reports are written as if the people involved had just finished reading the relevant literature and saw a need for a particular question to be answered. It generally looks as if these scientists thought a great deal about the best way to answer the question and then designed their research accordingly. [Our] research . . . does not conform to this pattern. Instead, it resulted from an explicit, self-conscious attempt to design a study utilizing a specific method, which, at the time, was relatively underused in psychology. In fact, in this case, the content that was eventually studied [horn honking] was selected only because it was amenable to the method of interest. (Doob & Gross, 1976, p. 487)

Studying horn honking (an unobtrusive measure) in a natural setting allowed the researchers to set up an experiment in which they were able to measure individuals' level of frustration (number of horn honks) as follows:

We thought about a number of different ways to frustrate people, eventually thinking about one of the day-to-day frustrations that most urban people experience, that of traffic jams . . . it did not take long until one of us . . . realized that it is easy to frustrate someone in traffic simply by not moving when a traffic light turns green. In a few minutes, then, we had developed our ideas for our dependent variable. We would simply time how long it would take for the driver behind us in line to honk his or her horn. (Doob & Gross, 1976, p. 488)

Perhaps one of the most common paths to obtaining a research problem involves a review of the literature on a given topic. David Karp is a sociologist at Boston College who has written several books about depression. For Karp a literature review served as the bridge between his interests and an area of inquiry ready for investigation. Let's join David Karp behind the scenes.

Behind-the-Scenes With David Karp

Well, it struck me as odd, when I looked at all this literature on depression; a literature that has really important stuff to say about which independent variables were linked to rates of depression, etc. But depression is a feeling disorder. It is an affective disorder. And so, here I was, reading all of this stuff and I wasn't hearing the feelings of the people who have had the disorder. It struck me as a kind of paradox that that was the case. And, as I said a moment ago, one goal for me, at least of qualitative work, is to let people speak, to acknowledge that the people you are interviewing are really the experts. You talk to them *because* they are the experts. So, I had work to do here, because their voices weren't being heard. There was a journal over there in the O'Neill Library. . . . I was wandering in the stacks one day, and I came upon a journal called *The Journal of Affective Disorders.* It takes up about five feet of our shelf at the library, and there isn't one voice, not one word from a person who actually suffers from depression. I said, "Wow, I've got a thing to do here." That was the start.

While this section is not intended to go over the particulars of *how* to conduct a literature search, we discuss the variety of ways that a review of research literature can serve to help you formulate your research question. Locke, Spirduso, and Silverman (2000) provide us with a useful metaphor for thinking about the literature review process when they note that it is like an "extended conversation" (p. 63).

> The process of locating the voices of individual conversants, for example, is called *retrieval*. That involves searching through the accumulated archive of literature to find out what has been said (when, by whom, and on the basis of what evidence). The process of listening carefully to the ongoing discourse about a topic of inquiry is called *review*. That involves studying items previously retrieved until both the history and the current state of the conversation are understood. (p. 64)

First, if you are *vague* about your topic and want some idea of what is out there in order to begin to narrow down the range of possible things to study, perusing your topic via a literature review might be a good way to begin. You might first want to familiarize yourself with the specific computerized retrieval systems for literature searches that may be available to you, including the large variety of specific databases currently available online and offline. Many of these databases contain abstracts (summaries) of articles and reports which will enable you to quickly obtain an overview of the works. You may also want to think of some important "key words or phrases" that you can input into these databases that will best describe the topic under consideration.

- How do the authors of these articles define their topic?
- What key terms and phrases do they employ?

Keep a list of these so that you can build up a useful set of terms to input into your databases.

- How have other researchers approached your topic?
- What has been the history of research on this topic?
- What are the research controversies within this literature?
- Where is there agreement and disagreement?
- What specific questions have been asked?
- What has been found out?
- What findings seem most relevant?
- What remains to be done, that is, what burning questions still need to be addressed concerning your topic?
- Where do you find gaps in the literature?

Returning to the metaphor of the literature review as an "extended conversation," you may find that in answering many of these questions you are given an opportunity to listen and ultimately be part of the conversation about a given topic. If you already *narrowed* down your topic to some specific questions, the literature review can provide you with a context within which to place these questions and will allow you to tweak them on the basis of what you find out in your literature review. Perhaps you will discover that several researchers have already asked a similar question: How will this affect how you pursue your topic? Will you decide to replicate their study, will you extend your study to a different population, or, will you decide to alter your question somewhat to pursue an uncharted area?

In a qualitative research design it is important not to think of the literature review as occurring at a *fixed point* within the research process, as is often the case in quantitative research, where an exhaustive literature review is often conducted at the beginning of a research project and often serves as a justification for why the researcher asks a particular question and its research significance. Quantitative researchers run the risk of "drowning in the literature" because they may feel they cannot begin a project without leaving a single stone unturned. An inflexibility toward revising their literature review may occur, and it is usually only at the final end of their project that they may again revise their literature review to incorporate unexpected findings.

Given the iterative nature of the qualitative research process, with its emphasis on discovery, the literature review may in fact occur at multiple points in the research process, as new discoveries are made within the data and the researcher looks to the literature to provide a context within which to understand their findings. As a result, the qualitative literature review may take many "twists and turns" as the researcher is led by his or her data analysis to ask new questions that may lead to a different set of research literatures. Sometimes qualitative researchers find it hard to follow a standard (quantitative) research proposal design that asks for a somewhat lengthy literature review when what they propose to do is to discover a given set of questions and/or issues, rather than "test" specific hypotheses they have gleaned from their literature review. Review of the literature then may serve very different functions within qualitative as compared to quantitative analysis.

RESEARCH DESIGN ●

Research questions, as we have shown, are grounded in a *philosophical* standpoint regarding the nature of reality, but they are also guided by a range of factors such as academic and personal interests, abilities, social values, as well access by the researcher to particular economic and lifestyle resources. All of these determine the type of *research trajectory* that a given research project has.

In choosing a research design (a plan for how the researcher will carry out the research project), perhaps one of the most important questions one needs to ask is:

- What theoretical traditions characterize my research problem (interpretation? critical theory? positivism? What?)

A POSITIVIST RESEARCH DESIGN: AN EXAMPLE ●

The following research question derives from a positivist/postpositivist tradition and asks the following question:

What is the relationship between gender and eating disorders among college students?

This research question/problem states the relationship between two variables; one is termed the *independent* (that which we believe to be the cause) variable (here, gender) and the other is termed the *dependent* (that which we believe needs to be explained) variable (here, eating disorders). In the positivist/postpositivist framework the researcher is after a "cause" and an "effect." In order to determine causality, it is important for the independent variable to precede the dependent variable in time, and that there is a relationship between the two, and that there be no third variable, such that if it is "controlled" for (taken into account), the original relationship between the independent variable and dependent variable will not disappear. In pursuing this research question you need to determine *who/what* you will research and *where* the research is going to be pursued. In answering the "*who*" or "*what*" aspect, you will need to determine the "unit of analysis" of your study: Will it be individuals, nation-states, organizations, or what? You will then need to list the behaviors and circumstances and settings you are interested in studying (Golden, 1976, p. 6).

To pursue this research question, we would most likely come up with something like the following:

This study is based on responses from 1,000 male and 1,000 female college students. Students were selected from a random sample of five U.S. Ivy League colleges. A self-administered questionnaire was given to each student to fill out, which covered eating habits, dieting, attitudes toward self, family, friends, school, and related issues. Included in the questionnaire were two different measures of eating-disordered behaviors, namely the Eating Attitudes Test (EAT) and the Eating Disorders Inventory (EDI). These two measures were scored to classify students into either normal or abnormal categories of eaters.

In the above example our unit of analysis is the individual male and female college student. The setting is Ivy League colleges and the behaviors covered are eating attitudes (dependent variable) and values and other factors involved in determining eating-disordered behaviors (dependent variable). A series of hypotheses can be derived from this initial question:

H1. Women are more likely than men to diet.

H2. Women are more likely than men to binge eat.

H3. Women are more likely than men to express that they want to lose weight.

H4. Women will express higher rates of body dissatisfaction than men.

H5. Women will have higher rates of eating-disordered behavior than men.

Once an initial research question and a set of hypotheses are formulated, it is important to consider the following:

- How will you go about "measuring" these ideas? That is how will you "get at" them in the concrete social reality?
- How do you determine if your research subjects have an eating disorder?

Measurement is the process whereby we turn *concepts* like "eating disorders" into *variables*. The process of turning concepts into variables is termed *operationalization*. Some variables like "gender" are more easily measured and can often be "gotten at" through asking a simple question such as: What is your gender? The answer provided by the respondent in your study serves to categorize them (turn them into variables) regarding gender status. Other concepts such as "eating disorders" are much more abstract and may require a great deal of conceptualization concerning what we mean by the term and its various dimensions. Eating disorders have both a *behavioral* and *psychological* set of dimensions that must be measured. This requires asking a number of questions in order to get at the range of behavioral manifestations of the disorder, such as bulimic behaviors, anorexic behaviors, dieting behaviors, as well as a range of psychological dimensions, such as "maturity fears," "perfectionism," etc. One might come up with a set of questions in the form of an inventory (scale) called the Eating Disorders Inventory (EDI), which consists of a range of items that captures the behavioral and psychological dimensions of eating-disordered behaviors (Garner, Olmsted, & Polivy, 1983). One would administer these questions to the selected population, and the answers would determine the extent to which one would be categorized as manifesting eating-disordered behavior.

VALIDITY AND RELIABILITY ●

An important issue that positivists/postpositivists are concerned with in relation to the topic of measurement is the question of the validity and reliability of measures. The positivistic tradition's view of social reality as "knowable" is wedded to a classic concept of validity, defined strictly in terms of measurement:

- Does the measure measure what it is supposed to?
- Is there a correspondence between the measure and the objective social reality?
- Example: Is the EDI a valid measure of eating disorders?

Kvale (1996) notes that,

In a positivist philosophy, knowledge became a reflection of reality: There is only one correct view of the independent external world, and there is ideally a one-to-one correspondence between elements in the real world and our knowledge of this world. (p. 239)

The term *validity* is associated with the field of psychology known as "psychometrics."

In psychology, validity became linked to psychometrics, where the concurrent and predictive validity of the psychological tests were declared in correlation coefficients, indicating correspondence between test results and some external criteria. (Kvale, 1996, p. 238)

So, for example, Scholastic Aptitude Test (SAT) scores would be used to predict success in school (*predictive validity*). The measure of success would be a student's grade point average (GPA) in college (external criteria). *Construct validation* measures the validity of more abstract concepts such as "authoritarianism" by hypothesizing what it might be related to (theoretically) if it is a valid measure. So for example, we would expect an authoritarian measure to be related to untrustworthiness and suspicious behavior (see Deutsch & Krauss, 1965).

Researchers within a positivistic paradigm are also concerned with issues of reliability. Reliability asks the question: If I administer the EDI to a group of students on Day 1 will I also get the same response from the same students on Day 2? If there is no reason to suspect any real change has taken place in a student's life from one day to the next, I should expect the EDI to show consistent results in my student respondents from Day 1 to Day 2. If not, then I would be concerned with how reliable the measure was. If there are discrepant results, then there may be something inherent in the way that I am asking particular questions that makes them unreliable and prone to error. This is different from the issue of validity. The EDI measure may be valid, but not reliable. The reason for unreliability may be, for example, in the way I have physically set up the questions in the questionnaire that makes it difficult for individuals to check off the proper box each time. This is not due to the substance of the measure but to the way it has been administered. It may be that to make some measures more reliable, I have to sacrifice detail in the measure, perhaps by asking fewer, less complicated questions to create a more simple set of choices that are less prone to inconsistencies in checking off choices. In this case I would sacrifice some validity for a gain in reliability. That is, I would create a measure of eating disorders that may not be the most comprehensive in capturing all dimensions of eating issues, but is one that is more simple and easier to administer and cuts down on problems of reliability. As a researcher, I am constantly weighing the reliability of a measure against its validity. Ideally one should try to strike a delicate balance between these two concerns.

SAMPLING ●

The second issue a researcher contends with is the decision regarding sampling: What population do you wish to study? Do you want to make generalizations about college students—if your goal as a positivist qualitative researcher is to infer generalizations, then you need to concern yourself with randomly sampling your population. The idea of drawing a random sample from a wider population is that one can draw inferences about the wider population. If a sample is drawn at random, one can use the laws of probability to calculate how closely the sample's value resembles the true population on a given study variable. There is also a range of probability samples (random, stratified, cluster, and multistage sampling) and non-probability samples (such as purposive or judgment samples or quota samples). In purposive sampling the researcher may not be concerned with the representativeness of the sample with regard to the wider population, and, in fact, there may be no idea of what the wider population is. For example, if I were interested in making generalizations about eating disorders among homosexual college students, it might be more difficult for me to obtain a "master list" of students from which to sample because of issues of homophobia and identity protection.

A QUALITATIVE RESEARCH DESIGN ●

If we decide to follow a different research trajectory and want to study eating disorders among college students from a *feminist standpoint qualitative perspective* our research goal becomes an *understanding from the point of view of those we are studying*.

- *What is the* "lived experience" of college men and women's relationship to food and to their body image?

A *feminist perspective* is especially interested in uncovering any "subjugated" or "hidden" aspects of individuals' experience that may have been missed by researchers. Asking survey questions gleaned from the research literature on this topic and administering eating disorder scales like the EDI would *not* capture the "lived experiences" of these college students. What is their story? We would not then start out with a set of concepts or "measures"; instead we would derive these from the respondents' themselves. From these concepts we would then hope to understand the process by which eating and body issues become gendered and perhaps even begin to build some *theoretical ideas* concerning this topic.

Given this research trajectory, issues concerning validity, reliability, and sampling are quite *different* compared to the positivist qualitative approach we first spoke about.

● VALIDITY IN QUALITATIVE RESEARCH

The question regarding whether college students' relationship to food and their bodies is valid hinges on a different conception of what we mean by truth. If the perspective of most qualitative research is that social reality is "socially constructed," then using the concept of "validity" as "correspondence" with the "objective" reality will not work. Then what will?

> . . . validity is ascertained by examining the sources of invalidity. The stronger the falsification attempts a proposition has survived, the more valid, the more trustworthy the knowledge. (Kvale, 1996, p. 241)

Validity takes the form of subjecting one's findings to competing claims and interpretations and providing the reader with strong arguments for your particular knowledge claim (Kvale, 1996, p. 240).

When you are finished reading a qualitative study, ask yourself: What are the factors that make you resonate with the research findings? Does the researcher capture an understanding of the social reality of the respondents he or she has studied? Kvale (1996) has come up with three criteria of validation for any given qualitative study. He defines these as (1) validity as the quality of craftsmanship, (2) validity as communication, and (3) validity as action (p. 241).

VALIDITY AS CRAFTSMANSHIP ●

"Validity as craftsmanship" has to do with how you perceive the credibility of the researcher and the research. Does the researcher have "moral integrity" (Kvale, 1996, p. 241)? This integrity and credibility is built up through the perceived actions of the researcher. How well has the research been checked? How well has the researcher investigated the findings under consideration? Have the findings been checked, questioned, and theorized? Validation as checking can cover a range of procedures performed on qualitative data (such as looking for negative cases in one's study, going back to respondents when you may not be clear about a point they have made, perhaps sharing your ideas with your respondents to obtain their point of view, making sure that your sampling procedures match your given research question, etc.). As we mentioned, an important aspect of checking your data is that of *"negative case analysis."* Very often this is done as an ongoing procedure throughout one's study, especially if one is using a more grounded theory approach to research (Glaser & Strauss, 1967). To validate is to look for "negative" cases within the study. If you think that you have come up with an idea in your data—a key relationship you found, for example—you must go out of your way to look for negative instances in your data where it does not hold up. So, for example, in the study of eating disorders and body image among college students, we derived a concept termed *"watching it."* This is an abstract concept which describes the range of ways women talk about their bodies being surveyed by themselves and others throughout their everyday activities. For example, Helene, a college student interviewed for a project on college women's eating issues, provides an example of what is meant by this concept from *her* standpoint:

> When I'm home I drop weight, because my mother is always on my back.
> When I go out to eat she tells me what I should order. When I look fine,
> my mother says nothing about my body, not even a compliment. But when
> I start gaining weight, the criticism begins. (Hesse-Biber, 1996, p. 73)

This concept appeared to be strongly related to how women talked about their relationship to food, more specifically what they ate and how much. In order for us to validate this claim, we would want to go through the interviews and look for instances in which this was not the case. If we found a "negative case," we would want to understand why this relationship did *not* hold for this particular individual. Analyzing negative cases provides researchers with feedback concerning the extent to which their initial theoretical claims are validated by their data. As one researcher notes:

Another important type of checking involves going out of your way to provide alternative theoretical explanations for your given findings and attempting to critically examine the relative strengths and weakness of your argument and alternatives to your argument. (Kvale, 1996, p. 242)

Another important aspect of validity as craftsmanship is the ability of the researcher to theorize from their qualitative data (Kvale, 1996, p. 244). Is the researcher able to tell a convincing story? That is, is he or she able to fit the data to a given theoretical framework and make it credible to the reader? In the case of the study of college students' attitudes toward food and body image, has the researcher derived important theoretical insights from the data? Have you learned more about how women and men relate to their bodies and do you have a fuller understanding of these issues? Have important aspects of a given issue been left out?

● COMMUNICATIVE VALIDITY

A second form of validation is communicative validity. One can think of this as a dialogue among those considered legitimate knowers who may often make competing claims to knowledge building. The idea here is that each interpretation of a given finding is open to discussion and refutation by the wider community of researchers, and sometimes this extends to the community in which the research itself was conducted. There is a give and take of dialogue surrounding meaning, a move toward the idea of "intersubjective" understanding of meaning through dialogue. Not all researchers agree on who can share in this dialogue or who has the right to interpret knowledge and how disagreements should be resolved (Kvale, 1996, p. 244). If I were to practice a form of communicative validity, I might ask the students interviewed in the eating attitudes study to comment on my research findings. Do they agree with my interpretation of their interviews? What if they disagree? How will alternative points of view into these findings be resolved?

● PRAGMATIC VALIDITY

Communicative validity attempts to reach an understanding concerning knowledge claims within the wider research community and beyond. Pragmatic validity goes a step further and looks to see the extent to which research findings impact those studied as well as changes which occur in the wider context within which the study was conducted. Depending on the type of study conducted and the findings, one would expect to look for certain "action" outcomes. For example, in the study of the relationship between gender and eating disorders among college students, we found that the problem of eating disorders was much more prevalent among women than men and that there were certain factors within the college community that contributed to women's problems with food. Several of these factors had to do with the types of food available in the school cafeteria and in vending machines. Other factors had to do with the scheduling of cafeteria hours. One might look to see what impact the research findings had on the wider college community as a result of this report. Did the college food service change its food policies? Was there dialogue in the college newspaper around these issues and did other students push for changes in school cafeteria policies, for example, asking that low-fat foods be readily available in the dining halls? Are research subjects empowered to make changes within their lives as a result of their experience with and knowledge of this project? It is important to keep in mind the power dynamics involved in pragmatic validation. As Kvale notes,

> Pragmatic validation raises the issue of power and truth in social research: Where is the power to decide what the desired results of a study will be, or the direction of change; what values are to constitute the basis for action? And, more generally, where is the power to decide what kinds of truth seeking are to be pursued, what research questions are worth funding? (1996, p. 251)

Researchers should consider these issues if they are hoping for some sort of social change to result from their research.

TRIANGULATION AS A VALIDITY TOOL ●

One important check on the validity of research findings is to employ the technique of methods *triangulation*; that is, using two different methods to get at the same research question with the goal of looking for "convergence" in research findings (Greene, Caracelli, and Graham, 1989). If two methods come up with the same finding, this serves to enhance the validity of research results. So, for example, we might utilize a mixed-methods approach to study the eating attitudes of college students by combining a qualitative design (interviewing) with a quantitative design (a survey) to see if the results concerning body image attitudes hold up using two separate methods. There are other forms of triangulation beyond using two different methods. We might use two different theoretical perspectives (a feminist approach and a critical theory approach) to study the same problem (*theoretical triangulation*) as well as using different data sources (*data triangulation*) within the same study to enhance the validity of research results. We may also have different investigators studying the same phenomenon (*investigator triangulation*). So, for example, to obtain data triangulation in our study of student eating attitudes, we might include field notes drawn from observations conducted in the student cafeteria and combine this data with interviews from college students in order to more fully understand the impact of college life on student eating attitudes. We might have two different investigators collect (investigator triangulation) these data sources. A feminist perspective could be applied to understand student attitudes toward food and body image, focusing on potential gender differences. A critical theoretical perspective would look at the power and influence of wider cultural factors, such as the mass media, in order to understand gender differences in student eating and body image attitudes. Utilizing *both* these theoretical perspectives may shed *more* light on our understanding of gender differences in eating attitudes with the goal of enhancing the validity of our findings (see Denzin, 1989, pp. 236–247). It is important to note that obtaining validity in qualitative analysis is not a specific entity or end/goal "out there" waiting to be captured by the researcher. Validity is a *process* whereby the researcher earns the confidence of the reader that she or he have "gotten it right." Trustworthiness takes the place of truth. Lincoln and Guba (1999) note:

> The basic issue in relation to trustworthiness is simple: how can an inquirer persuade his or her audiences (including self) that the findings of an inquiry are worth paying attention to, worth taking account of? What arguments can be mounted, what criteria invoked, what questions asked, that would be persuasive on this issue? (p. 398)

There are some guidelines to navigate the important "threats to validity," such as researcher bias and measurement bias. However, there is no specific litmus test we can administer that will apply a stamp of approval to any given qualitative research project.

There are some qualitative researchers who have developed a specific set of "core characteristics" to ascertain the validity of any qualitative study (see Spencer, Ritchie, Lewis, & Dillon, 2003) and this raises an important question:

- Should qualitative researchers follow a set of core criteria for assessing the validity of their research?

The search for some specific criteria with which to assess qualitative findings may be harkening back to a positivistic model of the research process that assumes there is a "truth" out there waiting to be found out. Qualitative research stresses the importance of interpretation—that is, how individuals experience their lived reality. In fact, some qualitative researchers might view our discussion of triangulation as a validity tool for convergence of research findings as only one function of triangulation. Triangulation can also serve to capture alternative and multiple perspectives on the social reality! Doubts are also raised concerning whether such "core" validation factors can apply across different qualitative methods. For example, is assessing the validity of a content analysis study the same as ascertaining the validity of findings from an interview project? Studies that seek to develop specific core criteria, in fact, do not always agree with each other on what these factors should be (compare Seale and Silverman, 1997, with Popay, Rogers, & Williams, 1998).

All measures of validity are not without their issues, nor is it clear that employing all of the above validity checks will result in a one-to-one convergence of research results. What these validity practices can move us toward is the more systematic practice of "rigor" and "trustworthiness" in the research process, so that we can "broaden, thicken, and deepen the interpretive base of any study" (Denzin, 1989, p. 247).

RELIABILITY IN QUALITATIVE RESEARCH ●

Neuman (2003) talks about the issue of reliability in terms of gathering data from observations of individuals or events within a field setting. He refers to the "internal consistency" of field observations: Is the data you gathered reasonable? Does it fit together? Does your data add up? Is there consistency in your observations "over time and in different social contexts?" (p. 388). External consistency refers to "verifying or cross-checking observations with other divergent sources of data" (p. 388). The researcher who is concerned with external consistency goes out of his or her way to look for other evidence that will confirm his or her findings. Neuman notes:

> Reliability in field research depends on a researcher's insight, awareness, suspicions, and questions. He or she looks at members and events from different angles (legal, economic, political, personal) and mentally asks questions. (p. 388)

As you can see, both validity and reliability are important and complex issues in qualitative research, though conceived of differently than in positivist work. The following is a reliability checklist for qualitative studies: Gay and Airasian (2003, p. 536) adapted from Schensul, Schensul, and LeCompte's (1999) ethnographic volume that you might want to employ in thinking about conducting a qualitative research study, especially one that involves gathering data from interviews, or conducting an ethnographic participant observation study.

● GAY AND AIRASIAN'S CHECKLIST IN EVALUATING RELIABILITY IN QUALITATIVE STUDIES

- "Is the researcher's relationship with the group and setting fully described?"
- "Is all field documentation comprehensive, fully cross-referenced and annotated, and rigorously detailed?"
- "Were the observations and interviews documented using multiple means (written notes and recordings, for example)?"
- "Is interviewer's training documented?"
- "Is construction, planning, and testing of all instruments documented?"
- "Are key informants fully described, including information on groups they represent and their community status?"
- "Are sampling techniques fully documented as being sufficient for the study?" (Gay & Airisian, 2003, p. 536)

In order to gain a deeper insight into these issues, let's go behind the scenes with sociologist David Karp and see how these issues impact his research practice.

Behind-the-Scenes With David Karp

Well, I guess I would disagree with those who say that people who do qualitative research can't generalize. I make a distinction in my mind between what I think of as "empirical generalizations" and "analytical generalizations." I don't think you will find this in a textbook, but to me an empirical generalization is sort of what people do when they do statistical analysis. They are generalizing from a sample to some larger universe. Analytical generalizations, in my mind, come sort of close to what Georg Simmel talked about when he talked about "social forms"—the discovery of underlying social forms. The kind of generalization that I'm trying to make in my work is the Simmel-type generalization. And I think it is possible to do that kind of analytical generalization with smaller samples of qualitative data. But there are dangers. I wouldn't discount them. The article was based on 35 interviews. My book, *Speaking of Sadness,* eventually was based on 50. The "Dialectics of Depression" was an article that I wrote along the way. It was absolutely my first effort to say something from the data. You're always trading off breadth for depth. I mean, the great value of survey research is breadth. You truly can, within known probabilities of error, make generalizations about a larger universe of people. It's a very, very powerful thing to be able to do. So, really, the method you use must be dictated by the problem. You don't use a hammer when you need to use a saw. Well, one could say about the 35 people in this study, that they aren't representative, and I can hear that. They're largely white people. I think I had a couple of people in the study who were non-white. And, I think, properly one could say, "Well, might the experience of depression be different for Hispanic people, different for African-Americans, and so on?" I say, "Absolutely!" And there you go. Take my work and move beyond it, and do something else with it. No study is self-contained from beginning to end. Every study, whether it's a statistical study, or an in-depth interview study, with 50, 60, 100, 200 people, is going to have limitations in terms of generalizability.

In the end, the test of validity, of whether you have been well-disciplined by the data, whether you really have discovered some underlying social forms, is whether the real experts, those you've studied, when they read your work say, "You've captured it!" See, to me, the ultimate test of validity is when people have read the work—this is very gratifying—and say, "You know, you really captured my experience. You found a way to convey my experience. It lets me understand my own life more deeply." Truly, I think that the power of sociological work is that when you have an experience as an individual, especially something like depression, you feel so much like nobody else could possibly understand, but when I step back and listen to people, and listen well, and look for those patterns, those forms, I can see things that the individual can't see in her own life; because they have only their own life to generalize from. So, to me, if the generalization thing is off-base, people will dismiss your work. They will say, "This is off the wall. You're trying to write about depression, but it's so distant from my experience that your analysis just doesn't work."

As you can see, validity, in practice, is also linked to issues of representation and generalizability. This brings us to sampling.

● SAMPLING IN QUALITATIVE RESEARCH

The logic of qualitative research is concerned with in-depth understanding, usually working with *small samples*. The goal is to look at a "process" or the "meanings" individuals attribute to their given social situation, not necessarily to make generalizations. We investigate women's attitudes toward their bodies not to make overall generalizations about *how many* women have problems with their body image, but to understand how women *experience* being overweight, for example, in a thin culture. Here we would be interested in the process by which women do or do not cope with their body image and the ways in which they interact with cultural messages of thinness from the media and significant others in their lives.

Qualitative researchers are often interested in selecting *purposive* or *judgment samples*. The type of purposive sample chosen is based on the particular research question as well as consideration of the resources available to the researcher. Patton (2002, p. 242), in fact, has identified 16 different types of purposive samples, and more than one purposive sampling procedure can be used within any given qualitative study. We will select a few examples of how researchers use some of these particular qualitative samples in their studies.

Katherine Hendrix (1998) wanted to study how the credibility of a professor is communicated in the college classroom and how race influences a student's perception of a professor's credibility. She notes:

> The participants in the study represented a "purposeful rather than random" sample. My goal was to obtain the participation of male dyads reflecting professors who worked in the same division and possessed comparable years of teaching experience at the collegiate level. However, three of the professors would be Black and three would be White. (p. 43)

Hendrix (1998) also wanted to interview a sample of students from each of these courses who had volunteered to be interviewed. These students were selected according to their class year, race, and major using a random procedure. However, with a limited number of students volunteering, the random procedure was revised to ensure a diverse pool and students were selected to match specific criteria, such as race (p. 44).

Hendrix used several different *sampling procedures* in carrying out her research project. The first decision to sample came directly from her research problem: in her review of the literature on the topic of teacher communication, she noted that there were particularly difficult "restricted interactions" between black faculty and their white students. Hendrix speculated that within a predominately white university she might find "particular challenges to building credibility and acceptance . . . for the Black teacher and professor" (p. 43). She wanted to follow up on this idea. She therefore chose a large 4-year university that had a predominately white college student population. She selected a "*homogenous* sample," a *university* with a predominately white population, which enabled her to reduce the variation in race of the student population in order to study her problem. However, when it came to sampling six *faculties* and a diverse group of students to interview from their classes, she employed a *stratified purposive sample* in order to ensure that certain "characteristics" of the faculty and students were included. Sampling for these differences was crucial in carrying out her stated research goals.

Sometimes, however, sampling follows no logical plan; it just happens. Circumstance provides the researcher with an "opportunistic sampling" possibility. One anthropologist recalls his research in West Pakistan and how a sequence of events led to the unintended selection of individuals to interview:

> I recall the use of opportunistic sampling during my first ethnographic trip to West Pakistan. The abundant visitors who voluntarily came to my home served as respondents for innumerable questions; I sought to plumb their motivations and other personality characteristics, and in some cases begged them to take the Rorschach test. Occasionally I solicited my guests with my interview schedule (that had been prepared for a random sample). . . . My wife and children also utilized invitations to the homes of relatively well-to-do or high-ranking families as opportunities to observe certain aspects of domestic life and to obtain other information. . . . (Honigmann, 1982, p. 81)

An important part of conducting fieldwork is having access to informants who can serve as "guides" to provide information concerning the research site. Very often, however, researchers find the selection of informants boils down to who is available, who has some specialized knowledge of the setting, and who is willing to serve in that role. This type of sampling is known as a "*convenience sample.*" There may not be an opportunity to sample among a group of informants according to some given criteria such as age, sex, or social class, for example. Ethnographer Michael Agar's field research among a poor migrant group known as the Lambardi, who resided in a village located in the state of Karnataka, India, notes how the researcher may have no choice in the selection of an informant. He or she is usually earmarked by the community to handle "strangers" and in fact Agar gives informants the name "professional stranger-handlers." He notes:

Among the Lambardi, the professional stranger-handler was an older man named Sakrya. He was the first who came up to talk with me when I entered the tanda [settlement]. He pleasantly explained, for example, that the tanda was overcrowded. Therefore, I had to understand that it would be impossible for me to live there. It was Sakrya who suddenly appeared whenever I began doing something bizarre in the early days of fieldwork, like drawing a map or measuring the dimensions of a tanda hut. After a couple of months, it was partly Sakrya's decision that I was trustworthy that opened up the tanda to me. (Agar, 1996, p. 135)

Another important type of purposive sample is known as *"theoretical sampling."* This kind of sample is often used as a part of a "grounded theory" approach to research. Glaser and Strauss (1967) define theoretical sampling as "the process of data collection for generating theory whereby the analyst jointly collects, codes and analyzes his data and decides what data to collect next and where to find them in order to develop . . . theory as it emerges" (p. 45). Theoretical sampling implies that the researcher decides who or what to sample next, based on prior data gathered from the *same* research project in order to make comparisons with previous findings. Analyses of findings in your current analysis of the data and the theoretical insights you come up with provide you with new sampling questions like: Who will I talk with next? What additional sources of data should I explore? What data will challenge or confirm my theoretical understanding of this finding? (See Glaser & Strauss, 1967; Guba & Lincoln, 1989; Lincoln & Guba 1985; and Patton, 2002.) Anthropologist Michael Agar (1996) provides the following example of theoretical sampling:

Say you've worked with four men on agriculture. You've talked with them about their interpretation of the flow of events that constitutes agricultural work, and you've made several observations working with them in the fields. Now you seek out four more men for shorter interviews and observations who live on the other side of the village. You select them for the purpose of checking similarities in the accounts given by your original sample. (p. 172)

Agar notes that if the researcher finds the results are the same for this group of individuals and learns nothing new by sampling again from this population, then a point of *"theoretical saturation"* or " data adequacy" (see Morse, 1995) on this group of individuals is reached. The researcher may then opt to interview another group in the village, perhaps those who do not own land, to see if a different angle of vision onto the issue of agriculture is ascertained. By doing this, one enhances understanding through seeking multiple perspectives (Agar, 1996, p. 172). Janice Morse (1995), a noted qualitative researcher, provides the following insights to guide your sampling procedure that involves a delicate balance between numbers and insight, in other words, "statistical significance" does not mean "theoretical significance."

> . . . in quantitative methods the significance of numbers is carefully taught, and statistical significance is based on frequencies, averages, and the distribution of data. *Frequency* is central to the analysis, and if a particular instance is too abhorrent, it may even be deleted from the data set as an "outlier" or an error. On the other hand, in qualitative analysis, the converse is true. It is often the infrequent gem that puts other data into perspective, that becomes the central key to understanding the data and for developing the model. It is *the implicit* that is interesting. (p. 148).

Janice Morse (see boxed text) provides a set of "principles" to follow when thinking about sample size and how to capture issues of "difference" in our qualitative research project.

Sampling and Qualitative Research

• "Select a cohesive sample. The greater the cohesiveness of the sample, the faster saturation will be obtained, but the less generalizability of the project. This includes using a culturally cohesive sample and a sample that shares (with least variation) the characteristics that address the research topic."

• "Saturation will be achieved most quickly if theoretical sampling is used. Snowball, or a convenience sample, will result in saturation being achieved more slowly. With a random sample, saturation may never be achieved because the sample may be theoretically inappropriate, or poor informants, whose stories replicate rather than provide new information, may be randomly selected."

• "Sample all variations appearing within the data until each 'negative case' perspective is saturated. When constructing a theory, locate every possible "hypothetical" negative case, and give these data equal attention as the mainstream storyline."

• "Saturated data are rich, full, and complete. The resulting theory makes sense and does not have gaps."

• "The more complete the saturation, the easier it is to develop a comprehensive theoretical model." (from Morse, 1995, pp. 147–149)

● QUALITATIVE RESEARCH INQUIRY: A DYNAMIC DANCE

Qualitative research design relishes a tight link between *epistemology* (viewpoint on the social reality) and *methodology* (theoretical perspective into the social world). This is the research nexus we explained in Chapter 1. These factors help shape the *research trajectory* of a qualitative project—the types of problems selected, what sampling procedures are utilized, and the types of data analysis and interpretation strategies (which we will discuss in greater detail in Part 3 of this book) that a researcher employs. There is a dynamic interaction between these elements of the research process. While we have separated out the parts to look at each individually in this chapter, we can now step back and look at these parts as a whole and how they often influence one another. In order to do so, working within the qualitative tradition, we will compare the dance routines of a qualitative research design with its quantitative counterpart.

Typically the quantitative research process is presented as a "wheel" or a circle. The various parts of the research process make up the circumference, and one can begin one's research at different parts of the wheel. The process is also presented as a series of steps (Crabtree & Miller, 1999, p. 9).

Diagram of the Quantitative (Positivistic) Research Process (Adapted from Crabtree & Miller, 1999):

Step 9: Revise Hypotheses
↑
Step 8: Conclusions
↑
Step 7: Data Analysis
↑
Step 6: Data Collection
↑
Step 5: Instrumentation and Sampling
↑
Step 4: Research Design (methods)
↑
Step 3: Hypothesis Formulation
↑
Step 2: Literature Review
↑
Step1: Define Research Problem

Crabtree and Miller (p. 8) note that this figure can best be understood "metaphorically" as "Jacob's Ladder." In this form of inquiry, most closely associated with the natural sciences, the researcher "climbs a linear ladder to an ultimate objective truth" (p. 8). You will notice that the arrows point only in one direction, always moving up the ladder. The quantitative process becomes cyclical when the researcher's conclusions (step 8) lead to a revising of the initial hypothesis, and the process begins again at step 1 with a redefining of the research problem, and so on. Ideally, within this model all conclusions are open to confirmation (the theory/hypothesis has been subjected to testing and it endures) and for some researchers the hypothesis is also opened up to refutation through seeking alternative explanations and testing these against the original hypothesis (see, for example, Karl Popper's (1935) concept of "falsificationism"). Most positivist inquiry is now moving to a more postpositivist conception of reality by altering the definition of "truth," which is now phrased in terms of "probabilities." As Crabtree and Miller note, "The postpositivist perspective seeks successive approximations to reality but understands the unlikelihood of getting to ultimate reality" (p. 9).

- How would this model be revised if one were to move to a qualitative model of social inquiry?
- What elements would remain, what elements would be added, or discarded?
- How would you relate elements of the process to each other in a holistic manner?

Based on what you have already learned in this chapter, we can immediately begin to see glaring omissions in this diagram. Perhaps the first element that is missing from this process is some acknowledgment of the influence a particular *philosophical substructure* (paradigm choice) has on the research process. Although qualitative research paradigms may differ in terms of their assumptions regarding the extent to which knowledge can be "objective," most qualitative paradigms agree on the importance of the *subjective meanings* individuals bring to the research process and acknowledge the importance of the social construction of reality. In the qualitative research process there is a *dynamic interaction* between the research problem and the literature review. One's research questions are tentative and most often *not* phrased in terms of hypotheses. The goal is one of *theory generation.* Having said that, this does not mean that qualitative researchers have no interest in "testing" out their ideas. In fact, some qualitative researchers, especially those employing a *grounded theory* (Charmaz, 2000) perspective, stick close to their data and are constantly testing out their ideas as their data is being collected. There is an *iterative process* between data collection and data analysis and theory generation in a process known as *analytical induction.* As one collects data, one is interpreting it and formulating a range of ideas to test out on additional data collected and so on. There is a dynamic interaction between steps 6 (data collection), 7 (data analysis), and 3 (hypothesis formulation). Data collection (step 6) and data analysis (step 7) can lead to the creation of ideas/hypotheses concerning the data. This in turn might lead the researcher to collect specific types of data via a particular sampling procedure (step 5), that is, sampling specific cases to test out these ideas (theoretical sampling). The researcher moves back and forth in the steps of research almost as if he or she is doing a dynamic dance routine, whose steps are often unstructured, subject to whatever type of music one happens to be listening to (the data), and the researcher is open to new routines at a moment's notice (see also Crabtree & Miller, 1999). There is no one right dance, no set routine to follow. One must be open to discovery. There is no linear dance routine to this model; this form of inquiry doesn't work that way.

Barrie Thorne is a Professor of Sociology and Women's Studies at the University of California–Berkeley and has written extensively about ethnography. The dynamic dance that often characterizes qualitative inquiry is exemplified by Thorne's approach to research. Let's join Thorne for a behind-the-scenes view.

> ### Behind-the-Scenes With Barrie Thorne
>
> I start with fairly broad questions, strategically choose a research site (with a case study logic in mind), and proceed to observe, and, in my current work, interview, and also gather relevant statistics (about the area of Oakland I'm studying), e.g., from the census and the school district. Further questions, reworked questions are "emergent," that is, there is a continual back and forth between the conceptual themes I brought in and have developed and the empirical data; it's a honing and inductive process, with a lot of discovery and reformulation along the way. (Discovery, opportunities for serendipity—those are also distinctive features of some types of qualitative research.)

● CONCLUSION

At this point in the book we hope that you are getting a sense of the complexity of qualitative research on both a theoretical and practical level. In particular, every researcher operates from within a paradigm or, world view. This perspective impacts all phases of a research project and forms the philosophical substructure of the research project. The research nexus (the combining of epistemology, theory, and method) is where the philosophical underpinnings of the project intersect with the research techniques you will use. The many issues pertaining to research design that we have reviewed in this chapter are all impacted by these underlying issues. In this way, qualitative research truly is a holistic activity where the varied layers of research, as well as the varied phases, interact with each other. But having said this, one ongoing component to qualitative research has yet to be properly addressed, and that is ethics. In the next chapter we turn to a discussion of the ethical substructure of research and why qualitative scholars are committed to dealing with ethics in a holistic manner.

GLOSSARY ●

Analytical Induction: Iterative process between data collection and data analysis and theory generation.

Construct Validation: Measures the validity of more abstract concepts such as "authoritarianism" by hypothesizing what they might be related to (theoretically) if they are valid measures.

Constructive-Interpretive Approach: This is one of the three interpretive paradigms in qualitative research. If I take a *constructivist* or *interpretive* approach to research I would assume a reality that is subjective and consists of stories or meanings produced or constructed by individuals within their "natural" settings. Constructivists in particular assert that there is no "objective" social reality "out there" waiting to be found out.

Convenience Sample: Very often, researchers find the selection of informants boils down to who is available, who has some specialized knowledge of the setting, and who is willing to serve in the role. This type of sampling is known as a convenience sample.

Critical Approach: One of the three interpretative paradigms in qualitative research; a critical paradigm deals with how power, control, and ideology dominate our understanding of reality.

Feminist Perspective: A feminist perspective is especially interested in uncovering any "subjugated" or "hidden" aspects of an individual's experience that may have been missed by researchers.

Grounded Theory: In fact, some qualitative researchers, especially those employing a grounded theory (Charmaz, 2000) perspective, stick close to their data and are constantly testing out their ideas as their data is being collected.

Interpretive Perspective: This perspective developed as a direct challenge to positivist epistemology and its interpretation/application of objectivity. The interpretive epistemology is based on the interpretation of interactions and the social meaning that people assign to their interactions (Nielsen, 1990, p. 7). This perspective epistemologically believes that social meaning is created during interactions and by people's interpretations of interactions. The implication is that different social actors may in fact understand social reality differently, producing different meanings and analyses. Research of this kind involves the building of relationships between the researcher and research participants who are collaborators in the research process.

Materialist-Realist Ontology: Reality is viewed here as "representational" rather than "real" or "the truth."

Operationalization: The process of turning concepts into variables.

Philosophical Assumptions: These assumptions may often go unstated and unexamined, but they are crucial underpinnings to the research enterprise and help shape its process. The philosophical substructure of a research enterprise guides us and our interpretation of reality in some core metaphysical issues.

Philosophical Substructure: A paradigm choice.

Positivism: The positivistic tradition's view of social reality as "knowable" is wedded to a classic concept of validity, defined strictly in terms of measurement.

Postmodernist Research: This perspective questions the very foundation of what one means by "reality." A postmodernist examines how social life is produced and privileged by those in power.

Predictive Validity: For example, Scholastic Aptitude Test (SAT) scores would be used to predict success in school (*predictive validity*). The measure of success would be a student's grade point average (GPA) in college (external criteria).

Purposive Sample: Also known as *judgment samples,* qualitative researchers are often interested in selecting these kinds of samples; the type of purposive sample chosen is based on the research question at hand as well as consideration of the resources available to the researcher.

Research Trajectory: Research questions are grounded in a philosophical standpoint regarding the nature of reality, but they are also guided by a range of factors such as academic and personal interests, abilities, social values, as well as access of the researcher to particular economic and lifestyle resources. All of these determine the type of research trajectory for a research project.

Sampling Procedures: The systematic selection of a pool of participants.

Small Samples: The logic of qualitative research is concerned with in-depth understanding, usually working with small samples. The goal is to look at a "process" or the "meanings" individuals attribute to their social situation and not necessarily to make generalizations, which is why small samples are often appropriate.

Subjective Meaning: Although qualitative research paradigms may differ in terms of their assumptions regarding the extent to which knowledge can be "objective," most qualitative paradigms agree on the importance of the subjective meanings individuals bring to the research process and acknowledge the importance of the social construction of reality.

Theoretical Sampling: Another important type of purposive sample; this kind of sample is often used as a part of a "grounded theory" approach to research. Glaser and Strauss (1967, p. 45) define theoretical sampling as "the process of data collection for generating theory whereby the analyst jointly collects, codes and analyzes his data and decides what data to collect next and where to find them in order to develop . . . theory as it emerges."

Theoretical Saturation: Agar (1996) notes that, if a researcher finds the results are the same for a group of individuals and she or he learns nothing new by sampling again from this population, then a point of theoretical saturation on this group has been reached.

Theory Generation: This occurs when a researcher uses her or his data to develop a theory about the social world or some specific aspect of it.

Validity: Researchers working within the qualitative paradigm conceptualize validity differently than traditional positivist conceptions of the term. Generally speaking, validity is one of the issues researchers address as they make a case or argument for the knowledge they have produced being valid. In other words, that the knowledge produced reflects some aspect of the social world and/or is compelling.

DISCUSSION QUESTIONS ●

1. What is a worldview and how does it impact the research process holistically?

2. How is research design impacted by philosophical and practical considerations?

3. Why is it important for a researcher to be open to modifying a research project in terms of both theory and methods?

4. How do qualitative researchers think about issues of validity, reliability, and generalizability?

5. What considerations are important when selecting a sample?

6. What does it mean to say that qualitative researchers use a "dance" model of inquiry rather than a "step" model?

● SUGGESTED WEBSITES

Resources for Qualitative Research

http://www.qualitativeresearch.uga.edu/QualPage/

This website is dedicated solely to qualitative research, with useful links such as publications, discussion forums, methods, papers, and organizations and interest groups.

Qualitative Research in Information Systems

http://www.qual.auckland.ac.nz/

This website aims to provide qualitative researchers in IS—and those wanting to know how to do qualitative research—with useful information on the conduct, evaluation, and publication of qualitative research.

● REFERENCES

Agar, M. (1996). *The professional stranger: An informal introduction to ethnography* (2nd ed.). New York: Academic Press.

Banks, J. A. (1976). Comment on "A content analysis of the black American in textbooks." In M. P. Golden (Ed.), *The research experience* (pp. 383–389). Itasca, IL: F. E. Peacock.

Becker, H., Geer, B., Hughes, E., & Strauss, A. (1961). *Boys in white: Student culture in medical school.* Chicago: University of Chicago Press.

Charmaz, K. (2000). Grounded theory: Objectivist and constructivist methods. In N. Denzin & Y. Lincoln (Eds.), *Handbook of qualitative research* (2nd ed.) (pp. 509–535). Thousand Oaks, CA: Sage.

Crabtree, B. F., & Miller, W. L. (1999). The dance of interpretation. In B. F. Crabtree & W. L. Miller (Eds.), *Doing qualitative research* (2nd ed., pp. 127–143). Thousand Oaks, CA: Sage.

Denzin, N. K. (1989). *The research act: A theoretical introduction to sociological methods,* (3rd ed.). Englewood Cliffs, NJ: Prentice Hall.

Denzin, N., & Lincoln, Y. (Eds.). (2000). *Handbook of qualitative research* (2nd ed.). Thousand Oaks, CA.: Sage.

Denzin, N., & Lincoln, Y. (Eds.). (1998a). *The landscape of qualitative research: Theories and issues*. Thousand Oaks, CA: Sage.

Denzin, N., & Lincoln, Y. (Eds.). (1998b). *Strategies of qualitative inquiry*. Thousand Oaks, CA.: Sage.

Deutsch, M., & Krauss, R. M. (1965). *Theories in social psychology*. New York: Basic Books.

Diaz, J. (1999). Blood money: Life, death, and plasma on the Las Vegas Strip. *Electronic Journal of Sociology, 4*(2). Retrieved from: http://www.sociology.org/content/v01004.002/diaz.html

Dobb, A., & Gross, A. (1976). Status of frustration as an inhibitor of horn-honking responses. In M. P. Golden (Ed.), *The research experience* (pp. 481–486). Itasca, IL: F. E. Peacock.

Garner, D. M., Olmsted, M. P., & Polivy, J. (1983). Development and validation of a multidimensional eating disorder inventory for anorexia nervosa and bulimia. *International Journal of Eating Disorders, 2,* 15–34.

Gay, L. R., & Airasian, P. (2003). *Educational research: Competencies for analysis and application* (7th ed.). Upper Saddle River, NJ: Merrill/Prentice Hall.

Glaser, B. G., & Strauss, A. L. (1967). *The discovery of Grounded Theory: Strategies for qualitative research.* Chicago: Aldine.

Golden, M. P. (Ed.). (1976). *The research experience*. Itasca, IL: F. E. Peacock.

Greene, J. C., Caracelli, V. J., & Grahan, W. F. (1989). Toward a conceptual framework for mixed-method evaluation deisgn. *Educational Evaluation and Policy Analysis, 11*(3), 255–274.

Guba, E. G., & Lincoln, Y. S. (1989). *Fourth generation evaluation*. Newbury Park, CA: Sage.

Gubrium, J. F., & Holstein, J. (1997). *The new language of qualitative method*. New York: Oxford University Press.

Heidegger, M. (1962). *Being and Time*. New York: Harper & Row. (Originally published in 1927).

Hendrix, K. (1998). Student perceptions of the influence of race on professor credibility. *Journal of Black Studies, 28*(6), 738–763.

Hesse-Biber, S. (1996). *Am I thin enough yet: The cult of thinness and the commercialization of identity?* New York. Oxford University Press.

Honigmann, J. (1982). Sampling in ethnographic fieldwork. In R. Burgess (Ed.), *Field research: A sourcebook and field manual* (pp. 79–90). London: George Allen & Unwin.

Jones, S. B. (1976a). Geographic mobility as seen by the wife and mother. In M. Golden (Ed.), *The research experience* (pp. 315–326). Itasca, IL: F. E. Peacock.

Jones, S. B. (1976b). Personal reflections on the research process. In M. Golden (Ed.), *The research experience* (pp. 327–339). Itasca, IL: F. E. Peacock.

Kvale, S. (1996). *Interviews: An introduction to qualitative research interviewing.* Thousand Oaks, CA: Sage.

Lincoln, Y., & Guba, E. (1985). *Naturalistic Inquiry.* Beverly Hills, CA: Sage.

Lincoln, Y., & Guba, E. (1999). Establishing trustworthiness. In A. Bryman & R. G. Burgess (Eds.), *Qualitative research*, volume III (pp. 397–434). Thousand Oaks, CA: Sage.

Locke, L., Spirduso, W. W., & Silverman, S. (2000). *Proposals that work. A guide for planning dissertations and grant proposals.* Thousand Oaks, CA: Sage.

Miller, W. L., & Crabtree, B. F. (1999). Clinical research: A multimethod typology and qualitative roadmap. In B. F. Crabtree & W. L. Miller (Eds.), *Doing qualitative research* (2nd ed.) (pp. 3–30). Thousand Oaks, CA: Sage.

Morse, J. (1995). The significance of saturation. *Qualitative Health Research, 5*(2), 147–149.

Neuman, W. (2003). *Social research methods: Qualitative and quantitative methods*, (5th ed.). Boston: Allyn & Bacon.

Nielsen, J. M. (Ed.). (1990). *Feminist research methods.* Boulder, CO: Westview Press.

Patton, M. (2002). *Qualitative research and evaluation methods* (3rd ed.). Thousand Oaks, CA: Sage.

Popay, J., Rogers, A., & Williams, G. (1998). Rationale and standards for the systematic review of qualitative research in health services and research. *Qualitative Health Research, 8*, 341–351.

Popper, K. R. (1959, 1935). *The logic of scientific discovery* (Originally published in German in 1935). New York: Basic Books.

Rosaldo, R. (1989). *Culture and truth: The remaking of social analysis.* Boston: Beacon.

Schensul, S. L., Schensul, J. J., & LeCompte, M. D. (1999). Essential ethnographic methods: Observations, interviews and questionnaires. In S. L. Schensul, J. J. Schensul & M. D. LeCompte (Eds.), *Ethnographer's handbook*, volume 2, pp. 278–289). Lanham, MD: Alta Mira/Rowman & Littlefield.

Schutz, A. (1967). *The phenomenology of the social world* (G. Walsh & F. Lehnert, Trans.). Evanston, IL: Northwestern University Press.

Seale, C., & Silverman, D. (1997). Ensuring rigour in qualitative research. *European Journal of Public Health, 7*, 379–384.

Simmel, G. (1971). *On individuality and social forms* (D. Levine, Ed.). Chicago: University of Chicago Press.

Spencer, L., Ritchie, U., Lewis, J., & Dillon, L. (2003). *Quality in qualitative evaluation: A framework for assessing research evidence.* London: Government Chief Social Researcher's Office.

Strauss, A. L., & Corbin, J. (1998). Basics of qualitative research: Techniques and procedures for developing grounded theory (2nd ed.). Thousand Oaks, CA: Sage.

Vaughan, D. (1990). *Uncoupling: Turning points in intimate relationships.* New York: Vintage Books.

CHAPTER 3

THE ETHICS OF SOCIAL RESEARCH

THE TUSKEGEE SYPHILIS STUDY ●

The Tuskegee Syphilis Study was conducted by the United States Public Health Service (USPHS) beginning in 1932. The study examined untreated cases of latent syphilis in human subjects to determine the "natural course" of the disease. Three hundred and ninety-nine black males from Tuskegee, Alabama, who already had late-stage syphilis, were recruited for this study along with a matched sample of 201 noninfected males. The subjects were not asked to provide their informed consent in order to participate in this project. Those infected with syphilis in the early 1930s were given the standard treatment at that time, which consisted of administering heavy metals. However, those men participating in the study were not treated. In fact, the doctor in charge of the study noted "everyone is agreed that the proper procedure is the continuance of the observation of the negro men used in the study with the idea of eventually bringing them to autopsy" (Jones, 1993, p. 132). However, when antibiotics became available in the 1940s and it was evident that this treatment would improve a patient's chances for recovery, antibiotic treatment was withheld from the infected subjects, even though the researchers knew that if left untreated the disease would definitely progress to increased disability and eventually early death. According to some reports, "on several occasions, the USPHS actually sought to prevent treatment" (Heintzelman, 1996, p. 49). The experiment lasted over 4 decades, and it was not until 1972, in large part prompted by exposure from the national media, that government officials finally ended the experiment. By that time "74 of the test subjects were still alive; at least 28, but perhaps more than 100 had died directly from advanced syphilis" (p. 49). There was a government investigation of the entire project launched in mid-1972, and a review panel "found the study 'ethically unjustified' and argued that penicillin should have been provided to the men" (p. 49).

● ETHICAL LESSONS LEARNED FROM THE TUSKEGEE BIOMEDICAL EXPERIMENT: INFORMED CONSENT

At no time in the course of this project were subjects asked to give their consent to participate in the study. They were not told about the particulars of what the study would entail. In fact, those who participated did not volunteer for the project! Instead, they were deceived into thinking that "they were getting free treatment from government doctors for a serious disease. It was never explained that the survey was designed to detect syphilis. . . . Subjects were never told they had syphilis, the course of the disease, or the treatment, which consisted of spinal taps" (Heintzelman, 1996, p. 51). We have reproduced a copy of the original recruitment letter that was first issued in 1933 from the "Macon County Health Department" and the "Alabama State Board of Health and U.S. Public Health Service cooperating with Tuskegee Institute." As you read this letter you will notice that it makes no mention of spinal taps as a standard treatment, but instead claims subjects will receive "special treatment," and even have "people wait on you." You can imagine if you are living in dire poverty and with a serious illness, this letter might seem like a "gift" of life.

In his book *Bad Blood: The Tuskegee Syphilis Experience,* author James Jones notes that the subjects in the Tuskegee experiment had a blind trust in the medical community. As one subject from the experiment notes:

> We trusted them because of what we thought they could do for us, for our physical condition. . . . We were just going along with the nurse. I thought [the doctors] was doing me good. (Jones, 1993, as cited in Heintzelman, 1996, p. 50)

There is also a question of whether or not the researchers took advantage of a vulnerable population whom they knew did not have the resources to afford medical treatment or the education to question their medical expertise. In addition, the researchers' stereotypical racist attitudes about black males made it easier to justify their decision to not provide them with treatment:

𝔐𝔞𝔠𝔬𝔫 𝔆𝔬𝔲𝔫𝔱𝔶 𝔥𝔢𝔞𝔩𝔱𝔥 𝔇𝔢𝔭𝔞𝔯𝔱𝔪𝔢𝔫𝔱

ALABAMA STATE BOARD OF HEALTH AND U.S. PUBLIC HEALTH
SERVICE COOPERATING WITH TUSKEGEE INSTITUTE

Dear Sir:

Some time ago you were given a thorough examination and since that time we hope you have gotten a great deal of treatment for bad blood. You will now be given your last chance to get a second examination. This examination is a very special one and after it is finished you will be given a special treatment if it is believed you are in a condition to stand it.

If you want this special examination and treatment

you must meet the nurse at _____ on

_____at _____ M. She will bring you to the Tuskegee Institute Hospital for this free treatment. We will be very busy when these examinations and treatments are being given, and will have lots of people to wait on. You will remember that you had to wait for some time when you had your last good examination, and we wish to let you know that because we expect to be so busy it may be necessary for you to remain in the hospital over one night. If this is necessary you will be furnished your meals and a bed, as well the examination and treatment without cost.

REMEMBER THIS IS YOUR LAST CHANCE FOR SPECIAL FREE TREATMENT. BE SURE TO MEET THE NURSE.

Macon County Health Department

This letter is reproduced from an educational website at the University of Illinois's Poynter Center for the Study of Ethics and American Institutions (http://poynter.indiana.edu/sas/lb/facts.html).

The rationale was that the conditions existed "naturally" and that the men would not have been treated anyway, according to the premise that shaped the study—that African Americans, being promiscuous and lustful, would not seek or continue treatment (Brandt, as quoted in Heintzelman, p. 49).

Poor decisions on the part of the researchers, influenced by bigotry, allowed this to happen. But this kind of research is simply unacceptable. It demonstrates how racism can lead to inhumane treatment of human subjects. It is argued that the effects of this experiment have to some extent created a long-lasting impact on the black American community, casting a "long shadow on the contemporary relationship between African Americans and the biomedical community" (Gamble, 1997, p. 1773).

● THE CENTRALITY OF ETHICS IN THE RESEARCH PROCESS

Ethical discussions usually remain detached or marginalized from discussions of research projects. In fact, some researchers consider this aspect of research an afterthought. Yet, the *moral integrity* of the researcher is a critically important aspect of ensuring that the research process and a researcher's findings are "trustworthy" and valid.

The term *ethics* derives from the Greek word *ethos* which means *character*. To engage with the ethical dimension of your research requires asking yourself several important questions:

- What moral principles guide your research?
- How do ethical issues enter into your selection of a research problem?
- How do ethical issues affect how you conduct your research—the design of your study, your sampling procedure, etc.?
- What responsibility do you have toward your research subjects? For example, do you have their informed consent to participate in your project? What ethical issues/dilemmas might come into play in deciding what research findings you publish? Will your research directly benefit those who participated in the study?

A consideration of ethics needs to be a critical part of the substructure of the research process from the initial conception of your problem to the interpretation and publishing of the research findings. Yet this aspect of the research process does not often appear in the diagrams of the models of research we discussed in Chapter 2. A brief history of the ethical aspects of research will better help us understand why this still remains the case.

● A BRIEF HISTORY OF RESEARCH ETHICS

Formal consideration of the rights of research subjects grew out of the revelations of the terrible atrocities that were performed in the guise of scientific research on Jews and other racial and ethnic minority groups in Nazi concentration camps during World War II. One result of the revelations of these appalling medical experiments perpetrated *in the name of science* resulted in the creation, in 1949, of the *Nuremberg Code,* a code of ethics, which starts off with the stipulation that all research participation must be voluntary. Other codes of ethics soon followed, including the *Declaration of Helsinki* (1964). This code was specifically developed "in part as an alternative to the Nuremberg Code, which dealt exclusively with nontherapeutic [research promising no direct benefit to the subject] research" (Alvino, 2003, p. 896). This code protects research subjects in both therapeutic and nontherapeutic contexts. The Declaration of Helsinki notes several central procedures that should be applied in biomedical research:

> Every biomedical research project involving human subjects should be preceded by careful assessment of predictable risks in comparison with foreseeable benefits to the subject or to others. . . . The right of the research subject to safeguard his or her integrity must always be respected. Every precaution should be taken to respect the privacy of the subject and to minimize the impact of the study on the subject's physical and mental integrity and on the personality of the subject. (pp. 896–897)

The Council for International Organization of Medical Sciences (CIOMS) was also created for those researching in developing nations (Beyrer & Kass, 2002). Throughout the history of scientific research, ethical issues have captured the attention of scientists and the media alike. While extreme cases of unethical behavior are the exception not the rule in the scientific community, an accounting of these projects can provide important lessons for understanding what can happen when the ethical dimension of research is not considered holistically within the research process.

GUIDELINES AND LAWS GOVERNING ● THE RESEARCH PROCESS

Unfortunately, when the Tuskegee experiment began, there was no institutional review board (IRB) to oversee the goals of the project. It was not until the mid-1960s that the federal government began the process of developing a set of "official rules" governing the treatment of research, partly in response to such medical abuses as the Tuskegee experiment and others (see Beecher, 1966; Jones, 1981), which ultimately led to the passage by Congress in 1974 of the National Research Act. This act set up an Office for the Protection of

Research Risks (OPRR) and was housed in the National Institutes of Health (NIH). The act called for the establishment of a "Commission on Protection of Human Subjects of Biomedical and Behavioral Research" (Alvino, 2003, p. 897). These ethical principles were released by the Commission in 1978 in a report known as the "Belmont Report," which was later revised to incorporate additional protections for young children who participate in the research process (p. 898). In 1991, these revised guidelines, known as the Common Rule, received widespread adoption by federal agencies (p. 898). The Common Rule mandated, among other things, that any institution receiving federal funds for research must establish an institutional review committee. These committees, known as *Institutional Review Boards* (IRBs), have the job of watching over all research proposals that involve working with human subjects and animals. Universities and colleges, for example, that receive federal funding for research on human subjects are required by federal law to have review boards or forfeit their federal funding. IRBs are responsible for carrying out U.S. government regulations for human research. They must determine whether the benefits of a study outweigh its risks; that consent procedures have been carefully carried out and that no one group of individuals has been unfairly treated or left out of the potential positive outcomes of a given study (Beyrer & Kass, 2002). This is, of course, important in a hierarchically structured society where we can't simply assume racism, sexism, homophobia, and classism won't make their way into research. Certain types of research, for example, educational research dealing with "instructional strategies," may have an "exempt status" and a full review by an IRB may not be required (DHHS, 1989).

It is noteworthy that over the course of more than 4 decades, even after the USPHS had finally set up a Code of Research Ethics for the treatment of research subjects, the Tuskegee experiment was still allowed to continue (Heintzelman, 1996, p. 52). This raises questions about how effective and accountable research projects are to IRBs as well as about the effectiveness of the range of professional ethics codes that are part of most professional associations and currently serve as guidelines for conducting research (see, for example, the American Sociological Association, 1992; the American Psychological Association, 1981; see the APA website, http://www.apa.org/ethics/homepage.html).

● HOW WELL ARE RESEARCH SUBJECTS PROTECTED TODAY?

It has been over 30 years since the government issued its regulations for protecting human subjects in research studies receiving federal funding, yet there continue to be cases involving human subjects that have resulted in harm and death. As one researcher notes, "The history of research involving human subjects has been described by ethicists as one of 'progress propelled by scandal'" (Alvino, 2003, p. 895). Concerning the current scandals in the field of biomedical research, Alvino says:

> . . . the highly publicized death of Jesse Gelsinger, a research subject who died as a result of his participation in a gene therapy trial at the University of Pennsylvania, aroused significant media attention and public concern regarding the safety of clinical trials. His story is far from unique. . . . Medical research suffered another blow . . . when it was discovered that researchers and pharmaceutical companies involved in research at Cornell and Tufts had failed to notify the National Institutes of Health that six gene therapy research subjects had died during experiments over a nineteen-month period. (p. 902)

At the center of many of the debates regarding the protection of human subjects is the question of whether informed consent procedures are *sufficient* to protect human subjects, and the ability of IRBs to *oversee the research process* in their home institutions. Why didn't the IRBs report the deaths of research subjects to the federal agencies involved in funding these projects? Were the research subjects given proper information regarding the side effects of the study? In the case of Jesse Gelsinger, he was an 18-year-old college student at the time he participated in the University of Pennsylvania study in 1999. An investigation of his death showed that (1) he in fact was not a good candidate for the study in the first place, and (2) he was not provided with adequate information concerning the extreme adverse side effects that other participants in the study had experienced (p. 908). Jesse's father notes: "[I]t looked safe. It was presented as being safe . . . I was misled" (*Chicago Sunday Times*, February 3, 2000, p. 23). This has too often been the case.

Professional associations such as the American Educational Research Association (AERA), the American Sociological Association (ASA), and the American Psychological Association (APA) also outline general ethical guidelines for their members. Each of these associations has a website that discusses a range of specific ethical concerns in each of these professions. The American Psychological Association's website (http:://www.apaorg/ethics/code2002.html), for example, outlines specific ethical categories of conduct, from general principles of professional conduct that deal with issues such as integrity and justice to more practice-specific concerns such as privacy and confidentiality of patients and research subjects. There are also ethical guidelines on record keeping and fees as well as ethical guidance on issues that may come up in a therapeutic situation, such as those especially pertaining to sexual intimacy with clients and therapy with former sexual partners. There are also guidelines for resolving ethical issues, such as how to handle complaints and discrimination.

Thus far we have been focusing on biomedical research. To what extent do the ethical issues in the sciences carry over into the *behavioral* and *social* sciences? Researchers conducting biomedical studies often present a "protocol" that outlines the specific steps they will follow in conducting research on human subjects. Qualitative research is, by its very nature, open to discovery and change in research goals. It may be nearly impossible for the qualitative researcher to account for all of the happenings in the research setting, and it may be hard to go back and forth to a Human Subjects Committee (like an IRB) for approval each time a project takes an unexpected turn. Adler and Adler (2002) argue that obtaining informed consent hits those researchers practicing participant observation the hardest:

> Participant observation has a fuzziness about what is research and what is not, as ethnographers are observers of everyday life and may be generating insights and gathering data from people in all kinds of situations (a waitress at a restaurant, a fellow passenger on an airplane, a person whose child is the same age as one's own). They may not know in advance what information will drift their way and that may prove explicitly useful, either currently or in the future. (p. 40)

In addition, there is often a very personal engagement with research subjects that is often not found to the same extent in biomedical research, raising even more prominently the possibility of undue power, influence, and authority being wielded in the research process.

There are some "classic" examples of extreme violations of ethics in the annals of behavioral and social scientific research as well. Perhaps one of the most egregious comes from a 1963 research project on "obedience to authority," conducted by psychologist Stanley Milgram. Milgram wanted to understand the conditions under which individuals obey authority figures. His research protocol called for deceiving volunteer subjects into thinking they were involved in an experiment on the impact of punishment on memory. Volunteers first read a series of word associations to the individuals (confederates) under a variety of experimental conditions: (1) where they could not see or hear the confederate; (2) they could hear the confederate protest but not see the confederate; (3) they could hear and see the confederate; (4) same conditions as (3) except the subject was required to place the confederate's hand on a shock plate. If confederates were unable to repeat the words, volunteers were asked to administer an "electric shock" to them, increasing the voltage for each wrong answer in order to enhance learning. Subjects had a fake voltage meter in front of them with readings "from slight to severe shock," with a sign warning of the danger in using the equipment posted next to the meter. Some subjects protested upon hearing confederates complain about pain and other medical problems. Even though some volunteers wanted to quit the experiment, the researcher in charge insisted that they continue, saying that he (the researcher) would take responsibility. Some subjects, however, did not protest and even went on to administer what they considered the "highest," most lethal, shock to a confederate, even when they had received no feedback that the person was even alive (Milgram, 1963).

Milgram's experiment deceived his volunteer subjects and failed to obtain their informed consent. The protocol of this experiment did not allow subjects to quit even when some protested and asked that it be stopped. In addition, some subjects experienced psychological distress knowing they actually could administer what would be considered a lethal shock to another human being.

THE ETHICAL DILEMMA OF COVERT RESEARCH ●

Some researchers argue that their research must be conducted in a "covert" manner in order to obtain the information they need to understand certain social phenomena. For example, researchers have gone undercover to study such underground cultures as the drug culture (see Williams, 1996) and used deception in order to find out about the inner workings of the social life of drug dealers and drug takers, often observing individuals engaging in illegal activities and sometimes finding themselves asked to engage in these same activities. There would be no point in asking for the informed consent of the members of this closed society, since they would most likely not want their organization studied. Williams, who did participant observation on a subculture of cocaine users and dealers in the after-hours clubs in an inner city, notes the following concerning his undercover activities:

> I was in a Brooklyn club where I was already conspicuous as a nonuser of cocaine. It seems that I was also overzealous. In the sense that I was staring too much and asking too many questions. One of the club's owners came over to me and said "Listen, my man, if you're undercover, I got people that'll take care of that." I was not sure whether he meant force or bribery, but in any case I stopped going to that club. . . . As a researcher,

I knew what data I needed: information on cocaine users and the associated nightlife, street myths about use. . . . But as most researchers know there is a quid pro quo in every research situation. . . . I was asked to do a variety of favors, such as lending money and finding social workers. . . . On many occasions I was asked to engage in illegal acts. . . . This and similar requests put me in an awkward position. (Williams, 1996, p. 30)

- Is it ethical to go undercover?
- Is it ethical to engage in illegal activities under the guise of research?

One can imagine those social scientists studying deviant behaviors, such as life in the underground drug trafficking world, and how difficult it might be to obtain the informed consent of everyone involved in order to study the inner workings of the illicit drug trade.

- What does the researcher do when he or she confronts information or situations where individuals are observed to engage in major violations of the law?
- Is the researcher ethically obligated to report such activity?
- What about the risks the researcher is taking in terms of his or her own life if he or she does so?

Deception in research doesn't have to occur by going "undercover" in carrying out research projects. The Milgram experiment was a study in deception. From the start, Milgram did not truthfully explain the nature of the experiment, and he deceived subjects into thinking they were in fact applying electrical shocks to another human being. Some qualitative social science research methods, like fieldwork, also require some type of deception between the researcher and the researched. Sociologist Herbert Gans, conducting fieldwork in Park Forest, a suburb near Chicago, in Boston's West End, and in Levittown, a New Jersey suburb, relates his personal reflections on the anxiety he experienced in what he finds is "the deception inherent in participant observation":

Once the fieldworker has gained entry, people tend to forget he is there and let down their guard, but he does not; however much he seems to participate, he is really there to observe and even to watch what happens when people let down their guard. He is involved in personal situations in which he is, emotionally speaking, always taking and never giving, for he is there to learn and, thus, to take from the people he studies, whereas they are always giving information, and are rarely being given anything. Of course they derive some satisfaction from being studied, but when they ask the participant observer to give—for example, help or advice—he must usually refuse in order to maintain his neutrality. Moreover, even though he seems to give of himself when he participates, he is not really doing so and, thus, deceives the people he studies. He pretends to participate emotionally when he does not; he observes even when he does not appear to be doing so and like the formal interviewer, he asks questions with covert purposes of which his respondents are likely to be unaware. In short, psychologically, the participant observer is acting dishonestly; he is deceiving people about his feelings and in observing when they do not know it, he *is* spying on them. (Gans, 1982, p. 59)

Herbert Gans represents a particular point of view on the role of the researcher as participant in the fieldwork experience. The idea that the researcher should remain neutral and "detached" from the research subject tells us that he or she aspires to the goal of "objectivity" in the research process. This objectivity then is enhanced by deception. Yet, as we have seen, this frame on the research process is one of many *paradigms* one can bring to the fieldwork experience. There are those who believe the researcher does not need to maintain distance between the researcher and the researched. Ann Oakley (1981), in fact, critiques this model of neutrality and instead argues for bridging this divide through empathy and affinity. Other ethnographers feel that this form of closeness between researcher and researched also has its problems and that one can become too close to respondents. This in turn can create a series of conflicts and deceptions. Ethnographer Judith Stacey comments:

. . . the irony I now perceive is that the ethnographic method exposes subjects to far greater danger and exploitation than do more positivist, abstract, and "masculinist" research methods. And the greater the intimacy—the greater the apparent mutuality of the researcher/researched relationship—the greater is the danger. (1991, p. 114)

Stacey notes that the further involved she became with her respondents the further exposed she became to situations within the field that left her open to the possibility of manipulating and betraying her respondents (p. 113). So we can see that issues of disclosure and trust are actually very complex.

Some might argue that a certain amount of "strategic" deception is needed when researchers are especially interested in "studying up" (see Korn, 1997). The study of elites is not a common practice within the social sciences (for exceptions, see Hertz & Imber, 1995, and Odendahl & Shaw, 2002). The elite and semi-elite population hold key positions within society, yet their activities and power remain invisible to the average citizen. Elites often protect their privacy through a myriad of self-imposed barriers, ranging from unlisted phones and email accounts to the hiring of staff to screen their calls and contacts and security personnel to prevent unwanted contact with those outside their elite culture. Adler and Adler (2002) note that current IRB and professional associations who fear lawsuits have developed codes of ethics that now ban all aspects of covert research, using the argument that it is almost impossible to obtain informed consent. In addition, these boards cannot protect the researcher from revealing the identity of their respondents if they are asked to do so by officials investigating their research findings. Adler and Adler (2002) note:

> Clearly, if we are being told that we cannot protect our own subjects from official investigation short of our or their going to jail, which not everyone is willing to do, some changes are necessary. Is the new system the best way? If you fundamentally shut down research there is no risk to subjects because researchers will not know anything. (p. 42)

Johnson and Altheide (2002) reflect on professional ethics, given their 65 years of combined experience as university scholars. They note the lack of legal protection of social scientists regarding the confidentiality of their sources as a "political" and not a moral issue:

> In the United States, the first amendment of the Constitution protects journalists by guaranteeing free speech and a free press. Social scientists lack such protection regarding confidentiality of sources, however, and we surmise that this is best seen as a political, rather than a moral one. If social scientists had such protection, we speculate that we might be addressing a different set of ethical issues—perhaps ones such as how social scientists abuse their constitutional protection. (p. 69)

Adler and Adler (2002) argue that ethics boards have overstepped their function, which has resulted in the unanticipated outcome of favoring the dominant classes over the weaker: "Powerful, elite groups can now better hide their mechanisms of control, while weak and powerless groups have lost the ability to tell their stories from their own perspective" (p. 40). These researchers lament the fact that covert research, such as that done by Erving Goffman (1961) in his classic work, *Asylums,* which provides readers with a bird's-eye view of the treatment of the mentally ill by those who care for them, and that carried out by Gary Marx (1988) on the activities of control agencies such as the police, will no longer be possible under the new ethics guidelines.

Haggerty (2004) has identified what he terms an "ethics creep" that has taken over social science research "in the name of ethics." He defines this term as follows: "This is characterized by a dual process whereby the regulatory system is expanding outward to incorporate a host of new activities and institutions, while at the same time intensifying the regulation of activities deemed to fall within its gambit" (p. 391).

RESEARCHER FOR SALE?: CONFLICTS OF INTEREST IN THE RESEARCH PROCESS

Academics are under financial pressures from their universities to obtain grants for research. More and more of these grants are coming from commercial institutions such as drug companies:

> The sharp increase in privately funded (i.e., industry sponsored) research has created an atmosphere that breeds conflicts arising from compelling financial incentives. These conflicts may arise from researchers' financial relationships with companies whose products they are studying, whether the research is sponsored by the government or by the company itself. (Alvino, 2003, p. 906)

In some cases, universities are becoming enmeshed with industrial research interests. Angell (2000) points out the problem of academic medicine being "for sale." She notes:

> Academic medical institutions are . . . increasingly beholden to industry. . . . Some academic institutions have entered into partnerships with drug companies to set up research centers and teaching programs in which students and faculty members essentially carry out industry research. Both sides see great benefit in this arrangement. For financially struggling medical centers, it means cash. For the companies that make the drugs and devices, it means access to research talent, as well as affiliation with a prestigious brand. (p. 1516)

It is possible that in some cases members of a university's own IRB boards can have a vested interest in the very studies they have oversight on. Alvino notes:

Although IRB members are supposedly foreclosed from participating in review of any project or study in which they have a conflicting interest . . . there is no way to ensure that the research facility or individual researchers are not operating under such conflicts. (2003, p. 902)

An article in the *L.A. Times* cited a Yale University study which remarked that "one quarter of the biomedical researchers at universities had commercial ties serious enough to raise questions of financial conflict" (Hotz, 2003, p. 14, as cited in Alvino, 2003, p. 902).

- What are the ethical implications of accepting funding for research?
- How can academics and IRBs work together most effectively?
- How can funding sources, such as the National Science Foundation (NSF) or the National Institute of Mental Health (NIMH), help alleviate the tensions between funding research and ethics?

● ETHICAL DILEMMA: DIVIDED LOYALTIES

Bell and Nutt (2002) talk about their "divided loyalties" in terms of how their professional and occupational commitments pull them in many different directions, creating ethical dilemmas arising from the multiple roles they bring to a research setting. Nutt describes how her professional role as a social work practitioner who is "bound by general social work codes of practice" (p. 79) conflicted with her role as researcher:

As she was leaving the home of a new carer following the research interview Linda Nutt noticed an unambiguously sexually explicit picture in the hallway. For most researchers this would not be an issue; art is a matter of personal taste. But Linda Nutt wasn't just a researcher she was also a practitioner. Frequently when children are placed in foster homes little is known about their life experiences so new carers are instructed to assume that all children have been sexually abused unless specifically told otherwise. . . . There is a statutory responsibility to disregard confidentiality where children are at risk. Nonetheless, because she wanted to keep the roles clear and separate—to act as a researcher (and be in receipt of information) and not as an employee . . . (who could give them information), Linda Nutt chose not to tackle this issue with these new carers but spent several days considering this ethical dilemma. In the end the social worker practitioner identity overcame that of the researcher identity and Linda Nutt informed the local authority of her unease regarding the picture and its potential impact upon the foster children. (p. 79)

Some researchers employ research techniques that raise ethical issues regarding how human subjects are treated. Homan notes what he calls the "softening up" techniques to get at more personal information from respondents who may be unwilling to talk:

The insidiousness of softening-up techniques is demonstrated by some impertinent questions reserved for the latter and more compliant stages of the interviews and questionnaires: having scrupulously sought and obtained a general consent from respondents and their parents. (1992, p. 328)

By its very nature, qualitative research often requires emotional engagement with those with whom we build knowledge. Jean Duncombe and Julie Jessop (2002) discuss how some researchers can lack sympathy for their respondents and "fake" their interest and concern for those they research. Duncombe describes how she wound up treating some of her respondents in a research project she was conducting:

. . . we found it more difficult to achieve rapport where we did not spontaneously feel empathy with our interviewees. For example in an early study of Youth Training Schemes (YTS), Jean felt she established a "genuine," if shallow rapport with the YTS trainees and with the more conscientious employers who took training seriously, because she was "on their side." But with the more exploitative employers and trainers (who provided neither jobs nor training), she knew she was faking rapport to "betray" them into revealing their double standards, and sometimes whilst smiling at them she almost smiled to herself, thinking: "What a revealing quote." . . . Julie felt uncomfortable and personally compromised when she found that, in order to obtain a "good" interview, it seemed necessary to smile, nod and appear to collude with views she strongly opposed. (Duncombe & Jessop, 2002, p. 115)

Researchers are human just like everyone else. Accordingly, we all bring our own likes, dislikes, emotions, values, and motivations to our research projects. It is unrealistic to expect that you will always like those you research, or that you will always naturally feel 100% engaged. This being said, bear in mind that it is you, the researcher, who has initiated this process and involved others (your subjects). Consider this carefully as you contemplate your ethical obligations to your research participants, but as you think through these issues, do so with your own "humanness" in mind—be realistic and fair to all involved.

● IS INFORMED CONSENT THE SOLUTION FOR ETHICAL ABUSES IN RESEARCH?

A major principle underlying many of the ethical policies which have historically grown up around the issue of how to treat research subjects has been the use of "informed consent," the right of subjects to decide anonymously whether they will be involved in a research endeavor (Faden & Beauchamp, 1986). Some ethicists question the extent to which informed consent has lived up to the promise of anonymity for research subjects (Cassileth, Zupkis, Sutton-Smith, & March, 1980). Research has pointed out that subjects do not always understand the medical aspects of the clinical project they are participating in, and some do not even know that they may in fact be participating in a research trial (Lynoe, Sandlund, Dahlqvist, & Jacobsson, 1991; see also Appelbaum, Roth, Lidz, Benson, & Winslade, 1987). As we have seen earlier in this chapter, there are many instances in which there is failure to fully disclose to research subjects the full extent of the risks and benefits of participating in a study, and this has led to some disastrous research outcomes for some of those who participated in clinical trials and biomedical research. There is, then, a *practice* and a *reality* to providing informed consent. There exists a wide variation in how well researchers carry out the policy of informed consent in their ongoing research projects. For example, we present two types of letters on informed consent a researcher might write to parents regarding their child's participation in a research project on body image. We observe that "Letter A" contains a much more detailed account of the research problem, including several research goals and an explanation of how the research will be carried out.

Letter A

Dear Parents:

My name is _____ and I am a sociologist and teacher at _____College. I have previously conducted several studies on self-esteem in young girls. Currently, I am conducting a study on body image and self-esteem among African American and white preteen and adolescent girls. I firmly believe that it is essential to include a sample of African American girls. It has been my experience that the attitudes and beliefs of this important group have been all too often left out. They need a voice and this is why I am writing to you today, to ask for your help and permission to interview your daughter. I would also like to take a moment to tell you a little more about the study.

I plan on having the girls meet at the Health Center for pizza and soda after school in groups of three or four to chat about self-esteem and body image. If your daughter chooses to participate, with your permission, the interview will take no more than 45 minutes and her participation will be completely voluntary.

This research project will study preteen and adolescent attitudes about body image and self-esteem. Some of the questions that we will explore are:

1. From whom and where do preteens learn perceptions of body image and self-esteem? For example, what role do peers and the mass media play in influencing preteens' and adolescents' attitudes about their weight and body image?

2. What factors (if any) appear to "protect" preteen and adolescent girls against feelings of low self-esteem, and what factors (if any) contribute to a depressed sense of body esteem?

I envision this study as a unique opportunity. As I said earlier, we need to give young black women and the black community a stronger voice. I believe that my project can accomplish that. Yet even more importantly, I believe that providing an opportunity for the girls to get together to chat with friends and peers about issues of black identity and self-esteem will serve as a mechanism for black female empowerment.

Attached you will find a consent form which, upon agreement, is to be signed by your daughter and yourself and brought to the Health Center the day of the interview.

If you have any questions or concerns, please feel free to call me at home: _____ or work: _____.

Thank you for your time and I look forward to hearing from you soon.

Sincerely,

_____ Ph. D.
Chair, Department of Sociology
Professor

* * * * *

CONSENT FORM

I, _____ , understand that I will be a participant in Dr. _____research project on body image and self-esteem among white and African American preteens and adolescents.

I also understand that my participation is completely voluntary and that if I feel it necessary, that I may discontinue the interview at any time.

Taking into account all that has been said above, I, _____ , agree to give you, _____, my interview, trusting that all information shall be kept strictly confidential.

* * * * *

If the maker of the above agreement is under the age of 18, this consent form must also be signed by her parent/legal guardian.

I, _____ , understand that my daughter,

_____ , has in the above lines, agreed to participate in Dr. _____ research project on body image and self-esteem among white and African American preteens and adolescents.

I also understand that her participation is completely voluntary and that, if my daughter or I feel that she should discontinue the interview, she may do so at any time.

Taking into account all that has been said above I, _____ , give you Dr. _____, permission to interview my daughter, trusting that all information shall be kept strictly confidential.

"Letter B" is much shorter and provides few details concerning the research goals, and, from it, it would be difficult to ascertain very much about the substance of the research project goals.

Letter B

Dear Parents:

My name is _____ and I am a sociologist and teacher at _____ College. I am conducting a study on body image and self-esteem among African American and white preteen and adolescent girls.

I plan on having the girls meet at the Health Center for pizza and soda after school in groups of three or four to chat about self-esteem and body image. If your daughter chooses to participate, with your permission, the interview will take no more than 45 minutes and her participation will be completely voluntary.

Attached you will find a consent form which, upon agreement, is to be signed by your daughter and yourself, and brought to the Health Center the day of the interview.

I appreciate the opportunity to interview your daughter. If you have any questions or concerns, please feel free to call me at home: _____ or work: _____.

Thank you for your time and I look forward to hearing from you soon.

Sincerely,

* * * * *

CONSENT FORM

I, _____, understand that I will be a participant in Dr. _____ research project on body image and self-esteem among white and African American preteens and adolescents.

I also understand that my participation is completely voluntary and that if I feel it necessary, I may discontinue the interview at any time.

Taking into account all that has been said above, I, _____ , agree to give you, _____, my interview, trusting that all information shall be kept strictly confidential.

* * * * *

If the maker of the above agreement is under the age of 18, this consent form must also be signed by her parent/legal guardian.

I, _____, understand that my daughter,

_____, has, in the above lines, agreed to participate in Dr. _____ research project on body image and self-esteem among white and African American preteens and adolescents.

I also understand that her participation is completely voluntary and that if my daughter or I feel that she should discontinue the interview, she may do so at any time.

Taking into account all that has been said above, I, _____, give you, Dr. _____, permission to interview my daughter, trusting that all information shall be kept strictly confidential.

"Letter B" contains the minimum information that can be given to respondents. Both letters ensure respondent *confidentiality,* that is, their names cannot be used in any written material concerning the research or in discussions of the research project, and interview materials will also be stored in a safe place free from disclosure. This means the researcher and others working on the project will not know the identity of the respondent, for example, a respondent will return a survey questionnaire with no name on it.

These letters, however, point out some of the *political dimensions* involved in creating an informed consent letter.

- Why do researchers differ in how much they reveal of research project goals?

It may not always be in the interest of the researcher to be forthcoming regarding full disclosure. Some researchers may even go out of their way to explain the research project as a "*cover story*," and this may be built into the original design of the research project:

> The selection or invention of details to constitute the cover story and convince intended respondents is an element in the design of a research project. That requires skills of persuasion. Investigators develop a sense of what details allay fears and what prompt suspicions. As in other types of negotiation, such as bargaining over salaries, the initiating party uses a gambit declaring a position which it may concede and which supposes an opposition of interests between the negotiating parties. The investigator will reveal further information if required but in many cases subjects will not be briefed to ask pertinent questions and the project will move on quickly from negotiation to interview. (Homan, 1992, p. 324)

If respondents initially refuse to participate in a research project, rather than accepting the right of the researched to act autonomously, this is often viewed as a failure on the part of the researcher, and there is a tendency of the researcher to break down "the defenses of respondents" through a variety of means, from group pressure to exploitation of friendships. To this issue, Homan says:

> In various ways research projects trade upon a relationship with agencies in power or authority. Sutherland was able to research the secretive and exclusive Rom community, which was normally hostile to representatives of the world outside it by exploiting her role as teacher of its children. (p. 325)

There are even times when following ethical guidelines may not always be in the best interests of your research respondents. Baez points out the ethical conundrum he experienced in maintaining the *confidentiality* of his respondents. Baez interviewed 16 minority faculty members regarding their personal experiences with the tenure and promotion process at one private university. He notes that maintaining confidentially can be a double-edged sword. Keeping the interviews confidential, especially for untenured faculty, allowed him to obtain candid data regarding racism and sexism within this university. On the other hand, confidentiality prevented him from reporting "serious contradictions within an institution that, through institutional documents and public comments by key administrators, purported to be supportive of racial and cultural diversity . . . I could not do so without feeling that I would be identifying my respondents to others in the institution" (2002, p. 39). Bear in mind that you often don't know what your research will teach you, and it can be very difficult not to try and effect social change in some situations.

Patton (2002) notes that respondents are now maintaining their right to "tell their stories" (p. 411) without hiding their identities, especially when they see the project as an opportunity to gain empowerment through telling their stories and perhaps becoming a catalyst for social change. Patton suggests a number of important ethical dilemmas that flow from this new viewpoint on confidentiality:

- Should the researcher "impose confidentiality against the wishes of those involved?"
- Are human subjects committees "patronizing and disempowering" if they turn down those respondents who wish to reveal their identities?
- Does the research subject make the choice independent of others in their social context? What about the privacy of significant others in their lives, such as children, spouse, and extended family members? (p. 411)

Beyond all of these considerations, some researchers are very cognizant of ethics in practice, attempt to use informed consent, and still experience challenges. Sarah Maddison is a feminist sociologist at the University of New South Wales in Australia where she focuses on gender and social policy. Maddison encountered several problems when trying to use informed consent in her ethnographic work with a feminist student group. Let's join Maddison behind the scenes.

Behind-the-Scenes With Sarah Maddison

A couple of years ago I was engaged in a project researching a group of young student feminists drawn from various university campuses in New South Wales. The Cross Campus Women's Network (CCWN) was a loose coalition of women who met on a fortnightly basis. At each meeting there would be between five and 10 women and, with the exception of the convenor, these could often be a different group of women each fortnight. It was this changing roll call at each meeting that created a major obstacle for the ethical conduct of this research: although I had carefully explained the purpose of my research and sought permission to attend and participate the first time I went along, there were women at subsequent meetings who missed out on my spiel and became very suspicious of my presence and my intentions.

(Continued)

(Continued)

So they kicked me out! The convenor emailed me and asked me not to attend any more meetings until they had resolved this issue between themselves (apparently there were differing views about the merits of my research within the group). I was allowed to send an email to the group explaining myself again and then I just had to sit and wait. Time to reflect on power (shared), clarity (and confusion) and consent (given—and taken away again).

I have to say I felt pretty foolish—but in actual fact it was my fear of *appearing* foolish that had put me in this situation to begin with. As a researcher wanting to begin the "participant" part of the participant observation process I was reluctant to continually draw attention to my researcher status by outlining my project every time I saw a new face. I really wanted to blend into the group and participate in meetings like I was "one of them" not an outsider. More than anything I wanted them to forget what I was doing there so that I could somehow observe, participate and consume what "really" went on in their meetings. I rushed in there with the arrogant assumption that the merits and importance of my research were obvious to all and the belief that no one would *not* want to participate.

So stupid—and so wrong. They were right to kick me out because I was behaving very badly, and totally unethically. I had forgotten for a moment that the presence of a researcher always and inevitably changes the dynamics and practices of a group and that my very presence made the group a *different* group to the one that had existed before I strutted through the door. More importantly, I had deluded myself that, as a participant observer, I could somehow, sometimes take off my researcher hat and be "one of them." Of course I knew all these things before I began, but in my enthusiasm to get the project started I had left my ethical practice at the door as I barged on through.

My delusions of invisibility made me forget the first and most golden rule of any sort of research—*consent*. How could my research have any integrity if even one member of the group did not realise I was a researcher? How dishonest of me! How misleading! I could really only be grateful that these young women were feisty and confident enough to boot me out while they considered their choice to participate in the project. There would be many other groups of potential research subjects who would not have the confidence to ask a researcher to leave their group. This awareness made me reflect anew on the significance of power in research relationships and the role that consent must play in clarifying these power relationships.

After a few weeks I was informed that they had decided to let me come back, and I returned gratefully and with my tail between my legs. I had learnt my lesson. Even though I had thought I had been completely open and transparent about my project, I had been careless about ensuring that *every* member of the group had a good understanding of who I was, why I was there and what the research might achieve—an essential step for ethical research in which informed consent is crucial to the legitimacy of the entire project. This is not a lesson I will forget in a hurry and I am thankful for these young women's patience in helping me learn it again.

There is a great deal we can learn from this example. Specifically, Maddison shows how ethical practice is an ongoing consideration. Moreover, ethical issues and informed consent provide the researcher with an opportunity to learn about themselves and develop as researchers—ethics are a doorway to reflexivity.

THE PRACTICE OF ETHICS IN SOCIAL RESEARCH ●

Ethics exist within a social context. The ethical dilemmas we discussed in this chapter serve to remind us of the importance of including an ethical perspective in the very foundation of our research project. Ethical rules cannot possibly apply to all events that can happen in a given project. Rubin and Rubin (1995) note that ethical guidelines do not begin to cover all of the ethical dilemmas you may face in the practice of social research:

> You cannot achieve ethical research by following a set of preestablished procedures that will always be correct. Yet, the requirement to behave ethically is just as strong in qualitative interviewing as in other types of research on humans—maybe even stronger. You must build ethical routines into your work. You should carefully study codes of ethics and cases of unethical behavior to sensitize yourself to situations in which ethical commitments become particularly salient. Throughout your research, keep thinking and judging what are your ethical obligations. (Rubin & Rubin, 1995, p. 96, as quoted in Patton, 2002, p. 411)

A useful distinction we might keep in mind here is the difference between what Homan (1992) terms *ethical codes* and *ethical values*. Agreeing to comply with ethical codes as outlined in an informed consent proposal does not absolve the researcher from adhering to the underlying ethical values contained in these codes, yet very often "they invite observance in the letter rather than in the principle" (p. 325). Homan (1992) reminds us that the danger is that many researchers think their moral obligation begins and ends with the signing of the letter of consent. In some cases an informed consent letter is seen as one protecting the researcher more than the researched. One anthropologist notes:

> I fear that informed consent, when mechanically applied using a form or some verbal formula, becomes more of a protection for the researcher than the researched. Informed consent obtained in this way is unilateral rather than bilateral and protects the researcher against charges from participants that they did not understand fully the intent or outcome of the research. (Fluehr-Lobban, 1998, p. 199)

Ethics does not exist in a vacuum. As King, Henderson, and Stein (1999) note:

> . . . the ethics of human subjects research may be universal but is at the same time deeply particularized, so that what autonomy or informed consent or confidentiality or even benefit and harm *means* depends on the circumstances. The circumstances do not determine whether any of these "Western" moral concepts applies, but *how*. (p. 213)

● EMERGENT ISSUES IN ETHICS RESEARCH: ARE WE MOVING TO A NEW "ETHICS" PARADIGM?

King, Henderson, and Stein's (1999) observations on ethical behavior point to a shift in thinking about how ethics is incorporated into the research process. They discuss a paradigmatic shift in thinking of ethics as based on moral principles (principalist paradigm) largely independent of specific circumstances, to one based on a view of ethics embedded in contextual relationships (relationship paradigm). A principalist might be concerned about the inherent "relativistic" point of view contained within a relational ethics perspective, while a relationalist might charge a principalist with "moral imperalism, paternalism and absolutism" (see King, Henderson, & Stein, 1999, p. 217).

Ethics viewed through each of these paradigmatic lenses asks different types of questions, and it weighs in differently on what priorities should be stressed in a discussion of the ethics of human subjects research. Up to now, a principalist paradigm has guided the development of the ethics guidelines for IRBs and professional associations. What is needed to move the discussion of ethics forward is a more concerted dialogue between these two perspectives, and perhaps, some say, even a synthesis. King, Henderson, and Stein (1999) suggest some important questions that might be fruitful to address in such a dialogue:

> To whom do we turn for moral argument? How shall we constitute the community, or communities, to examine these things together? The language of the question is significant. It means, "With whom are we in a moral relationship of equals?" Not "who will adjudicate this for us? Who will tell us the rules?" But, "With whom can we talk? With whom can we work toward an answer?" (King Henderson, & Stein, 1999, p. 224)

CONCLUSION ●

Integrating ethics into the research process, starting with the selection of the research problem, to carrying out research goals, to the interpretation and reporting of research findings, is critical to ensuring that the research process is guided by ethical principles beyond informed consent. This chapter challenges us as researchers to become aware of the range of ethical dilemmas researchers confront in the carrying out of the day-to-day tasks of any research project. An important step beyond securing informed consent lies in the researcher engaging in self-reflexivity, by asking:

- What is my "ethical standpoint" on the research process?

You may find the following checklist of questions useful in uncovering your own ethical perspective on the research process:

- What type of ethical principles guide your work and life beyond the professional code of ethics you are bound by through a given discipline or professional association?
- Where do your ethical obligations to the researched start and end?

Knowing your own ethical standpoint as a researcher is an important internal guide as to how to proceed in your research. Michael Patton (2002) provides an "ethics checklist" (p. 409) to take into account as you proceed with your research project. We have adapted Patton's list to include a range of research inquiries.

PATTON'S CHECKLIST OF QUESTIONS FOR ● CONDUCTING AN ETHICAL RESEARCH PROJECT

- How will you explain the purpose of the inquiry and methods to be used in ways that are accurate and understandable to those you are researching?
- Why should the researched participate in your project?
- In what ways, if any, will conducting this research do harm (psychological, legal, political, becoming ostracized by others)?
- What are the reasonable promises of confidentiality that can be fully honored?

- What kind of informed consent, if any, is necessary for mutual protection?
- Who will have access to the data? For what purposes?
- How will you and your respondent(s) likely be affected by conducting this research?
- Who will be the researcher's confidant and counselor on matters of ethics during a study?
- How hard will you push for data?
- What ethical framework and philosophy informs your work and ensures respect and sensitivity for those you study, beyond whatever may be required by law? (Adapted from Patton, 2002, p. 408)

A good example of ethical reflection within the research process comes from a study conducted by Huber and Clandinin (2002). They interviewed inner-city elementary school children and relate the ethical "give and take" they engaged into the process of understanding the lives of inner-city youth. They cite the importance of creating an "ethic of relational narrative inquiry" that goes beyond the requirements of signing a consent form.

> From a nonrelational research ethics perspective, we had met the ethical requirements, but this was not sufficient. . . . When we felt disease around who we were as researchers in relation with Azim [a respondent the researchers' study] we realized we needed a different way of understanding what it means to live out ethical research with children as coresearchers in relational narrative inquiry. (p. 794)

They found that a "relational model" of inquiry requires a great deal of "reflexivity" on the part of the researcher (especially when studying a vulnerable population). Putting their reflexive experience into the research process enables them to engage in a dialogue with their own ethical standpoint and to ultimately confront their own personal biases as researchers as well as teachers of elementary school children. In the end, they became more attentive to the complexities of co-creating meaning and the necessity of living within the tensions they experienced as coresearchers:

> As we entered into coresearcher relationships with children, we began to be very thoughtful about what plotlines were shaping us as teacher researchers, as researcher teachers, as researchers. Attending to the maintenance of relationships with children, now and in the future, became, for us, a first consideration . . . we need to reframe ethical concerns into

concerns of relational responsibility. We realized that our attentiveness to relationship could conflict with dominant stories of what "good" teachers and "good" researchers do. Plotlines for good researchers do not often attend to the aftermath for children's lives as their first concern. As relational narrative inquirers engaged with children as researchers, we realized that it was here that we needed to attend. (p. 800)

It is our hope that this chapter provides you with an awareness of the importance of the ethical dimension in the research process. We also offer some of the tools you'll need to enhance your awareness of your own ethical standpoint and its application in your ongoing research endeavors. The various components of ethical practice continue to come up throughout the following chapters, including a discussion of emergent ethical concerns linked to computer-driven research (see Chapter 10).

GLOSSARY ●

Confidentiality: This means that research subjects are protected by remaining unidentifiable. That is, their names may not be used in any written material concerning the research or in discussions of the research project. Any interview materials must be stored in a safe place.

Cover Story: Researchers who choose to use deception may even go out of their way to explain the research project as a cover story (this may be built into the original design of the research project).

Deception: Researchers may be dishonest about who they are or what they are doing and thus use deception in order to conduct their research.

Disclosure: A researcher may or may not reveal, or disclose, his or her identity and the purpose of his or her research. In accordance with ethical considerations, we advocate full disclosure whenever possible.

Ethical Codes: These are codes of conduct set in place to protect the research subjects and their setting—neither of which should be harmed by the research process. By agreeing to comply with ethical codes, as outlined in an informed consent proposal, the researcher is absolved from adhering to the underlying ethical values contained in these codes, yet very often "they invite observance in the letter rather than in the principle" (Homan, 1992, p. 325).

Ethical Values: *See* Ethical Codes.

Informed Consent: Informed consent is a critical component in ethical research which uses human participants. Informed consent means that participants fully understand what the study is about, how the results will be used, that their participation is voluntary and can be stopped at any time, and that their identity will be protected.

IRB: Institutional review boards (IRBs) ensure that studies using living subjects are ethical and will not cause harm.

Moral Integrity: The moral integrity of the researcher is a critically important aspect of ensuring that the research process and a researcher's findings are "trustworthy" and valid.

Nuremberg Code: A code of ethics, which starts off with the stipulation that all research participation must be voluntary.

● DISCUSSION QUESTIONS

1. What is the "ethical substructure" of the research process and why must ethics be attended to holistically?

2. Although informed consent is a critical component of ensuring the ethical dimension of your research project, there have been instances in which there was a failure to fully disclose to research subjects the full extent of the risks or benefits of participating in a study. Therefore, who do you believe is responsible for any unintended consequences?

3. The questions brought up in this chapter include: Where do your ethical obligations to the researched start and end? What responsibility does the researcher have to the participant after the research process has "ended"? Does the researcher still have a responsibility for any emotional and psychological problems that ensue in part because of the research project? What do you think about these issues?

4. IRBs were created to oversee the research process and ensure that "no one group of individuals has been unfairly treated or left out of the potential positive outcomes of a given study." However, as discussed, IRBs have proved ineffective in certain cases where members of IRBs have a vested interest in the very studies they oversee. Therefore, do you believe IRBs to be an effective resource in ensuring ethical centrality in research processes? If not, what is your suggestion for improving the assurance of the ethical dimension of the research process? To your mind, what would be the most effective means of ensuring "ethical consideration/safety" in research projects conducted in universities?

5. As noted in this chapter, informed consent does not absolve the researcher from all ethical issues. Why is this? What are some ethical considerations one must keep in mind when conducting "covert research" or "participant observation"? What are some other ways of making sure that the ethical dimension is given its proper place in your research project?

6. Do you believe it is the responsibility of the researcher to reveal information concerning the research participant if he or she feels it benefits the subject? Why or why not?

7. If a researcher imposes confidentiality in the research process, do you see this as a way of disempowering research participants who want to reveal their identities? Do you believe it is the sole responsibility of the researcher to determine whether information should be kept confidential? Should the issue of confidentiality be a collaborative effort? To what extent should it be collaborative?

8. If a sociologist is interested in studying underage teenagers' drinking and driving behaviors—what are some of the ethical considerations the researcher would have to keep in mind? Discuss some of the ethical dilemmas you would encounter. How would you structure your research project (bearing in mind the centrality of ethics in the structuring of your research process)?

SUGGESTED WEBSITES ●

National Science Foundation

http://www.nsf.gov/bfa/dias/policy/docs/45cfr690.pdf

This link is to the current law regarding informed consent/IRBs/human subjects: "The Common Rule for the Protection of Human Subjects for Behavioral and Social Science Research."

http://www.nsf.gov/bfa/dias/policy/hsfaqs.htm

This is a list of "frequently asked questions" concerning the above legislation.

http://www.hhs.gov/ohrp/humansubjects/guidance/belmont.htm

This is a link to "The Belmont Report: Ethical Principles and Guidelines for the Protection of Human Subjects of Research."

http://www.nsf.gov/bfa/dias/policy/guidance.htm

This site has a section entitled "Human Subjects" with information concerning the basic principles of human subject protection as well as information about IRBs.

Online Ethics

http://onlineethics.org/

This is a link to the "Online Ethics Center for Engineering and Science." They claim that their mission is "to provide engineers, scientists, and science and engineering students with resources for understanding and addressing ethically significant problems that arise in their work, and to serve those who are promoting learning and advancing the understanding of responsible research and practice in science and engineering."

If you click on "Contents of the Online Ethics Center (OEC)" and then "Research Ethics":

http://onlineethics.org/reseth/index.html

This page contains cases, discussions, guidelines, and regulations that place responsibility on the researcher and how she or he conducts research (including information about both issues of research integrity and the treatment of research subjects). It also includes useful links to reference materials concerning research ethics (with a list of websites and governmental sites devoted to this topic).

National Institutes of Health

http://ohsr.od.nih.gov/

This is a link to the Office of Human Subjects Research, which provides information about the existing legislation concerning the use of human subjects and research (as well as the ethical dilemmas involved). It also provides links to other governmental websites dealing with the issue.

http://www.nih.gov/sigs/bioethics/IRB.html

This link is entitled "Human Subjects Research and IRBs." It contains links to policies and regulations, guidance for investigators, IRB resources, short courses on bioethical issues in human studies, research resources, and human subjects research tutorials.

http://www.nlm.nih.gov/pubs/cbm/hum_exp.html

This is a link to a very extensive list of references, all dealing with ethical issues in research involving human participants. The table of contents (you have to scroll down the page a little to get this) breaks down the page into different categories, making it easier to find your specific topic. The bibliography contains information regarding reference materials, including journals, books, government documents, etc.

U.S. Department of Education

http://www.ed.gov/about/offices/list/ocfo/humansub.html

This is a link to the "Protection of Human Subjects in Research" page. This page includes links to general information concerning human subjects in research and the regulations and legalities surrounding using human subjects in research. It also contains information about "Guidance and Educational Materials" (with links to "The Belmont Report" and the "Institutional Review Board Guidebook").

American Sociological Association

http://www.asanet.org/memberfs/ecostand2.html.

This is a link to the ASA's *Code of Ethics*. The *Code of Ethics* is available on the site, and there is also a downloadable PDF version.

American Psychological Association

http://www.apa.org/ethics/homepage.html

This link discusses the APA's new Ethics Code. It has three downloadable versions of the code as well as links to ethics in the news and ethics resources/reference materials.

American Association for the Advancement of Science

http://www.aaas.org/spp/sfrl/projects/intres/main.htm

This is a link to the "Ethical and Legal Aspects of Human Subjects Research in Cyberspace," which contains a link to the report prepared by the AAAS staff (which was created after a workshop was convened in collaboration with the NIH concerning Internet research involving human subjects).

Indiana University's Poynter Center for the Study of Ethics and American Institutions

http://poynter.indiana.edu/links.shtml

This site contains links to ethics centers, publications, research ethics, research policy, and general information about ethics. As stated on the website, the Center's mission is "dedicated to studying a broad range of ethical issues in American public life. Interdisciplinary in aim, the Center uses the full resources of Indiana University to initiate research and teaching across traditional academic boundaries." The site contains very useful resources for teaching research ethics. Of particular interest is their online interactive teaching module titled "The Least of My Brothers," which explores the ethical issues surrounding the Tuskegee Syphilis Experiment. There is a detailed Instructor's Manual that accompanies this module. See their sublink: http://poynter.indiana.edu/sas/lb/.

International Sociological Association

http://www.ucm.es/info/isa/about/isa_code_of_ethics.htm

This page contains the American Sociological Association's Code of Ethics. This code consists of a preamble as well as four sets of specific ethical standards.

● REFERENCES

Adler, P., & Adler, P. (2002). Do university lawyers and the police define research values? In W. C. Van Den Hoonard (Ed.), *Walking the tightrope: Ethical issues for qualitative researchers* (pp. 34–42). Toronto: University of Toronto Press.

Alvino, L. A. (2003). Who's watching the watchdogs? Responding to the erosion of research ethics by enforcing promises. *Columbia Law Review, 103,* 893–924.

American Sociological Associations' Ethical Standards: http://www.asanet.org/memberfs/ecostand2.html. This list consists of topics such as informed consent, use of deception as a research practice, etc. *See also:* Guidelines for the Conduct of Research Involving Human Subjects at the National Institutes Of Health: http://www.helix.nih.gov.8001/ohsr/guidelines.html

Angell, M. (2000). Editorial, Is academic medicine for sale? *New England Journal of Medicine, 342,* 1516–1518.

Appelbaum, P. S., Roth, L. ., Lidz, C. W., Benson, P., & Winslade, W. (1987). False hopes and best data: Consent to research and the therapeutic misconception. *Hastings Center Report, 17,* 20–24.

Baez, B. (2002). Confidentiality in qualitative research: Reflections on secrets, power and agency. *Qualitative Research, 2*(1), 35–58.

Beecher, H. K. (1966). Ethics and clinical research. *New England Journal of Medicine,* 1354–1360.

Bell, L., & Nutt, L. (2002). Divided loyalties, divided expectations: Research ethics, professional and occupational responsibilities. In M. Mauthner, M. Birch, J. Jessop, & T. Miller (Eds.), *Ethics in qualitative research* (pp. 70–90). Thousand Oaks, CA: Sage.

Beyrer, C., & Kass, N. E. (2002). Human rights, politics and reviews of research ethics. *Lancet, 359*(9328), 246–251.

Cassileth, B. R., Zupkis, R. V., Sutton-Smith, K., & March, V. (1980). Informed consent— Why are its goals imperfectly realized? *New England Journal of Medicine, 302,* 896–900.

Department of Health and Human Services (DHHS). (1989). Code of Federal Regulations (45 CFR 46) Protection of Human Subjects. Washington, DC: National Institutes of Health, Office for the Protection from Research Risks.

Dunconmbe, J., & Jessop, J. (2002). 'Doing rapport' and the ethics of 'faking friendship.' In M. Mauthner, M. Birch, J. Jessop, & T. Miller (Eds.), *Ethics in qualitative research* (pp. 106–122). Thousand Oaks, CA: Sage.

Faden, R. R., & Beauchamp, T. L. (1986). *A history and theory of informed consent.* New York: Oxford University Press.

Fluehr-Lobban, C. (1998). Ethics. In H. R. Bernard (Ed.), *Handbook of methods in cultural anthropology* (pp. 173–201). London: Alta Mira Press.

Gamble, V. N. (1997). Under the shadow of Tuskegee: African Americans and health care. *Am J of Public Health, 87*(11), 1773–1778.

Gans, H. (1982). The participant observer as a human being: Observations on the personal aspects of fieldwork. In R. G. Burgess (Ed.), *Field research: A sourcebook and field manual* (pp. 53–61). London: Allen & Unwin.

Gene therapy's risks hidden. (2000, February 3). *Chicago Sun Times,* p. 23.

Goffman, E. (1961). *Asylums. Essays on the social situation of mental patients and other inmates.* Garden City, NY: Doubleday Anchor.

Haggerty, K. D. (2004, Winter). Ethics creep: Governing social science research in the name of ethics. *Qualitative Sociology, 27*(4), 391–414.

Heintzelman, C. (1996). Human subjects and informed consent: The legacy of the Tuskegee Syphilis Study. *Scholars: Research, Teaching and Public Service, Fall,* 23–29.

Hertz, R., & Imber, J. (1995). *Studying elites using qualitative methods*. Thousand Oaks, CA: Sage.

Homan, R. (1992). The ethics of open methods. *The British Journal of Sociology, 43*(3), 321–332.

Huber, J., & Clandinin, D. (2002). Ethical dilemmas in relational narrative inquiry with children. *Qualitative Inquiry, 8*(6), 785–803.

Hotz, R. L. (2003, January 22). Medical tests are skewed, study finds. *Los Angeles Times*, p. 14.

Johnson, J. M., & Altheide, D. L. (2002). Reflections on professional ethics. In W. C. Van Den Hoonaard (Ed.), *Walking the tightrope: Ethical issues for qualitative researchers* (pp. 59–69). Toronto: University of Toronto Press.

Jones, J. H. (1993). *Bad blood: The Tuskegee syphilis experiment*. New York: Free Press.

King, N. M. P., Henderson, G. E., & Stein, J. (1999). Regulations and relationships: Toward a new synthesis. In N. M. P King, G. E. Henderson, & J. Stein (Eds.), *Beyond regulations: Ethics in human subjects research* (pp. 213–224). Chapel Hill, NC: University of North Carolina Press.

Korn, J. H. (1997). *Illusions of reality: A history of deception in social psychology*. New York: SUNY.

Lynoe, N., Sandlund, M., Dahlqvist, G., & Jacobsson L. (1991). Informed consent: Study of quality information given to participants in a clinical trial. *British Journal of Medicine, 303,* 610–613.

Marx, G. T. (1988). *Undercover: Police surveillance in America*. Berkeley: University of California Press.

Milgram, S. (1963). Behavioral study of obedience. *Journal of Abnormal and Social Psychology, 67,* 371–378.

Oakley, A. (1981). Interviewing women: A contradiction in terms. In H. Roberts (Ed.), *Doing feminist research* (pp. 30–61). London: Routledge and Kegan Paul.

Odendahl, T., & Shaw, A. (2002). Interviewing elites. In J. Gubrium and J. Holstein (Eds.), *Handbook of interview research: Context and methodology* (pp. 299–316). Thousand Oaks, CA: Sage.

Patton, M. (2002). *Qualitative research and evaluation methods* (3rd ed.). Thousand Oaks, CA: Sage.

Rubin, H., & Rubin, I. (1995). *Qualitative interviewing: The art of hearing data*. Thousand Oaks, CA.: Sage.

Stacey, J. (1991). Can there be a feminist ethnography? In S. Gluck & D. Patai (Eds.), *Women's words: The feminist practice of oral history* (pp. 111–119). New York: Routledge.

Williams, T. (1996). Exploring the cocaine culture. In C. D. Smith & W. Kornblum (Eds.), *In the field: Readings on the field research experience* (2nd ed., pp. 27–32). Westport, CT: Praeger.

PART II

METHODS OF DATA COLLECTION

CHAPTER 4

IN-DEPTH INTERVIEW

In-depth interview, also known as intensive interview, is a commonly used method of data collection employed by qualitative researchers. In-depth interview uses individuals as the point of departure for the research process and assumes that individuals have unique and important knowledge about the social world that is ascertainable through verbal communication. In-depth interviews are a particular kind of conversation between the researcher and the interviewee that requires *active asking* and *listening*. The process is a meaning-making endeavor embarked on as a partnership between the interviewer and his or her respondent. The degree of division and hierarchy between the two collaborators is typically low, as researcher and researched are placed on the same plane, though variations occur.

Qualitative interviews can be used to yield exploratory, descriptive, and explanatory data that may or may not generate theory. Likewise, they can be used as a stand-alone method or in conjunction with a range of other methods such as surveys, focus groups, or ethnography. Ethnographers, as we will see in Chapter 7, commonly conduct interviews when in the field. There is a natural link between these two forms of inquiry, and multimethod approaches are standard fare. In-depth interviews are generally less time consuming than field work, and so when the topic under investigation is not linked to a particular setting (Warren, 2002, p. 85), but can be ascertained from individuals in a prearranged setting (as opposed to the indivdual's natural setting), in-depth interviews may be appealing and appropriate. Typically researchers who conduct in-depth interviews are looking for patterns that emerge from the "thick descriptions" of social life recounted by their participants. In this sense, qualitative interviews are designed to get at "deep" information or knowledge (Johnson, 2002, p. 104). In this vein, in-depth interviews yield large amounts of data in the form of interview transcripts, which are later reduced through the analytical and interpretive process. Qualitative interviews thus differ from quantitative interviews, which consist of standardized questions (often closed-ended, meaning that they have a finite range of possible answers) in search of standardized data.

When is it appropriate to use in-depth interviews? In-depth interviews are *issueoriented*. In other words, this method is useful when the researcher has a particular topic he or she wants to focus on and gain information about from individuals. As we will see in the next chapter, this differs from the oral history method of interview where a respondent's entire life story may be covered in the interview sessions. In-depth interviews typically occur in one session with a particular interviewee (though more than one session can be used), and the interview centers around a specific topic that the researcher is interested in. For example, a researcher interested in how single parents balance family and work or how young girls experience body image issues may find in-depth interviews extremely appealing. The goal of intensive interviews is to gain rich qualitative data, from the perspective of selected individuals, on a particular subject.

For example, in our research on body image among different populations we became interested in how gay, lesbian, and bisexual people experience body image. While our literature review revealed that there is some data indicating a different range of body image issues across sexual orientation, the data available is minimal and does little by way of *explaining* these differences in a nuanced way. Some questions we wanted to address included: How do lesbian women feel about their physical selves? What are the standards by which they feel judged in the gay community and the straight community? How do our participants feel about these standards and how do the standards make them feel about themselves? How do they view attractiveness? What esteem issues do they experience and why? What, if any, differences do they perceive in body ideal between the gay and straight communities? How has primary group support or lack of support regarding their sexual orientation impacted their body image? These are just some of the questions that can be explored using in-depth interview. This kind of study can yield both descriptive and explanatory data and is also appropriate in exploratory research where little is known in a field. Let's take a look at a transcript excerpt from an interview with a middle-aged lesbian respondent who has suffered from compulsive overeating and see the kind of information gleamed by this method (note: OA stands for Over-Eaters Anonymous).

Interviewer: Do you think, overall, women who are straight as opposed to women who are lesbians have more or less "issues" with their bodies?

Respondent: I think straight women have more, but there are definitely exceptions. Like I had a girlfriend who was totally obsessed with it. I met her in OA so already she has straight up body stuff. And I know quite a few lesbians, well that might be an exaggeration, but who have a lot of body image issues, a lot are really grossed out by fat people.

Interviewer: How does that manifest itself in a meeting, as far as . . . ?

Respondent: It doesn't at a meeting, they wouldn't, well some people do talk about it, fat serenity, they call it. People who they consider fat but say they are abstaining from compulsive overeating, they think they are diluting themselves, they call it fat serenity, I hate it when they say that.

Interviewer: Mmmmm.

Respondent: So anyway, people aren't critical of other people at meetings, they would never say that. These are things people say outside of meetings. But in general, I would say in terms of the lesbian community, which is a huge generalization again.

Interviewer: Yeah.

Respondent: Less emphasis on having the right body shape or size.

Interviewer: Um hmmm.

Respondent: That has sort of been my experience. Like if you go to a lesbian function, you'll see a lot more women with different body sizes, bigger, small, all ranges in between.

Interviewer: Right.

Respondent: I think that you would, well that's not true, the general population is getting bigger and bigger, but more accepted as different body sizes. Yeah I definitely think that's true, but there are definitely exceptions.

Interviewer: Yeah.

Respondent: Well I'm sure like a lot of whatever you grew up feeling about yourself, before you even discovered your identity that would probably still affect people.

Interviewer: Yeah, in *Am I Thin Enough Yet?*, white college straight women were obsessed with being thin, really thin, thinner than they could even be basically.

Respondent: I know a few lesbians like that. But most lesbians I know aren't like that. They are pretty easygoing about the whole subject. I mean what they feel in their hearts about it, I don't know, but just in terms of conversation and interactions.

Interviewer: Yeah.

Respondent: And I think part of that is that you're not buying into a lot of the cultural stuff.

Interviewer: Yeah.

Respondent: And a lot of thin women thinking they need to be thin so they get a guy.

Interviewer: Mmmm.

Respondent: I mean I think a lot of it, to feel good about themselves they need to be thin, but I think a lot of it is that message that you have to be thin to get a boyfriend.

Interviewer: Right.

Respondent: So, um, and I think in the lesbian community, that's not, ya know you don't get that message as strongly. Tons of women who are bigger have partners.

Interviewer: Mmmmm.

Respondent: So it's not such a strong issue, I think.

Interviewer: Um hmmm. Are you part of, do you have like a gay community or like is it more of like scattered friends, or is there a group of friends?

Respondent: No I don't anymore. I have some gay friends, most of my friends are in OA now, some of who are lesbians, some of them straight. I have some gay friends, I have these two friends Gladys and Anita I have been friends with for like 25 years.

Interviewer: Um hum.

Respondent: They are a happily married couple, well not legally married, but happy couple. When I was in my 20s I hung out with this group of lesbians, um, when I stopped drinking and I sort of moved away from that group. But I see them once in a while.

Interviewer: Yeah.

Respondent: Go to a birthday party or something. But no I don't really have a group of gay people that I hang out with for the most part.

In looking at this bit of transcript, several points can be made. First, in-depth interview is a way of gaining information and understanding from individuals on a *focused topic.* In this instance we were interested in understanding a lesbian woman's body image issues as well as her perspective on body image issues within both the gay and straight communities. Second, the in-depth interview is a very particular kind of interaction, a particular kind of conversation. A "normal" conversation would have much more back and forth between the two people, both communicating their ideas to each other. An in-depth interview is a different kind of dialogue. The researcher begins by asking a question and then serves as active listener. As you can see in the above example, the researcher actually said very few words but showed her engagement in the conversation through gestures and probes. The respondent did most of the talking, though the researcher is very present in the dialogue and resulting transcript. Last, the respondent speaks on two levels: from her experience and her perceptions. She speaks about her own experience in terms of weight struggles and body image issues, and she also speaks to her perception of social pressures on homosexual and heterosexual women based on her experience in the culture.

In-depth interviews are also very useful for accessing subjugated voices and getting at subjugated knowledge. Those who have been marginalized in a society, such as women, people of color, homosexuals, and the poor, may have hidden experiences and knowledge that have been excluded from our understanding of social reality. Interviewing is a way to access some of this information. Shulamit Reinharz (1992) explains how interviewing is a way feminist researchers have attempted to access women's hidden knowledge:

. . . interviewing offers researchers access to people's ideas, thoughts, and memories in their own words rather than in the words of the researcher.

This asset is particularly important for the study of women because in this way learning from women is an antidote to centuries of ignoring women's ideas altogether or having men speak for women. (p. 19)

The same is true for interviewing people of color and homosexuals, who have long been left out of the research process. Accessing the invisible experience of lesbian women and their relationship with their body was one of the motivators in the study we excerpted earlier.

Now that you're beginning to get a sense of what an in-depth interview is and when it is an appropriate method to address your research topic and question, let's look at research design.

● DESIGNING AN IN-DEPTH INTERVIEW STUDY

Most of the research design techniques discussed in Chapter 2 apply to constructing an in-depth interview study. First, the researcher needs to select a research topic and form a research purpose (and, ultimately, now or later during initial data collection, a research question). Next, participants, sometimes called "informants" or interviewees, must be selected. Sampling can occur in any of the ways discussed in Chapter 2, such as probability sampling, theoretical sampling, or "snowball" sampling (also known as *convenience samples*. The individuals selected to participate in the study should have the kind of knowledge or experience or information that the researcher wants to know about. Sometimes researchers pay respondents a small sum or give them a gift (such as a gift certificate) to thank them for their participation, though this usually isn't necessary. The best interviews occur with respondents who want to share their story and knowledge, and, ideally, the interview situation is a rewarding experience for them in and of itself.

Once a respondent is lined up for an interview, a time and a location need to be arranged. Often in-depth interviews occur in the researcher's office or in the respondent's home, though any private space is suitable as long as both parties feel comfortable. These in-person intensive interviews typically last 1 to 2 hours, though some may be shorter. Interviews can also be conducted over the telephone or by email. Telephone interviews are different because they are not happening face-to-face, and thus gesturing, eye contact, and other means of showing interest and building rapport are not possible. In addition to these issues, email interviews are a different kind of dialogue altogether, one in which the exchanges happen with a time delay compared to the flow of in-person or telephone interviews. Likewise, people write more slowly and differently than they speak, so responses are apt to be more thought out, less spontaneous, and shorter. We recommend that these methods only be used when time, money, and other pragmatic factors make an in-person interview impossible. In this chapter, we're going to focus on in-person interviewing, though we want to bring these other options to your attention.

Informed consent should be explained in advance and executed either in advance or at the time of the interview. Even though the study and the participant's informed and voluntary participation have been discussed in advance, it is important to reiterate this prior to beginning the interview. Interviewees should be given every opportunity to ask questions. This brings us to the unique aspects of in-depth interviews. For starters, there are different kinds of in-depth interviews that vary in terms of structure.

Depending on your research question and corresponding research goals, you may design a study with either structured interviews or semi-structured or open-ended interviews. A *structured interview* means that you will ask each participant the same series of questions. If the participant strays too much from the topic at hand, or says some interesting things but things that aren't directly relevant to the study, the interviewer guides the conversation back to the interview questions. Researchers working from postpositivist theoretical perspectives may employ such a structure with their interviews. When in-depth interviews are being used to confirm and augment data gained by other methods, such as surveys, structured interviews may also be appropriate. Ultimately a structured interview allows for a greater degree of comparison between interviews because the resulting data has a higher degree of standardization. The interviewer has acted, relatively speaking, the same during all interviews and asked the same questions. Comparisons between respondent's can thus be made. It is also easier to generalize (if applying standard "scientific" expectations of generalizability) from data that was obtained in a more uniform fashion. Having said all of this, most qualitative researchers think of in-depth interviews as an opportunity to allow the words of the respondent, and his or her experience and perspective, to shine through. In other words, qualitative researchers are generally more inclined to impose less structure on their interviews and thus opt for semistructured to open-ended (or low-structure) interviews. Additionally, as seen in our Behind-the-Scenes With David Karp in Chapter 2, qualitative researchers frequently have different ways of conceptualizing generalizability, allowing them to use less-structured interviews and still make larger inferences and generate social theory.

Semi-structured interviews rely on a certain set of questions and try to guide the conversation to remain, more loosely, on those questions. However, semistructured interviews also allow individual respondents some latitude and freedom to talk about what is of interest or important to them. In other words, while the researcher does try to ask each respondent a certain set of questions, he or she also allows the conversation to flow more naturally, making room for the conversation to go in new and unexpected directions. Interviewees often have information or knowledge that may not have been thought of in advance by the researcher. When such knowledge emerges, the researcher using a semistructured design is likely to allow the conversation to develop, exploring new topics that are relevant to the interviewee. In *low-structure* or completely *open-ended interviews*, this is taken even further. While the researcher has a particular topic for the study, he or she allows the conversation to go wherever the research participant takes it, and each interview becomes highly individual. The data produced from these kinds of interviews are nonstandardized (Reinharz, 1992, p.18). In a low-structure interview, the researcher asks very few, broad questions and allows the respondent to take the discussion in whatever directions he or she wants. This approach is highly congruent with the tenets of the qualitative paradigm.

> Open-ended interview research explores people's views or reality and allows the researcher to generate theory. In this way it complements quantitatively oriented, close-ended interview research that tries to test hypotheses. (Reinharz, 1992, p. 18)

The *degree of structure* imposed during the interview impacts the *researcher's role* in the interview situation. The more structure sought the more *control* the researcher imposes.

Next, researchers can prepare for the interview by constructing an *interview guide*. An interview guide is a set of topical areas and questions that the interviewer brings to the interview. Weiss (1994) suggests beginning with a "substantive frame" and then using that to create a guide. When thinking about constructing an interview guide it is helpful to think topically prior to creating specific questions. In other words, guides can be constructed by beginning with broader, more abstract areas of inquiry from which questions are developed. To begin, write down a "topics-to-learn-about" list (Weiss, 1994). Each topic listed is a *"line of inquiry"* or *"domain of inquiry"* that you want to pursue during the interview session. Interview questions can then be constructed to "get at" information in each of these "lines." Ultimately the interview guide is a list of topics with or without specific questions under each topic that speak to the "lines of inquiry" suggested during the initial drafting of the guide (Weiss, 1994, p. 48). The process of creating an interview guide, even if it remains unused, is important preparation for the interview (Weiss, 1994) because it helps the researcher identify key issues and think about the kinds of things he or she may like to ask respondents. Pilot interviews are an opportunity for researchers to test out the effectiveness of their research guide (Weiss, 1994):

- Is the guide clear and readable?
- Does the guide cover all of the topical areas you are interested in?
- Are there any topical areas or general questions missing from the guide?

Based on early experiences with an interview guide, you can then modify the guide to better suit your needs.

David Karp talks about creating interview guides as an *analytical process* in the following Behind-the-Scenes:

Behind-the-Scenes With David Karp

Looking for major themes, what I think of as "domains of inquiry." Of course, they don't just come out of nowhere, because I've done so much preliminary work before this. And this is really critical, because too often when people do in-depth interviews, they see putting together the interview guide as, "Well, I've got to get this out of the way." And I see this task of discovering the areas of inquiry as an incredibly important analytical step in the process of doing this work. And if we talk about the full process, when you get to the point of writing, in my case books or articles, it comes full circle because the amount of time and energy that I put into getting this interview guide together really previews what will be the central pieces that I ultimately will write about. Now, in the end, it's just a guide, and in any interview maybe 60% of the questions I ask are not on that guide. You're sitting, having a conversation with a person, and the artfulness of doing that in-depth interview is to know when to follow-up on what a person is saying in the moment. By the end of the interview I want to make sure that all the areas that I want to have covered are covered. But you would be missing the whole deal if the only questions you asked were the questions on your guide.

It is important that interview guides are not too lengthy or detailed. They are meant to serve as aides to the researcher but ideally will not be heavily relied upon because too strong a focus on the interview guide itself can distract a researcher from paying full attention to the respondent. An interview guide is meant to be glanced at when needed and ideally remains unused or as a prompter for the researcher (Weiss, 1994, p. 48). The guide can also serve as a "check-list" for the researcher at the end of the interview, as a way of making sure all of the topics under investigation have been addressed even if not in the sequence suggested by the guide (Weiss, 1994, p. 48).

An interview guide is essential to a successful interview and the preparation of an interview guide is particularly helpful for novice interviewers. Once sampling and structural decisions have been made and an interview guide constructed, data collection can begin. There are many tips that can be given for successful interviews; however, we encourage you to try to learn by practice. In-depth interviewing is a skill and craft and as such, one gets better with experience.

● THE INTERVIEW: CONDUCTING IN-DEPTH INTERVIEWS

In-depth interviews are a *meaning-making partnership* between interviewers and their respondents. These sessions provide an opportunity for researchers to learn about social life through the perspective, experience, and language of those living it. Respondents are given an opportunity to share their story, pass on their knowledge, and provide their own perspective on a range of topics. Qualitative interviews are thus a special kind of *knowledge-producing conversation* that occurs between two parties. The relationship between the interviewer and respondent is critical to the process of constructing meaning.

As discussed in Chapter 1, qualitative researchers working from theoretical and epistemological positions that fall under the interpretive umbrella are concerned with the co-creation of meaning. In other words, qualitative researchers generally attempt to reduce any hierarchy between the researcher and researched. During the in-depth interview situation researchers have the ability to place themselves on the same plane as their respondents and work together cooperatively as they construct social scientific knowledge. In this pursuit, the relationship between interviewers and interviewees can be characterized as *reciprocal*. Furthermore, interviewees are given authority over their own stories, which means that they are seen as "experts." In order for reciprocity and shared authority to be possible, the two parties must feel comfortable with each other. Researchers help respondents share their stories by building *rapport*. Respondents must feel safe, comfortable, and as though what they are saying is valued. In order to accomplish this, researchers need to take the role of active listener while the interviewee is speaking. Showing genuine interest is critical to the establishment of rapport. Researchers are not there to judge their respondents, but rather to help them flesh out what they see as the critical aspects of the story they are sharing. Eye contact and appropriate gesturing (such as nodding) are important to the building of rapport and foster productive interviews. Picking up on *markers* is another way to show a respondent that you are interested in what he or she is saying.

Likewise, markers are a valuable source of information and often lead to the kinds of thick descriptions that characterize qualitative interview data.

Markers are important pieces of information that a respondent may offer as they are talking about something else. Weiss (1994) explains markers and how they might appear as follows:

> . . . a passing reference made by a respondent to an important event or feeling state . . . Because markers occur in the course of talking about something else, you may have to remember them and then return to them when you can, saying, "A few minutes ago you mentioned . . ." But it is a good idea to pick up a marker as soon as you conveniently can if the material it hints at could in any way be relevant for your study. Letting the marker go will demonstrate to the respondent that the area is not of importance to you. It can also demonstrate that you are only interested in answers to your questions, not in the respondent's full experience. . . . Respondents sometimes offer markers by indicating that much has happened that they aren't talking about. They might say, for example, "Well there was a lot going on at that time." It is then reasonable to respond, "Could you tell me about that?" (p. 77)

To examine markers more closely let's take our example of interviewing lesbian women about the relationship between their sexual identity and body image. If a respondent is telling you about her parent's reaction to her "coming out" and in the midst of this story says, "well it was partly due to my sister's stuff and all that craziness . . ." and then continues on with *her* story, you need to make a mental (or even written) note of this marker. It is probably not appropriate to query the respondent while she is in the middle of an important and difficult story; however, you want to go back when she is done and say something like; "earlier you mentioned your sister was going through something at this time that bore on what was happening with you, can you tell me a little about this?" Using the same example, your respondent could be talking about her experience in compulsive overeaters anonymous and say something like; "the group wasn't really helpful but I was so depressed about other stuff anyway and so . . ." and then continue talking about the OA meetings. When she finished you could follow-up by asking; "you mentioned being depressed about other stuff during that time, can you please expand on this?" This shows your respondent that you have been carefully listening to her speak and also has clued you in to some potentially important information that you otherwise wouldn't have known to ask about.

Probes are also critical to a good interview, and it is important to be able to distinguish between when a marker has been dropped that you want to pick up on, and when you should probe further into a respondent's response. Probes are, typically, needed consistently during an in-depth interview, particularly if it is a low-structure interview where perhaps you ask fewer questions but delve deeper into what the respondent is choosing to talk about. A probe is the researcher's way of getting a respondent to continue on with what they are talking about, to go further or to explain more, perhaps by virtue of an illustrative example. Sometimes a probe is simply a sign of understanding and interest that the researcher puts forward to the interviewee. Let's look back to a snippet of our transcript from earlier to see this kind of probe.

Respondent: And a lot of thin women thinking they need to be thin so they get a guy.

Interviewer: *Mmmm.*

Respondent: I mean I think a lot of it, to feel good about themselves they need to be thin, but I think a lot of it is that message that you have to be thin to get a boyfriend.

Interviewer: *Right.*

Respondent: So um and I think in the lesbian community, that's not, ya know you don't get that message as strongly. Tons of women who are bigger have partners.

Interviewer: *Mmmmm.*

Respondent: So it's not such a strong issue, I think.

The interview merely has to say "right" and, at times, simply make a sound (and perhaps simultaneous gesture such as a nod) to show the respondent that she is listening, understands, is empathetic, and *wants her to continue.* As a result, the respondent does continue without the need for the interviewer to ask another question. This is critical because qualitative interviewers want as much of the interview material as possible to come from the interviewee.

At this point, let's join David Karp behind the scenes to get a glimpse at how he conducts an interview and addresses some of the following issues.

- How do you get someone to start talking?
- Is it hard to be an active listener while in the role of interviewer?
- Do respondents want to share their stories?
- What do respondents get out of this process?

Behind-the-Scenes With David Karp

Well, I think you should be making it easy on people. You should begin by asking the easy questions. You know, "What religion did you grow up with, etc.?" And to not ask threatening questions, and to give people a sense about what you're doing. Because what they're trying to figure out, just like in any interaction, is, who is this guy? What is he after? Is he genuine? Are his intentions good? Does he listen? Does he seem to care about what I'm saying? And when you do an interview, you must make that person feel that they are the only person in the world at the time that you are talking to them. I could never do more than one interview a day, never! Because the amount of energy that is required to really listen, to really pay attention, is enormous. And to know just when to ask a lot of questions.

Part of this conducting thing is to reach a balance between . . . You should be respectful of the story that the person you're interviewing wants to tell. See, people come into your office and they have a story that they want to tell. And when they walk in, at the beginning, maybe they want to talk about how medicine screwed them over, or something like that. That's what they really want to talk about. I have to go with that at the beginning. I'm not going to turn them off. I'm not going to say, "Well, I didn't want to talk about that until two hours into the interview." And I think it's reaching balance between allowing people to be heard, to tell the parameters of the story that they really want to tell—and every story is to some degree idiosyncratic in meaning—and at the same time, as I said, to know what you want to get covered before you're done with this person.

I find in doing interviews that if you ask the right question at the beginning of the interview, once you really get into the substance of it, you often don't have to ask much more. In the depression stuff, the first question I typically asked people was, "You may not have called it depression, but tell me about the first moment it entered your head that something was wrong. What was the first time there was any kind of a consciousness that something was wrong?" Sometimes I didn't have to say much of anything else for the next 3 hours. People had a way of telling their story, and they spontaneously covered all of those domains of inquiry that I wanted to have covered. And the other thing I would say about this, is that people really do want to tell their stories. Almost invariably, people thanked me at the end of their interview for giving them a chance to tell their story. And to have a sociologist ask them questions . . . They often got a different perspective on their life than they could have gotten through years of therapy, because I was asking questions that only a sociologist would ask.

As you can see, the process of in-depth interviewing is a process of communication involving asking, listening, and talking. By beginning with good opening questions and showing enthusiastic listening, an interviewer can gain a wealth of data by doing little more than fostering a respondent's storytelling process. Intensive interview is a collaborative process of getting at knowledge that requires a unique relationship between the researcher and interviewee, based on mutual interest, respect, and compassion. When most effective, the process is rewarding for both partners, and both widen their perspective through the experience.

● ISSUES OF DIFFERENCE

Qualitative researchers view social reality as complex and multidimensional, and this shapes how they think about the interview process. The researcher and the researched often come to the interview situation with different backgrounds in terms of their gender, ethnicity, and sexual preference, as well as class status and many other differences. Researchers working from a positivist tradition often pay scant attention to how these differences can impact the interview situation. Traditional positivistic research deals with the issue of difference through *minimizing* its effects. Positivistic researchers do this by standardizing their participation in the interview situation by being "objective," that is "bracketing off" these differences in their positionality vis-à-vis their respondent, so as not to influence the interview process itself. They seldom ask such questions as:

- Can a single white middle-class male researcher interview a black working-class mother?
- Can a middle-class white female interview a woman from the Third World who is living in poverty?
- Can a straight white middle-class male interview a gay working-class male?

Qualitative researchers, on the other hand, argue that it is not so easy to "bracket" off attitudes and values that emanate from any given individual's mix of positional ties. In fact, it is the acknowledgment of difference—how we are the same or different from our respondent—that allows the researcher to take account of difference and its impact on the interview situation. Issues of difference impact all phases of the research process—starting with the selection of a particular research question, what hypotheses we test out on our data, and the overall process of data collection, analysis, interpretation, and the

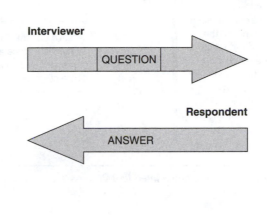

Information flows in both directions with the researcher asking specific questions and respondent 'answering each question'. There is no give and take in terms of a conversation between the researcher and researched. The interviewer must remain "distanced" from the interview situation by sticking to his or her agenda and avoid revealing any of his or her personal values and attitudes.

Figure 4.1   Model of the Interview Process: Quantitative Model

writing up of our research findings. As discussed in Chapter 1, Sandra Harding (1993) introduces the concept of "strong objectivity" and argues that by taking difference into account in all phases of a research project the researcher in fact "*maximizes* objectivity" by ensuring that our respondent's voice is represented, listened to, and understood. Sandra Harding urges researchers to examine the questions they pose in the interview situation and notes that these are not "value free" but very often reflect the values, attitudes, and agendas of the researcher. Those researchers who practice "strong objectivity" ask questions such as:

- How do my values and attitudes and beliefs enter into the research process? Do I only ask questions from my perspective?
- How does my own agenda shape what I ask and what I find?
- How does my positionality impact how I gather, analyze, and interpret my data: From whose perspective?

A positivist scenario of the interview process is one where the researcher "asks" questions that the respondent then answers. While communication flows in both directions, the object of the interview is to obtain "information" that is often in the form of standardized or semistandardized questions. There is a specific agenda that the interviewer has in mind.

Interview flows more like a "conversation." There is a give and take between interviewer and respondent. There is in fact a "co-creation of meaning." If the researcher has an agenda, this does not take precedence over the specific issues the respondent wants to bring up. There is a premium paid on listening to the respondent instead of one's own agenda.

Interviewer

"Give and take" in the interview process. The researcher and researched are co-participants.

Respondent

Figure 4.2 Model of the Qualitative Interview Process

A qualitative model of interviewing, on the other hand, allows for information to flow in both directions. Qualitative researchers do not maintain a view of social reality as "out there" waiting to be captured by the social researcher if only they are objective. As mentioned earlier, the interview is often seen as a *co-creation of meaning*. The researcher's job is to listen intently to what the researched has to say and be prepared to drop his or her agenda in response to what takes place during the interview. Kathryn Anderson, a speech communications expert, wanted to document the lives of rural farm women living in northwest Washington State for the Washington Women's Heritage Project (1991). During the course of her research, however, her focus on the attitudes and feelings of rural farmwomen was often displaced by her need to produce specific descriptions of farm life that depicted women's activities on the farm in order to provide sufficient material for an exhibit. She notes:

> In retrospect, I can see how I listened with at least part of my focus on producing potential material for the exhibit—the concrete description of experiences that would accompany pictures of women's activities. As I rummaged through the interviews long after the exhibit has been placed in storage, I am painfully aware of lost opportunities for women to reflect on the activities and events they described and to explain their terms more fully in their own words. (Anderson & Jack, 1991, p. 13)

Let's listen in on an interview conducted by Kathryn Anderson. She interviews a farm woman named Verna. During the course of this interview Verna reflects upon how difficult life has been for her as a mother. Verna begins to open up to Anderson in the following excerpt. Notice Anderson's response to Verna's emotional remarks:

[Verna:] there was times that I just wished I could get away from it all. And there were times when I would have liked to have taken the kids and left them someplace for a week—the whole bunch at one time—so that I wouldn't have to worry about them. I don't know whether any-body else had that feeling or not but there were times when I just felt like I needed to get away from everybody, even my husband, for a little while. Those were times when I just felt like I needed to get away. I would maybe take a walk back in the woods and look at the flowers, and maybe go down there and find an old cow that was real and gentle and walk up to her and pat her a while—kind of get away from it. I just had to, it seems like sometimes . . .

[Anderson:] Were you active in clubs? (Anderson & Jack, 1991, p. 16)

From the above interview excerpt, we can observe how Anderson was single-minded in her pursuit of her agenda and does not really "listen" intently to what Verna was conveying to her. Instead, she has an "agenda" she follows, and the next question on her interview schedule deals with membership in clubs. Anderson's question fails to acknowledge Verna's outpouring of feelings concerning motherhood.

The qualitative interview is more of a conversation between copartici-pants, and information flows back and forth during the course of the interview. The researcher's primary role is to listen intently to the researched. And while the researcher may want to pursue some specific questions of interest to them, their primary focus is to take their cue from the researched. The heart of the qualitative interview requires much *reflexivity,* that is, sensitivity to the important "situational" dynamics between the researcher and researched that can impact the creation of knowledge. Anderson and Jack (1991, p.24) provide us with a guide to sharpening our "listening" skills during the interview process, especially listening across our differences. They provide the following questions/issues you might consider regarding the type of interview schedule that promotes listening:

- Have an open-ended interview style to enable your interviewees to express their attitudes and feelings.
- Probe for feelings, not just facts. For example: How does the respondent understand what is happening? What meaning does he/she give to the course of events in his/her life?
- What is not said?

Anderson and Jack (1991) also suggest the following checklist you might consult *before* you conduct your interviews:

- Be mindful of your own agenda.
- Go with your own "hunches, feelings, responses that arise through listening to others" (p. 24).
- If you are confused about something, don't be afraid to follow-up on an issue or concern.

What about your own discomfort and how this might affect the interview situation? Can your personal discomfort also provide you with a clue as to where you need to look at "what is being said" and what the respondent is feeling?

Insider or Outsider?

One strategy researchers have used to overcome the impact of difference in the interview process is to "match" some of their important status characteristics (race/age/gender/sexual preference) so that they can take advantage of their *insider status* in gaining access to an interview and obtain cooperation and rapport within the situation in order to expedite understanding their respondents. The researcher, after all, is an insider and should be familiar with the respondent's group's situation. It is also important that such a balance in some of these status characteristics also decreases the possibility of power and authority imbalances in the interview situation (Oakley, 1981). The standard thinking on difference in the interview situation suggests that if the interviewer is an *outsider* this might make it more difficult to gain access and to understand the situation of "the other." Does an "insider" status ensure a more valid and reliable interview? How does difference impact the research process?

Doing Difference: An Example of Taking Account of Difference in the Research Process

The Problem: What is the economic and social impact of globalization on Third World women?

Taking into account difference, it is important to ask:

What women are we talking about?

We need to account for the diversity of women's experiences within the global marketplace. Some important characteristic dimensions of the woman worker we might consider are: (1) the geographical region in which the woman worker resides (rural/urban/suburban). Also: Is she is a recent immigrant to the area?; (2) at what point is she in the life cycle?—for example, young, not married, or with a partner and no children versus married with a partner and middle-aged, etc.; (3) level of education; (4) ethnicity; (5) if married or with a significant other, is that person employed full or part time? These and other factors are important because they will help the researcher to understand that globalization can impact women workers differently, depending on a woman worker's positionality along these critical socioeconomic dimensions. For example, Helen Safa (1981), in her classic article "Runaway Shops and Female Employment: The Search for Cheap Labor," notes that the impact of women's employment in export processing zones (EPZs) on the division of labor in the home "varies with the degree of male unemployment and intensity of patriarchal tradition." For example, Safa states that in Mexico the disruption of the traditional family pattern was very problematic as a result of women's involvement in the Maquiladoros (Border Industrial Program). She argues that women became the "primary breadwinners" of the family because the men were not employed and resented this and did not help out at home. On the other hand, in other areas such as Jamaica, female employment did not affect the division of labor at home. It is also noted by Safa that age of entering EPZs is also important. Older married women who had children fared better than younger unmarried women who were more exploited (by their families and the corporation) (Safa, 1981, p. 427).

Embedded in this difference example is the realization that from the beginning of our research project, what we chose to study and who is grounded in an appreciation of difference. *What* and *Who* we study are impacted by how we as researchers approach and are cognizant of difference issues. An appreciation of difference allows us to ask the question: Which women? Are all women around the world the same? How are they different and what differences are important to my research question?

Difference is also critical in terms of the *interview situation*. Can a researcher from a First World country truly understand the plight of women working in the global marketplaces in the Third World? Suppose the researcher is a white middle-class male conducting this research. How will his gender, race, ethnic background, and social class impact the interview process? Can the researcher "overcome" differences between him- or herself and those he or she researches?

It is easy to conclude that if the interviewer and interviewee are of the same gender, class, and ethnic background, this might go a long way towards establishing an open dialogue between researcher and researched and provide a maximum opportunity for the voice of the respondent to be heard and represented. To some extent this is a reasonable supposition. In her field research among Gullah women (African American women who reside in the Sea Islands of South Carolina and Georgia). Beoku-Betts (1994) found that fully informing her participants of her social positionality and background—that she too was raised in a rural community with similar cultural practices—enabled her to make contacts and gain data that would otherwise have not been available. Kath Weston (2004) is very reflexive about her identity as a lesbian and how it influenced her research. She writes that although she still would have studied gay families, the project would have been very different if she were not a lesbian. Weston also recognizes that her position within the homosexual community was the reason she had little trouble finding lesbian participants, while lesbians had remained virtually invisible to men conducting sexuality research. She notes:

> In my case, being a woman also influenced how I spent my time in the field: I passed more hours in lesbian clubs and women's groups than gay men's bars or male gyms. (Weston, 2004 , p. 202.)

Sometimes sharing some insider characteristics with our respondent is not enough to ensure that the researcher can capture the lived experience of those they research. Catherine Kohler Riessman's research on divorce narratives (1987) notes that in her interviews with divorced women, just being a woman was not enough to understand the divorce experience of women whose class and ethnic background differed from hers. Her positionality as an Anglo, middle-class, highly educated individual prevented her from fully comprehending the particular ways these women structured their divorce narratives (episodically instead of chronologically). It became a challenge in the interview situation not to place the researcher's cultural expectations of what a narrative should look like onto individuals of different ethnic and class backgrounds. Likewise, Beoku-Betts (1994) confronted a similar scenario in her field research among Gullah women. Beoku-Betts is a black West African female researcher, and in terms of her race she was definitely an insider among the black community she was studying. Beoku-Betts relates how one of her respondents told her that: "she preferred a black scholar like myself conducting research in her community because 'black scholars have a sense of soul for our people because they have lived through it'" (Beoku-Betts, 1994, p. 416). However, Beoku-Betts found that her insider status was intertwined with other factors such as differences in class and cultural background. She found herself having to overcome some resistance within the community toward her fieldwork activities:

> My shared racial background proved instrumental in providing access to research participants and in reducing the social distance at a critical stage of the researcher process. However, my identity as an outsider was also defined by other subgroups within that identity. For example my gender, marital status (unmarried), and profession status as a university researcher often operated separately and in combination with my race to facilitate and complicate the research process. (p. 420)

She notes that in one of the communities she studied, her status as an unmarried female created some tensions in the research process. She relays two incidents that happened in the field around the fact that she was unmarried.

> In one community a local man visited the family with whom I was staying. When we were introduced, he recalled that he had heard about me and shared with me the rumor in the community that I was there to look for a husband. . . . Another incident occurred in church one Sunday with an African American minister who invoked the topic of the Anita Hill/Clarence Thomas hearing after I was asked to introduce myself to the congregation. At first the minister was very supportive and welcomed me warmly into the community as an African coming to study aspects of a common historical heritage. However, he soon switched to the Hill/Thomas hearings and began to remark on the fact that Anita Hill was also an educated woman who had used that privilege to accuse and embarrass Clarence Thomas (whose hometown was not far from this community). (Beoku-Betts, 1994, p. 428)

Beoku-Betts finds she must negotiate her differing statuses if she wants to obtain interviews with her respondents that reflect how they actually feel about her. It was not until she completed the negotiation process that she had full access to some of the research subjects and could begin to co-create meaning and understanding.

Having said all of this, being an outsider can actually be an advantage, depending upon the research problem and population you are studying. By not belonging to a specific group, you may be viewed as more unbiased by your respondent. Likewise, you may be more likely to ask things that you would otherwise take for granted as "shared knowledge" and in fact learn that your participants have their own way of viewing a given issue. Sociologist Robert Weiss comments on issues of difference between the interviewer and respondent as follows:

> One way to phrase this issue is to ask to what extent it is necessary for the interviewer to be an insider in the respondent's world in order to be effective as an interviewer. . . . It is difficult to anticipate what interviewer attributes will prove important to a respondent and how the respondent will react to them. . . . There are so many different interviewer attributes to which a respondent can react that the interviewer will surely be an insider in some ways and an outsider in others. . . . I have generally found it better to be an insider to the milieu in which the respondent lives, because it is easier then for me to establish a research partnership with the respondent. But some of my most instructive interviews have been good just because I was an outsider who needed instruction in the respondent's milieu. (1994, p. 137)

What is interesting to observe is that one's status as insider/outsider is fluid and can change even in the course of a single interview. On some interview issues, you may share a given role/status with your respondent; at other times, you may find stark differences according to the particularities of your research question or topic of conversation. A good example of such a situation comes from research conducted by Rosalind Edwards.

Edwards is an educated middle-class white woman who is interested in conducting unstructured interviews with Afro-Caribbean mature mothers who are also students (1990). She wants to understand the lived experiences of these women around issues of education, work, and family life. She describes the difficulty she had in gaining access to this population and gaining trust within the interview relationship. It was not until she openly acknowledged these differences with her respondents that they began to talk more openly with her. During the course of the interview Edwards relays the ebb and flow feeling of being both an insider and an outsider depending on the issues she discussed with her respondents. She notes that when the discussion turned to being a mother she felt more like an insider: "the black women did indicate some common understandings and position between us" (p. 488). Yet, when the discussion reverted to a more "public" realm like their educational experiences, even though the author also shared the positionality of having been a mature mother and student, the conversation became one where "black women were least likely to talk to me about what we had the most in common" (p. 488).

Reflexivity and Difference

Researchers can use the process of *reflexivity* as a tool to assist them with studying across difference. Reflexivity is the process through which a researcher recognizes, examines, and understands how his or her own social background and assumptions can intervene in the research process. The researcher is a product of his or her society and its structures and institutions just as much as the researched. Our beliefs, backgrounds, and feelings are part of the process of knowledge construction. It is imperative for the researcher to be aware of his or her positionality—the set of attributes that he or she brings with them into the research project—his or her gender, race/ethnicity, class, and any other factors that might be of importance to the research process. The research projects we recounted above required each researcher at some point during his or her research project to become aware of how he or she is similar and different from his or her respondents. *Doing reflexivity* in fact empowered both the researcher and researched within the interview situation. Reflecting on difference allowed Beoku-Betts (1994), Edwards (1990), Riessman (1988), Weston (2004), and Weiss (1994) to *negotiate their differences and similarities* with their respondents in order to *gain access* and *obtain data* that would not necessarily be available to them and to *gain new insight* into their data. Weston's (2004) reflectivity concerning her lesbian identity and how it impacts her research allowed her to easily obtain access to the lesbian community. Edwards' (1990) recognition of both how she is similar and different from her Afro-Carribean population provides her more in-depth understanding of how her population talks about public and private issues. Weiss (1994) and Edwards (1990) also realize that the categories of insider and outsider are not fixed but fluid, depending upon the given research topic and the individual ebb and flow of the interview itself.

Reflexivity also reminds us that we need to be mindful of the importance of difference to our research project as a whole. Difference enters into the projects we select, the questions we ask, the way data is collected, analyzed, written, and interpreted. Difference needs to be explored, not disavowed.

● ANALYSIS AND INTERPRETATION OF INTERVIEW DATA

We go into detail about the analysis and interpretation of data in Chapter 10. However, we will provide you with some general thoughts about generating analysis from your interview data. Sociologist David Karp (personal communication) provides us with a step-by-step approach (see text box below) to how you might begin the analysis of your interview data. He stresses the importance of beginning your analysis right after you begin data collection. Qualitative data analysis is an *iterative process* of data collection along with data analysis. These two processes almost proceed simultaneously. Karp stresses the importance of "memoing," that is, taking stock of where you are in your thinking about your project by writing down your hunches and your ideas about how your data fits or does not fit together. If you do come up with what you consider an important breakthrough, reflect on this. Memoing also functions to help the researcher become more reflexive about his or her own positionality and how it may impact what he or she is researching. Karp also points out the importance of going out of your way to look for "negative cases," things that don't seem to fit together or that are problematic, by asking yourself: What doesn't support my interpretation?

Tips on Analyzing Interview Data From David Karp

1. "Remember that the analytical work you do along the way is every bit as important as the task of data collection. Never subordinate the task of data collection to thinking about and analyzing your data. The great strength of methods such as in-depth interviewing is that you can engage simultaneously in the processes of data collection and analysis. The two processes should inform each other."

2. "Start writing memos with the very first interview. Let your early data tell you which of your ideas seem sensible and which ones ought to be reevaluated. Especially at the beginning you will hear people say things that you just hadn't thought about. Look carefully for major directions that had just not occurred to you to take. The pace of short memo writing ought to be especially great toward the beginning of your work. We advocate "idea" or "concept" memos that introduce an emerging idea. Such memos typically run two to three pages."

3. "Reevaluate your interview guide after about 10 interviews. Ten interviews ought to give you enough information to do a major

---

assessment of what you are learning or failing to learn. This is probably a good point at which to take a close look at your research questions and emerging themes."

4. "If you think that you have been able to grab onto a theme, it is time to write a "data" memo. By this we mean a memo that integrates the theme with data and any available literature that fits. By a data memo I mean something that begins to look like a paper. In a data memo always use more data on a point than you would actually use in a research paper. If you make a broad point and feel that you have 10 good pieces of data that fit that point, lay them all out for inspection and later use. Also, make sure to lay out the words of people who do NOT fit the pattern."

5. "Once themes begin to emerge, go out of your way to find cases that do not fit. You must try as hard as you can to disprove your ideas. Do not be afraid of complexity and ambiguity about themes. The world is complicated and your writing must reflect that complexity. There is a tendency of social scientists to describe patterns as if they were uniform and monolithic. To do that slights the complexity of things. Don't fall in love with early, plausible theories."

6. "After 15–20 interviews it is probably a good idea to create coding categories. Here the task is to begin by creating as many categories as you can that seem sensible. Coding is another way of "getting close to the data" and telling you what you know. You can eventually use these codes as you go through the data for paper and memo writing."

7. "Write a fairly complete memo every time your work takes on a new direction (say, a major change in sampling procedure). Provide a full explanation for changes in analytical directions. Your memos can constitute an "audit trail" for people who want to retrace your steps. People who do qualitative research should be as fully accountable for their procedures as those who employ more standardized procedures."

8. "If you think you have a theme significant enough to write a paper on for publication, do it. Getting papers published is very affirming and brings your ideas to a point of high refinement. You don't have to wait until all your data are in to write papers. You will find that some of your papers will be on "subsamples" within the larger sample."

9. "Periodically, write outlines for what a book, thesis, or report from your data might look like. Draw up preliminary prospectuses. Pretend that you were about to sit down and write a book. This is a good exercise that requires you to paint the total picture."

10. "Do not get crazy about getting exactly the same data from every respondent. You will find that each respondent's story is to some degree unique. In your writing you will want to point out here and there the unique story. It is probably a good idea to write up a summary sheet of about one page that describes the main themes in each interview."

11. "Test out your hypotheses on your respondents. Incorporate your hypotheses into questions ("You know, several of the people with whom I have talked tell me that . . . Does this make sense to you?"). There is no reason to hide or conceal hypotheses, ideas, and concepts from subjects."

12. "Pay attention to extreme cases, as they are often the most informative. Be on the look-out to do "deviant case analysis."

● CONCLUSION

In-depth interview is a wonderful method for getting at the lived experiences and perspectives of people. Qualitative interviews require the building of rapport and reciprocity in the interview situation. Many factors influence how a conversation will go, and as we saw, difference cannot be ignored but should be incorporated into the research design and data gathering process from start to finish. Other issues such as sharing authority and co-creating a narrative, which were mentioned in this chapter, will be discussed at greater length in the next chapter on oral history interviews.

● GLOSSARY

Co-creation of Meaning: This occurs when the researcher and research participant create meaning or knowledge collaboratively. The interview is often seen as a site for the co-creation of meaning. The researcher's job is to listen intently to what the researched has to say and be prepared to drop his or her agenda in response to what takes place during the interview.

Focused Topic: A particular contained topic the researcher is studying.

In-Depth Interview: A qualitative interview where the researcher seeks knowledge from the respondent's point of view.

Insider Status: This is a trait or characteristic or experience the researcher has in common with his or her research participants. One strategy researchers have used to overcome the impact of difference in the interview process is to "match" some of their important status characteristics (race/age/gender/ sexual preference) so that they can take advantage of their *insider status* in gaining access to an interview and obtaining cooperation and rapport within the situation in order to expedite understanding their respondents.

Interview Guide: A list of topics and/or questions constructed prior to the interview to be used at the discretion of the researcher.

Knowledge-Producing Conversation: The qualitative interview is a special kind of knowledge-producing conversation that occurs between two parties. The relationship between the interviewer and respondent is critical to the process of constructing meaning.

Line of Inquiry: Also known as *domain of inquiry*, each topic listed on the interview guide is known as a line of inquiry that you want to pursue during the interview session.

Low-Structure Interview: *See* Open-Ended Interview.

Markers: Markers are important pieces of information that a respondent may offer as he or she talks about something else. It is important to remember and return to markers as appropriate.

Meaning-Making Partnership: In-depth interviews are a meaning-making partnership between interviewers and their respondents. These sessions provide an opportunity for researchers to learn about social life through the perspective, experience, and language of those living it.

Open-Ended Interview: In this type of interview, the researcher has a particular topic for the study, he or she allows the conversation to go wherever the research participant takes it, and each interview becomes highly individual. This is also referred to as a *low-structure* interview.

Outsider Status: This refers to major differences between the researcher and research participants, such as a difference in race, gender, social class, sexual orientation, educational level, and so on. The standard thinking on difference in the interview situation suggests that if the interviewer is an *outsider* this might make it more difficult for him or her to gain access and to understand the situation of "the other."

Probe: The researcher's way of getting a respondent to continue with what he or she is talking about, to go further or to explain more, perhaps by virtue of an illustrative example. Sometimes a probe is simply a sign of understanding and interest that the researcher puts forward to the interviewee.

Rapport: Researchers help respondents share their stories by building *rapport.* Respondents must feel safe, comfortable, and as though what they are saying is valued. In order to accomplish this, researchers need to take the role of active listener while the interviewee is speaking. Showing genuine interest is critical to the establishment of rapport.

Reflexivity: Reflexivity is the process through which a researcher recognizes, examines, and understands how his or her own social background and assumptions can intervene in the research process. It is sensitivity to the important situational dynamics between the researcher and researched that can impact the creation of knowledge. Researchers can use the process of reflexivity as a tool to assist them with studying across difference.

Semistructured Interview: Semi-structured interviews rely on a certain set of questions and try to guide the conversation to remain, more loosely, on those questions.

Structured Interview: A structured interview means that the researcher asks each participant the same series of questions. If the participant strays too much from the topic at hand, or says some interesting things that aren't directly relevant to the study, the interviewer guides the conversation back to the interview questions.

● DISCUSSION QUESTIONS

1. When is in-depth interview appropriate? What kind of questions is this method suited to answer and when should it be used instead of ethnography?

2. What kind of dialogue occurs in the in-depth interview situation?

3. Explain the different degrees of structure an interviewer can impose and when it is appropriate to use a more or less structured approach. How do qualitative interviews differ from quantitative interviews?

4. What is an interview guide? How does one construct an interview guide and how, ideally, should a guide be used?

5. Explain the importance of building rapport in the interview situation. In this vein, what does it mean to say that qualitative interviews rely on the co-construction of meaning?

6. What is the difference between a marker and a probe? Why are these important to the successful interview?

7. Discuss issues of difference in intensive interviews. What are the benefits of having insider status? What are the benefits and drawbacks of outsider status? Explain how these statuses exist on a flowing continuum in actual research practice.

SUGGESTED WEBSITES ●

Education Online "Collecting data by in-depth interviewing"

http://www.leeds.ac.uk/educol/documents/000001172.htm

This is a paper/presentation on the basics of in-depth interviewing. The author explains how to collect data by walking through the process of her own study. There is an extended section on what types of questions to ask. The paper ends with a large bibliography.

Audience Dialogue

http://www.audiencedialogue.org/kya10.html

This website is put out by "Audience Dialogue" to provide useful information for communicators everywhere. This URL leads to Chapter 10, which is about in-depth interviewing. The site breaks down the process and describes what needs to be accomplished before, during, and after this form of data collection.

REFERENCES ●

Anderson, K., & Jack, D. C. (1991). Learning to listen: Interview techniques and analysis. In S. B. Gluck & D. Patai (Eds.), *Women's words: The feminist practice of oral history* (pp. 7–11). New York: Routledge.

Beoku-Betts, J. (1994). When black is not enough: Doing field research among Gullah women. *NWSA Journal, 6*(3), 413–433.

Edwards, R. (1990). Connecting methods and epistemology: A white woman interviewing black women. *Women's Studies International Forum, 13*(5), 477–490.

Harding, S. (1993). Rethinking standpoint epistemology: What is "strong objectivity"? In L. Alcoff & E. Potter (Eds.), *Feminist epistemologies* (pp. 49–82). New York: Routledge.

Johnson, J. M. (2002). "In-depth interviewing." In J. F. Gubrium and J. A. Holstein (Eds.), *Handbook of interview research: Context & method* (pp. 103–119). Thousand Oaks, CA: Sage.

Kohler-Riessman, C. (1987). When gender is not enough: Women interviewing women. *Gender and Society, 1,* 172–207.

Oakley, A. (1981). Interviewing women: A contradiction in terms. In H. Roberts (Ed.), *Doing feminist research* (pp. 30–61). London: Routledge and Kegan Paul.

Reinharz, S. (1992). *Feminist methods in social research.* New York: Oxford University Press.

Riessman, C. K. (1988). Worlds of difference: Contrasting experience in marriage and narrative styles. In A. D. Todd & S. Fisher (Eds.), *Gender and discourse: The power of talk* (pp. 151–173). Norwood, NJ: Ablex.

Safa, H. I. 1981. Runaway shops and female employment: The search for cheap labor. *Signs, 7*(2), 418–433.

Warren, C. A. B. (2002). Qualitative interviewing. In J. F. Gubrium and J. A. Holstein (Eds.), *Handbook of interview research: Context & method* (pp. 83–101). Thousand Oaks, CA: Sage.

Weiss, R. S. (1994). *Learning from strangers: The art and methods of qualitative interview studies.* New York: The Free Press.

Weston, K. (2004). Fieldwork in lesbian and gay communities. In Sharlene Hesse-Biber & Michelle Yaiser (Eds.), *Feminist perspectives on social research* (pp. 198-205). New York: Oxford University Press.

CHAPTER 5

ORAL HISTORY

A Collaborative Method of (Auto)Biography Interview

"To speak is to preserve the teller from oblivion."

—Alessandro Portelli

Storytelling is a natural part of the human experience. Human beings communicate meaning through talk. Oral historians have harnessed this tradition of transmitting knowledge and created an important research technique that allows the expression of voice. While storytelling has a deep history, the adaptation of this human process into a legitimated research method is relatively new.

Oral history was established in 1948 as a modern technique for historical documentation when Columbia University historian Allan Nevins began recording the memoirs of persons significant in American Life. (North American Oral History Association, as quoted by Thomson, 1998, p. 581)

Some researchers find it helpful to distinguish between "oral tradition" and "oral history," the former being the umbrella category in which the oral history method can be placed. "Oral tradition" among many Native American people refers to stories handed down for multiple generations that can also involve nonhuman subjects (Wilson, 1996, p. 8). This differs from the more recent academic use of the term "oral history," in which personal stories are collected from an individual.

As we will show in this chapter, oral history is a very unique kind of interview situation because the process of storytelling on which it is based is distinct. There are moments of realization, awareness, and, ideally, education and empowerment during the narrative process. When conducting an oral history with a college-aged woman struggling in a serious battle with anorexia nervosa, there was a point, two long sessions into the life history project, when the interviewee noted the moment in her life that culminated in a turn toward anorexia. It was a significant moment in her life narrative that could only have come through by the autobiographical telling of her story. Not only did this represent a major turning point in the respondent's self-awareness, but it also helped elucidate and expand on existing substantive knowledge about eating disorder vulnerability and the onset of such disorders. The clarity with which Claire notes the moment she turned toward body obsession and the way in which it initially occurred could only have happened through the telling of her story from childhood on.

I kind of focused more on my circumstances and the lack of opportunities that had been available to me. Like, all these things that I had, put up waiting, you know, I had waited for, for so long, and everyone was like, "one day, one day," and then, that day was here and nothing was happening. You know? And so that was hard. Um, but I and actually it was at that time when I knew I was staying at school, that I remember thinking, ok, obviously I can handle the academics. You know, the friends, maybe I won't be developing my closest friends at college, but I still have my ones from high school. You know, what am I going to do with this time? Like I was sitting here looking at, a three-year period going, what am I going to do with three years of my life? You know? And I think that was the other disappointing thing, is that with the exception of perspectives, my other classes were like high school. They were very structured, very like, rote memorization, as opposed to: what ideas do you have? Like, do you think this is, a good idea? How do you feel about this? And so I was kinda like, what am I gonna do with three years? And I can remember that day, thinking to myself, well, at least I can come out with what I want to look like. Like, part of being successful to me, like, I had a certain image in my head, and that image was not like, a woman with baby fat on her face. You know? It was very in-shape; it was funny because I never wanted to be skinny. But I wanted to be strong. I always,

I mean, especially growing up with guys, I wanted to be able to take them on in basketball. And I wanted to be able to go skiing, you know? I just wanted to be in really good shape. And I was just like, ok, well at least I can, I can control my health. You know? Even though I don't really have much I can do about this decision, and now looking back I can see that I, you know, that I did have a voice. I could have said forget it, I'm just leaving, you know? But when I weighed the pros and the cons, especially because I was always someone to keep the peace in my house, to disrupt a balance, or to make unnecessary trouble, wasn't something I was willing to do. So I, you know, I remember saying to myself, well, I'll just start exercising, to watch what I eat, you know, I mean, it was the first time I wasn't in organized sports, so like, I wasn't going from season to season. ***And um, I was just like, ok, that's what I'll do***. [Leavy, 1998, interview two with Claire (pseudonym), emphasis added]

What a powerful moment in the research process—the revelation of when and why what would become a life-threatening body obsession began two years earlier.

As you can already begin to see, oral history is a special kind of intensive biography interview. During an oral history project a researcher spends an extended amount of time with one respondent in order to learn extensively about her life or a particular part of her life. The preceding excerpt is taken from a project which used oral history as a way to understand how otherwise successful female college students with eating disorders became so focused on their bodies—what life experiences webbed together in a way that created body image obsession vulnerabilities in Claire and others? But it is not enough to say that we learn about the lives of our respondents as with other qualitative methods of interview and observation, oral history allows researchers to learn about respondents' lives from their own perspective—where they create meaning, what they deem important, their feelings and attitudes (both explicit and implicit), the relationship between different life experiences or different times in their life—their perspective and their voice on their own life experiences. Oral histories allow for the collaborative generation of knowledge between the researcher and the research participant. This reciprocal process presents unique opportunities, continual ethical evaluation (heightened in the electronic age), and a particular set of interpretive challenges. Predominantly a feminist method, oral history allows us to get at the valuable knowledge and rich life experience of marginalized persons and groups that would otherwise remain untapped, and, specifically, offers a way of accessing subjugated voices. Beyond contributing to social scientific knowledge substantively, the oral history process can be a rewarding and empowering experience for both the participant and researcher, as in the case of Claire, who later reported feeling empowered by gaining insight regarding pivotal moments in her life.

● ORAL HISTORY AS DISTINCT FROM IN-DEPTH INTERVIEW

What is oral history? As we have already said, oral history is a special method of interview where the researcher and research participants spend extended time together engaged in a process of storytelling and listening. In other words, it is a collaborative process of narrative building. However, this alone does not distinguish oral history from other forms of qualitative interview. So the real question is: what makes oral history special? What is unique about this method, how do qualitative researchers use this method, and what does it add to our knowledge of the social world? In order to explicate the special qualities of oral history, we must differentiate it from in-depth interview, which is the closest alternative.

As we saw in the last chapter, in-depth interviews are an excellent way to gather rich qualitative data from the perspective of the people being studied. The same is true in an oral history. However, when using in-depth interviews an interviewer will typically have a focused topic for the interview and will follow an interview guide which, as we saw, may be semistructured or relatively unstructured. Interviewees may or may not be asked identical questions, depending on the design and goals of the project. Oral history interviews differ in that, while the researcher is studying a specific topic, the organization of the topic is likely to be far less focused. For example, if you are interested in studying the body image issues women experience while in college, in-depth interviews may be the appropriate method for focusing on that issue while still allowing respondents ample room to qualitatively explain what is important in that regard, from their perspective. Now let's say that you want to study body image issues among college-age women as a part of their life process. Meaning, if you are interested in the life of the respondent from childhood on, such as the various life experiences that may have webbed together to create particular body image vulnerabilities once in college, oral history may be appropriate. This was the case in the study Claire participated in. Oral history allows you to study a long period of a person's life or even their entire life. You can narrow down the topic, such as body image, work experiences, parenting experiences, etc., but ultimately you will get a much more in-depth story from each individual participant. This depth may sacrifice some breadth as they start to detail particular experiences at the exclusion of others, but we will discuss this more soon.

It is not enough to say that you are studying a longer period of time with oral history; in fact, in some cases this may not even be true. What is really underlying the strength of the method is that you can study *process*. If you are studying a woman's life from childhood through college in order to understand her body image issues at the present time, what you will learn about is not only what she is currently experiencing and her perspective on that, but the *process* that led her there. Likewise, historical processes and circumstances will underscore her narrative in ways that help us understand individual agency within the context of social and material environments. So, while oral history focuses on the individual and her narrative, it can be used to link micro- and macrophenomena and personal life experiences to broader historical circumstances. Accordingly, oral history is a critical method for understanding life experiences in a more holistic way as compared with other methods of interview. This is congruent with the tenets of qualitative research and can yield not only rich descriptive data but also knowledge about social processes. Some topics simply lend themselves more to one method. History-driven topics are highly congruent with oral history. For example, if you are interested in studying a historical event or a historical time period and how a certain population experienced that event or lived in that period, oral history may be the best method.

Botting (2000) used oral history as a way to understand the experiences of a particular group of working women in the 1920s and 1930s. Specifically, she was interested in domestic servants who had migrated from coastal communities to a mill town in Newfoundland for employment purposes. She used oral history as a way to understand the experiences of both migration and domestic work for that group of female workers, who at the time represented a large proportion of women workers in that area. This kind of research is essential in filling gaps in our current knowledge base of what it means to be a woman from a particular social class in a given time, place, and industry, from the woman's own perspective. There are numerous examples of how experiences that have not yet been researched could begin to be understood from the vantage point of those who have lived them by using oral history in the way that Botting did. In this way previously excluded groups can share their valuable knowledge with us. In addition to these kinds of expansive experiences, oral history is invaluable in coming to understand how people have experienced historical events of import.

Crothers (2002) launched a fascinating project at Indiana University Southeast in which undergraduate students extensively interviewed community residents about historical events. Specifically, World War II and Korean War veterans were interviewed as were people who lived during the Great Depression. The study had an immeasurable positive effect on both the interviewers and interviewees. One dimension of this outcome could be categorized as community-building because the community learned more about its constituent members. In terms of direct educational benefits, students learned about the relationship between individual experience and sociohistorical conditions, allowing the importance of a historical perspective to emerge during the experience of doing qualitative research.

> After interviewing World War II and Korean War veterans, students no longer view Pearl Harbor, Normandy, Iwo Jima, Hiroshima, and Inchon as distant locations on a map but as places where young Americans like themselves fought and died in miserable conditions and often without recognition. Students learn that though the veterans invariably remembered their service with pride, most had no desire to repeat the experience. Veterans left permanently disabled, both physically and psychologically, and those who were prisoners of war reinforce the lesson that war, even a "good war," should be entered only with trepidation. In short, interviews made a profound impression on students. (Crothers, 2002, p. 3)

Additionally, research participants were given a voice and the opportunity to tell their story to interested listeners. This too is a profound and important part of the oral history experience.

> Students also interact directly with some of the community's most undervalued members, senior citizens, who share the richness of their lives and experiences. As one student noted, "I think the older people [involved in the project] were made to feel important. *They had a story to tell* and I think college students taking the time to investigate their experience made them feel like someone cared about their sacrifice. (Crothers, 2002, p. 3, emphasis added)

When used in these ways, oral history can meet ideals of education and empowerment as well as substantive knowledge building. There are also examples of using oral history as a way of understanding current events of import from the perspective of those experiencing them while they are still fresh.

Merely days after the terrorist attacks of 9–11, "The September 11, 2001, Oral History Narrative and Memory Project" was initiated at Columbia University. Bearman and Marshall Clark were cofounders of this institutionally supported longitudinal research project. Within 7 weeks after the event the researchers had collected oral history interviews from almost 200 people, and within 6 months they had collected an additional 200 oral history interviews, including those with volunteers, rescue workers, survivors, and others who lived or worked in the area of Ground Zero. The researchers were interested in understanding the construction of individual and social memory. Specifically, they wanted to understand the role of the mass media and government in the interpretative process of individuals regarding coming to terms with the events that had transpired. Furthermore, as their interviewees were ethnically diverse, they wanted to understand how a heterogeneous group of people who were at the epicenter of the event has interpreted it and filtered the information and images they were receiving from the larger culture. How did feelings of patriotism and alienation impact the construction of individual memory during the immediate aftermath? In the minds of those there, does 9–11 qualify as a "turning point" in American history as it has repeatedly been portrayed by media analysts and political leaders? These were amongst the questions the researchers had as they listened to the stories of 9–11 from those who had experienced it and were now trying to make sense of it. Oral history became an important way of understanding memory construction as it was actually occurring.

The researchers found that political imagery was an important component in early memory construction. The researchers ended up determining that there were various recurring categories of interpretation that people placed on their experiences in order to make sense of them. These can also be likened to frames through which people come to interpret their experience of the tragedy. Categories/frames included patriotism, flight and refuge, consolation, and solace (p. 7). The frame of interpretation that the researchers were most interested in was the idea of 9–11 as an "apocalypse."

> Perhaps the most important for our ultimate considerations of the significance of September 11 as an axis of national as well as international understanding, the attacks were perceived in direct and indirect ways as an apocalypse. It was registered, in that sense, as a moment that stood outside of time and an event that ended history as we had previously understood it. The interviews we conducted with survivors and eyewitnesses were frequently shot through with religious analogies and metaphors and with apocalyptic imagery from films and movies, demonstrating the ways that many wrestled with questions of good and evil, life and death outside the frame of history as they had previously understood it. (Marshall Clark, 2002, p. 7)

The ability of oral history to tap into the intersection of personal experience, historical circumstance, and cultural frame is clear in the 9–11 oral history study. Moving away from these specific examples, we can make some comments about the relationship between biography, history, and culture as revealed by oral history.

In a general sense, oral history provides a way to invite people to tell their story—of their past, a past time, a past event, and so on. However, their individual story is always intimately connected to historical conditions and thus extends beyond their own experience. Oral history allows for the merging of individual biography and historical processes. An individual's story is narrated through memory. This means that their recollection of their experiences, and how they give meaning to those experiences, is about more than "accuracy;" it is also a process of *remembering*—as they remember, they filter and interpret. Having said this, there is a tension between history and memory, the collective recorded history and the individual experience of that collective history, that can be revealed, exposed, and explicated though oral history. In this vein Richard Candida Smith (2001) says: "memory and history confront each other across the tape recorder" (p. 728). As we will expand on in our conclusion to this chapter, you can see that oral history is becoming increasingly important in the growing interdisciplinary research on collective memory.

Similar to the study of historical or current events, oral history is also very useful for studying the individual experience of social change and merging social and personal problems. Slater (2000) used oral history in order to understand how four black South African women experienced urbanization under apartheid. The women, as perhaps would be expected, had both shared and individual experiences which are brought out during the life history process. The data show how structural constraints shaped these women's economic realities in profound ways (p. 38). However, these women also illustrate that their own agency ultimately impacts their lives, as does the social reality that they share.

> . . . life histories enable development researchers to understand how the impact of social or economic change differs according to the unique qualities of individual men and women. This is because they allow researchers to explore the relationship between individual people's ability to take action (their "agency"), and the economic, social, and political structures that surround them. (p. 38)

Slater makes a case that oral history can be an integral method in development research.

As globalization and our study of it increases, oral history can continue to be used to study political, social, and economic changes. In this time of world change, oral history can help us understand both the shared and the personal impact of social upheaval on the individuals living within it. For example, oral history would be a wonderful method for understanding how individuals within Iraq are experiencing the U.S. occupation, political regime shift, and rebuilding of their country. How do individuals adapt to these major social changes? What are individual coping strategies? How do individuals filter and respond differently to these changes? How has social change impacted people's personal relationships, including marriage, courtship, and parental relationships?

Oral history is also often used to study the experience of oppression—the personal experience of being a member of an oppressed group. Sparkes (1994) conducted an oral history interview project with a lesbian physical education teacher in order to examine the ways that discrimination and heterosexism shaped her workplace experiences. Personalizing the shared experience of oppression is a strength of oral history.

When using oral history researchers may interview fewer people in total but spend more time with each participant, which is likely to occur over several preplanned interview sessions. Qualitatively inclined researchers who work with human subjects, particularly in fields such as sociology, are likely to be drawn to both in-depth interviews and oral history interviews. A choice between the two should be based on the fit between the research goals and research method. When comparing in-depth interviews with oral history interviews, the appropriateness of the method is related to the topic you are pursuing and the number of respondents and depth of data that you are looking for. It is important not to privilege one method over the other but rather to focus on the strengths of each. Likewise, the two methods can be combined in multimethod designs, though this is pretty uncommon due to their similarities and the fact that they are both very time-consuming.

Now that you are getting a better handle on how oral histories are distinct from traditional in-depth interviews, it is important to examine more closely why oral histories are special and why feminists in particular have worked so hard to revive, study, broaden, and legitimate their use.

ORAL HISTORY: RAPPORT, LISTENING, AND STORYTELLING AS RESEARCH TECHNIQUES ●

Building Rapport and Dealing With Difference

During data collection, oral history relies on recording verbal communication between the researcher and research subject. We can break this down further and say that oral history is dependent on two techniques which foster the flow of data: talking and listening. Before a story is even told the interviewer and interviewee can begin to understand how to listen and talk in the context of producing a life narrative. It is important that the interviewer and interviewee begin to create a rapport prior to the first recorded interview session (if possible), a rapport which they must attend to throughout the interviewing process. While rapport is always dialectical, the primary responsibility is with the researcher who has initiated the research process. This may mean some preliminary discussions so that both parties feel comfortable with each other and begin to become familiar with each other's "talk style."

> Prior to the initial meeting, interviewers can discard their own research-oriented time frame in favor of narrators' temporal expectations. Taking time to know another means more than a preliminary interview; it entails meeting for an extended session or more. Congruent with good oral history practice, researchers take the opportunity to solicit narrators' comments and suggestions about the project, including names of potential narrators, other resource persons, and sources for photos, artifacts and written materials. However, the purpose of the initial contact is not just a preliminary interview to obtain data; the meeting is an opportunity to promote collegiality and to engage in mutual self disclosure. (Minister, 1991, p. 36)

The process of gaining rapport and building collegiality is vital to the successful interview process. Linguistic practices are also a part of this. As we will see later in our section on storytelling, there are various structures people use to tell their stories, and both parties must be comfortable with each other's style.

Although we have discussed rapport and reciprocity as critical in the use of all interactive qualitative research methods, these issues are perhaps heightened in the oral history situation—particularly for researchers who envision the process holistically. This is because, as a researcher, you are not simply asking the research participants to allow you to observe naturally occurring behavior that is independent of the research process (as in field research). Likewise, you are not asking a set of questions on a clearly defined topic (such as with in-depth and focus group interviews). When you ask someone to participate in an oral history project you are asking that person to narrate his or her life story and, through words, to share him- or herself on a deep level. Depending on the nature of the project you may be asking him or her to revisit difficult times in his or her life without any guarantee that once you have triggered their memory, he or she will be able to "turn it off" at will. Likewise, you may have no idea what directions the person's story will go in once the narrative takes off. Thus you cannot define all of the topics that will be covered in advance—you simply don't know them yet. Rapport is therefore essential in the oral history process because the interviewee gives a high level of trust over to the researcher and makes themself vulnerable to a range of emotions, feelings, and thoughts that may stretch from very positive and joyous to difficult and painful. When a foundation for trust is established the collaborative process of oral history can proceed and the research participant will know that the researcher is truly there with them for the ride. As you will see, oral history is an intimate process of two people working together in order to produce a meaningful biographical narrative.

Given the collaborative nature of oral history, who can do it? Who can be an interviewer? As with all interactive research, issues of difference are an inseparable part of the research process. As such, to what extent can the researcher and narrator differ from one another? For example, some researchers suggest that because different groups within the social order have particular experiences and particular ways of expressing those experiences, "sameness" is integral to a successful oral history interview. Minister (1991) explains that women communicate differently than men and without supportive communication in return some women may be muted. As such, women must interview women because they share in a particular sociocommunication subculture and understand how to talk with other women. Other researchers actively incorporate difference into their research but practice reflexivity throughout the project in order to avoid claiming authority over another. For example, Sparkes (1994) conducted an oral history project with a lesbian despite the fact that he differed in terms of both gender and sexual orientation. As such, he did not share in the experience of oppression (and multiple oppressions) that framed his respondent's life. As a part of reflexive practice Sparkes wrote about the experience of interviewing someone who does not share in the unearned social privileges that he enjoys. By incorporating this difference into the entire research endeavor, including the write-up, Sparkes demonstrates that social privilege can be used to help give voice to those typically silenced within the culture (1994). There is much debate in academia about who can be a knower, who can understand the words of another, and so forth. Ultimately, these are personal choices that the researcher must make. In thinking through some of these issues as you select your topic and design your research project, you'll have to consider your epistemological beliefs regarding the relationship between the researcher and researched. When writing up your results, you'll need to consider to what extent you are able to have authority over the life story of another, particularly if you do not share a vital social status (i.e., the experience of oppression due to race, ethnicity, social class, gender, or sexuality).

● LISTENING

During the interview process the researcher assumes the role of active listener. This role is not simply the role of listener we all enact with friends, family, and colleagues. As the interviewer in an oral history situation, the researcher must learn to listen with a completion and attentiveness that is far more rigorous and in tune with nuance than most of us use in daily life. As such, we must train our minds and ears to *hear* the story of others, not just the words, but also the meaning, the emotion, the silence. We must listen to the narrator and to ourselves. This process may involve the questioning and disavowing of previously held concepts and categories that frame our understanding of social reality, making the process potentially transformational for the researcher as well. Feminist scholar and oral historian Dana Jack explains that the complexity of "listening" experienced in oral history is *the very thing* that makes this method unique. Let's join her behind the scenes.

Behind-the-Scenes With Dana Jack

What I think the unique aspects are is that what it does is it allows the researcher to situate herself or himself right in the middle between the culture and the individual. And what I mean by that is as we listen to a person, what we hear is an individual's life story in its full idiosyncrasy, with all of the details and all of the sort of particulars of that person's life. But as a researcher you're also listening for the culture and so you also know that the very words that the person uses to explain their life and their situations also come from the culture and so they're explaining their life through um, culturally available stories. And yet, when we listen carefully, you can hear how the individual also participates in all those cultural stories but also brings their different experiences and so what you're listening for is how—to me I'm listening for so many things. One is how the person, the individual, the idiosyncratic story relates to the larger cultural story and how the narratives are available and how those cultural narratives can sometimes obliterate a person's meaning, a person's experience, and then they have to sort out what they think and feel in relation to the larger story, and so I guess what I love about the oral history method is that it lets you listen to the individual really carefully while also still understanding the larger cultural narrative and how the person participates in that. And of course there are many larger cultural narratives . . .

So it lets, let's see how to say this, well, I don't know (*laughs*). It just lets us, it lets us listen to at least two large voices, one is the individual and the other is the cultural narrative that they dip in and out of. And then how, where's the tension? Where are the questions? Where's the person um, feeling confused by how their own experience relates to these larger narratives? How and why are they trying to distinguish their experiences or does the larger narrative try to you know, seem to obliterate it and what happens then? How do they feel? So I'm always listening for not just one voice, not to that subject's voice only, but how it intertwines and distinguishes itself and is in conflict with other narratives, other larger narratives.

As qualitative researchers engaged in research involving human participants, we are searching for meaning from the perspective of those being studied. In order to get at this kind of meaning we must become nonjudgmental and open listeners. The researcher needs to be right there with the person narrating their story. In this way we need to "immerse ourselves in the interview" (Anderson & Jack, 1991, p. 18) in order to hear meaning from the perspective of the person speaking. But how are we to know if what we are hearing is the person's perspective? How do we know that our own life experiences and categories of understanding are not filtering the meaning we take from the experience? While, of course, as imprinted human subjects ourselves, we can't simply disavow our own understandings of social reality, there are techniques that we can apply to the oral history interview in order to better get at meaning from the respondent's perspective.

Jack (Anderson & Jack, 1991) suggests three techniques aimed at helping us become more effective listeners. These are specific things we can *listen for*—places where meaning, from the narrator's viewpoint, can be found. First, researchers can listen to a person's "moral language" (p. 19). These kinds of comments tend to be self-evaluative. How a person evaluates him- or herself can tell us a lot about where the person is placing emphasis in his or her life, and how they use cultural constructs of success, failure, attractiveness, promiscuity, etc. as measures in his or her own live and identity formation. These comments also provide insights into a person's emotional center, places of self-confidence and self-scrutiny.

Although very different in tone, these moral self-evaluative statements allow us to examine the relationship between self-concept and cultural norms, between what we value and what others value, between how we are told to act and how we feel about ourselves when we do or do not act that way. (Anderson & Jack, 1991, p. 20)

For example, if you are conducting an oral history with a woman and you are talking about some joyous event in her life, such as a special birthday party or other family celebration, and in the midst of her talking she says, "the cake was really beautiful with ornate decorations and it was so good but of course I felt guilty about having so much right there," this would clue you in to several things. This is an example of using moral language—the language of guilt—to impart meaning. This may serve as a signal to the interviewer that there are some body image issues going on or that the respondent has concerns about her weight and how she appears to others. Her statement is not, however, occurring in a vacuum, but rather in a cultural context that puts a premium on thinness and self-control, particularly for women. So here you can start to make some links between the respondent's self-concept and the larger culture in which she lives. Both what she has said and the way she has said it are important. Such statements may also provide the interviewer with probes to be pursued later or even at a different session with the respondent (as to not interrupt the flow of what the narrator wants to say).

The second thing to actively listen for is what Jack terms "meta-statements" (Anderson & Jack, 1991, p. 21). These are places in the interview where the interviewee will stop and double-back to critically reflect on something they just said. They have made a statement, but now they are going to return to that statement in order to comment on it. This may illustrate a change in their thought process, a moment of self-realization or discomfort with how their statement may have been perceived and thus an internal desire to support their words.

Meta-statements alert us to the individual's awareness of discrepancy within the self—or between what is expected and what is being said. They inform the interviewer about what categories the individual is using to monitor her thoughts, and allow observation of how the person socializes feelings or thoughts according to certain norms. (p. 22)

For example, someone who has just made a comment about race may then double-back to clarify, explain, or support their original statement. This kind of cycling back may be a reflection of historically specific societal norms, such as appearing nonracist, and the interviewee's awareness that they may have violated those norms in the eyes of the interviewer. Such statements are then one potential space for understanding how individuals feel about and adjust to societal norms, values, and expectations.

Finally, we must learn to listen to the "logic of the narrative," paying particular attention to consistencies and contradictions and "recurring" themes (p. 22). More specifically, the way that themes are brought into the person's narrative and their relation to other themes is important data. The placing of emphasis through recurring themes and both consistencies and conflicts within statements can give us insight into the logic the person is using to tell their story. For example, what assumptions do they hold to be true that inform how they interpret their own life experiences? What thoughts, beliefs, values, and moral judgments are underlying their interpretive and narrative processes?

Beyond using these listening techniques, Anderson and Jack (1991) also encourage researchers to learn to listen to themselves, and, in our experience, this is a critical part of the listening process in oral history. As you listen to the narrator you must listen to your own internal monitor—your feelings, confusions, questions. These are areas that may require clarification, elaboration, and exploration. You do not want to interrupt the narrator to answers these questions; remember, your primary job is that of listener. However, when pauses and transitions arise you may want to cycle back and probe based on the various thoughts and feelings you experienced while listening. It is a fine line that through practice you will learn how to navigate. On the one hand, to be an active listener in this collaborative narrative process you can't just "be in your own head" having an internal conversation; however, you want to be listening to your own gut reactions while you listen to the respondent.

When we choose to practice oral history we are making a commitment to understanding meaning from the perspective of those being interviewed. We want to know what they think, how they feel, how they filter and interpret in the ways that they do. In order to do so, we become highly engaged listeners. So far, we have been talking about listening to the content of what a respondent is saying—the main kinds of statements that emerge as people tell their stories. As important as the substantive content of oral history narratives is the form through which people tell their stories. In other words, the narrative style. In this vein, the nuances in the way a person narrates her story are also an important data source. We recommend that you come up with a consistent way of transcribing data that allows you to note pauses, laughter, the raising or lowering of voice, tonal changes, the elongation of words, and so forth. All of this can alert you to where a person places meaning and how that person is feeling at a particular point in the interview. Putting such remarks in italics, bold print, parentheses, etc. is an easy way to retain this valuable data in your initial transcript. We will discuss this more later when we talk about transcription and analysis.

In terms of listening, what is missing from their story, silences, absences, feelings for which there are no words, are also components to knowledge that emerge in oral history form. We will talk about narrative style more when we discuss storytelling and "talking" as a method of data building, but for now we will elaborate on what we mean by listening for "silences," remembering that we are meaning-seekers.

What is left out of the narrator's story can give us insight into his or her struggles and conflicts, such as differences between his or her explicit and implicit attitudes, but also the impact of the larger culture on the person's biography and retelling of that biography. Clear omissions, for example, may indicate that there is a disjuncture between what the person thinks and what he or she feels is appropriate to say. This may be the result of his or her perception of social norms and values or his or her feeling that he or she is in violation of normative ways of thinking, feeling, and behaving. For many researchers who practice oral history, such as feminist and multicultural researchers, the research project is imbued with an intent to access subjugated voices—the perspectives and people who are forced to the peripheries of a given social order. In this circumstance, listening for silences may also indicate that the categories and concepts we use to interpret and explain our life experiences do not in fact reflect the full range of experiences out there. The silence therefore indicates something about the culture at large and a gap between ways of framing experience and the experience of the individual. In other words, culture may not be providing everyone with appropriate tools with which they fully and freely express what meaning something has for them. For many, this is the very reason why listening to the voices of individuals, particularly those long excluded from the production of culture, is imperative.

At the heart of the collaborative process of data collection is both an emphasis on listening and talking. The form talking takes is that of storytelling and narrative.

Storytelling and Narrative Styles

During the oral history interview the research participant assumes the role of narrator and tells their story. This is a collaborative process of storytelling involving both the narrator and interviewer. The narrator tells his or her story, but the interviewer fosters the narration through the listening and observational techniques described earlier. In addition to the spoken word itself, the way in which a participant tells his or her story is itself recognized as an important knowledge source by oral historians.

Qualitative researchers are generally concerned with attending to the meaning people attribute to their life, but oral historians are interested in attending to the experience and voice of those they study in a comprehensive way, unique to the practice and historical development of oral history methodology. Williams (2001) distinguishes between voice and Voice within the research process, using the capital "V" to denote a holistic conception of the term *voice*. Voice in this sense includes nonverbal gestures, intonation, expressions, bodily movements, speech patterns, and silences (p. 43). These components of the interview are a part of the interviewee's full expression of him- or herself. In other words, we must attempt to retain and learn from the *performative* aspects of the storytelling and not allow this to be lost during transcription and analysis (p. 46). Williams encourages researchers to attend to the Voice of the participant more than simply the spoken word provided by an unembellished or "clean" transcript. The researcher can then use his or her listening and observational skills (p. 45) to take "field notes" or "memo notes" during the interview or transcription process, respectively. Returning more specifically to the role of the participant as narrator and even performer, let's examine storytelling techniques and speech patterns, central components of data building in oral history.

People have different styles for telling their stories. These different communicative styles result in various kinds of narratives. In this vein, the researcher needs to focus on the "narratology" or narrative structure (Williams, 2001). As feminist and other critical scholars have long explained, narrative form and language choice also provide important data about the narrator. In this way the language and speech style used by the narrator do not merely frame the substantive content of the interview but are also an integral part of it. A holistic approach to oral history emphasizes all aspects of the process. Oral historians, who often work from feminist, multicultural, and Third World theoretical perspectives, are interested in understanding the experiences of those marginalized within the society. How has their position within the culture influenced their life experiences as they interpret them and how have these experiences in turn impacted their approach to storytelling? Etter-Lewis expresses these issues:

> Language is the invisible force that shapes oral texts and gives meaning to historical events. It is the primary vehicle through which past experiences are recalled and interpreted. Attention to language, its variations and categorical forms, enriches narrative text analysis beyond strictly linguistic concerns. On a most fundamental level, language is the organizing force that molds oral narrative according to a narrator's distinct style. Styles vary as widely as individuals, but recurring patterns indicate more than speakers' personal quirks. Speech patterns inherent in oral narrative

can reveal status, interpersonal relationships, and perceptions of language, self, and the world. In the case of black women, we must ask what their narrative patterns reveal about their lives. How do their unique experiences influence the manner in which they tell their own life stories? (1991, pp. 44–45)

To be successful at the art of oral history means, for the critical researcher, to understand, accept, and embrace different narrative styles and, moreover, to recognize their importance rather than disavowing the meanings implied by such difference. This is not without its difficulty. First, scholarly oral history developed within a patriarchal context. Second, those whom we wish to hear from may themselves be accustomed to the silence. Let's examine each of these intertwined issues.

In a male-dominated world, male forms of communication are normalized and communicative expressions that differ from this model are assumed to be less valid. Qualitative interviewing, including oral history, has not been immune to the culture in which it is practiced. The academy is deeply entrenched in male ways of thinking about knowledge construction. Even nonpositivistic research methods have been influenced by male ways of thinking about language, and this includes qualitative interviewing.

> What needs to be altered for women's oral history is the communication frame, not the woman. Oral history interviewing, influenced by its ties to academic history and by the practice of interviewing in general, has developed in the context of the male sociocommunication system. Because in an andocentric world male speaking is the norm, any other kind of speaking is subnormal. . . . (Minister, p. 31)

Given our immersion in our culture, we are accustomed to male forms of communication (this could of course be broadened to include the privileging of all hegemonic ideals including white and middle/upper-class styles of communication). So, in order to perform our role of enabling others to tell their stories, we must be attentive to diversity in communicative styles and narrative forms, which includes being reflexive about how our culture has already influenced our assumptions about "the right way to tell one's story."

When engaged in this process many scholars explain that we will be confronted with gender differences in communication styles. Specifically, as embodied actors within a larger social order, women communicate differently then men. Furthermore, women's communicative styles have not been legitimated by the academy or society in general. As such, when interviewing women, the researcher must understand the participant's storytelling process and legitimate it.

Although some women narrators have adapted well to this male interviewing system that female oral historians must acquire, we will not hear
what women deem essential to their lives unless we legitimate a female
sociocommunication context for the oral history situation. . . . We will not
be able to hear and interpret what women value if we do not know how to
watch and how to listen and how to speak with women as women. We first
need to know consciously how women do communicate privately and with
each other. (Minister, 1991, p. 31)

When working within the assumptions of standpoint epistemology, this
idea of communication subcultures is heightened. Standpoint acknowledges
different perspectives based on differential positions within a hierarchical
social order. One's experiences, visions, and voice are thus earned through
their experience of being located at a particular point in the social order.
Communication strategies may differ based on the intersection of race, ethnicity, class, gender, sexuality, religion, and nationality. In the context of a
large oral history project involving the collection of oral history interviews
from multiple participants, it is important to bear in mind that there may be
differences across and within genders. Take this into account as you prepare
to meet with each participant. You cannot assume that based on one characteristic alone a person will mirror the storytelling practices of a previous
interviewee. Having said this, despite these differences, there are patterns by
which people tend to tell their own life history. We refer to these patterns as
narrative structures.

Etter-Lewis (1991) identifies three major narrative styles encountered
in the life history interview process: (1) unified, (2) segmented, and (3) conversational. To this we would add a fourth category, which Kohler-Reissman
calls episodic storytelling. As with all narrative forms, the way your respondent tells her or his story may largely be influenced by factors such as race,
class, and gender. Related to these characteristics are education, work, and
geographic location.

Often researchers may have the expectation that the respondent will
hear a topic or guiding question and respond by chronologically explaining
their experience regarding the topic, providing in-depth examples to illustrate their experience, and remaining focused on the topic or question. This
is the "unified" narrative style.

Contiguous parts of the narrative fit together as a whole, usually in the
form of an answer to a particular question. Words and phrases all are
related to a central idea . . . the narrator supports her answer as completely as possible by providing several relevant examples. The result is

a stretch of discourse unified by its focus on a particular topic. (Etter-Lewis, 1991, p. 45)

A person who uses such a style of talk may also be telling us something about how she sees herself and how she interprets her life experiences. For instance, a unified approach may indicate that a participant sees the topic clearly and has a cohesive response to it. Beyond the topic at hand, a unified approach may indicate that on a more general level the narrator experiences her life as cohesive and clearly defined. This differs in significant ways from the segmented narrative form.

Continuous parts of a narrative characterized by a diverse assortment of seemingly unrelated utterances. (Etter-Lewis, 1991, p. 46)

This form of storytelling may be counterintuitive to some researchers who are not used to this form of talk. As such, the initial meetings between the researcher and respondent, where listening and talking skills are worked on, through the building of rapport, become critically important for the researcher to become comfortable with the narrator's speech (and vice versa).

A segmented approach to oral narrative can also reveal meaning from the perspective of the person sharing her story. For example, the narrator may feel fragmented or that the various components of herself or her experiences are disconnected. This may be true for people who have experienced multiple oppressions due to race, class, gender, and sexuality, which frame their life experiences. In this situation a discussion of female body image disturbances may result in a black narrator talking about how her female mentors taught her coping strategies for dealing with racism that in effect helped give her the high self-esteem needed to also combat a deeply sexist culture that reduces women to their physical bodies. Her experience of sociocultural female body pressures brings her to a discussion of race, because in her experience, these are inter-linked. Her narrative may shift around, but in ways that are inextricably linked to her experience of the topic being discussed. There are alternative reasons a narrative may be segmented. If the narrator has never been given the oppor-tunity to reflect on the many experiences that comprise her life, the process of sharing her story may also be an intimate process of self-discovery. Thus her narrative style may reflect "a putting together of the pieces" for herself and simultaneously the researcher. What may initially appear as off the subject may actually be quite connected to the issue under discussion. This is intimately tied to our earlier contention that many of those we ask to speak may in fact be used to being muted due to their marginalization within the society. Those denied access to the social tools by which to tell their stories due to their race, ethnicity, social class, gender, or sexuality may simply not have previous experience telling their story. In this vein feminist oral historian Armitage says, "We will learn what we want to know only by listening to people who are accustomed to talking" (as quoted by Minister, 1991, p. 32). We can see this in pop culture forms as well, such as Eve Ensler's play *The Vagina Monologues*, in which some women stated that they had difficulty talking about their sexual experiences simply because no one had ever asked before. They didn't know what to say and were surprised that someone was interested. A segmented approach to narration may in these cases be the result of unearthing thoughts and feelings that had previously been untapped. A process of making the internal orally available for external use may involve a negotiation expressed through words.

Narrators may also recount past conversations as a means of providing an answer to questions. Such an approach may result in an indirect but very important and descriptive answer to a question posed by the researcher.

A contiguous part of a narrative identified by the reconstruction of conversations as they probably occurred in the past. Conversational elements are used to illustrate an idea or event. The narrator modifies voice, tone, and pitch in order to represent different speakers and different emotions (e.g., high pitch for anger or surprise). (Etter-Lewis, 1991, p. 47)

Etter-Lewis (1991, p. 47) asserts that the narrator may choose to recount a past conversation instead of directly answering a question as a way of mediating painful or otherwise difficult feelings that come to the surface as a past experience is recalled. In this way it is a defense mechanism for tapering uncomfortable or particularly strong emotions. It is vitally important to enable this kind of self-protection, since, as discussed earlier, neither the researcher nor research participant can know the extent to which the oral history interview process will bring any given emotion to the surface. Participants need the freedom to deal with unexpected emotions in a way that works for them. To the ethnographic interviewer, the performative repetition of conversations may provide the details and descriptions the researcher is most interested in. Etter-Lewis explains that these recollections may actually serve as a "magnifying glass through which details can be highlighted" (p. 47).

Drawing similarities to segmented and conversational styles of storytelling, some people may use an episodic frame through which they share their story. Kohler-Riessman (1987) contrasted the episodic and linear ways women narrated their marriage life histories. Episodic narrative differs from a unified approach where a teller uses a linear (temporally ordered) model of storytelling. In episodic narration a participant speaks by telling stories as episodes within their life. Their speech pattern relies on recounting experiences as episodes that are not chronologically ordered but are rather thematically driven.

Research participants may use more than one of these storytelling techniques as they share their knowledge with you. Shifts in narrative frames may be important indicators of a narrator's feelings or where they place emphasis. In keeping with the goals of understanding social meaning from the perspective of those creating it, truly developing one's craft as an oral historian involves understanding the various frames through which people communicate ideas and paying attention to nuance, such as a shift in narrative form. In this regard the interview process results in more than the flat words on the transcript page, but a complex understanding of the person's story as it was told to you.

● COLLABORATION AND AUTHORITY: ISSUES OF VOICE, INTERPRETATION, AND REPRESENTATION IN ORAL HISTORY

In 1990 Michael Frisch coined the term *shared authority*, which put a name to an issue of particular salience in the oral history process: the extent to which oral history is collaborative. Frisch used the term shared authority to denote the collaboration of the researcher and narrator during interpretation and representation (Thomson, 2003, p. 23). While the last chapter of this book details the broad issues of interpretation, analysis, and representation that are central to qualitative research, given the particulars of the oral history method, it warrants its own discussion of interpretation.

When using the oral history method the data collection component of the research process is collaborative. The researcher and research participant create knowledge together through the creation of a life narrative. The researcher initiates the process and facilitates the narrator's telling of his story. Typically, the researcher then transcribes the interview(s) and may add his or her memo notes to the transcript in order to account for the performative aspects of the narration and/or add his or her own feelings, thoughts, questions, and so forth. So in the end, put simply, the researcher and narrator work together to produce the raw data: the oral history transcript (and any additional material). But what happens once the interview has been collected?

Does the collaborative process that shapes data collection continue during analysis and representation? Who gets to put their mark on the story that emerges out of this process? Who has authority over the narrative? What does shared authority mean in practice? Is it always possible or even desirable? What are the ethical considerations involved when determining the scope to which a project will be collaborative? What impact does collaboration have on the researcher, narrator, and the research? Generally speaking, how do we think about interpreting oral history data? These are just some of the questions the oral historian must consider. Thinking about the qualitative research process holistically requires the researcher to consider issues of interpretation during research design and continue to revisit these questions throughout the research process, since qualitative research often involves an openness to change.

At its core questions regarding collaboration beyond the data collection stage are really questions regarding authority and what we refer to as the oral history matrix: the intersection of method, ethic, and politic. Who has authority over the data? Is this authority shared between the researcher and narrator(s)? The complex question of authority is where the oral history matrix of method, ethic, and politic is most clearly seen. Due to its historical development and current uses within the social sciences and humanities, oral history merges a research tool with a particular set of ethical considerations and social justice politics. When writing about the phrase *shared authority*, Shopes says:

> . . . this resonant phrase neatly captures that which lies at the heart of both the method and the ethic—or perhaps one should say the politics—of the oral history enterprise: the dialogue that defines the interview process itself and the potential for this dialogue to extend outward—in public forums, radio programs, dramatic productions, publications, and other forms—toward a more broadly democratic cultural practice. (2003, p. 103)

This raises important questions about the extent to which the knowledge that flows from the oral history storytelling process is collaborative in terms of development and subsequent availability and use. The collaborative potential of oral history is not simply a choice about methodology but also carries with it a set of politics and a host of ethical considerations. Central to these issues is the question posed by Frisch: "Who is the author of an oral history?" (2003, p. 113). In fact Frisch goes on to call our attention to the connection between the words *author* and *author*ity demonstrating how representation is imbued with power (2003, p. 113). The person who interprets, formats, and presents the narrative has a certain authority over the data—this person controls the construction of knowledge. So what does it mean for a researcher to "author" another person's story? How involved can the narrator be in this process? What options do qualitative researchers have?

As with all research projects, we recommend that the particular goals of the research project dictate the extent to which the interpretive phase is collaborative. Some projects will lend themselves more to sharing authority during all phases, while other projects will make this impossible or undesirable.

Your epistemological beliefs about the relationship between the researcher and researched will help frame these decisions, as will your ethical and political motivations, but ultimately the research process must mesh with your goals and resources. All oral history interviews contain collaborative dimensions; however, interpretive strategies can employ a variety of perspectives. It may be helpful to think of oral history as existing on a collaborative continuum—projects can vary from being collaborative exclusively during data collection to being thoroughly collaborative from initial research design through representation. In this regard Frisch makes an important point:

> . . . sharing authority is an approach to doing oral history, while a shared authority is something we need to recognize in it. (2003, p. 113)

Let's examine some of the pros and cons of using a shared authority approach to oral history by looking at various oral history research projects and how researchers have theorized and negotiated collaboration and authority in diverse ways.

Decentering Authority and Democratic Practice

Holistic collaboration, that which engages the researcher and narrator during all phases of knowledge production, is often appealing to those working from critical theoretical perspectives, including the feminist and multicultural frameworks. Likewise, this approach may be appropriate for research projects with the objective of creating social change or prompting social activism. Accordingly, as critical perspectives and social movement research are both on the rise, we are seeing an increase in collaborative research. This raises the question: Why are these folks particularly attracted to sharing authority?

Oral history is unique because it has the potential for decentering authority (Frisch, 1989; Shopes, 2003). As discussed in Chapter 1 historically the researcher has been privileged as the knowing party and he has had control over the research process and resulting knowledge. The researcher's authority over the data included analysis, representation/writing, and the dissemination of the resulting knowledge. For example, will the results be published? Where? How will they be used? Oral history assumes that the research participant has life experiences, thoughts, and feelings that can help us to better understand social reality or some aspect of it. In other words, the research participant has unique and valuable knowledge. The narrator alone has access to his or her own story and accordingly assumes the role of narrator. This method thus allows the research participant to maintain authority over their knowledge during data collection. The oral history method inherently challenges positivist and postpositivist conceptualizations of the researcher/ researched relationship, and moreover, necessarily shifts at least some authority to the research subject. Scholars working from critical theoretical perspectives are committed to destabilizing relations of oppression and making those historically at the peripheries of the social order the center of the knowledge construction process. Feminist and multicultural scholars are interested in decentering authority as well so that women and people of color are given a central and authoritative position within the knowledge building process. Furthermore, feminists are concerned with accessing women's voices. By changing the locus of knowledge and constructing engaged researchers and narrators, oral history lends itself to collaboration and the oppositional possibilities inherent in a collaborative knowledge-building process. The resistive dimension of sharing authority is also inextricably linked to ideas regarding democratic knowledge production which may be particularly resonant for social movement scholars.

The use of collaborative approaches to oral history bears traces of the earlier paradigm shift that prompted the development of qualitative research and wide-ranging changes in our conceptualizations of knowledge and the knowledge-building process. Some oral historians working in the area of social movements, public policy, and social activism advocate sharing authority during all phases of the research project in order to create democratic knowledge production, which can most effectively benefit those groups for whom we often conduct our research. This is because collaboration allows us to speak *with* our participants instead of *for* them. This democratic approach to knowledge construction relieves some of the questions of social power that permeate traditional research while allowing those we wish to empower to teach us how to accomplish our goals. Kerr (2003) argues that sharing authority "can play a significant role in movement building" (p. 31). Referring to Frisch's work, he writes:

He argues for "a more profound sharing of knowledges, an implicit and sometimes explicit dialogue from very different vantages about the shape, meaning and implications of history." He argues that this dialogue will "promote a more democratized and widely shared historical consciousness, consequently encouraging broader participation in debates about history, debates that will be informed by a more deeply representative range of experiences, perspectives and values." I would add that the dialogue built on this basis needs to go beyond the way we view history, but also influence the way we view history but also influence the way we design public policy and more importantly, the way we reproduce the social organization of the communities we live in. (p. 31)

In this vein, a collaborative approach to oral history analysis and representation extends beyond incorporating multiple voices and visions into our writing of history and can help shape the organization of our communities and the formulation of public policy. In this way oral history can promote multidirectional change. It is not surprising that social movement scholars have embraced this approach.

Kerr (2003) designed an oral history research project using collaborative analysis in order to study homelessness. As a part of his dissertation research Kerr spent years working on the Cleveland Homeless Oral History Project. This research, which involved multimedia interviews, is an excellent example of applying a shared authority approach holistically because it effectively enables the research objectives of an investigation. Kerr wanted to conduct research that could create meaningful dialogue among homeless people in Cleveland, which could foster the development and *implementation* of public policy changes aimed at reducing homelessness in U.S. urban centers. Kerr argues that traditionally the research on homelessness has failed to create conversations on a street level and, thus, without substantive input from the homeless themselves, resulting data hasn't garnered the support needed to both create and execute effective social policy.

Advocates and academics studying homelessness in the United States have primarily sought an audience of public officials, civic leaders, and middle and upper class progressives, who they believe have the power to create change. In part this focus has been structured by the public officials themselves who have encouraged this approach, seeking advice on the homeless problem almost exclusively from social service providers and academic experts. There is little incentive for academics to work collaboratively with the homeless. Those who have had the most success having their voice heard at the national policy level . . . have devised solutions without the input and oversight of the homeless and have done little to generate support for their solutions among the homeless. (p. 28)

The failure to produce knowledge that has successfully been used to alleviate homelessness is largely a result of two factors: (1) researchers cannot study misery from a neutral and detached position of authority, and (2) homelessness has a structural dimension supported by powerful interests who benefit from maintaining the system (Kerr, 2003, p. 30). Accordingly, Kerr had to give up the traditional privileged position of the "researcher as knower" and work collaboratively with the homeless in order to reveal trends, generate theory, advocate sensible policy changes, and, effectively implement them.

> By broadening the scientific community through the process of sharing authority with the homeless, one does not give up objectivity; rather one produces more objective and effective research. Theories and solutions that garner support are effectively implemented, and successfully address common problems [that] are objectively better than those that do not (p. 32)

In this circumstance, sharing authority was clearly the logical approach to the oral history process and promoted the integration of the researcher's ontological, epistemological, theoretical, and methodological choices, creating a robust and layered body of applicable knowledge. This knowledge cannot be separated from its democratic process of production and, thus, in every way signifies the issues it implicitly raises about *who gets to participate in the construction of our communities.*

Additionally, Kerr reported that the research participants were empowered through their participation. The process helped the homeless to become agents for social change in an arena that is directly relevant to their daily lives rather than remain victims of a reified system.

Empowerment, Ethics, and Conflict Within Collaboration

It is not difficult to understand how sharing authority has the effect of narrator empowerment. Certainly people are more likely to feel empowered when they are fully included, valued, and are operating on an even playing field. Rickard (2003) writes that the research participants in her collaborative study of British sex workers also felt empowered by the oral history process. Rickard's work is important because it raises key ethical questions about empowerment, advocacy, and sharing authority.

Is it always ethical to empower our research participants? What if they are engaged in illegal activity or an activity that we find morally or politically troublesome? As engaged researchers, where is the line between empowerment and advocacy? If we feel an obligation to benefit our research participants by empowering them (if possible), do we necessarily endorse their behavior? These are questions Rickard had to face when she shared authority with

British sex workers, including using one as an interviewer. Rickard openly adopts a "sex positive" perspective, which has opened her scholarship up to scrutiny. Some likened her collaborative research design to promoting prostitution (p. 53).

> Hence, by undertaking oral history in this area, I had to align myself with the "pro-sex work" political lobby and to become involved with the activities of national and international activist groups who support sex workers rights. The activist involvement also came from the deep concern with sharing authority. To ensure people's stories were recorded and collected I had to be prepared to use a position of academic privilege to offer political and practical support to interviewees, to facilitate communication through international networks, and to use oral history material for political and educational purposes. For me, this has led to a number of offshoot projects, such as the organization of a U.K. conference for sex workers, and the initiation of a health education project using extracts of OHP tapes as the basic resource. It has also involved me in local and national activist meetings and the use of oral history material as an educational resource for health workers. Over time, I have slowly realized that other sex work oral history has always tended to be carried out from a similar "sex positive" perspective to my own and nearly always in a context of personal and political advocacy. (p. 54)

Rickard is reflexive about her personal political alignment with her narrators and discloses how this impacts data analysis and her resulting scholarship. While we do not think it is necessary to comment on Rickard's research choices per se, we think it provides a valuable example from which we can contemplate our own research. By engaging in a thorough discussion of both the context of discovery and the context of justification, readers of Rickard's work are given enough information about the research process and the researcher's relationship to the work that they can interpret her work as they deem fit. And in this way she has done her job and also provided a robust case study for examining how we all engage in the oral history matrix of method, ethics, and politics. This brings us to a host of additional issues surrounding collaborative interpretation.

While some research projects necessitate heightened collaboration, others may be impeded by attempts to share authority. Likewise, collaborative interpretation may alter the scholarship in ways the researcher is uncomfortable with. As interpretation is a fundamental component of sense-making or meaning construction, collaboration deeply impacts knowledge building and is not necessarily desirable.

. . . collaboration is a responsible, challenging and deeply humane ideal for some oral history work, but in certain kinds of projects, beyond a basic respect for the dignity of all persons, it seems not an appropriate goal. . . . Taking the full measures of views other than your own is one thing; failing to subject them to critical scrutiny is yet another. Is presenting differing views in point/counterpoint fashion itself a form of critical inquiry? Is it enough? We need to think more about the limits and possibilities of oral history work with those with whom we do not share a fundamental sympathy. (Shopes, 2003, p. 109)

Shopes raises several important points while reaffirming that a holistic application of shared authority is only one approach to oral history. It is perfectly reasonable and often appropriate for the researcher to retain authority over the interpretive process. As researchers we can maintain feminist and other human-rights perspectives without placing the interpretive views of our narrators at the same level on which we place our own analysis. We need not invite the narrator to participate in the research process beyond the interview sessions if our project doesn't warrant it. Our scholarship and/or our emotional well-being may require that we do maintain strict intellectual authority over the process of representation.

For example, the body image oral history project that opened this chapter necessitated a separation between the researcher and narrator during data analysis. "Claire" was still deeply in the throws of anorexia nervosa and her health was rapidly declining at the time of the project. Despite her obvious ongoing battle, Claire repeatedly insisted that she was now healthy and had "clarity" over her "former" disorder. In the case of anorexia, it is clear that this kind of mind-set is common among women in the thick of an eating disorder. Her ability to judge the situation in a useful way was seriously hampered by her illness. In addition to her deep-seated denial, she was physically failing (which also had an apparent impact on her mental faculties). All of this made a collaborative analysis impossible and undesirable. In this type of situation, the researcher has to maintain intellectual authority over the data in order to generate meaning that is true to the story told by the narrator. This can be hard if you have a strong connection to your narrator; however, as the researcher you need to think of the overall process and the eventual knowledge, which may mean making a difficult decision. In our example, at the time Claire did not have the ability to effectively help interpret the web of pressures that culminated in her body image disturbance. Even in situations where a narrator is "able" to participate in the interpretive process, it simply may not be something the researcher is interested in. This is fine too.

At a basic level, I do think that the interview dynamic is collaborative. But I also think we need to think carefully where we wish to share intellectual control over our work and where we don't. We do need to be clear where and how we want to differ with narrators, perhaps in the interview itself, more likely in what we write based on interviews. We need to be clear when we wish to be critical of narrators, when there is no room for a shared perspective. (Shopes, citing herself in 2002; 2003, p. 109)

For example, what if your narrator is racist, sexist, or homophobic? If we are committed to the spirit of social justice then there are times when shared authority simply isn't an option. Regardless of whether or not we share a "fundamental sympathy" (Shopes, 2003, p. 109) with those we interview, we need to seriously consider the place of our own intellectual voice within our work. This requires us to construct, question, negotiate, and renegotiate the boundaries of collaboration within any particular project—always reflecting on the fit between our choices and our research objectives. Likewise, we think it is important for qualitative researchers to write openly about this process to assist others in thinking through the complexity of collaborative research and make informed decisions about where on the continuum any given project will fall. Let's look at an example that illustrates the importance of staying true to one's voice and the potential pitfalls of ill-defined collaboration.

Sitzia (2003) wrote a case study about the relationship she had with her oral history narrator as they tried to share authority while producing his auto-biography over a 6-year period. Her experience illuminates the rewards and dangers inherent in collaboration.

Sitzia shared important insider traits with her narrator, Arthur, particularly a working-class background, and common interests, which together facilitated a wonderful data-building rapport between the two.

This constant dialogue between me and Arthur enriched the process of working on another's life story. I quickly moved from being an interviewer to a facilitator in helping Arthur uncover his past. The development of the dialogue within the process was only possible through our relationship. (p. 94)

The kind of mutual engagement with, and shared ownership of, the project produces data that may otherwise remain hidden. However, the engagement required for collaboration has an emotional price and can at times be overwhelming. Likewise, while some scholars feel their work is enriched through shared interpretation, others may experience an unwanted loss of intellectual authority over their research, as Sitzia explains.

When our work began . . . I felt very pleased with the way the project was progressing . . . as . . . we drew closer to the publication of a book, Arthur began behaving aggressively; putting substantial pressure on me to work more quickly, threatening to complete the work with another editor, and most importantly, raising issues of ownership: "our" book became only "Arthur's" book. This situation was made worse by the fact that Arthur was going through a severe emotional and mental health crisis, which also meant that he became very dependent on me, calling in varying states of distress at all times of the day and night. I felt—and still do feel—a huge responsibility for Arthur and felt I should help him resolve his crisis, but did not feel equipped to do this. On reflection, these complications partly arose because of the experimental nature of the project: neither I nor Arthur had worked in such a collaborative way before. My approach to the project was an informal learning experience . . . I now believe that it is crucial to define clear boundaries and guidelines when embarking on a project of this nature. At the beginning of this collaboration I directed the work to a large extent and certainly had a "voice;" one consequence of this lack of clarity is that as the project progressed I felt that I gradually lost authority, that Arthur became more and more dominant—and in fact bullying—and my own voice seemed to be lost. (p. 97)

This illustrates the tensions a researcher may face when trying to determine where to place a project on the continuum of shared authority. In the end Sitzia came to understand that, in the case of her project, both she and Arthur could "own" it by being open to multiple outcomes from the one study. She and her narrator are thus free to draw on the work in various ways and, through those unexpected avenues, they can each make their own mark on the knowledge they have created. Sitzia uses aspects of the project in her writing while Arthur is able to use it in his performance pieces. This required them to let go of the idea that "one book" would be the outcome of this process and consider multiple outcomes. We think it is important to remain open to the data being used in multiple ways, as was the resolution here; however, we caution that this is not always appropriate and must be carefully contemplated by the researcher. Make choices and find resolutions that make sense in a particular circumstance.

Despite the difficulties that can arise, collaboration can be a worthwhile or necessary practice. It is therefore helpful to be proactive, design your study well, and remain open to modifications as practice dictates. If you decide to share authority with your narrators, we suggest the following strategies for dealing with the specific challenges you may encounter.

- Create clear boundaries regarding the relationship between the researcher and narrator. In other words, devote some substantial time to defining your relationship. Talk this through together so there is mutual clarity. Continue to have these conversations throughout the various phases of the process so you are constantly reinforcing your definitions and expectations (while modifying them as appropriate to growth in the relationship). This relationship must be tended to holistically.
- Set up precise expectations regarding each person's role(s) in the collaborative process. Things to discuss and come to an agreement on include:
  - The transcription process
  - Field notes and theoretical memo taking
  - Analysis procedures
  - Interpretation and theory building
  - Writing and/or representation
  - The use of the results (including how many possible outcomes are expected)

- Construct practical ideas for how to deal with potential interpretive conflicts.
  - What degree of difference does each party expect to have included in the final write-up?

By thinking these things through, you can avoid many potential pitfalls—this is time well spent. You can thus be open to less traditional approaches to oral history that may allow the asking and answering of new social scientific questions. Don't be afraid to create new methodologies as long as you remember that experimentation necessitates openness and rigor.

Archiving Oral Histories

As you have already seen, qualitative research in general, and oral history in particular, demand a high degree of ethics in practice. The archiving of oral history transcripts and/or projects is an important part of the oral history process. The American Historical Association says that arranging to deposit oral history interviews in an archival repository is a part of ethical research. The archiving of oral history materials, which makes them available for any host of future uses, may influence the research process in many ways. If a participant is well informed about the research and its outcomes, as they should be through informed consent, then the knowledge the interview will be archived may influence their storytelling. This is particularly salient when unedited interviews will be archived as narrators understand their initial telling of their story will be documented and made available forever.

> The deliberate consideration of what can and should be said, and how it should be said, is pronounced when interview transcripts are specifically prepared for archival purposes because narrators will seek to prepare their narratives for an undetermined public audience. This has a double-edged effect. On the one hand, it can produce more accurate recollections and fuller accounts if narrators take the time to refresh their memories by consulting old documents, and/or other people who experienced the same events. On the other hand, however, it may produce more of a "canned speech," or a more carefully crafted statement that is sensitive to wider implications of what is said. (Wilmsen, 2001, p. 72)

Edited interviews, intended for archival deposit, present their own set of challenges.

Analyzing, interpreting, and writing up your data is always a part of meaning making. Producing a version of the work can be equated with producing meaning itself—creating knowledge. Editing is thus tied up with the construction of meaning (Wilmsen, 2001). As the researcher, how are you going to edit the transcript? Will you "clean it up" in terms of pauses, "ums," "likes," and the other informal ways people speak? Will you fix grammar? Will you change the particulars of their way of speaking, and, if so, what implications does this have in terms of meaning construction? Will you delete or add emphasis to convey meaning? And, if so, meaning from whose perspective, yours, the narrator's or your interpretation of the narrator's meaning? How is all of this influenced by social class, race, gender, and other characteristics? In other words, what are the implications in changing the grammar of a narrator from a lower socioeconomic background? What are the implications of changing, or adding your own explanations for slang words, which may be the product of ethnic background and other social characteristics? These are all considerations when determining how to edit the transcript. Wilmsen (2001) cautions that these choices are interlinked with social power—the power to construct and disseminate knowledge.

> A significant feature of the social relations of oral history interviews is the power relations between the interviewer and the narrator. Gender, class, race, and other social considerations enter into every interview situation to a greater or lesser extent. They affect editing through narrator and interviewer/editor perceptions of the social status similarities

or differences between them, which in turn shape their understandings of their respective roles. The importance this has for editing is the way in which power relations are interwoven with differing experience with the written word. The fact that narrators have varying experience with the written word, the world of publishing, research archives, libraries, et cetera, affects what editing decisions are made, who makes them, and why. (p. 75)

As with all of the choices a researcher makes when thinking about interpretation and representation, editing is an important arena in which meaning production occurs. Reflexive researchers must consider issues of difference and research power relations as a part of ethical praxis.

The extent to which the research process is collaborative will also impact the editing process. If the narrator is involved in the interpretive process they will likely have input upon reflection. In other words, when reviewing the raw transcript, it is very likely that the narrator will recall things that were forgotten at the time of the interview that they may want to add. Likewise, they may want to elaborate or edit parts of the transcript. As a part of ethical practice we encourage you to share your transcripts with your narrators for their approval and input; however, we caution that this of courses raises many possible responses. Ultimately, the degree of influence the narrator will have on the editing process is linked to the issues of authority previously discussed.

● AUTOETHNOGRAPHY

Sometimes researchers use themselves as the subject of their research. In this way, one can conduct an oral history project using oneself as the narrator. For example, if you are interested in your own personal experiences and how they are situated in a cultural context, this approach may help you meet your goals. Qualitative researchers often use autobiographical data in both explicit and implicit ways. For instance, field researchers often keep a journal, ethics diary, or reflective diary where they document their thoughts, feelings, emotions, and so forth (Tenni, Smyth, & Boucher, 2003, p. 2). In this way autobiographical data is a part of the research process. Additionally, particular theoretical and epistemological positions may influence a researcher to explicitly include autobiographical data. When using standpoint epistemology as conceptualized by Sandra Harding, and thus using "strong objectivity," the researcher necessarily discloses information about her own biography and how it is informing the knowledge-building process. There are many examples of researchers incorporating their own experience into their projects, including doing so implicitly by imposing categories on their data derived from their own life experience. Autoethnography is a particular approach to oral history in which the research explicitly constructs data from their own life history. Furthermore, many researchers merge autobiographical writing with fiction as they write up their autoethnographies. This method thus allows researchers to fictionalize aspects of their work and create characterizations.

But it is insufficient to say that autoethnography is simply an oral history interview that you do to yourself. There is a key distinction between oral history and autoethnography. The difference is that a traditional oral history interview is based on talking (verbal narration that is recorded) whereas an autoethnography is based on writing (Maines, 2001, p. 109). Oral history interviews produce transcripts which replicate narration (Maines, 2001, p. 109). In the case of using oneself as the data source, talk is replaced by writing (Maines, 2001, p. 109). Talking and writing are entirely different modes of communication and thus deeply impact the data produced. People talk faster than they are able to write, produce more detail, and are less likely to censor themselves talking (Maines, 2001, p. 109). Additionally, speech patterns, gestures, tone, and all of the other nuances of the narrative process we discussed earlier are removed from the writing process where the author retains total control and may place emphasis differently than if speaking. Now that we have reviewed the major difference between biographical and autobiographical oral histories, let's looks more closely at the kind of writing process that constitutes autoethnography.

The term *autoethnography* can mean different things depending on how it is applied and what theory is applied to it; however, in this section we are focusing on autoethnography as a very general form of autobiographical oral history.

> *Autoethnography* refers to writing about the personal and its relationship to culture. It is an autobiographical genre of writing and research that displays multiple layers of consciousness. (Ellis, 2004, p. 37, quoting Dumont, 1978)

Ellis (2004) expands on this definition in order to illustrate the richness of this method and variability in representational forms it can utilize, which includes books, essays, poems, plays, novels, and performance pieces.

> What is autoethnography?" you might ask. My brief answer: research, writing, story, and method that connect the autobiographical and personal to the cultural, social, and political. Autoethnographic forms feature concrete action, emotion, embodiment, self-consciousness, and introspection portrayed in dialogue, scenes, characterization, and plot. Thus, autoethnography claims the conventions of literary writing. (p. xix)

This method allows us to use our own experiences, thoughts, feelings, and emotions as data to help us understand the social world. Through this approach we are able to link our personal stories to the larger society, which is the structural backdrop against which we experience everything. We can also fictionalize aspects of our project for the sake of the narrative told. This kind of research can be empowering for the researcher-subject and raise our self-consciousness and reflexivity. Having said this, these potential rewards carry their own burden.

As stated earlier, the oral history process is intellectually and emotionally draining. When conducting an oral history interview we can never be fully prepared for what the narrator might say. Nor can we fully prepare our narrators for the range of possible emotions that could flow from telling their story. The same is true for when we use ourselves as the subjects of our research.

> The engagement with what is going on for us must be physical, emotional and intellectual. It is with the physical and emotional in particular, that we often get the first clue that something is happening and may be worthy of exploration. So our annoyance, discomfort, restlessness, sadness, excitement, triumph, tense neck, scratchy eyes or feeling of serenity is also data that alert us to something. This process may cause some degree of distress so having supports in place (such as a supervisor, colleague or support group) is important. (Tenni et al., 2003, p. 3)

Heightened emotions during the research process can be markers of important data that we need to flesh out and try to make sense of. These moments also represent times where we may need additional support because the strains of the research process may be more than we can comfortably handle alone. Keeping track of one's emotions during the process can thus serve as both data and signals to the researcher about how he or she is coping with the autobiographical process. The data analysis process may also require external assistance. Differing from traditional supervisory roles of detachment and purported neutrality, supervisors engaged in assisting with autoethnography must be invested and engaged (Tenni et al., 2003, p. 3). The person or people invited to help the researcher gauge the process and interpret the data must be invested in the process, because it is, after all, about the life of the researcher, who may be their friend or colleague. Having an external dialogue (Tenni et al., 2003, p. 3) can help the researcher stay grounded and also help alleviate some of the concerns about validity that are often raised when researchers use personal data. Additionally, an external party, but one who is committed to the project, can add complexity and nuance to the data analysis process—he or she may help the researcher "see" more broadly, enhancing both the data and what the researcher takes away from the project in terms of self-consciousness.

Autoethnography can also be challenging, as you are opening up your own experiences for "public" consumption and perhaps the scrutiny that comes along with that. In other words, this method requires a level of vulnerability on the part of the researcher. Author Carolyn Ellis explains how she had to deal with this issue as she performed autoethnography. Let's join Ellis for a behind-the-scences look at the reality of confronting this process.

Behind-the-Scenes With Carolyn Ellis

More than a decade after writing and publishing an autoethnographic story with my partner Art Bochner about an abortion that occurred early in our relationship, I received this e-mail from a professor, who had assigned our story in an undergraduate class. "I gave the students the opportunity to write about it. Would you like to see what they wrote?" he e-mailed. I said yes, though I felt some anxiety when the responses arrived the next day.

The assistant professor begins this e-mail with:

> The students were asked to write about how they felt while reading the text. This was optional, but many students indicated that the text was extremely evocative and I wanted to provide a space where they could express how they truly felt. So several decided to send me an e-mail while others chatted with me outside of class.

Scrolling down, I note the comments continue for six pages. I take a deep breath and read. Addressing her letter to Art and me, the first respondent describes the narrative as being very touching. She likes the openness of emotion and reflection. Acknowledging crying several times while reading the story, she thanks me for expressing the turmoil, reality, and emotional confusion associated with pregnancy and abortion. She continues:

> Short of actually having experienced what you did, I don't think I could understand or feel the reality of abortion more clearly. While I was uncomfortable in some parts, I think that the way in which the forbidden topic was portrayed was informative and beneficial. It was necessary to make the readers feel awkward in order to convey the emotions you felt.

She asks several questions:

(Continued)

(Continued)

> What made you pick this intimate experience to share openly with so many people? Outside of the academic discipline, what was your purpose in writing on the topic of abortion? Very few people care to acknowledge their experience, let alone write about it. I was also wondering how the abortion impacted your relationship with the father? Our professor informed us that you are still together, but did it strengthen your love for each other or create some obstacles to overcome? What are your present views on abortion? Do you view the circumstances the same way after these years?

I feel relieved and pleased. The student shows an understanding of what we were trying to do in the story and an empathy for the difficulty of our choices. As I contemplate answering her questions, my eyes fall on the word *father* and my stomach involuntarily contracts. I move to her questions. A part of me wants to avoid revealing anything about my current relationship; another thinks she deserves a thoughtful and deep response. I type in her e-mail address, thank her for her astute and empathetic response, then say:

> We wrote this primarily to work through our own relationship and the pain brought on by having the abortion. I'm happy to say that we have a wonderful relationship, now 10 years later, and that writing about the experience brought us closer together.
>
> We would make very different decisions now if we had the opportunity. I try not to allow myself to second guess the decision we made in 1990. It felt like the best decision then. I feel very different about abortion for myself now, and would have serious difficulties ever having another one, though I still think women should have the freedom of choice—and I think we should try to educate everyone to be responsible regarding pregnancy. My husband and I would have liked to have had a child, but we did not have another opportunity. Nevertheless we are very happy with our family of four dogs.

I then scroll down to the second response. This student thinks the article is an insightful portrayal of emotions and especially appreciates hearing from the male in the experience, but she feels that as a reader she can only partially enter the story because each person's story is so different. She objects to my referring to the pregnancy as a problem and interprets that to mean that I was not ready to be a parent.

I continue reading. The responses get more negative and I wonder if the professor of the class has organized them that way to soften the blow. If so, it doesn't seem to be working. Without signing a name, the third student states that he or she is pro-life and found the article very difficult to read. This student appreciates hearing the father's view and empathizes with the woman's pain, but finds it disturbing to read what the baby went through given that he or she loves children so much.

The fourth student identifies himself by name and says he could feel every emotion and kind of physical pain as he read. He wonders, What if it was my parents who had to make a decision like that? What if I was a burden on them? He asks how Alice and Ted [the names we gave ourselves in the story] could possibly look themselves in the mirror for their actions. They, along with the doctor, played God, he says. At the same time, he professes to understand how tough the decision was and how heart wrenching and emotionally consuming this was.

I hesitate. It's hard reading these things about Art and me, things that people ordinarily won't say to you directly. This is certainly not the way I see myself. I take a deep breath and continue. The last one is the most critical. Though the student does not say, I think the response is from a male. A devout, anti-abortion Catholic, he is appalled at the disregard for human life and the inability for anyone to look at this situation from the unborn child's perspective. This decision, he continues, was made out of convenience. They both seem too wrapped up in their own careers to face up to the circumstances that they created for themselves. The arguments continue for several paragraphs and end with, "Taking this life is murder."

I am trembling by the time I finish. I want to dismiss these responses but, similar to the actual abortion experience, I push myself to face them. I know people react in these ways, but it doesn't dull the pain of seeing the condemnation in print, a pain that is part of the cost of doing autoethnography deeply and honestly.

A few days later, I get an additional response from another student in the class. I am relieved when he tells a story—rather than condemns—about an experience in which the writer, at age 16, thought his girlfriend was pregnant. Since he tried to talk her into an abortion, he empathizes in particular with Alice. I do not take comfort in his empathy.

I write back to the teacher and thank him for sending the responses. I admit the responses were painful, but add that I welcomed pain as part of the lived experience, a truthful response but one no doubt engendered as well by my concern that he not feel badly for having sent the e-mails. I wonder how he, a religious grandson of a minister, responds to the story; how his religious beliefs affect how the story is given to and received by the students. Does being gay make him more open to this kind of complexity, or not? He doesn't say; I don't ask. I do ask him to thank his students for responding and to tell them I learned from what they said. As I click "send," I wonder what it is that I did learn. I already knew that people usually had one of three responses to the piece—right to life, right to choose, or a complex emotional response that incorporated the lived experience of both positions.

(Continued)

I write Art an e-mail message asking if he wants to see the students' responses. I found them painful to read, I warn. Though I don't say so, I fear they will be even more painful for him. He writes back that he'd like to see them. Other than acknowledging that they were difficult to read, we don't discuss them, bringing back briefly memories of the silence we endured immediately after the abortion, which was one of the reasons for writing this story in the first place.

When Art reads the paragraph I have written above, he writes in the margin: My sense was there was nothing more to say about them. I felt a closure at the time and know that my memory and feelings are significantly influenced by my immense love for you, what *we* have become together, and the occasional absence I feel from not having children. If there was silence, it was not the same kind of numbing silence I experienced after the abortion, at least not for me.

Nor for me, I think, in retrospect.

Not long after I received these student responses, I get an e-mail from Christine Kiesinger, a former student, who also had used the abortion story in a segment on relationship studies in her undergraduate Introduction to Communication class. Would you like to see what they said? she asks, and I respond that I would. She writes that their reading of the abortion story had occurred in the context of reading other autoethnographies, including a piece I had written on taking care of my mother, called *Maternal Connections*. The students had looked at the way Art and I had negotiated through our relationship dilemma, focusing on how the issue of choice is experienced as a constraint for both partners and on the relative newness (ten weeks) of the relationship and how it impacted the decision. Additionally they discussed the often contradictory feelings both characters experience—knowing you are going to terminate, yet rubbing your belly, knowing something living exists inside—the pull between fantasizing about a child, having and raising a child, and simultaneous need/decision to terminate. The students, she said, were not convinced that Ted wanted to end the pregnancy, and empathized with him, yet admired his stance to support Alice, regardless.

When I wrote *Maternal Connections* five years after the abortion narrative, I talked about desiring a child. Christine's students felt that, in retrospect, I regretted the decision to abort. This, she said, made for very interesting classroom time. According to Christine's interpretation, only one student struggled with the decision to terminate and that was Sara, self-defined as a feminist, whose philosophy included a pro-choice stance. This was the first time she felt torn, Christine said, as she thought about you as a character in *Maternal Connections* who later desired a child. . . . It bothered her to think that you might have some lingering regret or pain about the choice to terminate.

Throughout the semester, Christine writes me later, our names often would come up as the students struggled with some tough issues about intimacy:

What do you think Art and Carolyn would do in this circumstance? they began to ask. It was as though, Christine reports, they really identified with Ted and Alice as a couple engaging in a very conscious, very communicatively strong relationship—a couple who might have insights and ideas that would assist others in moving through their own relationships. While I hardly wanted to be a role model, her message reminded me of the usefulness of this piece as a pedagogical device and as a point of comparison for discussing how to live.

Note: See *The ethnographic I: A methodological novel about autoethnography* (C. Ellis, 2004, Walnut Creek: AltaMira Press), from which this piece is partially excerpted, for a fuller discussion of this topic. For the original story, see Ellis, C. and Bochner, A. P. (1992). Telling and performing personal stories: The constraints of choice in abortion. In *Investigating subjectivity:Research on lived experience*, C. Ellis and M. Flaherty (Eds.) (pp. 79–101). Newbury Park, CA: Sage. Also mentioned in the text is: Ellis, C. (1996). Maternal connections. In *Composing ethnography: Alternative forms of qualitative writing*, C. Ellis and A. Bochner (Eds.) (pp. 240–243). Walnut Creek, CA: AltaMira Press.

CONCLUSION ●

As you have seen, oral history is an intense, rewarding, and variable research method. It is particularly useful for gathering rich data from the perspective of those who have traditionally been marginalized within the culture and excluded from their own representation. In this way, oral history allows narrators to use their voice and reclaim authority in an empowering context where their valuable life experiences are recognized as an important knowledge source. Oral history is also an excellent tool for situating life experience within a cultural context. In other words, personal stories can be interlinked with collective memory, political culture, social power, and so forth, showing the interplay between the individual and the society in which she or he lives.

Oral history is a collaborative process that must be conceptualized holistically. Special attention must be paid to the relationship between the researcher and narrator, and clear guidelines should be employed through a rapport-building dialogue that is revisited throughout the project. And as we have outlined, a researcher needs to consider the oral history matrix: interplay between the method or tool, ethical considerations, and politics.

GLOSSARY ●

Autoethnography: Research, writing, story, and method that connect the autobiographical and personal to the cultural, social, and political.

Autoethnographic forms feature concrete action, emotion, embodiment, self-consciousness, and introspection portrayed in dialogue, scenes, characterization, and plot. Autoethnographies may combine fiction with nonfiction.

Narrative Structures: There are three major narrative styles encountered in the oral history interview process: (1) unified, (2) segmented, and (3) conversational. To this we would add a fourth category, which Kohler-Reissman calls episodic storytelling. As with all narrative forms, the way your respondent tells her or his story may largely be influenced by factors such as race, class, and gender. Related to these characteristics are education, work, and geographic location.

Oral History: A method of open-ended interview, usually occurring in multiple sessions, where a researcher aims at interviewing a person about her or his life or a significant aspect of it. This is a highly collaborative interview method resulting in a co-created narrative.

● DISCUSSION QUESTIONS

1. Discuss some of the differences between oral history and in-depth interviews.

2. In what ways does oral history benefit the researcher and participant?

3. What is the significance/importance of building rapport with your research participant? How does the establishment of a good relationship between the researcher and research participant contribute to a successful oral history?

4. What is "shared authority" and how is it distinct in oral history? We note a few instances in which a shared authority would not be beneficial to the research process. Can you think of any other instances? What are some of the problems that can arise?

5. What are some things a researcher should keep in consideration when deciding whether to use a collaborative strategy? What are some of the ethical considerations a researcher must keep in mind when determining the degree to which an oral history project will be collaborative? What kind of guidelines can help collaborative research work effectively?

6. How does oral history help us to bring about social change and aid in social activist efforts?

7. What is autoethnography? Why use this method? How can this data be represented creatively? How can external assistance be beneficial to both the researcher and research project in an autoethnography?

8. Do you believe the collaborative process that shapes data collection should continue on during the analysis and representations phases of the research project?

9. In what ways can society impact the ways in which a person tells his or her story, and why is it critical for the researcher to cue into this?

10. Oral history can be an empowering experience for both the researcher and research subject. In what ways can this be true?

11. If, for example, you were interested in how teenage females internalize images of female beauty in American society, how would the use of oral history be beneficial as opposed to an in-depth interview method?

SUGGESTED WEBSITES ●

The General Commission on Archives and History

http://www.gcah.org/oral.html

This website is a clear-cut, easy-to-understand guide to oral history interviewing. It gives the steps of interviewing as well as useful tips and a reference list of books and articles.

How to Collect Oral Histories

http://www.usu.edu/oralhist/oh_howto.html

This website explains what recording oral histories entails. It also has a link to other useful websites dealing with collecting oral histories.

Oral History Interviewing

http://www.cps.unt.edu/natla/web/oral_history_interviewing.htm

This website gives a step-by-step easy guide to understanding and conducting oral histories. It also has a link to a sample release form and sample interview questions.

Center for the Study of History and Memory

http://www.indiana.edu/~cshm/oral_history.html

This site has links to techniques for oral history interviewing, resources, newsletters, and forms. The most useful link at this site is the techniques link, which provides a lengthy description of techniques for oral history.

Center for Oral History

http://www.lib.lsu.edu/special/williams/index.html

This website offers a list of publications including some online publications. It also has links to projects, forms, other sites, and its newsletter. The mission of the Williams Center is to collect and preserve, through the use of tape-recorded interviews, unique and valuable information about Louisiana history that exists only in people's memories and would otherwise be lost.

American Sociological Association

http://www.asanet.org/public/IRBs_history.html

This link contains information about oral history interviews and protection provisions.

● REFERENCES

Anderson, K., & Jack, D. (1991). Learning to listen: Interview techniques and analysis. In S. Gluck & D. Patai (Eds.), *Women's words: The feminist practice of oral history* (pp. 11–26). New York: Routledge.

Botting, I. (2000). Understanding domestic service through oral history and the census: The case of Grand Falls, Newfoundland. *Feminist Qualitative Research, 28*(1, 2), 99–120.

Candida Smith, R. (2001). Analytic strategies for oral history interviews. In J. Gubrium & J. Holstein (Eds.), *Handbook of interviews research: Context & method* (pp. 711–733). Thousand Oaks, CA: Sage.

Crothers, A. G. (March, 2002). Bringing history to life: Oral history, community research, and multiple levels of learning. *The Journal of American History, 88* (4). Retrieved May 27, 2003, from http://www.historycooperative.org

Dumont, J. (1978). *The headman and I: Ambiguity and ambivalence in the field-working experience.* Austin: University of Texas Press.

Ellis, C. (2004). *The ethnographic I: The methodological novel about autoethnography.* New York: AltaMira Press.

Etter-Lewis, G. (1991). Black women's life stories: Reclaiming self in narrative texts. In S. Gluck & D. Patai (Eds.), *Women's words: The feminist practice of oral history.* New York: Routledge.

Frisch, M. (2003). Commentary: Sharing authority: Oral history and the collaborative process. *The Oral History Review, 30*(1), 111–113.

Frisch, M. (1989). *A shared authority: Essays on the craft and meaning of oral and public history.* New York: State University of New York.

Kerr, D. (2003). We know what the problem is: Using oral history to develop a collaborative analysis of homelessness from the bottom up. *The Oral History Review, 30*(1), 27–45.

Kohler-Riessman, C. (1987). When gender is not enough: Women interviewing women. *Gender and Society, 1,* 172–207.

Leavy, P. (1998). Claire oral history session two transcript.

Maines, D. (2001). Writing the self versus writing the other: Comparing autobiographical and life history data. *Symbolic Interaction, 24*(1), 105–111.

Marshall Clark, M. (2002). The September 11, 2001, oral history narrative and memory project: A first report. *The Journal of American History, 89*(2), 1–9.

Minister, K. (1991). A feminist frame for the oral history interview. In S. Gluck & D. Patai (Eds.), *Women's words: The feminist practice of oralhistory.* New York: Routledge.

Portelli, A. (1991). *The death of Luigi Trastulli and other stories: Form and meaning in oral history.* Albany: State University of New York Press.

Rickard, W. (2003). Collaborating with sex workers in oral history. *The Oral History Review, 30*(1), 47–59.

Shopes, L. (2003). Sharing authority. *The Oral History Review, 30*(1), 103–110.

Shopes, L. (1994). When women interview women—and then publish it: Reflections on oral history, women's history, and public history. *Journal of Women's History, 6*(1), 98–108.

Sitzia, L. (2003). A shared authority: An impossible goal? *The Oral History Review, 30*(1), 87–101.

Slater, R. (2000). Using life histories to explore change: Women's urban struggles in Cape Town, South Africa. *Gender and Development, 8*(2), 38–46.

Sparkes, A. (1994). Self, silence, and invisibility as a beginning teacher: A life history of lesbian experience. *British Journal of Sociology of Education, 15*(1), 93–119.

Tenni, C., Smyth, A., & Boucher, C. (2003). The researcher as autobiographer: Analyzing data written about oneself. *The Qualitative Report, 8*(1), 1–12.

Thomson, A. (2003). Introduction: Sharing authority: Oral history and the collaborative process. *The Oral History Review, 30*(1), 23–26.

Thomson, A. (1998). Fifty years on: An international perspective on oral history. *The Journal of American History, 85*(2), 581–595.

Williams, R. (2001). "I'm a keeper of information": History-telling and voice. *Oral History Review, 28*(1), 41–63.

Wilmsen, C. (2001). For the record: Editing and the production of meaning in oral history. *Oral History Review, 28*(1), 65–85.

Wilson, A. (1996). Grandmother to granddaughter: Generations of oral history in a Dakota family. *American Indian Quarterly, 20*(1), 7–14.

CHAPTER 6

FOCUS GROUP INTERVIEWS

As we've seen from our real-world research examples in earlier chapters, there is a lot of available research on females and body image, particularly white middle-class females. Let's say that we want to research men and body image. What are the specific issues in regard to body image that men experience? Do men suffer from body image disturbance? If so, which men, in what ways, and why? What unique body image concerns do gay men have and why? Are gay men more conscious of their appearance than heterosexual men or just differently concerned? Are self-esteem and sexual identity related to body image in male populations? What criteria do men use to evaluate their own bodies? These may be some of the questions guiding our research process, and as we will share later, these are among the research questions we are exploring in our current research. As with any new project, we would begin by conducting a literature review to see what research we already have available in this area. Our initial literature review indicates that very little research has been done on men and body image, with even less on gay men and body image. As such, focus groups may be an important method to gain exploratory qualitative data that can stand on its own or then be used to shape future research, such as qualitative in-depth interviews or quantitative surveys.

In a focus group, multiple respondents are interviewed together, making the focus group distinct from the one-on-one methods of interview we have been discussing up until now. Focus groups have a distinct advantage over other available research methods when the researcher doesn't know what all of the issues are surrounding their topic. Focus groups can help the researcher inductively figure out what the key issues, ideas, and concerns are from multiple respondents at once. The data will be qualitative in nature and thus descriptive and process oriented, giving the researcher depth and breadth to a subject very little is known about. In other words, focus groups can be used to gain needed exploratory data. This is one example of why a qualitative researcher may use focus groups. However, focus groups are used for more than just exploratory research because of the many unique qualities they bring to the research process. Qualitative group interviewing is not simply about interviewing several people at once but constitutes an entirely specific approach to research.

● SOME BACKGROUND ON FOCUS GROUPS

Focus groups developed in the 1940s (Betts, Baranowski, & Hoerr, 1996) and are used for a variety of purposes in many different fields. Although famed sociologist Robert K. Merton used focus groups in the 1950s, market researchers have historically most frequently used focus groups. This is because focus groups are an economical way to gather a relatively large amount of qualitative data from multiple human subjects.[1] In order to increase the vendibility of their products, companies often employ market researchers to conduct focus group interviews with consumer target groups. This strategy is used to evaluate a product's likability, to help market new products, and to aid in the advertising of new, old, and "improved" products. Researchers conducting these kinds of focus groups may face unique pressures "to perform" as clients often watch the group from behind one-way mirrors. As we will see later, these pressures may significantly influence the structure of the group and level of researcher participation. In market research, focus groups are also frequently video recorded (Puchta & Potter, 1999, p. 318). Focus groups are an effective method of data collection in market research because they are good for exploring people's feelings, thoughts, and behaviors (Costigan Lederman, 1990). More specifically, Bristol and Fern (1996) outline three different purposes for which focus groups are used in market research: (1) clinical, (2) exploratory, and (3) phenomenological. They are used for "clinical purposes" to "uncover consumers' underlying feelings, attitudes, beliefs, opinions, and the subconscious causes of behavior" (Bristol & Fern, 1996, p. 186). When used for "exploratory purposes," which Fern and Bristol explain they are particularly well suited for, they help "generate, develop, and screen ideas or concepts" (p. 186). In terms of "phenomenological purposes" this is when a researcher is interested in "discover[ing] consumers' shared everyday life experiences, such as their thoughts, feelings, and behavior" (p. 186).

Focus groups are also a common method of data collection in evaluation research in academia and other organizations. They are used when a program of some kind needs to be evaluated in order to help measure its success, strengths, and weaknesses, and also to help qualitatively *explain* the nature of what is and is not working. For example, new educational programs are frequently evaluated through focus group research in order to understand their benefits and aid in strengthening them. Focus groups are also useful in developing the content of new programs. Likewise, focus groups are an effective method of evaluating a range of early intervention programs in a multitude of social welfare organizations and agencies (Brotherson, 1994). The qualitative data yielded is important because it can help us to develop an understanding of the issues that families, individuals, and agencies deal with (Brotherson, 1994). Focus groups are also employed to evaluate issues and programs within the criminal justice system (Matoesian & Coldren, 2002). For instance, Matoesian and Coldren (2002) discuss how focus groups were used to gain insight into a community-policing program. In that case, a small focus group was used consisting of three members of the community and a moderator who was a member of the community-policing program.

For the past 3 decades focus groups have been increasingly used across such academic disciplines as sociology, psychology, media studies, education, and healthcare. Kitzinger (1994) explains that focus groups are particularly useful in gaining data from populations traditionally referred to as "difficult" (p. 112). These people may feel unsafe, disenfranchised, or otherwise reluctant to participate in research. Examples of such groups include AIDS patients, welfare recipients, drug users, etc. Focus groups may become more valuable in medical sociology as a means of accessing stigmatized populations about a range of topics, such as fertility, grief, depression, and cancer (p. 112). Likewise, focus groups are an important tool for accessing the experiences and attitudes of marginalized and minority groups, including racial/ethnic minorities, sexual minorities, women, children, the mentally and physically challenged, and so on. The ability to access "subjugated voices" may be a part of the recent surge in focus group exploration by academics, which corresponds to increased attention to feminist, multicultural, postmodern, and critical perspectives. Overall, the wide use of focus group interviews indicates that they can be a part of research design for a breadth of research questions and agendas.

Focus groups are a profound experience for both the researcher and the research participants that generate a unique form of data. They tell the qualitative researcher things about social life that would otherwise remain unknown. In this chapter we will explain qualitative focus groups as a method and source of data. We will discuss the varied ways they are used across disciplines in contained and multimethod designs, why we feel they are a profound and distinctive experience, and what they contribute to our overall knowledge. Moreover, while they are a method of interview just like the in-depth interviews and oral histories we have examined in the last two chapters, focus groups are unique and different from in-depth interviews. As you will see, focus group interviews result in data that is not comparable to the sum total of individual interviews or oral histories. We will now move into a discussion of the data collection process as a unique endeavor, followed by research design and multimethod approaches, and finally data analysis and representation.

● THE DIFFERENCE BETWEEN FOCUS GROUP INTERVIEW AND IN-DEPTH INTERVIEW DURING DATA COLLECTION: FOCUS GROUPS AS A UNIQUE EXPERIENCE AND PARTICULAR DATA SOURCE

When thinking about why a researcher would use focus group interviews as a part of research design versus in-depth one-on-one interviews, we must look at the differences between the two methods of qualitative interview. While an obvious distinction is that focus groups are the only method of qualitative interview where multiple respondents are interviewed simultaneously, what does that actually mean in terms of the kinds of research questions focus groups can help us answer and the particular form of data generated by focus groups?

Focus group interviews are fundamentally different from in-depth interviews because data is generated in a group composed of the researcher and respondents. It is a dynamic process based on interaction between multiple people. This dynamic can be thought of as producing a "happening" that cannot be replicated. In other words, the interaction and conversation within any given group will not be reproduced in another group even if the interviewer is consistent. This is because respondents, even if they hold similar views, attitudes, and life experiences, are not merely responding to questions posed by a researcher, but are also responding to each other and the group dynamic as a whole. The same researcher could conduct two focus groups on the same topic, with respondents who share common characteristics, yet the data will differ because it is produced within a different conversation. Likewise, a conversation fosters kinds of communication that are unlikely to occur in an in-depth interview (and remain almost exclusively untapped by survey research). These forms of communication are an important source of data and can be a significant part of the knowledge-building process—particularly in qualitative research.

> Everyday forms of communication such as anecdotes, jokes or loose word association may tell us *as much,* if not *more,* about what people "know." In this sense focus groups "reach that part that other methods cannot reach"—revealing dimensions of understanding that often remain untapped by the more conventional one-to-one interview or questionnaire. (Kitzinger, 1994, p. 109)

Focus groups can be thought of as a happening in which a rich conversation occurs, but, while dynamic and unpredictable, this is never a naturally occurring conversation but always arranged for the purpose of research. It is important not to confuse the conversational structure of focus groups with naturally occurring talk, as focus groups are always constructed by a researcher. The fundamental characteristic of focus groups during data collection is that the group dynamic starts to create a story. The narrative produced by the group begins to take hold and guide the production of data. Accordingly, group interviews are extremely useful for identifying the language, definitions, and concepts that the research participants find meaningful as they navigate through their daily life experiences.

> Group work ensures that priority is given to the respondents' hierarchy of importance, *their* language and concepts, *their* frameworks for understanding the world. (Kitzinger, 1994, p. 108)

As we will discuss later, the production of this kind of data makes focus groups an increasingly common tool in survey question development. This aspect of group work, though, may also be very attractive to researchers working from "power-sensitive" theoretical perspectives such as feminism and postmodernism. In this vein, Frey and Fontana (1991) explain that group interviews can alleviate some of the concerns postmodern researchers have regarding the hierarchy between researcher and researched even in an in-depth interview. Typically the researcher is ultimately privileged as the "authoritative voice." However, focus groups create data from multiple voices, which together create a narrative (p. 178).

While we refer to the *context* of a focus group as a happening, the dynamic produced *within* the group is termed the *group effect* (Carey, 1994; Morgan, 1996; Morgan & Krueger, 1993). The group effect serves as an important and unique source of data and is why focus group data is not equivalent to the sum total of individual interviews.

> What makes the discussion in focus groups more than the sum of individual interviews is the fact that the participants both query each other and explain themselves to each other . . . such interaction offers valuable data on the extent of consensus and diversity among participants. (Morgan, 1996, p. 139)

When a respondent makes a comment that appears to indicate disagreement with another respondent's comment, the researcher may make a note of this, using it as a marker to return to later (Myers, 1998, p. 96) for clarification, elaboration, or additional questioning. While agreement and disagreement are interesting aspects of focus group data, as well as serving as potential stimuli within the group for the production of data, these are not the only kinds of data enabled specifically by the group effect. Respondents may also change their minds, challenge previously held attitudes or beliefs, or reconsider their own behaviors when they are reflected back at them by the mirror of the larger group.

Unique data develops as participants disagree, explain themselves, and query each other, often negotiating their original ideas with new thoughts resulting from the conversation. This form of data often helps to both elucidate *and* challenge taken-for-granted assumptions that, like water to a fish, are difficult to discern. One fairly common goal for sociologists in particular is to *denaturalize* commonsense assumptions about the social environment. Yet since culture becomes a second skin for social beings, this process of understanding normative ideas and customs is quite complicated for the researcher and research participants. This general challenge for the social sciences is another reason that focus groups are a useful method of data collection, particularly when the researcher is explicitly studying issues that are largely taken for granted by the research participants.

Frances Montell (1999) found focus groups to be highly effective in explicating assumptions about sex and sexuality in her study of gender, sexuality, and the mass media. Montell credits the group dynamic created in focus groups for fostering an informative discussion that exposed and challenged the closely held beliefs of different women.

> In a group, if even one person expresses an idea it can prompt a response from the others, and the information that is produced is more likely to be framed by the categories and understandings of the interviewees rather than those of the interviewer. Participants can help each other figure out what the questions mean to them, and the researcher can examine how different participants hear possibly vague or ambiguous questions. This is

important in studying sex and gender because these issues are "naturalized" to such an extent that it is very difficult to recognize one's own
preconceived notions, much less challenge others' taken-for-granted
assumptions. The expansion of the roles available to women in a group
interview, beyond the strict separation between "interviewer" and "interviewee" allows for interactions that are more likely to reveal and even
challenge these taken-for-granted assumptions. (Montell, 1999, p. 49)

In addition to encouraging participants to explain their recognizable
assumptions, given the generally private nature of the subject matter (sexuality), Montell used focus groups as a means of making the participants more
open to discussing this highly personal and taboo aspect of social life. While
at first glance it may seem that the group atmosphere would deter people
from discussing intimate issues, once a relaxed environment is created participants may feel more comfortable than in a one-on-one interview because
the "spotlight" is not constantly on them. Once a comfort level is established participants may actually feel less pressure within the group. Likewise,
Montell used the group dynamic to get at ideas and assumptions that underlie the attitudes the participants were cognizant that they held.

. . . I just wanted them to state ideas explicitly that usually "go without
saying," to articulate the beliefs and categories that underlie their conscious attitudes. It is very difficult for people to talk about these kinds of
attitudes and assumptions in an individual interview. In a group interview, however, the ways participants respond to and interact with each
other can provide richer and more complex data. . . . (p. 47)

In addition to exploring *attitudes,* the group dynamic can be equally
fruitful for encouraging group members to provide detailed explanations
of normative *behaviors* that are mundane to them. Picking up on the black
American body image study that we first introduced in Chapter 1, we find an
excellent illustration of group interview as a method for gaining "thick
descriptions" of routine behaviors. The group interaction allowed the girls
to weave together a robust description of normative behaviors as banal (to
them), but analytically important to us, as hair care.

Interviewer: Is that good for some girls and bad for others?

Sasha: Well some people don't look good in either cut, though.

Deb: Caesar cuts are like a man's hairstyle.

Interviewer: I understand.

Deb: If your head looks like a football it's not going to look right.

Interviewer: Do you spend a lot of time on your hair?

Michelle B: Yes.

Sasha: I know I do.

Jen: Only when its straight enough to do something . . .

Deb: . . . Right . . .

Jen: This morning I threw some curls in it, got in the shower, got out and called it a day.

Interviewer: What happens when you go in the shower . . .

Sasha: Shower cap.

Interviewer: Why do you have to wear a shower cap?

Jen: Because we don't have hair like y'all. No offense but we just can't get ours . . . if we go in the shower, it depends . . .

Interviewer: Tell me what happens when you go in the shower.

Jen: When you first get a perm and you in the shower your hair still comes out straight, but if you wash your hair continually, like get your hair wet every everyday . . .

Sasha: . . . You'll get bald headed . . .

Jen: . . . And you got a perm on Monday, it will be nappy, it will be an Afro, we just can't get in the shower.

Interviewer: Why don't you want an Afro here? Why wouldn't you want hair to be nappy?

Jen: It's not about wanting to have an Afro, if I was born to have one, or made to have one, if the lord wanted me to have one, I'd have one . . .

Deb: . . . He would have gave you one, and kept letting my hair fall out . . .

Jen: The lord wants my hair to be short because I've had my hair short for awhile. therefore this is just how it's going to be.

Deb: Afros don't look pretty on girls.

Sasha:	Rashina has an Afro, but that's an exception.
Deb:	Rashina?
Sasha:	Yes.
Interviewer:	So you can't wash your hair everyday is what you are saying to me.
Jen:	There's no reason to.
Sasha:	It breaks.
Jen:	There just isn't a reason to. There's just no reason why I have to wash my hair everyday. I go to the hairdresser's every two weeks.
Interviewer:	You go to the hairdresser?
Jen:	I get a perm every six weeks.
Sasha:	I go home and shower, every two weeks I wash my hair. I get my perm every eight weeks, but at the present time I'm letting my hair grow until August because I'm getting my hair cut. I'm getting my haircut.
Interviewer:	You say you went to get a perm; what does that mean?
Sasha:	A relaxer . . .
Deb:	. . . You get a relaxer to get your hair straight . . .
Jen:	. . . A relaxer straightens your hair.
Interviewer:	It does straighten your hair.
Sasha:	Chemical-bound relaxer.
Interviewer:	When we're talking permanent we usually say it curls your hair, but your permanent relaxes your hair is what your saying.
Jen:	Exactly. If you got a perm, your hair would be curly. . . .
Sasha:	. . . or wavy . . .
Jen:	. . . If we got a perm our hair would straight.
Interviewer:	I understand. Why is it important to have straight hair?
Deb:	Because its nappy. You can't do anything with it.
Jen:	It's not necessarily important, it's just your image. You don't have to have straight hair. I wouldn't want to walk around. . . .

The preceding transcript is actually a brief snippet of the data elicited on this subject alone. As you can see, the group atmosphere fosters detailed descriptions of mundane experiences.

The dynamic produced within a group is very different from the experience of a one-on-one interview. Interaction influences all members of the group (the researcher as well as respondents, which we will talk about more when we discuss the role of the moderator in the focus group interview). Focus group participants often change their mind based on the influence of the attitudes and values in the group—this is a key part of the dynamic and it is an important part of the data collection process. As we saw in the chapter on in-depth interviews, what a person says in the context of a one-on-one interview is only influenced by the researcher and the rapport created between the researcher and that particular respondent.

> Comparisons to other methods have thus lead to the conclusion that the real strength of focus groups is not simply in exploring what people have to say, but in providing insights into the sources of complex behaviors and motivations. (Morgan & Krueger, 1993, as cited in Morgan, 1996, p. 139)

In the case of focus group interviews, what any given participant says is mediated by the group and subsequently reflected through the eyes of the others in the group as they continue the conversation. For example, in an exploratory study about gay men and body image, Jesse might explain why he feels the pressure to work out in order to be valued in the gay community, but his comment is then thrown back into the conversation by the other members of the group who respond to the statement and/or are influenced by the statement when they comment on their own experience. It is for *all* of these reasons that the data produced within a focus group differs from in-depth interview data.

The group dynamic is impacted by many research design choices and impacts data collection and analysis. The researcher's role in creating the group dynamic through the level of moderation they provide as well as the level of structure they impose is important and will be discussed in detail. Likewise, the dynamic is brought to bear during analysis when the researcher decides at what level analysis occurs and when she or he interprets the data and uncovers patterns that emerge from the data. These aspects of the group will be fleshed out later in this chapter. First we will discuss research design, where choices about moderation and structure as well as many other considerations, are made. Through an examination of how to design a focus group study some more of the unique aspects of this method will become clear.

DESIGNING A FOCUS GROUP ●
STUDY: THE RESEARCH QUESTION

As we saw in Chapter 2, the research design process, including methodo-logical decisions, should always be guided by the research question. The research design process is about formulating research procedures (Krueger, 1994, p. 43) linked to your research purpose. The importance of the fit between the research question and methodological design becomes even more salient in a project using focus groups because of the sheer multiplic-ity of design options for data collection alone. Morgan (1996) finds it helpful to distinguish between "project-level" design issues and "group-level" design issues. We caution you that while conceptualizing qualitative research as a holistic process in the ways we have explained, some of the distinctions between "project level" and "group level" become artificial in actual practice. This artificiality in practice may also be linked to the theoretical framework of the study. For example, a study using a grounded theory approach may merge some of these design choices in practice. Having said that these categorizations are not always so clear cut in practice, Morgan's model is very helpful when considering the design of your focus group project.

Considerations to be made at the *project level* include (1) multimethod frameworks, (2) group selection (sampling), and (3) standardization of data collection procedures. Sampling and standardization are related decisions, so we will discuss them together. At the group level the most important design consideration has to do with the role of the researcher. Specifically, what degree of moderation will the researcher provide in regard to managing the group dynamic and structuring the flow of topics? Issues of moderation, as we will see, are ultimately about structuring the proper balance between control and flow to produce the best results from the group for the specific research purposes. The researcher's role as the moderator is the distin-guishing characteristic of focus groups in comparison with other methods of interview. All of these research design issues, at both the project and group levels, should be worked through in relation to the research question and research goals.

Multimethod Designs:
Combining Qualitative and Quantitative Data

Focus groups can be used as a self-contained research method or as a part of a multimethod design (for a complete discussion of multimethod designs see Chapter 9). Most frequently, focus groups have been used in multimethod studies (Morgan, 1996, p. 133). Whether your study uses focus groups on their own or in conjunction with another method, either qualitative or quantitative, will depend on your research question. Linked to a congruency between the question and the method is the way in which a question is framed. For example, there are many questions that we could ask about male body image. The way we frame our research question will help determine an appropriate methodology, including whether focus groups will be used to help yield exploratory, descriptive, or explanatory data. Exploratory data raises the researcher's awareness about key issues in a new topic area. Descriptive data, a hallmark of qualitative data, provides richly detailed accounts of thoughts and behaviors. Finally, explanatory data helps explain social processes, cluing researchers into why and how things are experienced and how varied experiences may be linked. Let's review some of the most common multimethod focus group designs, using our research examples of gay male body image and black female body image as a means of illustrating the appropriateness of each option for different kinds of questions and purposes.

Creating research projects that use both focus groups and survey research is one of the most common methods of combining qualitative and quantitative techniques in multimethod designs (Morgan, 1996, p. 134). It is important to bear in mind that a holistic approach to knowledge construction necessitates that the methods are not simply used to generate a greater volume of data, but that the methods inform one another and are used in a reflexive way that creates a more complex understanding of social reality. Focus groups and surveys can be used with another research method in studies that practice *triangulation,* which is the use of three research methods; however, we are going to focus on two-method designs. It should also be noted that group interviews can also serve in a "pretest" capacity in order to make sure that the language of a survey is appropriate to the population (Frey & Fontana, 1991, p. 177). Morgan (1996) outlines the four *major* ways that focus groups can be used in conjunction with survey research. We will highlight how the methods can be combined in ways that encourage interaction between the qualitative and quantitative components, which will arguably be a significant part of the future of social research in general.

Survey research can be used to generate data that will guide the focus groups, from sample selection to topics and questions. Surveys are an effective method of generating large amounts of "flat" data from many respondents. The respondents can be stratified based on any number of characteristics, including race, sex, social class, age, and sexuality, through demographic questions at the beginning of a survey. This kind of information can be useful to a researcher who has not yet decided whether to use homogeneous or heterogeneous focus groups (as we will discuss later, these are groups with members who are similar or dissimilar, respectively). When surveys are used in this kind of preliminary capacity, they are essentially being employed to explore a topic that will then be fleshed out through qualitative focus groups. This kind of exploratory data is critical when a researcher is not sure what the key issues are.

For example, if we are to study gay men's body image and we decide to use focus groups as our primary method because of their usefulness in gaining exploratory and descriptive data and also in making participants feel comfortable discussing taboo subjects, we may want to use surveys as a preliminary way of discovering some key themes and patterns that we can use to shape our topics and questions. Although this is a perfectly legitimate way of combining these methods, it should be noted that one major weakness is evident. If in fact we know very little about gay men's body image, which is why we are going to use focus groups, then how are we going to create useful survey questions? Based on our literature review we would create a range of closed-ended questions that give respondents a limited choice of how to respond. While this data could certainly be used to guide the structuring of focus groups, it is important to realize that the survey data reflect our own categorizations—what *we* think some of the key issues may be. Since the entire study in our example is *exploratory* in nature, the data we derive from our surveys, which then guides our group interviews, may have framed issues in ways that are different from how our respondents *themselves* would have discussed them, may have distorted the importance of some issues over others, and may leave out many important issues altogether. The value of a survey rests solely on the ultimate usefulness of the questions asked, which is especially difficult to gauge in exploratory research.

A different and more common twist on this combination is to use focus groups as the preliminary method and surveys as the primary method. In this instance a researcher uses focus group data to help shape quantitative survey questions. Market researchers who ultimately want breadth to their data often use this economical structure. This framework is also useful in exploratory research when the researcher does not know all of the key issues and terminology, because the participants can create categorizations, choose what to emphasize, and explain their perceptions and experiences. Focus group data are very helpful when formulating survey questions whose value rests on their applicability to respondents' lives. Nassar-McMillan and Borders (2002) discuss the "highly effective" use of structured qualitative focus groups to generate and modify questions for the Volunteer Work Behavior Questionnaire. In this instance, survey respondents were educationally diverse but shared the experience of being "direct service volunteers." Focus groups were used to help find language and terms appropriate to the population. The focus group interviews resulted in substantial alterations in the survey instrument, which the researchers labeled an additional "quality control measure."

In our exploratory focus group interviews with gay men, the research participants had the opportunity to help guide the conversation, introduce their ideas, explain their meanings, clear up misconceptions, and educate the researcher. In this instance the participants helped the researcher to understand that gay subculture is not simply a source of body image pressure, but also acts as an important source of acceptance and positive self-esteem. The data we gathered would be very helpful for the generation of pertinent survey questions in the future.

> **Cliff:** Thanks to the gay subculture, I now am very self-conscious about things that I wasn't really self-conscious about, one of them being weight. Another being this whole question of genitals, which is so over emphasized. One of the most important things about my body to me is my heart and how that works; because emotions are physical, I experience this feeling and I don't know, these one-night stands are not, they don't tend to that. It's hard. So that's important—the physical relationship. (silence)
>
> **Tony:** I have changed quite a bit in the way I have dressed and the way that I think of myself before. . . . I used to wear clothes that did not look good on me at all, they looked terrible, black and dark colors, or bright colors. But since coming out and being more comfortable with myself, I have seen change in the clothing I buy now that aren't screaming out and saying look I'm very fashionable. I'm still well dressed (group laughter) but I have definitely noticed a change and I do feel much more comfortable with myself. (silence)
>
> **Jesse:** I think a lot of it has to do with confidence, which is a result of having come out. (pause) I used to hate my legs, because they seemed disproportionate to the rest of my body, which is very slim, and I have big tree trunks down here. I used to do a lot of cycling—whichever came first! (group laughter) I'm hyperconscious of putting weight on. It's less of an issue now. I don't know why. The only thing that has changed is that I have come out, and I'm more confident and what not.

The importance of gathering qualitative focus group data before constructing survey questions is also evident in our focus group study of black girls and body image. Many of the issues the principle investigator may have assumed to be of importance were in fact secondary issues to the girls. Given that the study was on body image and body disturbance, which the investigator had explored in-depth with white populations, there was a seemingly reasonable assumption that the girls might exhibit fear of being fat and desire to embody the media ideal of thinness, as white samples routinely did. However, weight was *not* a primary source of body concern for the girls.

Interviewer: How do you feel Keyett? You're 10 pounds [heavier] now, how do you feel?

Keyett: I feel fine. I feel on top of the world.

Interviewer: Come on now.

Keyett: No really, it won't make any difference, I may have to buy some new clothes and stuff, but otherwise it's not nothing.

Interviewer: If you were to gain 10 pounds tomorrow, how would you feel?

Joy: I'd be happy.

Tasha: I'd just go on feeling, but I mean, I'd probably change my way of thinking, but if I feel comfortable with it I'll just adjust to it, there is nothing else I can do.

The interviewer's assumptions were directly questioned and, as the transcript shows, she asked for clarification and confirmation with the phrase "come on now" in order to make sure that she understood the feelings of the participants that clearly challenged her own ideas.

The major concern qualitative researchers have with this way of combining qualitative focus groups with quantitative survey research is that by using surveys as the primary method of data collection the quantitative data is privileged. The resulting quantitative data has been intimately shaped by the qualitative data if questions were formulated that would otherwise have been excluded or worded differently. However, it is likely that when research results are reported/represented, the quantitative survey data, generally presented statistically, will be emphasized. This fails to take into account the interaction between the methods and the holistic nature of the research design. It is possible that the use of focus groups will be mentioned (in an introduction or appendix) and never elaborated on, masking the importance of the qualitative data. Likewise, the preliminary focus group data may not be discussed at all. Morgan (2002) explains that focus groups became popular in the social sciences when used with quantitative methods in evaluation research (p. 145). This trend gave qualitative researchers more legitimacy as well as access to funding formerly restricted to quantitative projects; however, these combinations were based on the privileging of the quantitative data, allowing researchers to ultimately remain within the conventions of quantitative approaches (p. 145).

The most common combination also uses surveys as the primary research method but employs focus groups during the later phase of data collection as a "follow-up" (Morgan, 1996, p. 135). This design is chosen so that researchers can employ the qualitative focus group data to aid in interpreting and analyzing their survey results. When applied in a manner that is appropriate to the research question, it can be a highly effective way of combining quantitative and qualitative data holistically—in a manner that expresses the different dimensions of the research. For example, a researcher may conduct survey research with white and black populations of college-age women in order to examine differences in body image perceptions and disturbances. Such data would likely indicate that black women have more positive body images and are less likely to exhibit body disturbances; however, the survey would not help us to understand *why* that is. By following up with respondents with qualitative focus groups, patterns or anomalies in their initial closed responses could be explained and clarified, adding descriptive and explanatory data to the statistical data. The two forms of data would "speak to each other" when represented, which is critical in holistic practice.

The final way of combining focus groups and survey research is when focus groups are used as the primary research method and surveys are employed in the follow-up manner we just described. What is appealing to us about this less common design is that qualitative data are conceptualized as the primary data form—this is rare and when it occurs exemplifies an important shift in thinking about the relationship between qualitative and quantitative data. A researcher may opt for this kind of design when she or he wants to see the pervasiveness of particular attitudes, behaviors, experiences, or themes. This may be a preplanned part of the research project, or a researcher may decide to go back and try to gain survey data from participants after the focus groups have occurred because she seeks clarification or some issues unexpectedly emerge from the transcript data. When a researcher presents their findings from this kind of project the quantitative data may in fact be used as an heuristic device. This means that the quantitative data is being presented as a means of highlighting themes within the qualitative data. With the advent of computer-driven qualitative data analysis programs (which we discuss in the chapter on analysis and representation) there are methods of accomplishing a similar end. Thus the rarity of this methodology may not only reflect epistemological issues but may also be linked to the availability of other ways of presenting qualitative data with similar quantitative augments.

Qualitative Multimethod Designs

Focus group interviews can be used in multiple method designs with other qualitative research methods. The possible combinations run the gamut of available qualitative methods. We will discuss the mixing of focus groups with in-depth interviews because this is the most typical and straight-forward pairing (nonetheless we encourage you to consider other creative combinations as your project dictates). For researchers asking qualitatively oriented questions that can be addressed via methods of interview, the benefits of combining focus groups and individual interviews are abundant. There are two major design strategies: (1) focus groups are used as a follow-up to in-depth interviews, and (2) individual interviews are used as a follow-up to group interviews. In both instances it is important to look at each method as a phase in the overall project. By conceptualizing the process in this comprehensive way the qualitative data yielded by the two methods can inform further data collection, analysis, and interpretation.

A qualitative researcher may design a study using these two methods because the research question requires both breadth and depth (Morgan, 1996, p. 134). In-depth interviews provide greater depth from individual respondents, while focus groups can give researchers a greater range of responses in a shorter time period. However, we caution you to take these as generalizations, because, as we have seen from the examples in this chapter, focus group data can also be quite rich. It is appropriate to follow up in-depth interviews with focus group interviews to verify individual interview data, examine how individual responses differ in a group setting, expose individual interviewees to the group dynamic as a means of education or empowerment, and to include larger populations that may not have been available for in-depth interviews.

A more common design strategy uses focus groups as the primary research method and follow-up intensive interviews with some or all of the focus group respondents. This methodology allows researchers to gain initial group data, which produces an overall group narrative, and then seek more data on specific components of the narrative. This design allows respondents to share their experiences in the group setting and then have individual time to elaborate on their personal experiences, attitudes, and beliefs, including any impact of the focus group. Additionally, although a focus group interview is "focused" on a particular topic, it is likely that many other issues come into the conversation. By following-up with intensive interviews the researcher is able to go back and gain more data where needed in order to best answer the research question. This was the strategy we employed in our study of black girls and body image. The principal investigator conducted the focus groups interviews, which provided a range and depth of data. She then conducted in-depth interviews with the focus group participants who wanted to continue their participation in the research. This allowed her to explore particular perspectives and themes at a greater depth. These interviews, however, were intimately shaped by the data gathered during the primary focus groups, and thus the two methods interacted in order to produce richer data.

Whether your project uses focus groups as a part of a multimethod design or uses focus groups in a self-contained format depends entirely on your research objectives and material constraints. We have provided you with some standard examples of how you may conceive of a multiple method design; however, these are simply models. There is a range of ways that focus groups can be employed, which is one of the appeals of this method. Beyond deciding the application of methods, there are many other choices that must be made when using focus groups.

Sampling and Standardization

Morgan identifies sampling and standardization as two of the key components in focus group design (1996, p. 142). Sampling addresses the question:

- Who comprises your focus group?

This question is intimately connected to your research purpose—what population or populations you are interested in learning about. However, other realities, not within your control, may also impact the selection of research participants. For example, what populations you can gain access to, your geographic location, and your timeline all impact recruitment and sample selection. The recruitment process is important in ensuring your design requisites are met. Morgan (1995) says that recruitment is about getting participants, and sampling is about getting the "right" participants (p. 519). He cites inattention to recruitment as the single greatest source of focus group failure (p. 517). While our holistic approach to the research process stresses the interconnection between all phases of the research project, it is also clear that recruitment procedures and group composition are key to success. Morgan (1995) suggests several strategies to proactively avoid the potential pitfalls of recruitment: overrecruit, send reminders, provide incentives (such as money). Moving beyond these structural realities and recruitment techniques, you should try to construct samples comprised of people who can best shed light on your topic through their personal thoughts and life experiences.

A major decision researchers confront is whether the focus groups will be *heterogeneous* or *homogeneous*. A heterogeneous group consists of dissimilar respondents. While these kinds of groups are relatively uncommon in academic research, heterogeneous groups are appropriate when the researcher wants a range of responses and is willing to sacrifice a more in-depth understanding of how a particular segment of the population experiences the topic under investigation. For example, let's say we are interested in how many different kinds of people think about the mass media's female body ideal. Heterogeneous focus groups would speak to this kind of research topic. Groups would be mixed in terms of gender, race, sexual orientation, social class, and perhaps age. The resulting data would not give us a deep understanding of why different people in the population have different attitudes about the mass-mediated ideal body type; however, this data would provide us with some insight into the different kinds of perceptions and attitudes prevalent in society at large. Such data, perhaps a preliminary phase of data collection, would be highly valuable in the thinking through of future research and could inform the development of subsequent focus group questions or other forms of data collection, ranging from in-depth interviews to quantitative surveys.

Generally qualitative researchers opt for homogeneous focus groups. These are groups with members who are similar to each other. Depending on the research question, it may be important that group members all share the same sex, race, sexual orientation, social class, age, occupation, educational level, medical condition, a particular life experience, or some combination of the above. Homogeneous groups are appropriate when the researcher wants to gain in-depth understanding about how members of a particular group experience or think about a given issue. For example, when we were interested in studying the unique ways gay men experience body image, it was important that we used homogeneous groups consisting of gay males—this is of course pretty clear-cut. In this instance, in terms of the initial research, we did not feel that the race of the participants was central, and thus our participants were racially dissimilar to each other. Homogeneous groups have an important built-in advantage, which is that they are typically helpful in creating a comfort level within the group that fosters fluid conversation. People tend to feel more comfortable speaking in a group when they have things in common with the other group members right from the start. This becomes more pronounced in the case of sensitive topic matters such as sexuality, body disturbance, violence, depression, addiction, racism, and so forth. As the group dynamic is integral to the development of the narrative, the advantage of homogeneity is significant.

Additionally, the composition of the group is likely to effect *who* will be more or less likely to fully express themselves. This happens in fairly predictable ways. Minority voices tend to be "muted" in majority populations (Kitzinger, 1994, p. 110). This process produces knowledge that is privileged from the position of dominance. In other words, unequal societal power relations along lines of race, class, gender, and sexuality are likely to be replicated in mixed-status focus groups. This is another reason why some researchers may opt for homogeneity, particularly feminists and other researchers committed to accessing the voices of marginalized groups who are typically silenced within our culture.

A widely used design feature that maximizes the benefits of homogeneity while allowing for comparison among populations is called *segmentation*. This occurs when each group consists of similar members, but the different groups within the study as a whole are different from each other. Put differently, segmentation is a way of stratifying groups based upon the particular traits in which you want to examine difference. Returning to the hypothetical study on perceptions of the mass-mediated female body ideal, let's say we wanted to be able to compare how men and women think about this issue. We could construct two solely female groups and two solely male groups. The study could be complicated further if we were interested in gender and racial differences—our literature review would indicate for example that race impacts the internalization of the media ideal in female populations. We might then construct two groups of each of the following: white males, black males, white females, black females. Depending on whether we think social class and age are relevant, we could control for these factors by making group members similar to each other in those ways. A major appeal of segmentation is that it creates a *comparative dimension* in the research (Morgan, 1996, p. 143). Our study of gay male body image would produce another level of knowledge if we also conducted focus groups with otherwise similar heterosexual males. This dimension of the research would give us a greater understanding of the link between body image and sexual identity and allow us to make powerful comparative claims. As exciting a design feature as segmentation can be, it also creates additional work (typically more groups and more complex data analysis), and thus time and other material constraints also come to bear on the feasibility of this decision. Sampling decisions always impact both the overall number of groups and the size of those groups. Ideally, sampling decisions should always be considered in relation to the research purpose.

The degree to which a *standardized approach* will be employed is also a critical issue when developing focus group-based research. Standardization refers to "the extent to which the identical questions and procedures are used in every group" (Morgan, 1996, p. 142). The degree of standardization used should be based on a logical fit to the research question. Market researchers typically maximize standardization because of the kind of information they are looking for—they want each group to stay on track and answer preconstructed questions. The main advantage of standardization, which is also appealing to academic researchers, is that it allows researchers to make "valid" comparisons between all of the groups in the study. This is particularly salient when dealing with segmented samples that presume comparability is a part of the research purpose.

Thinking back to the example of our gay male body image study, we saw how applying segmentation to our sampling procedures would add additional dimensions to our data. Specifically, such a design would help illuminate the relationship between sexual identity and body image within male populations. The emergence of any patterned differences between the homosexual groups and heterosexual groups would constitute very important contributions to our knowledge about sexual identity and male body image; however, clarity about differences between our groups based on sexual orientation alone requires a high level of comparability between the straight and gay groups. In other words, in order to link differences between the groups to the sexuality of group members—critical to how we have framed our research purpose— the groups must be similar on all other counts *and* have experienced a highly comparable interview situation. A quantitatively inclined researcher might refer to this as controlling for confounding variables, which can also be thought of as reducing mitigating circumstances. Despite the potential rewards of applying stringent standardization, particularly when comparison among groups is part of the research purpose, there are also considerable advantages to applying *open-ended* and *"grounded theory"* approaches to group interviewing and thus opting for less standardization.

While standardization fosters comparability, open-ended designs allow the respondents more freedom to speak to their own experiences and use their own language in ways that are meaningful to them. Likewise, open-ended formats allow the group dynamic to flow, creating a unique narrative whose power does not lie in conventional conceptions of generalizability. Less standardized approaches allow data to emerge from interaction. Furthermore, a more "learn-as-you-go" approach allows the researcher to apply what was learned in one group to the next. Thus, any errors or omissions in the interview guide don't impact every group in the study. The widespread appeal of open approaches is in many ways congruent to the appeal of qualitative research more generally.

Qualitative researchers are interested in understanding social life from the perspective of those experiencing it. Focus group interviews conducted in an open format allow participants to help shape the topic in ways that are meaningful to them. Research participants transform into coauthors of the emerging narrative. Researchers have the opportunity to allow important concepts and themes to emerge directly out of the interview situation. What is learned in one group can be used in later groups. Any theories about what is significant to the population develop *inductively* through data collection and are not merely constructed by the researcher and reflected by a firm research guide which will be used to yield data that likely supports previously held theories.

This way of conceptualizing the research process is often particularly appealing to feminist and multicultural and other politically motivated scholars committed to accessing subjugated voices, as was the case in our study of black girls' body image. Those focus groups were conducted in an open format so that the research participants could help shape the discussion in ways that were meaningful to them. Furthermore, applying a grounded theory approach to both data collection and analysis allowed themes to emerge directly from the girls, drawing directly on their ideas, language, and ways of understanding their own behaviors and attitudes. We were also working from a feminist perspective and were accordingly committed to creating knowledge *with* and *for* the research participants.

There are also ways to design your project that draw from the benefits of more and less standardized approaches. Morgan (1993; 1996) explains two mixed designs. One option is to apply a "funnel pattern" (1996, p. 143). In this instance each focus group begins with a high level of standardization (all groups begin with a fixed set of questions) and then the group becomes less controlled as subsequent topics are allowed to emerge (1996, p. 143). The other approach is to use the initial groups within a study in an exploratory way, thus applying a low level of standardization (1996, p. 143). The data collected is then used to develop a highly standardized research guide for subsequent groups. This kind of design is very similar to the use of focus groups as a means of developing survey research that is language- and concept-appropriate to the target population.

The Role of the Researcher in Focus Groups: Moderator

The researcher has a very particular and important role in focus group interviews that is different from the interviewer/listener role she or he takes on in the in-depth interview situation. In the context of a focus group the researcher assumes the role of *moderator.* The moderator greatly influences the flow of the conversation and thus the group dynamic and manner of the group narrative. Moderation styles can vary greatly, which is one of the general appeals of focus groups—they can be designed in many ways in order to meet the needs of a particular research objective. In fact, contrary to popular conceptions, some of the important work of moderation is actually done before the focus groups meet (Morgan, 2002).

Recruiting participants is not only linked to sampling, but also to moderation. This is because an open approach to the interview, in which respondents are allowed to speak freely, is a possible design option only if in fact the participants will speak extensively. In other words, low levels of moderation and researcher control are only viable in talkative groups. So, if you are anticipating employing a less structured approach to moderation (which we discuss in detail shortly), then it is vital to recruit participants who are deeply interested in the subject matter (Morgan, 2002, p. 149). Typically—we all have to face it—as researchers we are generally more interested in our particular research project than anyone else is likely to be. Having said this, we can go a long way to creating a range of possible design options by recruiting people who are also personally invested in the topic we are studying.

The interview guide is another critical component in the success of a focus group. Depending on the overall goals and research design, an interview guide can be a very detailed listing of major topics and subsets of specific questions, or an interview guide can be less rigid, with a set of general topics and/or some open-ended questions. Good questions, that is, questions that are designed to elicit the kind of data the researcher is looking for, are essential to focus group success. Accordingly, Morgan suggests pretesting questions (1995, p. 520). You can pretest questions with individual or group interviews depending largely on the time and resources you are able to allocate to validating the interview guide.

The opening question is perhaps the most important part of the research guide because it helps set the tone for the entire interview. A good opening question will prompt participants to speak and ideally lead them in additional directions that you already had in mind. In other words, a well-written question (especially the first question, but this is also true for all questions in an open-ended format) will not only ignite discussion but also suggest directions for the group conversation to continue in. When this occurs the moderator may have many of their interview questions answered without even having to ask them. We will talk more about this when we discuss level of moderator involvement, but for now it is important to note the significance of the opening question. However, a focus group interview, and thus the guide, may in fact begin with something other than a question. This is also a possibility the researcher must consider prior to meeting with the group.

Kitzinger (1994) suggests beginning groups with an exercise such as a card game or vignette. Such an activity serves as both a "common external reference point" and a "party game" that "warms up" the participants and helps make them feel comfortable in the group (p. 107). Kitzinger has used various kinds of card games that typically involve participants putting pre-made cards into piles. The cards have pictures, advertisements, opinions, accounts of events or people, etc. on them, and participants place cards into groups based on the level to which they agree or disagree with something the researcher says (p. 107). For example, participants may be given adver-tisements and asked to place them in a pile based on things such as how "effective" or "offensive" they find the ad to be (p. 107). This kind of game can be particularly helpful when the focus group is about a difficult topic. Kitzinger found the card game method very useful in her research on the effect of media images of AIDS.

We also found an "alternative" way of opening a focus group very effec-tive in our work on gay male body image. In that instance, the principal inves-tigator (Hesse-Biber) thought that using someone else to moderate the focus group would be beneficial. As the group was exploratory in nature, and the data is now being used to help shape other research we are working on, it was important for the group to feel as free and comfortable as possible. This is always particularly true when dealing with marginalized groups who are often victimized because of their status in a particular group, in this case, a sexual minority group. As an alternative moderator was available, who him-self is a gay male living in the same geographic region and is in the same age group as our participants, he was employed to moderate the group and was given a research guide consisting of 12 open questions. The opening of the guide however was actually a quote about gay male body image taken from a book published in 1980. The moderator started the group by reading the paragraph-long quote. He then introduced himself and went around the room allowing everyone to introduce themselves. Following the interview guide, he then asked for people's reactions to the quote. This opening was so effective in beginning an in-depth dialogue that the moderator barely had to ask any of the remaining questions—the conversation naturally supplied the answers. It is here that we start to move away from moderation prepara-tion to issues of moderation during the actual focus group interviews.

The way in which a researcher chooses to moderate during data collec-tion is intimately linked with decisions about standardization. In a research project with high standardization it is more likely that the researcher will maintain a high level of *control* as a moderator, whereas in more evolving designs the researcher may opt for less control and a more open style of moderation. Morgan (1992, 1996) identifies two main areas in which the researcher exercises a level of moderation, which can range from very high to very low. The moderator decides how much he or she will control the issues that are discussed. Will the moderator allow the group to veer off in its own direction as the conversation progresses, or will the moderator carefully control the topic flow making sure that participants stay on track answering a predetermined set of questions or focusing on predetermined topics? The moderator also acts as the manager of the group dynamic. Accordingly, the moderator can create a more structured conversation in which all participants have relatively equal speaking time, or the moderator can allow the participants and their group dynamic to lead the conversation. In the latter instance this means some people may dominate the conversation while others speak far less. As you can see, when we talk about the role of the moderator we are really talking about *structure* and *control*. Issues of moderation also exemplify the push-pull relationship that qualitative researchers using focus groups must come to grips with between *standardization* and *flow*.

In marketing research, moderators typically exercise a high level of moderation in terms of asking questions, controlling topics, and managing the group dynamic. Often in this kind of research the moderator will make sure that every research participant answers the same set of questions and the conversation does not stray off topic. The high level of moderator involvement reflects the goals of market research (Morgan, 1996, p. 145). Performing for paying clients, like we discussed earlier, may also prompt high moderator interaction and thus high control. According to Puchta and Potter (1999), since market researchers are typically after highly standardized data, focus group moderators have the task of "managing spontaneity." In order to address this particular undertaking a phenomenon has emerged in market research: focus groups often rely on "elaborate questions" (p. 319). By complicating questions through the use of additional question components, moderators help direct the responses they receive. Participants are more likely to stay on topic and answer questions in the ways anticipated by the researcher if the questions are complex, specific, and have possible answers or answer suggestions located within the question itself. Having said this, we are actually more concerned with how academic researchers deal with issues of moderation.

Social science approaches to focus group moderation can vary greatly but tend toward less control (Morgan, 1996, p. 145). Highly flexible approaches to moderation are sometimes viewed as more congruent with the main tenets of qualitative inquiry because they give participants more of a voice in shaping the topic and conversation. Low levels of moderation allow the research participants to do most of the talking, thus providing rich descriptions of social life and in-depth explanations of social processes. When the researcher does not stick to a rigid interview guide but rather allows the group to take hold of the narrative, the interview may move in directions that the researcher couldn't have anticipated. When this occurs the researcher is likely to learn about things that are of importance to the group being studied that he or she may not have known to ask. The group ends up placing emphasis on the areas that are significant to it and the researcher is given the opportunity to follow the group discussion in new and exciting directions. The resulting data are directly grounded in the experiences of the research participants as they perceive them. Additionally, if the group dynamic itself is a part of what's being studied, then it must be allowed to take its course freely. This would be true, for example, in a study about how members of dominant social groups and members of minority social groups interact in a group setting—who speaks freely, who dominates, who is silenced.

Another benefit of employing low levels of moderation is that the research participants are more likely to develop and shape the categories and concepts being used to understand their experience. In other words, if the researcher does little by way of providing the participants with language (aimed at guiding responses), the research participants will tell the researcher and other group members what language and concepts are appropriate to their group. For example, in our study of black girls and body image the moderator employed an open format with low levels of control. This allowed the girls to focus on the issues that were of importance to them as opposed to preconceived issues thought up by the researcher. This approach not only allowed the girls to shape the flow of topics but also to use language that was meaningful to them. In other words, it isn't just what is said, but the way that it is said—these are both influenced by the amount of control the moderator exerts. For example, there were times when the moderator did not understand a term the girls were using. All the moderator would have to say is, "I don't know what that term means" and the girls would provide a richly detailed explanation of the term and its significance. In their words, they would "break it down." Open formats are often used in exploratory research; however, for many qualitative researchers less structured formats that encourage participants to share their ideas, feelings, experiences, and language are simply most congruent with their qualitative projects.

> The ideal group would start with an opening question that was designed to capture the participants' interest, so that they themselves would explore nearly all of the issues that a moderator might have probed . . . one of the participants in the ideal group would spontaneously direct the others' attention to the topic for second question. . . . Anyone who has done much moderating has experienced this magic moment, as the group goes right where you want it to, without any help from you . . . the moderator could move toward closure with a typical wrap-up request, such as, "This has really been wonderful, and I'd like to finish by having each one of you summarize . . ." In this ideal version of a less structured group, the moderator would have to ask only the first and the last questions. Beyond that, the group itself would cover every topic on the guide. (Morgan, 2002, p. 148)

When the researcher has participants who are themselves deeply interested in the research topic and has created a conducive group composition, this kind of approach is possible. Again, this is why recruitment and the opening question (or opening exercise) are so important. Furthermore, the instructions given to the group are vital in open approaches (Morgan, 2002, p. 155). Most research participants have never been subjects of social research before. Because the researcher, who they may view as the "expert," recruited them, the onus is on the researcher to clearly explain that she or he has brought the group together because *they* are the experts on this topic and the researcher is there to learn from them. The best way to accomplish this is for the participants to speak freely and be as in-depth as possible. The researcher's role is that of active listener. This kind of direction is key if an open format is being employed. With any luck, beyond asking the first and last questions, the researcher will only have to say things like "can you explain that" or "what do you mean by that" from time to time.

The dynamic of a group is one of the most unique features of the focus group method. Given the significance of the group dynamic, the researcher's role as moderator deeply impacts the research process. Accordingly, great care must be used when considering how to moderate, which includes issues such as what level of structure will be imposed, how much control will be used, and how much the participants will be called upon to shape their own story. Moderation itself is a skill that requires time and patience on the part of the researcher. The best way to learn how to moderate effectively is to practice; you will get better and better over time.

Julia Johnson Rothenberg and Peter McDermott, education professors at the Sage Colleges, used focus groups to research education and parental involvement in urban schools (2000). Here's what Julia Johnson Rothenberg said about research design and moderation, in practice:

Behind-the-Scenes With Julia Johnson Rothenberg

Peter McDermott and I read several journal articles and reviews concerning focus groups after we had been questioning our work with subjects in our research on good teachers in economically distressed school districts. We knew we had strong feelings about our subjects and their work. It seemed that using the focus group approach in research would allow us to describe more fully our own biases and positions in the narrative of our research.

(Continued)

(Continued)

Another aspect to this became evident in our work with parents. These subjects were much more open with us when they were not described so much as "subjects" or "objects" of our research armed with questionnaires and questions already written. Seen as their allies and friends, they shared their experiences more openly.

Clearly the disadvantages are inherent in this plan: we do not have those objectively designed questionnaires, Likert-type scales, prearranged questions asked of all subjects . . .

It was extremely gratifying to be an advocate for the parents of urban school children. We have strongly held beliefs in equity and justice for children in school, and we were pleased to share these with parents. Likewise, they appeared to be gratified by our discussions. We thought the parents were honest in their discussions, too, as they freely disagreed with each other and also verified each other's data. One example of this was their talking about how teachers never visited their part of town, never came to community events. When we asked if there were any exceptions, all the group members named one kindergarten teacher who came to their community fairs and visited families in their homes.

There was one concern we had about the discussions and their veridicality, however. We were aware that people kind of urged each other on—especially in complaining. When we would intervene and ask more pointed questions, they persisted in their complaints about schools and teachers. Perhaps all this was true, but the effects of the group appeared to operate as well. I think we needed more time with them, over time, to establish communication patterns and group dynamics that reoccurred over time. I think this is the primary role of the researcher with focus groups, to assess the dynamics and determine where verification is needed.

● DATA ANALYSIS AND REPRESENTATION

Once focus group data has been collected and transcribed, it is time for data analysis and then representation. The most unusual aspect of this process, particular to focus group interviews, is determining the unit of analysis. At what *level* does analysis occur, the individual or the group? The short answer is, both. Just like the group "happening" and role of the moderator, focus group analysis is unique and exciting.

Focus group transcripts can be analyzed, in part, as a conglomeration of individual responses. In other words, analysis can occur, partly, on the *individual level.* This refers to what each individual group member has said and is similar to how one would analyze any interview transcript. What makes focus group analysis unique is that the transcript can also be analyzed at the *group level*. While individual accounts comprise the transcript, there is also a "group narrative" that emerges which is larger than the sum of its parts. In other words, the group dynamic and group interaction influences the data and becomes a part of the data.

When thinking about how to represent focus group data one must consider the following:

- What is the research question? What information am I trying to get at?
- At what level has analysis occurred (individual, group, or both) and how can this best be represented accurately?

Depending on the research question and kind of analysis employed (i.e., by hand, by computer) different kinds of representation will be appropriate. For an in-depth discussion on analysis and interpretation please consult Chapter 10 bearing in mind that focus group analysis differs as a result of the presence of data at the group level.

CONCLUSION ●

Focus groups are a valuable and time-efficient method for gathering qualitative interview data from multiple respondents at one time. Particularly useful in exploratory research when little is known about the topic under investigation, or as a part of a multimethod design, focus group interviewing allows the qualitative researcher to unearth individual narratives and a group narrative that is larger than the sum of its parts. In the context of focus group interviews the researcher serves as moderator and determines the degree of control and structure the interview will have. While this is a strength of the method it also presents many challenges as researchers try to manage a group dynamic and later make sense of it, including the extent to which group members may have influenced each other and the resulting data. As always, this method should be used when it serves the guiding questions posed by a researcher and his or her research objectives.

GLOSSARY ●

Comparative Dimension: A major appeal of segmentation is that it produces another level of knowledge by comparing groups that are similar in every way except the areas of difference that are relevant.

Denaturalization: The process of understanding normative ideas and customs by challenging taken-for-granted assumptions that, like water to a fish, are difficult to discern.

Exploratory Data: This is preliminary data that is used during the research design phase. In the case of focus groups, it is data that are derived from surveys and may serve as a guide for group interview questions.

Grounded Theory Approach: Allows themes to emerge directly from the data, in this case the subjects, drawing directly on their ideas, language, and ways of understanding their own behaviors and attitudes.

"The Group Effect": The dynamic produced within the group which impacts individuals and their responses.

Group Level of Analysis: The analysis is focused on the "group narrative" that emerges, which is larger than the sum of its parts. In other words, the group dynamic and group interaction influences the data and becomes a part of the data that is analyzed.

Heterogeneous: A group consisting of dissimilar respondents. This type of group is appropriate when the researcher wants a range of responses and is willing to sacrifice a more in-depth understanding of how a particular segment of the population experiences the topic under investigation.

Homogeneous: A group consisting of similar respondents. This type of group is appropriate when the researcher wants to gain an in-depth understanding about how members of a particular group experience or think about a given issue.

Individual Level of Analysis: The analytical focus is on what each individual group member has said.

Moderator: The researcher must take on this role in the focus group; she or he greatly influences the flow of the conversation and thus the group dynamic and manner of the group narrative. The main concerns of the moderator are *structure* and *control*. Highly flexible approaches to moderation are sometimes viewed as more congruent with the main tenets of qualitative inquiry because they give participants more of a voice in shaping the topic and conversation. Low levels of moderation allow the research participants to do most of the talking, thus providing rich descriptions of social life and in-depth explanations of social processes.

Open-ended Approach: Under this frame the moderator imposes less structure on the interview situation. In comparison to a standardized approach, the open-ended approach allows the respondents more freedom to speak to their own experiences and use their own language in ways that are meaningful to them.

Segmentation: A design feature that maximizes the benefits of homogeneity while allowing for comparison among populations; this is when each group consists of similar members but the different groups within the study as a whole are different from each other. Segmentation is a way of stratifying groups based upon the particular traits where you want to examine difference such as race or gender.

Standardization: Every research participant answers the same set of questions so the conversation will not stray off topic.

Standardized Approach: Standardization refers to "the extent to which the identical questions and procedures are used in every group" and allows researchers to make "valid" comparisons between all of the groups in the study.

Triangulation: The use of three research methods.

DISCUSSION QUESTIONS ●

1. How does data produced within focus groups differ from that which is produced in in-depth interviews?

2. In what ways do focus groups conducted for market research purposes differ from those conducted for sociological purposes?

3. How do group members influence each other in focus groups? How does this impact data produced by focus groups? What is the group "dynamic"?

4. In what ways can focus groups be disempowering for some members? How can focus groups be used to empower participants? What is the link between participant empowerment and the theoretical tradition that guides the research?

5. What is the role of the researcher in focus groups? What issues of control come up for the researcher and how are these issues informed by epistemological beliefs and research goals?

6. In what ways can survey research serve as a guide for structuring focus groups? How can focus groups and surveys be combined?

7. Discuss the strengths and weaknesses of conducting a less-structured focus group.

8. How does one sample for a focus group? Discuss the benefits of homogeneous versus heterogeneous focus groups. Discuss segmentation.

● SUGGESTED WEBSITES

Basics of Conducting Focus Groups

http://www.mapnp.org/library/evaluatn/focusgrp.htm

This website contains a comprehensive outline of how to set up a focus group, what questions to ask, and how to run the session, as well as what to do after the session is over. This website also provides a link to other useful focus group websites on the Internet.

The University of Surrey Social Research Update

http://www.soc.surrey.ac.uk/sru/SRU19.html

This website contains an article on focus groups written by Anita Gibbs, which appears in *Social Research Update*, issue 19. The article comments on the definition of focus groups, as well as how to run such a session, the benefits and limitations of focus groups, and the ethical issues that come to light when using this method.

Qualitative Research: Telephone Focus Groups, Face-to-Face Focus Groups

http://www.mnav.com/qualitative_research.htm

This website contains many links that deal with how to conduct various types of focus groups, as well as tips and strategies to use when dealing with focus groups, either in person or on the telephone. This website also introduces online focus groups. The articles mainly deal with marketing strategies but can be related to other areas as well.

Focus Groups

http://imwww.bhi.de/USINACTS/tutorial/focus.html

This website offers a tutorial on what focus groups are, how and why they are used, and their applications, as well as advantages and disadvantages.

Using Focus Groups for Evaluation

http://ag.arizona.edu/fcr/fs/cyfar/focus.htm

This website, based out of the University of Arizona, contains an article written by Mary Marczak and Meg Sewell. The article answers questions concerning what a focus group really is, what focus groups can demonstrate and cannot demonstrate, as well as how to set up a focus group. The article also addresses the advantages and disadvantages of this method.

NOTE

1. This is not to imply that arranging a focus group interview is easier than arranging in-depth interviews. In fact, the contrary may be true, as it may be very difficult to arrange a time when all of the interviewees are available. Additionally, sampling and recruiting may be particularly challenging in focus group research.

REFERENCES

Betts, N., Baranowski, T., & Hoerr, S. (1996). Recommendations for planning and reporting focus groups research. *Society for Nutrition Education, 8*(5), 279–281.

Bristol, T., & Fern, E. (1996). Exploring the atmosphere created by focus group interviews: Comparing consumers' feelings across qualitative techniques. *Journal of the Market Research Society, 38*(2), 185–195.

Brotherson, M. (1994). Interactive focus group interviewing: A qualitative research method in early intervention. *Topics in Early Childhood Special Education, 14*(1), 101–118.

Carey, M. (1994). Forms of interviewing. *Qualitative Health Research, 5*(4), 413–416.

Costigan Lederman, L. (1990). Assessing educational effectiveness: The focus group interview as a technique for data collection. *Communication Education, 38,* 117–127.

Frey, J., & Fontana, A. (1991). The group interview in social research. *Social Science Journal, 28*(2), 175–188.

Kitzinger, J. (1994). The methodology of focus groups: The importance of interaction between research participants. *Sociology of Health & Illness, 16*(1), 103–121.

Krueger, R. (1994). *Focus groups: A practical guide for applied research* (2nd ed.). Thousand Oaks, CA: Sage.

Matoesian, G., & Coldren, J. (2002). Language and bodily conduct in focus group evaluations of legal policy. *Discourse & Society, 13*(4), 469–493.

McDermott, D., & Rothenberg, J. (2000). Why urban parents resist involvement in their children's elementary education. *The Qualitative Report, 5* (3,4).

Merton, R. K., & Kendall, P. L. (1946). The focused interview. *American Journal of Sociology, 51,* 541–557.

Montell, F. (1999). Focus group interviews: A new feminist method. *NWSA Journal, 11*(1), 44–70.

Morgan, D. (2002). Focus group interviewing. In J. Gubrium & J. Holstein (Eds.), *Handbook of interview research: Context & method* (pp. 141–161). Thousand Oaks, CA: Sage.

Morgan, D. (1996). Focus groups. *Annual Review of Sociology, 22,* 129–152.

Morgan, D. (1995). Why things (sometimes) go wrong in focus groups. *Qualitative Health Research, 5*(4), 516–523.

Morgan, D. (1993). Future directions for focus groups. In D. Morgan (Ed.), *Successful focus groups: Advancing the state of the art.* Newbury Park, CA: Sage.

Morgan, D., & Krueger, R. (1993). When to use focus groups and why. In D. Morgan (Ed.), *Successful focus groups: Advancing the state of the art* (pp. 3–19). Newbury Park, CA: Sage.

Myers, G. (1998). Displaying opinions: Topics and disagreement in focus groups. *Language in Society, 27,* 85–111.

Nassar-McMillan, S., & Borders, D. (2002). Use of focus groups in survey item development. *The Qualitative Report, 7*(1), 1–11.

Puchta, C., & Potter, J. (1999). Asking elaborate questions: Focus groups and the management of spontaneity. *Journal of Sociolinguistics, 3*(3), 314–335.

CHAPTER 7

ETHNOGRAPHY

Reflections on fieldwork in the Trobriand Islands, Western Pacific early part of the 19th century:

Soon after I had established myself in Omarkana Trobriand Islands, I began to take part, in a way, in the village life, to look forward to the important or festive events, to take personal interest in the gossip and developments of the village occurrences; to wake up every morning to a new day, presenting itself to me more or less as it does to the natives. I would get out from under my mosquito net, to find around me the village life beginning to stir, or the people well advanced in their working day according to the hour or also the season, for they get up and begin their labors early or late, as work presses. As I went on my morning walk through the village, I could see intimate details of family life, of toilet, cooking, taking of meals; I could see the arrangements for the day's work, people starting on their errands, or groups of men and women busy at some manufacturing tasks. Quarrels, jokes, family scenes, events usually trivial, sometimes dramatic but always significant, from the atmosphere of my daily life, as well as theirs. It must be remembered that the natives saw me constantly every day, they ceased to be interested or alarmed, or made self-conscious by my presence, and I ceased to be a disturbing element in the tribal life which I was to study, altering it by my very approach. . . . In fact, as they knew that I would thrust my nose into everything . . . they finished by regarding me as part and parcel of their life, a necessary evil or nuisance, mitigated by donations of tobacco. (Malinowski, 1922, pp. 7–8)

Bronislaw Malinowski was a Polish-born British social anthropologist who conducted several fieldwork visits among the Trobriand Islanders from 1915 to 1916 and again from 1917 to 1918. Malinowski wanted to live among the peoples being studied. He felt that fieldwork must begin by "cutting one-self off from the company of other white men, and remaining in as close contact with the natives as possible which really can only be achieved by camping right in their villages" (p. 6).

Ethnographic research aims to get an in-depth understanding of how individuals in *different cultures* and *subcultures* make sense of their lived reality. The literal meaning of the word *ethnography* is "writing culture." Ethnographers "go inside" the social worlds of the inhabitants of their research setting, "hanging out" and observing and recording the ongoing social life of its members by providing "thick descriptions" (Geertz, 1973) of the social context and the everyday lives of the people who inhabit these worlds. Ethnographers provide detailed accounts of the *everyday practices and customs* of a culture, subculture, or group, often collecting artifacts and other cultural materials. They record and analyze the variety of social structures within their setting, paying attention to religious, familial, political, and economic life. This method is "up front and personal" and usually takes place in *natural settings*—those places where individuals go about their daily lives, rather than a prefabricated place "set up" by the researcher at a specific site. *Participant observation,* which is a primary research tool of ethnography and its practice, requires the researcher to live or make extensive visits to the setting they are studying, observing as well as participating in the activities of those they are researching.

The ethnographic method has often been associated with the field of *anthropology*, in which research is conducted on foreign cultures in order to capture understanding of the "native" population—the customs, values, artifacts associated with a given group and its wider culture. The sociological practice of ethnography dates back to the late 19th century and is rooted in the social reform movements that sought to understand and provide assistance to the underclass urban poor (Emerson, 2001). Early ethnographies by sociologists contained a variety of mixed methods, from survey research to field observations and intensive interviewing. Early ethnographic research was influenced by a "social survey movement." An example of this type of ethnography comes from the work of Charles Booth's study of London's underclass, his classic work *Life and Labour of the People in*

London (1902). Ethnographer Robert Emerson notes the following concerning Booth's work:

> In his studies, Booth combined statistical data, widespread interviewing, and direct observation to amass an extremely detailed and systematic description of the lives of the London poor. In their use of direct observation, Booth and his colleagues at times entered directly into the world of the poor. (Emerson, 2001, p. 9)

Writing over a half century later, sociologist Elijah Anderson (1976) relates his experiences in conducting field work in a poor black establishment on the South Side of Chicago he calls "Jelly's place." Jelly's was a bar and liquor store frequented by working and unemployed black males. Anderson also employs the technique of participant observation; however, he does not go to an isolated island in the Western Pacific, but, like Charles Booth, he is drawn to an urban setting; an American city, and to a part of American subculture whose life and activities remain hidden from the wider culture's purview—a subcultural island within the dominant culture of the city of Chicago. Anderson's purpose was to uncover the social life of Jelly's place—to understand the interactions among those who came to Jelly's. He describes his mode of participant observation as follows:

> My first few weeks at Jelly's were spent on the barroom side among the visitors and others. This side . . . was the place most accessible to new people, where strangers could congregate. It was also a place where I could be relatively unobtrusive, yet somewhat sociable. It was here that the process of getting to know Jelly's began, where increasingly I gained some license to exist and talk openly with people. Initially this meant getting to know the people and becoming somewhat involved in their relationships with one another; becoming familiar with the common, everyday understandings people shared and took for granted, the social rules and expectations they held for one another. (1976; 1996, p. 13)

Anderson's work in the inner city of Chicago has is roots in the fieldwork tradition known as the *Chicago School* of sociology, founded by Robert E. Park and Ernest W. Burgess. Both of these sociologists were influenced by the work of late 19th century social reformers, like Jane Addams, who founded Hull House, a social settlement institution, and they trained and supervised students in ethnography from around 1917 to the early 1940s (see Addams,

1910; Deegan, 2001). They urged their doctoral students to obtain first person accounts of the everyday lives of those individuals living in "natural areas" of the city. "Natural areas" were thought of as "concentric zones" that radiated from the city's center, with each zone containing individuals with different racial, ethnic, and social class backgrounds. Park and Burgess's students went on to produce a wide range of important ethnographies dealing, very often, with the city's "underside," invisible populations and issues such as homelessness (Anderson, 1923), gangs (Thrasher, 1927), taxi-dance halls (Cressey, 1932) and race relations (Frazier, 1932), to name a few of these studies. Park gave his students the following advice:

> You have been told to go grubbing in the library, thereby accumulating a mass of notes and a liberal coating of grime. You have been told to choose problems wherever you can find musty stacks of routine records based on trivial schedules prepared by tired bureaucrats and filled out by reluctant applicants for aid or fussy do-gooders or indifferent clerks. This is called "getting your hands dirty in real research." Those who counsel you are wise and honorable; the reasons they offer are of great value. But one more thing is needful: firsthand observation. Go and sit in the lounges of the luxury hotels and on the doorsteps of the flophouses; sit on the Gold Coast streets and on the slum shakedowns; sit in the Orchestra Hall and in the Star and Garter Burlesque. In short, gentlemen, go get the seat of your pants dirty in real research. (McKinney, 1966, p. 71)

Malinowski, Booth, and Anderson are part of this ethnographic tradition. They are concerned with the "everyday" world of activities and "rituals," looking for anything unusual. They are not there as interviewers, but as observers engaged in observation and conversation with those in the setting. They record their observations and interactions as *field notes,* which are written accounts of their everyday experiences in the field, sometimes jotting down notes on the fly, but usually writing up their field notes shortly after leaving the field. Ethnographers also conduct interviews with members in the setting and are interested in any documents that may give them insight into the lives of those in the research setting.

The concept of a *field* in ethnography differs depending upon the type of research project you pursue. For an anthropologist studying a foreign culture like that of Malinowski, the field is a *cultural* setting. For Anderson, studying a local bar or local neighborhood, the bar or neighborhood becomes the *field*. This type of research is often known as *urban ethnography*. Another classic example of urban ethnography is William Foote Whyte's

(1943) study of a neighborhood known as Cornerville. Cornerville is an Italian-American neighborhood located in the inner city of Boston. Sociologist William Foote Whyte wanted to understand the social interactions taking place within this community. The popular image of places like Cornerville was one of disorganization and suspicion on the part of the dominant culture. Especially during World War II, there was a feeling that the "Italian slum dweller might be more devoted to fascism and Italy than to democracy and the United States" (Gubrium & Holstein, 1997 p. 20). Through hanging out with local residents, Whyte was able to gain insight into the life of this neighborhood from the perspective of its inhabitants. Let's go behind the scenes with Whyte as he reflects on *Street Corner Society* (1943) 12 years after the publication of the first edition. Whyte talks about how he first got involved in studying Cornerville and some of the specific challenges this type of research project entailed.

Behind-the-Scenes With William Foote Whyte, Reflecting on *Street Corner Society*

I began with a vague idea that I wanted to study a slum district. Eastern City provided several possible choices. In the early weeks of my Harvard fellowship I spent some of my time walking up and down the streets of the various slum districts of Eastern City and talking with people in social agencies about these districts. . . .

I made my choice on very unscientific grounds: Cornerville best fitted my picture of what a slum district should look like. Somehow I had developed a picture of run-down three- to five-story buildings crowded in together. The dilapidated wooden-frame buildings of some other parts of the city did not look quite genuine to me. . . .

At the time I was completely baffled at the problem of finding my way into the district. Cornerville was right before me and yet so far away. I could walk freely up and down its streets, and I had even made my way into some of the flats, and yet I was still a stranger in a world completely unknown to me. . . . I sought out the local settlement houses. They were open to the public. . . . As I look back on it now, the settlement house also seems a very unpromising place from which to begin such a study. . . . However that may be, the settlement houses proved the right place for me at this time, for it was here that I met Doc. I had talked to a number of the social workers about my plans and hopes to get acquainted with the people and study the district. They listened

(Continued)

(Continued)

with varying degrees of interest. . . . In a sense, my study began on the evening of February 4, 1937, when the social worker called me in to meet Doc. She showed us into her office and then left so that we could talk. Doc waited quietly for me to begin, as he sank down into a chair. I found him a man of medium height and spare build. His hair was light brown, quite a contrast to the more typical black Italian hair. It was thinning around the temples. His cheeks were sunken. His eyes were a light blue and seemed to have a penetrating gaze. . . . I began by asking him if the social worker had told him about what I was trying to do. "No, she just told me that you wanted to meet me and that I should like to meet you." Then I went into a long explanation. . . . Doc heard me out without any change of expression, so that I had no way of predicting his reaction. When I was finished, he asked: "Do you want to see the high life or the low life?" "I want to see all that I can. I want to get as complete a picture of the community as possible."

"Well, any nights you want to see anything, I'll take you around. I can take you to the joints—gambling joints—I can take you around to the street corners. Just remember that you're my friend. That's all they need to know. I know these places, and, if I tell them that you're my friend, nobody will bother you. You just tell me what you want to see, and we'll arrange it." (Whyte, 1955, as cited in Whyte, 1996, p. 11–21)

● THE PRACTICE OF ETHNOGRAPHY

- When is ethnography appropriate to use as a method of social research?

As we have discussed in earlier chapters, the *research question* dictates the type of methods one pursues. If your research question requires an in-depth understanding of the social *context,* in particular the *culture* within which individuals engage in a particular set of behaviors, then ethnography is an important method for getting at this understanding through direct observation of behaviors and through interaction with others in your research setting. Ethnographic methods allow you to understand the social reality from the participants' perspective, which is why it remains a staple practice in qualitative inquiry. You have the opportunity to explore the range of activities that may even remain unconscious to those who participate in the setting. Ethnographers ask questions such as:

- How do individuals view their world?
- What is their story?
- How is a custom understood by members of a given culture?

Goffman wanted to study the social world of inmates at a mental institution. In *Asylums* he underscores the importance of getting at understanding the worlds of his respondents by immersing himself in their world.

> My immediate object in doing fieldwork at St. Elizabeth's was to try to learn about the social world of the hospital inmate, as this world is subjectively experienced by him. . . . It was then and still is my belief that any group of persons—prisoners, primitives, pilots, or patients—develop a life of their own that becomes meaningful, reasonable, and normal once you get close to it, and that a good way to learn about any of these worlds is to submit oneself in the company of the members to the daily round of petty contingencies to which they are subject. (1961, p. ix–x)

As we observed in Chapter 2, the selection of a particular research problem is related to a number of different factors. Your own biography may be *the* decisive reason for wanting to find out more about a given group or community. Perhaps growing up with a small town, inner city, or suburban lifestyle provides you with a set of specific ideas and interests or particular curiosities concerning aspects of the social world. It may be that a given research question becomes sparked by a personal or professional or academic experience, or even a memorable event, whether it be tragic or uplifting. Peggy Sullivan and Kirk Elifson happened to attend a church service run by a religious group known as "Free Holiness." This group was part of the Pentecostal Christian Church in a rural Georgia community that used serpent handling in their religious ceremony. They stumbled onto their research question almost by accident:

> What began as a curiosity visit grew into a two-year research project. Kirk originally went to the church with an undergraduate class he was teaching and later returned with graduate students from a sociology of religion seminar. Peggy was among those students. We arrived and sat on the last pew near the back door. Our curiosity was mixed with trepidation as we waited for the service to begin. . . . At first it was a half-joke-half-dare between us that we should conduct a participant observation research project focused on the church. Several days after the seminar group had visited the church we decided to learn if studying the church

would be possible. We knew practically nothing about rural Pentecostal religion and even less about serpent handlers. We had no idea whether we would be welcomed to the church enough to study it. (Sullivan & Elifson, 1996, p. 34)

There may be a set of economic and practical constraints that may determine whether or not you decide to conduct an ethnography. Ethnographic work is labor intensive and requires a good deal of time, energy, and resources.

An ethnographic perspective relies on a set of philosophical or epistemological assumptions concerning the nature of the social world. Ethnographic work relies, for the most part, on an *interpretative* versus a *positivist* perspective on the nature of social reality. The goal of this type of research is exploring and describing social phenomena. However, this does not mean that some ethnographers are not also positivists who employ quantitative methods to get at an understanding of their setting. Some ethnographers may also "test out their" preconceived hypothesis in the field as well. The ethnographic research question, however, is usually a *guiding* one that is not phrased in terms of hypotheses or a set of propositions. As we noted in Chapter 1, a positivist look onto a given social setting seeks "the truth" that is waiting to be understood by the researcher if only the researcher remains objective, not allowing their own attitudes and values to enter into the setting. The gathering of information is primarily a one-way street—with the researcher asking questions and those studied answering. There is little give and take between researcher and researched. An *interpretative approach* views the social world as constructed by those meanings/stories/accounts individuals provide concerning their understanding of their social world. There is dynamic interplay between the researcher and the researched. Multiple realities may exist within the same setting, depending on the views held by the range of inhabitants of that particular setting. There are also those ethnographers whose perspective goes beyond that of description and understanding. Some ethnographic field work is also activist and sets a goal of social change and empowerment of those within a given setting as well. This more activist ethnographic stance provides an interpretive as well as a *critical perspective*. The goal of a *critical ethnography* is to understand social life in order to change the way that those in power marginalize those with less power (Bailey, 1996, p. 25). Christine Sleeter (1992) studies multicultural education with the goal of wanting to change school systems: ". . . I have sought to understand why schools so consistently serve children from the dominant society better than children from poor families, families of color, and girls" (p. 55). She conducted a critical ethnography of an inner-city school system in order to understand the inner workings of multicultural education with the goal of developing social policy concerning multicultural education:

> The book . . . suggests why the mix of people who work in schools should reflect a much wider diversity of life experiences in order for teachers to generate for themselves richer concepts of what cultural diversity means. Diversifying the teaching force is a policy issue; this book addresses that issue . . . (p. 56)

There are a range of feminist approaches to ethnography, depending on the particular disciplinary perspective, theoretical stance, and political goals of any given feminist ethnographer. What unites these approaches, is a deep commitment to understanding the issues and concerns of women from their perspective, and being especially attentive to the activities and the "goings on" of women in the research setting. The work of early feminist ethnography did much to unearth the "invisible" aspects of women's roles in the ethnographic setting. A feminist ethnographer might look at Whyte's study of Cornerville, and ask: Where are the women in this setting? What is their story? While Whyte did much to illuminate life in this Italian community from the perspective of its male inhabitants, we know little about the lives of women who also inhabit this Italian-American enclave. The work of Patti Lather and Chris Smithies (1997) is an important example of feminist ethnography "giving voice" to women's concerns and issues. Lather and Smithies interviewed and participated in the ongoing lives of women they met through HIV/AIDS support groups in three cities in the United States. They study this epidemic by concentrating on the female HIV/ AIDS population, whose voice has remained muted, and provide in-depth accounts of women's experience living with HIV/AIDS.

Picking research topics of personal and political interest also means opening one's self up to a range of emotions. Carol Bailey, trained as an ethnographer, found this to be the case as she undertook an evaluation project.

Behind-the-Scenes With Carol Bailey

The client is a six-year-old, white male who has been diagnosed with ADHD, a possible mood disorder, and as being developmentally delayed. In his second year of kindergarten, he requires an aide from a school-based treatment program because of his disruptive and sometimes violent behaviors. The client already has had two stays in a psychiatric hospital. He refuses to obey any

(Continued)

(Continued)

rules set in the home, has tantrums daily in which he cries, screams, hits his brother, and destroys property. A neighbor sexually abused him last year. His mother is a substance abuser who allows different boyfriends to live with them from time to time. He is at imminent risk of out-of-home placement. Participation in the Virtual Residential Program is his only hope for remaining in his home.

The above description was modified to protect the client's identity, but none of the details were exaggerated. This client also is not atypical of other youth served by the Virtual Residential Program, an intensive, in-home intervention program for youth with severe mental illnesses and their families. The Virtual Residential Program is designed to reduce the client's inappropriate behaviors to acceptable levels and stabilize the client's home. The goal of VRP is to prevent the youth from being placed in a residential facility or psychiatric hospital because of the lack of appropriate alternatives.

I am currently doing a program evaluation of VRP at its request. This evaluation is an implementation, or formative evaluation, and an outcome, or summative evaluation. VRP has staff that are well trained and a manual with detailed protocols and procedures for its intervention. My task during the implementation evaluation is to see if the manual is being followed and if VRP is meeting its objectives. I use primarily qualitative data for the implementation evaluation. As the implementation evaluation proceeds and findings are communicated to program administrators, they make some of the changes suggested by my report. The implementation evaluation continues until VRP is satisfied with the level of program fidelity and the quality of its program.

The outcome evaluation explores the discharge status of the clients: did they remain or did they not remain in the home and whether the discharge status is similar for a diverse group of clients. Quantitative data is mostly used to measure outcomes. The outcomes thus far are excellent. Seventy-seven percent of the 98 clients served by VRP have remained in the community at discharge. No statistically significant differences have been found between the discharge rates for gender and race/ethnic groups.

This is a complex evaluation because VRP is located in several states, and the evaluation requires an analysis of the clients' records. However, complex evaluations are routine for evaluation researchers whose work is based within an interpretive paradigm. What makes this evaluation particularly problematic is that I have difficultly reading the clients' records without being flooded by emotions.

When I am reading comments written by the clinicians, I am supposed to be extracting data for the qualitative analysis. I should be watching for patterns and jotting field notes as ideas come to mind. Yet, I am not. I feel despair, helplessness, and anger.

(Continued)

The lives of family members and guardians of these youth are often in disarray. I get angry because I want to blame the adults and make them responsible for their children's pain. One mother increased her own drug use every time her daughter's behavior became more appropriate. How can I not say it is her fault that the child's progress stopped?

Because qualitative research usually entails data collected from more than one source, I have held informal interviews with VRP employees. The interviews gave me another interpretation of the data. The adults also are suffering and need help. Some of the parents have mental illnesses themselves and are victims of domestic abuse and poverty. Using a therapeutic perspective guided by family systems and multisystemic therapy, the clinicians see the adults and the youth as a unit, not one group pitted against the other. The insight of the VRP employees helped me widen my perspective as I returned again to the client data.

As I read, categorized, and analyzed the data again and again, looking for links between the theoretical frame, core values, and VRP procedures, I realized that the familiarity with the data had reduced my stark emotional reaction. I still had a sense of despair, but I also felt hope because of the amazing progress that occurred during the intervention for most of the clients.

Some who do only quantitative research accuse the qualitative researcher with doing work that is not objective and value neutral. While I can have rational discussions about objectivity, subjectivity, and inter-subjectivity, I find I have less patience with those who say that qualitative researchers are not value neutral. Of course I am not value neutral! How could I be?

I want VRP to work. I want these youth to have lives like children and adolescents without such severe problems. Every time I receive new data, I jump to the section that tells me if there is a "happy ending" for the client. I also want a "happy ending" for the treatment teams, supervisors, and director of VRP. I am impressed by how hard they work, how good they are at their profession, and how caring they are. Admittedly, I am glad that there is more good news than bad in the outcome summaries.

My caring about VRP employees, clients, and caregivers does not prevent me from engaging in a rigorous evaluation. I do not compromise my integrity. I tell the "truth," admittedly a "truth" that is unavoidably partial, multiple, and filtered through my analytical eyes. Evaluation research is not valid, or ethical, if the data, analysis, interpretations, and reports are manipulated to reflect the preferences of the researcher. I still ask research questions whose answers might identify what VRP needs to improve and what it is doing well. By doing so, I share in the efforts of a dedicated group of professionals whose services are sorely needed by clients and their families.

● CHOOSING A RESEARCH SETTING

As we saw with Peggy Sullivan and Kirk Elifson's participant observation study of a Pentecostal Church, familiarity with a setting may in fact propel an individual to be curious about the setting enough to want to research it. At other times the choice of a specific research question may determine what research sites are acceptable or not acceptable, it is imperative that you select a research site that will give you the information you need in order to address your research question(s). Sometimes you may need to select more than one setting.

Several factors may constrain or provide an opportunity in the selection of a specific research setting.

- Can you conduct research in this setting?
- How accessibility is determined is variable.

Some sites one might think are inaccessible settings, may, in fact, open up to the individual as a result of specific network ties the researcher has to that setting; other settings that one might think would be easy to enter can remain impervious to outsiders. Who is considered an "outsider" also depends on the type of setting. For example, some settings may restrict specific types of individuals based on their age, sex, or racial/ethnic and social class background. Terry Williams is a black American sociologist who is interested in the cocaine culture. Most researchers might find this culture quite inaccessible. Several factors were key in helping Williams gain access to after-hours clubs as a setting for his study. He notes:

In 1974, after completing several years of graduate study in sociology at the City University of New York, I accepted a teaching position at John Jay College of Criminal Justice. My first assignment entailed commuting from the main campus to Rikers Island to teach in the satellite program established by the college. After a year in this special program, I became friendly with several of the inmates, many of whom were serving relatively light sentences. Upon their release, three of them called me and offered to take me out on the town. They showed me the nightlife of New York City as I had never seen it before. In the small, intimate clubs known as after-hours spots, I was introduced to a bewildering variety of people—musicians, drug dealers, punk rockers, transvestites, secretaries, doctors, dancers, gamblers, actors, policemen, prostitutes—all of whom were there to share in a lifestyle based on the enjoyment of cocaine and the pleasure and excitement brought on by the intensity of their interaction. (Williams, 1996, p. 28)

Sometimes the selection of a research setting depends on a consideration of "practical issues" such as economics (How expensive will it be to conduct research in this setting?), time constraints (How much time do you have to spend in the setting? Does your research conflict with other obligations?), and potential risks to you as the researcher (Are you, for example risking bodily harm by entering a setting where illegal activity takes place?). Ruth Queen Smith provides an example of how one of these practical issues adversely impacted her ability to select a setting she was interested in. She was a doctoral candidate in education, and while she wanted to conduct research at a particular setting, her class schedule conflicted with her ability to make crucial observations in that setting:

> At first, I considered three different cultural settings for this ethnographic study. Two of the three choices involved researching people of poverty in racially integrated environments. These two research possibilities required that I conduct observations and interactions within the culture between the hours of 9:00 pm and 3:00 am because that was when the majority of sociocultural interactions were evident in the sites. Reality quickly awakened me. Both of these potential sites presented strong potential for engaging an ethnographic researcher. However, with a demanding doctoral student schedule, I know that it was not in my best interest to take either study at this time. I surrendered to practicality. This recognition created a reflective space in which I could discover my own process concerning the identification, selection, and ranking of research choices. (1998, p. 91)

Once a research question and site are chosen, the next step is to negotiate access into the setting as well as establish what role you as an ethnographer will take in this setting.

GAINING ENTRY AND DECIDING ● ON YOUR ROLE IN THE SETTING

How you gain *access* into a community or a group setting is critical in determining the type of data, if any, you will be able to collect and how difficult or easy the process will be. There are a myriad of ways to gain access to your setting, but a general way to begin is by making a *personal connection* to someone either who knows a member of the setting you wish to study or who can serve as a liaison to some key members of your setting. You might begin by thinking about how best to set up this contact. Would you write a permissions letter and/or make a call? What type of letter? How much do you reveal about your study? You will also need to think about how you will gain permission from a Human Subject's Committee, if there is one in the setting you propose to study, as well as the permission of the Institutional Review Board (IRB), if you are working within an organizational setting. Settings often contain *gate-keepers,* whose approval is crucial in order to gain access and acceptance. The gatekeeper(s) may not necessarily be the individual(s) who granted you permission to enter the research site. While formal permission is important, some in the setting may see your connection to a higher level official as threatening to them. What may matter more in gaining access is the approval support of *informal gatekeepers* who hold key positions in the setting and whose influence on others in the setting determines your level of access. Informal gatekeepers have the power to give your presence a "heads up" or "heads down." There are several factors that affect your ability to gain entry into a setting: The first is the degree to which the setting is *public* or *private.*

Public settings like cafés, bars, or laundromats will not create large problems with access. There are more private settings whose members are motivated to protect the boundaries of their setting. To what extent do members of the setting have a vested interest in keeping their affairs from outsiders? There are those settings where, for example, illegal activities may be part of the goings on. Gaining access may be next to impossible for the researcher, and entry into such a setting may place the researcher in harm's way. It may be in fact that the setting is quite public, like a restroom, but that there is a strong motivation by those in the setting to keep their activities under cover.

Several options are available for gaining access to more "private" settings. One role, of course, is to go "undercover" in the setting as a way of gaining entry. Laud Humphries (1976) studied the activities of male homosexuals who engaged in "illicit" sexual activities in public restrooms. Humphries was able to gain access to the setting covertly by assuming the role of a gay male and taking on the job of a "watch queen" or "lookout" who alerted the *insiders* (those engaging in illicit sexual activity) to the impending presence of *outsiders*, such as the police and those who only saw the setting as a public restroom. Humphries notes:

> By serving as a voyeur-lookout, I was able to move around the room at will, from window to window, and to observe all that went on without alarming my respondents or otherwise disturbing the action. Being a watch queen enabled me to gather data on the behavior of participants in homosexual acts. . . . (p. 104)

Another important strategy to gaining access to a setting involves establishing relationships with central figures who become *informants*. Some informants may in fact be the gatekeepers of the setting. Whyte (1996) notes the importance of Doc, a central figure in Cornerville with whom he struck up a friendship after being introduced to him by a social worker in the neighborhood.

> I had talked to a number of the social workers about my plans and hopes to get acquainted with the people and study the district . . . the head of girls' work in the Nortons Street House understood what I needed. She began describing Doc to me. He was, she said, a very intelligent and talented person who had at one time been fairly active in the house, but had dropped out. . . . If I wished, she would make an appointment for me to see him in the house one evening. . . . I jumped at the chance. . . . In a sense, my study began . . . when the social worker called me in to meet Doc. (Whyte, 1996, p. 20)

Through his initial contact and friendship with Doc, Whyte was able to find his way into the goings-on of this close-knit community. Doc in effect took on the role of informant:

> Doc introduced me as "my friend Bill" to Chichi, who ran the place and to Chichi's friends and customers. I stayed there with Doc part of the time in the kitchen, where several men would sit around and talk, and part of the time in the other room watching the crap game . . . when I went to the toilet, there was an excited burst of conversation in Italian and that he had to assure them that I was not a G-man. He said he told them flatly that I was a friend of his, and they agreed to let it go at that. (Whyte, 1996, p. 26)

Doc in fact provides Whyte with insightful interpretations of the social life of Cornerville:

> . . . without any training he [Doc] was such a perceptive observer that it only needed a little stimulus to help him to make explicit much of the dynamics of the social organization of Cornerville. Some of the interpretations I have made have been more his than mine, although it is now impossible to disentangle them. (Whyte, 1996, p. 28)

While Whyte relied on Doc for gaining a perspective into Cornerville life, depending too much on any *one* informant or becoming too aligned with a specific informant in the setting can have its drawbacks. Seeing the setting only through the eyes of a specific informant may serve to bias one's observations. Doc has a specific point of view on the setting, and, while his observations and interpretations helped greatly Whyte's understanding of Cornerville, *one way of seeing is also another way of not seeing.* For example, if Doc had made enemies in the setting, Whyte's close alignment with Doc may have served to alienate some important segments of the community from Whyte's research or may have prevented Whyte from seeking additional informants with a different perspective from Doc's or whose engagement with the community was very different from Doc's. Whyte was aware of these issues and did seek other allies in the community:

> While I worked more closely with Doc than with any other individual, I always sought out the leader in whatever group I was studying. I wanted not only sponsorship from him, but also more active collaboration with the study. Since these leaders had the sort of position in the community that enabled them to observe much better than the followers what was going on and since they were in general more skillful observers than the followers, I found that I had much to learn from a more active collaboration with them. (Whyte, 1996, p. 28)

Sometimes gaining access to a setting depends on the very attributes of the field researcher—their age, gender, social class, and racial/ethnic background. Some of these social attributes in and of themselves may make the researcher a perceived insider to the setting or an outsider. Interestingly enough, in any given setting the researcher's roles may become quite fluid, with the researcher taking on both insider and outsider roles. What specific social attributes matter depends upon how these attributes mesh with those of the setting. Anderson's ability to gain access to Jelly's bar and liquor store was probably enhanced because of his status as a black American male. He shared some *key attributes* with those who hung out at Jelly's (his race and gender). Although Anderson can be considered an outsider, especially in terms of his education (a Ph.D. student at the University of Chicago), he was able to move across some important social hurdles to gain entrance into the inner world of the regulars at Jelly's. Herman, an important group regular at Jelly's, befriended Anderson. Herman asks Anderson to become his "cousin." Anderson occupies a "fictive kin" role with Herman that allows him access to an insider status with Herman's friends and coworkers. Herman feels comfortable relating to Anderson as his "cousin" and gives him a way of explaining Anderson's presence in the setting. With Herman's guidance, Anderson was able to enter the inner sanctum of Jelly's and gain valuable information about the social world of working-class blacks on the South Side of Chicago.

Some researchers find that their gender can be an important impediment to their gaining access to the setting, especially when that setting is male-dominated. Arlene Kaplan Daniels wanted to study military officers but runs into trouble when she finds that they want her to maintain a traditionally feminine role, expecting her to exhibit a range of deferential behaviors. Some balk at being interviewed unless they place her in a subservient position such as that of a "mascot" (Daniels, 1967, pp. 285–286)! She notes:

I developed mediating and soothing strategies. . . . I learned the necessity of changing my tone. And, once I was in the field, I abandoned my picture of myself as the director of a research project and returned to the role of student and humble observer. . . . What I began to learn was that certain kinds of deference to the idea of superior male status had to be paid. Certain behavior was considered inappropriate or even insulting from women: a firm hand clasp, a direct eye-to-eye confrontation, a brisk, business like air, an assured manner of joking or kidding with equals were all antagonizing. (Daniels, 1967, p. 273)

Female researchers in settings that hold "traditional" expectations for women find that to offset these roles and gain access they need to be perceived as "nonthreatening." Exhibiting more "feminine attributes" like those described by Arlene Kaplan Daniels, or taking on specific roles in the setting like that of "daughter," may, in fact, increase a female researcher's probability of gaining access and information in more traditional male-dominated settings (Myerhoff, 1978).

WHAT ROLE WILL YOU TAKE IN ●
THE SETTING? ISSUES TO CONTEMPLATE

There are varying degrees to which a researcher participates in the research setting. There is often a tension between wanting to get close to those in the setting but at the same time maintaining the role of researcher, which involves a degree of detachment. Some research may require more attachment while other research may require less attachment or no attachment at all. Finding a balance between the two is crucial in most fieldwork settings, and, as a result, there are degrees of participation in a setting that range along a continuum from *complete observer, observer-as-participant, participant-as-observer,* to *complete participant* (Gold, 1958). There is no definite line between these roles; in fact a researcher may progress through each of these roles as their fieldwork progresses, by moving up and down the continuum between observation and participation, depending on the circumstances they bump up against in the setting.

Complete Observer

A complete observer role requires that the researcher's identity remain hidden; the researcher does not interact with those in the setting, but instead makes observations of the setting by using such devises as a hidden video camera or by remaining invisible behind a one-way mirror or a screen to avoid detection. The *complete observer* role allows the researcher to study a setting without interfering with its day-to-day operations, thereby minimizing the bias (or *reactivity*) that might result from the presence of the researcher interacting and possibly changing the very nature of social relationships in the setting. It is possible that those in the setting might change their behavior if they know a researcher is present.

Taking on the role of complete observer has its drawbacks. It does not allow the researcher to clarify meanings and answer questions concerning things that are not readily understood by the researcher.

- How do we know that our understanding/observation is shared with those we research?

The very physical location of our observations in a setting can limit our perspective. If we use a video camera to observe a particular field site, the very physical placement of the camera creates a particular angle of vision into the setting and may limit our ability to observe the entire setting. We also add our own unique bias when we observe a setting as well, since our observations are filtered by our own perspective and standpoint. We come to the research process with our own researcher positionality—our race, class, gender, and so on. Each of these factors can also influence what we observe and our interpretations of these observations. This is especially true when the researcher is not at all familiar with the customs and routines of a given setting.

Bearing these caveats in mind, observational studies are especially helpful in understanding the meanings of everyday behaviors. Erving Goffman (1967) was a keen observer of what takes place in everyday interactions between people, especially in public places. Goffman was interested in the roles we play with each other to sustain everyday microinteractions. He provides a *dramaturgical* perspective on everyday interactions. In essence we are "putting on a show" with each other in order to sustain these types of interactions. Goffman was especially interested in the social rituals we go through in order to carry out a variety of public behaviors, such as waiting in line, riding in a crowded elevator, or when we meet a passing acquaintance. For example, you might notice that when you are in a cramped elevator most people face forward and avoid eye contact when they are in close proximity to others, especially strangers. This is one way that individuals manage to be physically close, yet avoid intimacy with others.

The work of Robert Sommer is another example of studying everyday interactions. Sommer (1969) was interested in how individuals perceive and construct "personal spaces." A personal space is the region surrounding your physical body that you draw a boundary around which others (termed "invaders") are not supposed to cross. We all have personal boundaries regarding interpersonal space—how we draw those boundaries is linked to the type of relationship we have with those who enter our personal space. In fact, there is a science of studying personal space termed *proxemics*—the study of how individuals use space. Sommer describes a series of observational studies of the invasion of the personal space of students working at a study table at a university library. He noticed how they stake out their "territory" by placing numerous props like clothing or books in "their" space. He wanted to see what strategies students employ to defend their space and what they do when they perceive someone (in this case a person affiliated with Sommer's research project) violating their space by sitting too close. When students perceive their space to be violated, they react quickly by giving off several defensive gestures, shifting their body, or even moving away. Sommer notes: "If these fail or are ignored by the invader, or he shifts position too, the victim eventually takes to flight" (p. 35). There may be different reactions to "invasion" of personal space. Kaya and Feyzan (1999) are interested in observing how personal space is negotiated under conditions of crowding. They observed individuals who wait in line at ATMs in the city of Ankara, Turkey. They note that under conditions of high density (crowding), individuals will invade personal space much more often than under conditions of low density. They noted gender differences in invasion of personal space, with males more apt to infringe upon the personal boundaries of women.

Most fieldwork requires more than observation. It may not be easy for the researcher who is in the field to maintain the stance of "complete observer." There are those in the field who unwittingly draw the researcher into a more heightened participation level than the researcher may feel comfortable with, as Emerson and Pollner note:

Unlike laboratory researchers whose one-way mirrors provide distance and allow completely unengaged observation . . . fieldworkers cannot necessarily stand back and watch social interaction with absolutely no involvement with those engaged in that interaction. Nor can the field-worker simply declare a detached position by fiat: host members may resist the researchers' definition of his level of (non-) involvement and even ignore his self-definition as a researcher, analyst or observer. (Emerson & Pollner, 2001, p. 241)

- How can the researcher maintain distance in the setting so that the observer role is not compromised?

While we have talked about the importance of *gaining* entry in the setting, there are also strategies the researcher might need to employ in order to maintain a more observational role in the setting. As Emerson and Pollner (2001) note, there may be a need for field researchers to learn about "*doing distance*" in the field in order to maintain their research identity (p. 241). One threat to the observer role comes from those in the setting who entice the researcher into a more participatory role or who engage in interaction with the researcher other than as fieldworker (p. 242). "Remaining on the periphery" may be one way to offset this threat. This strategy may backfire, however, and serve to alienate those in the setting, especially if they have made overtures of inclusion they perceive are repeatedly rebuffed. Another, more indirect strategy is called *finessing*, where the researcher uses "diplomacy" and "evasive responses." Emerson and Pollner give an interesting example of "diplomacy" by a fieldworker who was asked to choose between two groups in the setting. When asked who was right, the fieldworker found that "throwing the question back to the disputants or pointing out the merits of either side, or making a joke of the entire dispute" was the best way of handling a difficult situation (p. 251).

Sometimes a more direct refusal is needed in order to maintain the researcher's identity and prevent the researcher from getting involved in activities they do not feel comfortable with. Some of these activities may be illegal; others may take the form of unwanted sexual overtures. Ping-Chung Hsiung (1996) conducted research in satellite factories in Taiwan. These are small-scale, family-centered operations. She wanted to understand how workers, particularly women workers, were treated by their male bosses. As an "uninvolved observer" working in the factory she found that she ran into several problems. She points out that while her role of observer on the periphery of the ongoing interaction in the setting provided the chance to listen to those on the shop floor, her position as a young married woman also created some problems:

. . . I see that my compliance with the role of uninvolved observer served two functions. By giving priority to the voices and actions of the people in the setting, it allowed incidents to unfold and events to take their full course. It also prevented me from imposing my feminist ideology on others. My efforts to be an impartial observer ran into difficulties, however. In my fieldwork, I was surrounded by and subjected to various forms of everyday sexism—daily norms and practices that were overtly oppressive toward women or covertly perpetuated gender inequality. . . . On my visits to factories, I was sometimes greeted with whistles and such remarks as "what a pretty woman," from male workers on the shop floor. . . . My gender took precedence over my academic credentials, for example, when a man who was supposed to help me get entry to a factory turned a factory tour into an incident of sexual harassment. He began by asking me what an American man would say to initiate a date. My indifferent response to his inquiry did not stop him. . . . When I refused his invitation for a date, he verbally insulted me: "What other fun can you have on Saturday afternoon when your husband is not around." (pp. 130–131)

Yet, given the social dynamics in the field, whether encouraged by others to take more of a participant role and/or the researchers' own enthusiastic embrace of opportunities for a fuller participation, researchers often try to strike a balance between intimacy and distance.

Observer-as-Participant

Along the continuum and moving toward more intimacy in the setting is that role of *observer-as-participant*. This role requires the researcher to reveal their identity in the setting, but the extent to which the researcher actively engages with the members of the setting is *limited*. Pamela Fishman's research on social interaction between married couples provides an example of this type of role identity. Fishman (1990) was interested in analyzing the power relations in conversations between couples in the privacy of their homes:

- How do couples interact with each other in their everyday lives?
- How are power and authority produced and maintained in an intimate relationship?

She intensively studied the conversations of three couples who agreed to have Fishman tape-record their conversations in their homes. She notes the following concerning her role:

The tape recorders were present in the apartments from four to fourteen days. I am satisfied that the material represents natural conversation and that there was no undue awareness of the recorder. The tapes sounded natural to me, like conversations between my husband and myself. Others who have read the transcripts agreed. All six people also reported that they soon began to ignore the tape recorder. Further, they were apologetic about the material, calling it trivial and uninteresting, just the ordinary affairs of everyday life. Finally, one couple said they forgot the recorder sufficiently to begin making love in the living room while the recorder was on. That segment and two others were the only ones the participants deleted before handing the tapes over to me. (p. 227)

While Fishman does have contact with the couples in her study, her presence in the research setting is invisible, but known. While couples are aware of her research presence by the intrusion of a tape recorder into their everyday lives, for the most part, Fishman's role remains very peripheral in the research setting.

Participant-as-Observer

The *participant-as-observer* participates fully in the ongoing activities of the research setting and the identity of the researcher is known to the members of the setting. There are *degrees of participation* in the research setting and degrees to which members of the setting view the researcher as an insider to that setting.

Whyte does some negotiating of his role in Cornerville. At times, Whyte himself is unclear about his degree of participation in the setting. While Cornerville residents know that he is a researcher who wants to know more about the life of Cornerville, it takes Whyte and the residents of Cornerville a bit of time to find a balance between these two roles:

At first I concentrated upon fitting into Cornerville, but a little later I had to face the questions of how far I was to immerse myself in the life of the district. I bumped into that problem one evening as I was walking down the street with the Nortons. Trying to enter into the spirit of the small talk, I cut loose with a string of obscenities and profanity. The walk came to a momentary halt as they all stopped to look at me in surprise. Doc shook his head and said: "Bill, you're not supposed to talk like that. That doesn't sound like you." I tried to explain that I was only using terms that were common on the street corner. Doc insisted, however, that

I was different and that they wanted me to be that way. . . . I learned that people did not expect me to be just like them; in fact, they were interested and pleased to find me different, just so long as I took a friendly interest in them. (p. 30)

Complete Participant

The *complete participant* actively engages with members of the setting; however, the researcher's identity is not known to the participants in the setting. The researcher participates in a *covert* manner, by not revealing their researcher identity in order to "pass" as an authentic member of that setting. Judith Rollins chose to go undercover in order to study the plight of domestic workers. She notes:

I began the field research process by working for a month as a domestic. . . . I chose to submerge myself in the situation before even designing the research in order to sensitize myself to the experience of domestic work and of relation to a female employer. . . . I obtained my jobs by placing advertisements in city-wide and suburban newspapers. (Rollins, 1985, p. 9)

Rollins's research raises important methodological issues you might consider when conducting covert participant observation. Those who favor deception argue that it is necessary because field research often would be impossible to do if the researcher's identity were revealed. Douglas goes so far as to suggest that covert researchers are *entitled* to do this type of work: "in order to achieve the higher object of scientific truth" (Douglas, 1979, p 17). Others point out that going undercover provides the researcher with an opportunity to study individual or group behavior that might otherwise remain invisible. Such is frequently the case with "studying up," as in the case of research done on elite groups such as surgeons (see Famradt, 1998) or studying those groups whose activities are often secretive, such as cult organizations (Galanter, 1989). For Rollins, the defining criterion for her decision to use deception in her participant observation of domestic workers and their employers hinged on whether the "gains" outweighed the "losses."

The immediate question became: is what can be gained worth the loss? I decided it was. I decided that because this occupation had been such a significant one for low-income women and because so little research had been done on it despite its presence throughout the world, the understanding that might be gained by my putting myself in the position of a domestic, even in this limited way was worth the price. (1987, p. 15)

Beyond the important ethical issues concerning deception in research that were discussed in Chapter 3, deception in the research process can sometimes interfere with the very in-depth understanding a researcher hopes to gain (Wax, 1971, p. 52; Bailey, 1996, p. 15). A researcher who goes under-cover may start to believe that they are in fact "one of the natives" and this in itself may serve to cloud a researcher's ability to understand the very setting that they are in. During her research, Rollins pretends to be a domestic only for a rather short period of time: "In all, I worked for ten employers: for seven of them I worked four weeks, one day . . . a week; by one, I was fired after the first day . . . and for two, I worked six months, one day a week" (p. 10). This length of time may *not* be sufficient for Rollins to gain an in-depth understanding of the everyday working conditions of domestic workers.

- To what degree is Rollins's experience as a domestic worker equiva-lent to the everyday realities of domestic working life?
- To what extent does taking on the "insider" role prevent/interfere with an understanding of the setting?

By assuming the role of insider, Rollins is prevented from asking ques-tions that might "blow her cover." Bailey notes: " . . . most people allow researchers to ask certain questions, such as those that are stupid or blunt, that are not allowed of insiders. . . . The role of researcher also allows one to go places that otherwise might be taboo" (1996, p. 15). Added to this is the increased inability of the researcher to readily jot down their observations "on the fly" in order to accurately capture their ideas and observations of what is happening in the setting. Waiting until there is an appropriate time to do so may result in loss of information and inaccurate accounting of impor-tant events (p. 15). In addition, by completely immersing herself in the setting and taking on the specific role of a domestic, Rollins' vision of her employer is limited. To what extent can Rollins get "outside" the role of domestic within the setting and reflect on the social interaction between domestics and their employers, from the point of view of the employer? The context of understanding the social interaction is missing the vantage point of the employer.

Most ethnographic fieldwork lies in between the observer–participant continuum. We can think of each of these as parts of a seesaw. At one end of the rise, we have the "observer" part of ourselves; at the other end the "participant" part. When the seesaw is not balanced—we might move too much to one side or the other. The researcher's selves may get out of balance—one self is in the air (participant role) while the other is on the ground (observer role). Each of these sides can become unstable, and the balance point is when both of these roles are grounded. The fun and understanding, however, sometimes lies in the constant interplay between each of these roles. These roles are *not fixed* in a research setting and it is possible for the researcher to seesaw up and down the continuum depending on the social situation and the demands of the research problem.

Whatever role(s) you take in the field, you should expect the unexpected. You should also expect to learn about yourself as you learn about others—this is one of the things that makes ethnography such a rewarding and unique experience. Sarah Maddison learned all of this firsthand as she conducted field research with a group of young feminists in Australia. Let's join Maddison behind the scenes.

Behind-the-Scenes With Sarah Maddison

I loved the year I spent researching young feminists in the Australian women's movement. During 2001 I was lucky enough to spend twelve whole months doing participant observation with two very different groups of young women in Sydney. Both groups were a lot of fun—I looked forward to the time I spent "hanging out" with them each week. The research data I gathered during this time were exciting and challenging. But the experiences I had with these amazing young women also gave me an opportunity to reflect on some questions of power and intimacy that can arise in this type of research.

One group I was researching was a network of "young women who were parents" (their preferred term) who were working in a women's health centre in a poor, outer suburb of Sydney. I spent one day a week with the Young Women Who Are Parents Network (YWWAPN), during which time we planned campaigns, did crafts and talked about parenting—all very enjoyable activities. I also participated in the training program that the young women were doing, known as Opportunities and Choices, by co-facilitating a session on gender issues.

(Continued)

(Continued)

One of the exercises that the young women were invited to participate in was to "draw a feminist," life-size, on butchers' paper. The outcome was fascinating. As I expected, one group drew a woman that conformed to all the well-known, negative media stereotypes of feminism. The other group, whose drawing also reflected some of these stereotypes but was far more flamboyant in other ways, confessed that they had drawn me—naked, except for big boots, dreadlocks and tattoos–not the way in which I usually presented myself to the Centre at all!1 When I asked why they had depicted me in that way the group members replied that they saw that my feminism had given me the freedom to say and be whatever I wanted because I was not afraid of the world.

The drawing was confronting but strangely flattering. Importantly, it made me reflect on my place in the lives of these young women and the resulting vulnerabilities in the research relationship. I developed a heightened awareness of the points of connection and similarity between me as a researcher, and the research participants, in negotiating the research relationship. There were significant biographical overlaps between my life and the lives of the young women in the study. Most obviously, perhaps, there was the fact that I was also a feminist and was known to be active in the women's movement. But with the YWWAPN the connections were also of a quite personal nature. It was important to these young women to know whether or not I was a mother and in what circumstances my mothering role had been experienced. Sharing with them the fact that I too had been a relatively young mother (23) at the time of my first child's birth, and that I had spent time as a single parent, increased their sense that I was someone they could trust, as I was not a complete stranger to their lives and experiences.

But I was also aware that, for some of these young women at least, I was seen as something of an aspirational figure in light of the fact that I had not finished high school, I had gone to university with two young children in tow, and was now engaged in academic research. Their view of me was a considerable responsibility and one that I had to take very seriously. For me as a researcher it was a moral imperative not to abuse or manipulate the trust that these young women placed in me and to remain clear about the boundaries in our relationship.

Ethnographic participant observation can be an enormous amount of fun. If you are lucky like me and find yourself researching a group of people who you like and respect and whose company you enjoy, then the "work" you are doing can seem a lot more like play. But herein lies the danger for the researcher. Having *too much* fun can mean forgetting why you are there and the power relationships involved. The sometimes intimate relationships that are a part of this research method must be treated with care and respect. Forgetting these rules could mean damaging your research participants in ways that you never imagined—and that would be no fun for anyone.

EXITING THE FIELD ●

The particular role you take on in the setting—how enmeshed you are in the day-to-day life of the setting—can determine how easy or difficult it is to depart. The ending of a project can happen for a variety of reasons. You might for example have to abruptly exit the field because of time constraints or economic or personal reasons; these are unforeseen constraints. Other factors may stem from unfortunate events in the setting that make it difficult for you to continue your work. What often occurs, however, is that you reach a *saturation point,* where you do not find anything new in the setting and where you may even feel that if you stay any longer you may start to lose your researcher perspective. Dorinne Kondo is a bilingual Japanese American conducting fieldwork in a confectionery factory in the city of Tokyo. She is particularly interested in the idea of treating workers as part of one's "family." Is the Japanese factory really like a family? Do the workers consider themselves part of a "family"? She spent almost 3 years in the field and she describes how difficult it was to finally leave: "I kept extending my stay at the factory; it became something of a joke, as the older women would tease me about my parents, whose 'neck must be soooooo long.'" She notes however, that one event really marked her final departure from the field:

> At a tea ceremony class, I performed a basic "thin tea" ceremony flawlessly, without need for prompting or correction of my movements. My teacher said in tones of approval, "You know, when you first started, I was so worried. The way you moved, the way you walked, was so clumsy! But now, you're just like an *ojosan,* a 'nice young lady.' Part of me was inordinately pleased that my awkward exaggerated Western movement had finally been replaced by the disciplined grace that makes the tea ceremony so seemingly natural and beautiful to watch. But another voice cried out in considerable alarm, "Let me escape before I'm completely transformed!" And not too many weeks later, leave I did. (2001, pp. 199–200)

There are degrees of exiting the field as well. Some researchers may depart abruptly, severing all ties to the setting. This may happen because the researcher and/or the researched may be feeling uncomfortable with their interactions in the setting, or perhaps personal or economic circumstances require that the research project end early. Ruth Horowitz wanted to conduct research on a Chicano gang; however, unwanted sexual overtures from gang members made it impossible for her to remain in the field. She notes: "As the pressures increased to take a locally defined membership role, I was unable to negotiate a gender identity that would allow me to continue as a researcher"

(Horowitz, 1986, p. 423). Others may maintain close ties to their setting, visiting and keeping in contact with the researched; some may even form friendships that last a lifetime. There are some important *exiting strategies* you might employ in leaving the field, such as being sure to let the researched know that your stay is only temporary, and even giving others a sense of your own research timetable. Inherent in the field research process is the forging of reciprocity (rapport) between the researcher and the researched. Those in the setting, for example, can come to rely on the researcher for emotional support and advice and, if and when this is withdrawn, it may create a sense of loss and abandonment for both the researched and the researcher. Maxine Baca Zinn (2001) conducted her field research on Chicano family life. She made initial contacts with families through her participant observations at a local community education program by attending workshops and participating in the activities for parents whose students were enrolled in educational programs. She notes how sometimes the researcher-researched relationship is not balanced, and those in the setting who come to depend on the researcher for social support, motivation, and friendship often feel let down when the project comes to an end. Baca Zinn related the following story concerning her exiting from the field:

> During the last stages of the research, the stage of breaking off relationships and preparing to leave the field, the uneven nature of the research relationship became clear. I tried to be honest with primary informant families once the research relationships had been established. I was frank about the amount of time I would be spending in the field, for example. Still, they know that I had accepted a university teaching position and eventually would be leaving the community. Nevertheless, some of the informants had come to depend on me. I know this is the final stages of the research, and I felt uncomfortable when I heard the informant say at a parent meeting, "I wish she was not leaving us. I couldn't have been (Parent Activities) chair without her help. I don't know how I'll manage when she leaves." (2001, pp. 159–166)

It was also difficult for Baca Zinn, a Chicana scholar studying a Chicano community, to leave this setting, especially when some in the setting wanted her to teach at a nearby college so that, as one of her informants notes: "When my children go to college, they should be able to take courses from their own people" (p. 166). Baca Zinn grapples with her own feelings of how much a researcher "gives to" and how much they "take from" (or some might even say "exploit") a given research setting. She notes that while she had a ready-made answer for this informant, she still grappled with the issue: "having to do with my career commitments and an answer which he accepted. Yet I did not have an answer for myself when faced with the disturbing question: was I, after all, one of those researchers who is never seen in the community again once the study is completed? It was and is a painful question . . ." (p. 166).

Whatever your reasons for leaving, it is important to come up with some strategies for your departure. It might be important to check in with others concerning your departure to get a sense of how they are feeling and perhaps to arrange with those in the setting some ways to mark your departure in a more public way—such as a party, ceremony, etc., as well as the type of follow-up you plan—whether that follow-up is a letter or a return visit.

GATHERING DATA IN THE SETTING ●

It is crucial for you to determine what type of data you want to collect in the setting and the best way to go about doing that. Your role in the setting will determine what types of data you will or will not be able to collect. Will you obtain data only through observing and/or participating? Will you collect data using other methods, such as interviewing those in the setting, both informally and formally? Will you rely on previous information about the setting collected by others (e.g., research studies, documents)? These are also choices about data collection. Most of these decisions should be guided by your research question.

If you are gathering data through observation and participation in the setting, it becomes critical that you collect data on an *ongoing* basis. Data collection and data analysis should proceed simultaneously. For the ethnographer in the field this means writing down your observations and ideas (data collection) and trying to figure out what is going on (data analysis). This is done each day as soon as you leave the field or, if possible, while you are in the setting. Otherwise it is easy to forget important details and events. Analysis of your field notes may lead to asking new questions and new observations and interactions in your setting.

- How do you observe?

It is important to remember that you cannot observe all interaction that is going on. It's important to ask:

- What particular part(s) of the setting do you want to observe?

There are multiple levels of observation contained within a setting and all cannot be observed at any one time. Some levels of observation you might want to consider are:

- What are people doing in the setting?
- What are their activities?
- What sensory observations can you make about the setting (e.g., specific sounds and smells)?
- What is being said (pay attention to language—write down specific quotes/phrases you feel capture the story of what is going on in the setting)?
- What is not said? Are certain things taken for granted? Sometimes what is not present is just as important as what is present.

How Do You Record Your Observations?

Not all ethnographers agree on what is the best way to do this. This section concentrates on how you might record the observations in the form of *field notes,* but you might use a tape recorder or even a video or digital recorder. Field notes are the "data" that you gather in order to make sense of your research setting and serve as an aid in writing your research results.

● DATA MANAGEMENT OF FIELD NOTES

First and foremost, in order to help with data management of your field notes, it is important to record the date, time, location, page number of all field notes. It also helps to create different types of field notes or divide or mark up your notes into different sections. Sometimes, however, these sections will run into each other in any given field note. Several researchers have suggested several types of field notes you might create for yourself (see especially Bailey, 1996, p. 80).

"On-the-fly" notes can consist of some key words or phrases to help you remember important events or ideas that occur while making your observations. They can be written on a small memo pad. Some researchers use whatever paper they can find, including the back of a matchbook cover or a paper napkin so that their ongoing observations in the field are not disrupted.

"Thick descriptions" of the setting are all the things that you can remember about exactly what took place in the setting. Be sure to record, whenever possible, the exact "in vivo" words or phrases of respondents, or as close to their words as you can get. Be sure not to forget the sensory observations in the setting: What do you smell? What about specific visuals? While you might think some of these details about activities and events are

very mundane, it's important that you not censor your descriptions but be open to the range of events and details in the setting. These notes and their relevance can be sorted out after you leave the field. Something you thought was unimportant may, in fact, be crucial once you fit some of these descriptive pieces together.

"Data Analysis" notes. In some sense you can think of these notes as linking notes you gathered *on-the-fly* and your "thick descriptions" from the setting. These are the "what does it mean?" notes to yourself. What things go together? What new questions do these observations bring up for you? What have you learned thus far and what does it mean at this juncture? These notes can also contain your innermost hunches. Allow your "analysis" self to have free reign here through the process of brainstorming (see also Bailey, 1996, and Lofland & Lofland, 1984).

"Personal Matters and Reflexivity" notes. This is a space for you to explore your own positionality as the researcher in the research process. What are you feeling about this setting? What are your concerns? How might you critique your role in the setting? Were you open to new ideas or were you shut down that day because the people you met were critical of you? Write down your emotions vis-à-vis those you are researching. For example: Are you limiting your observations of "X" because you really don't like them—he/she reminds you of your college roommate who went out with your ex-lover. What are you concerned about? What are your fears? What are the "to do" things you need to remind yourself of? Do you need certain research supplies like computer paper or index cards? These "to do's," while seemingly trivial are important to keep your project moving along (see Bailey, 1996, and Lofland & Lofland, 1984).

- "Accounting of what you collect each day and a more complete accounting at midpoint in your project observations" notes.

You also might want to conduct a mini accounting/summary of what data you gather on a *daily* basis by providing (1) a brief summary of what you found and (2) a short memo on what you think it means so far, by asking yourself, "What are the implications of (1) and (2) for how I will proceed the next day with my observations? What should I examine next?" etc. This mini accounting/summary doesn't have to be a long memo; a few paragraphs will do. About midway through your data collection you might provide a more substantive accounting by going over (1) all the data you collected from the beginning up to the midpoint and (2) a substantive memo on what you think it means, asking the same questions.

It's important to remember that there is no "perfect" formula for writing field notes; everyone's field notes take on a life of their own. Some of us may like to draw visual diagrams more than others. Some of us like to doodle as a way to get at some of our ideas. Some of us may cut and paste various clippings into the field notes that we acquired that day. Maybe someone gave you a newspaper article, a brochure, or even a letter or card that they wanted you to have. Remember field research can also consist of documents you gather in the field, and these also need to be analyzed.

● ANALYZING YOUR FIELD NOTES AND OTHER MATERIALS: THE ETHNOGRAPHIC PUZZLE

Let's go inside the research process and look at how one researcher writes up her field notes. Notice how description and analysis are running together in these notes. These field notes are written by a white middle-class research assistant who is observing in a predominantly black context. The following is an excerpt of field notes written shortly after she observed the activities at an inner-city community center in a predominately black neighborhood. She takes on the role of observer participant in the setting. She accompanied her professor to the research site called Cityville in order to locate black respondents for a research project on black identity and body image.

Field Note: Number 1
Date: July 1995
Place: Community Center, Cityville
Event: Mother-Daughter Day

It was so different to drive into Cityville, a neighborhood and part of the City that I have never seen before. The difference between where I live and go to school and Cityville is amazing. It is almost two separate worlds.

The Cityville public school was hidden back off a side road, you would never even know that it was there. The school itself was so much different than the schools that I have seen in my area. It was a huge school but very old and not very well taken care of. I was a little nervous about what we would find when we walked in.

The first thing that struck me was how white I felt. My professor and I were the only two white people in sight and I felt like everyone was looking at me and thinking "who is this stupid white girl and what the hell does she want?" I read an article in my Professor's class called the "Invisible Knapsack" and it talked about white privilege and the fact that no matter where we go, as white people, we can bet that the majority of the people around us will be white as well. So I have always been aware of what it must feel like to be black and to walk into an all white room but not as aware as I was when I walked into an all black room. The tables were turned and I have to admit, I didn't like it. I felt so uncomfortable and unwanted. I felt like I needed to show or prove to all the people there that I was the same as them, even though deep down I knew it wasn't true.

Well the second thing that struck me was what a huge commotion the place was. Kids were running everywhere, adults were shouting orders here and there. Then we walked into a room where tables were set up and a group of kids were practicing a stepping routine with their coach. A lot of people were all dressed up and as I sat there, I knew that this couldn't have been a normal day at the center. A few minutes later, my professor and I found out that there was going to be some type of show. Well this was a surprise. And the even bigger surprise was that my professor would be speaking at the show to all the kids and parents. So much for advanced notice.

As my professor got ready I watched the steppers continue to practice. They were really cute kids, ranging in age from about 7 to 14, and there were about 12 girls and 1 boy. Their coach was really into it. He was very stern with the kids and demanded their attention and precision, but stern in a very caring way. The kids were also very serious about the stepping and practiced very hard.

Well after a while the parents started pouring in and the steppers left. My professor and I got a pamphlet from one of the ushers and discovered that we were at the Mothers' and Daughters' Night. My professor's name was on the pamphlet as a speaker and in a few minutes she was going to be on.

We sat at a table with a mother, father, and sister of one of the steppers. There were some other families in the room and one of them was overweight. There was the mother and father of one of the steppers, the grandmother and her two daughters, and even some friends. The others were mothers and friends of the other girls. There was even a mother there to support her son who was an usher. The ushers were all dressed up with name tags and seemed to take their job very seriously.

Finally some other white people showed up, now I didn't feel like I stuck out as much. There was a mother and a sister of one of the singers, the only white girl in the group of kids that I saw. Very interesting! The two other white people who came were speakers as well.

Well, the show began. My professor spoke first, she was pretty brave because you couldn't have paid me to get up in front of that group. But she gave a great talk and most of the mothers seemed pretty interested. Then the new director of the center spoke about how happy he was to be the new director and about how excited he was to get some new programs going. Next came a group of singers. There was a lead singer about 10 or 12 and a group of back up singers of about 8 girls and 1 or 2 guys. They sang "You Have to Be Strong."

All of the parents looked very proud. Next one of the white women got up to speak about her Family Van. She is a doctor who drives around a van with a team of professionals and provides free health services to those who need it. She said that she wanted to introduce her van and make sure that the community really wanted it in Cityville and to ask if they had any questions. A few questions were asked and then she seconded what my professor said. Next came the steppers. They had matching outfits and they performed their routine to perfection. Their coach looked very proud and so did all of the parents. The mother at my table said "there's my baby" as her daughter marched out. The kids seemed really proud and pleased as well. At the end I saw their coach give them a big hug. Their message was about knowledge and success and trying your hardest, it was a powerful message.

A couple of women told my professor that they wanted to talk to her so she went off with the grandmother. I was a little nervous for her because I thought that she might tell her where to go but she didn't. In fact, she wanted to be interviewed and with her 2 daughters and her grandchild. She was very interested and she told my professor that black men and the black community are more accepting of big women.

I, myself, noticed such a difference between all the women in the room compared to a room full of white women. There were a few very large women but they were all well dressed, they all carried themselves with confidence, they all looked happy and they all looked at ease. I've never really seen that in the white community. Usually when people are bigger in the white community they carry themselves differently, they don't look confident and at ease. I know that this is a generalization but it is what I have noticed. These black women, big or little, all carried themselves the same.

As far as the young girls went, if they were thin, it looked like they were naturally that way. Some girls were of normal build and looked happy and comfortable and at ease, and some were even what would be considered big in the white community but they looked just as happy and confident.

There was so much pride and love and culture and strength in the room. It was overwhelming and amazing to be a part of this event, even as an outsider. I would like all the people who make comments and generalizations about blacks to go to a center like Cityville's for a day and see how wrong they are.

Another woman got up and spoke, she was a black woman and she brought her mother. It was interesting to listen to her speak as she called for "Amens" and to see how much more responding the audience was to her than to my professor and the other white speaker.

After this we left and as we were asking for directions a woman who was leaving offered to give us a ride to the trolley. She was very generous and also very friendly. She has lived in Cityville for 25+ years and runs a drug hotline/clinic.

On the trolley ride home the tables were turned back and I was the white majority again. Amazing how much more comfortable I felt.

Ethnographic data analysis takes place as an ongoing activity—you gather data, you think about it, you gather more data and you think about it. Data gathering and data analysis proceed as an upward moving spiral toward creating meaning. Ethnographers may also utilize quantitative techniques and statistical analyses to assist with this goal, although this type of analysis usually remains secondary to qualitative analysis.

THE ETHNOGRAPHIC PUZZLE ●

We can think of ethnographic analysis as an *inductive process,* that is, a process of discovering what the data you gather means. Description is the bedrock of ethnographic analysis and field notes are the record of the in-depth observations you garnered from the field that provide a window into the research setting—its people, the physical attributes of the setting, and so on. We can think of field notes as pieces of a puzzle. The object is to put these pieces together to create a puzzle picture (analysis) and then to tell the reader what you see (interpretation). How well do you organize this descriptive story? You might begin simply by reading over what you have gathered and ask some sensitizing questions, such as:

- What is going on in the setting?

Part of your analysis is to arrange these descriptive pieces into a story. Your analysis (how you organize these pieces into a whole puzzle picture) leads to interpretation (what does the puzzle mean?). As you know, there are false starts to solving a puzzle. We move the pieces back and forth, sometimes forcing pieces of a puzzle together! Certain problems may arise in your analysis journey. These are some sensitizing questions to ask yourself along the way:

- Am I moving too fast from description to analysis? If so, the picture may be blurred and your explanation too weak.
- Am I spending too much time at the level of description? If so, you may describe all of the pieces of the puzzle in accurate detail, but not have a clue as to what the puzzle is or what it means.

Analysis helps us to fit the puzzle pieces together. Analysis asks: What fits together? What doesn't? When certain pieces of the puzzle fit together, we have grabbed onto a *theme,* something that provides us with an idea of what the puzzle is and allows us to move forward toward our goal of completing the picture. You might consider "memoing" about how your analysis is going. *Analysis memos* are ideas that you write down to help you think through how you are going about your work, what something means. Just as with field notes there are a variety of memos you might write to assist with your analysis, and we will cover some of these techniques in the analysis and interpretation chapter (Chapter 10).

You might employ a variety of analysis methods for putting the pieces together. For example you could "code" each piece by its size (assign the code categories large, medium, or small to each of the pieces) and place (sort) all the pieces into these three categories. *Codes* are ways to organize your data. Codes can be useful or not useful. To do this you often compare the pieces with each other. We can think of this technique as employing the ethnographic analysis method called *constant comparative method* that is part of grounded theory (see Glaser & Strauss, 1967). We will talk about this method in more detail in Chapter 10. In effect this technique consists of looking at how puzzle pieces are the same or different from one another. This method asks:

- What is this piece?
- What does it mean?
- Are there other pieces like this?
- What makes piece "A" different from/same as piece "B"?

Comparing analysis to putting a puzzle together is meant to remove much of the jargon that has cropped up when researchers try to explain how to analyze and interpret data. To take this analogy and apply it to your project, you might begin by just reading over all your field notes and other written documents and interviews. You should try to reach a comfort zone about your data—the point at which you feel very familiar with the data you have before you. You might also begin by marking up the text as you go along; perhaps you would like to make notes or memos about what is happening and what you think are the important points you want to return to. You might also think about inputting your data into a computer software program such as HyperRESEARCH or Ethnograph to help you with this task (we will take up the issues with computer software and data analysis in Chapter 10). In the first "run through" of your data you might begin to see and identify some major categories or what we might term "codes," these can be literal to analytical codes (often called *categories* or *themes*). You might want to look at things that "go together" and things that don't seem to fit anywhere (*analytical comparison*). Think about this process and write about how codes are similar or different and why. Once you have grabbed onto what you feel is a potent theme/code, look for several independent sources that might support this idea—documents/interviews in addition to your observations. This is called *triangulating* your data between different sources. You might even have your respondents read over your ideas to see if they can corroborate your theories/perspective. Be sure to memo about your important theme idea. How is it related to other ideas you have also isolated? Doing this will help you see the links between various code categories. Little by little your story will emerge (see Hammersley & Atkinson, 1995, p. 157).

COMMON ANALYSIS AND INTERPRETATION PROBLEMS ●

In conducting an analysis you might find yourself becoming distracted on a given strategy of analysis. For example, you only focus on getting more and more puzzle pieces, but don't spend time or enough time linking the pieces.

Here memoing might help you to stop and think about how you might begin to code and categorize these pieces (sort them) as a way toward creating a more holistic picture of what is going on.

You are too quick to categorize and link your pieces, and as a result the picture you obtain is fuzzy and/or incomplete.

Here you might want to go back to the field to collect more specific data or go over notes you might have discarded. Maybe your code categories are not clearly defined. Examine how you are linking your codes/themes together. Memoing about this conundrum is often helpful.

You may leap to a great interpretation of the picture (what it means) with no idea of whether or not the puzzle is clear or even what its component parts are.

You might be short on analysis to support your interpretation. You may want to go back to triangulate your interpretation with other sources of information as well as share your interpretation with those in the setting. You might need to collect more data to corroborate your findings.

As a final tidbit of advice, it's also important to remember the process of analysis and interpretation goes back and forth. Pieces of the puzzle may or may not fit; in fact, they may even belong to another puzzle. If you get lost, remember that what often guides your puzzle making is the set of guiding research questions you started out with. It may be, however, that these pieces are really answering another question—and you may need to revise what it is in fact that you were asking, but didn't know it!

THE ISSUE OF REPRESENTATION: ●
THE ART OF STORYTELLING

It is important to consider the issue of representation—from whose perspective do we tell the story? John Van Maanen conveys the sense of early ethnography's attitude toward the researched, which often resulted in the point of view that one should always "let the ethnographer speak for the data" with minimum interpretation from the researched. He notes the following:

There once was a time—some might say a dreamtime—when ethnography was read as a straight-ahead cultural description based on the firsthand experience an author had with a strange (to both author and reader) group of people. Those who wrote ethnographies may have had their doubt about what the adventure of field work taught them and just how "being there" results in an ethnography, but few doubts surfaced in their written products. It seemed as if ethnography emerged' more or less naturally from a simple stay in the field. One simply staked out a group, lived with them for a while, took notes on what they said and did, and went home to write it all up. If anything, ethnography looked like a rather pleasant, peaceful, and instructive form of travel writing. (Van Maanen, 1995, p. 1)

Yet little by little, Van Maanen (1995) notes, this important premise of ethnography—the authority of the researcher to represent the subject—was itself the target of severe scrutiny. As he notes "a kind of ethnography of ethnography" is taking place out of textual studies and "new understandings are gradually altering the way we think about cultural representation practices both past and present" (Van Maanen, 1995, p. 17). Van Maanen notes that new questions are being raised:

- "What role does the researcher play in the process of interpreting his or her data?"
- "Should the qualitative researcher allow his or her feelings to enter into the interpretation process?"
- "Whose point of view is the ethnographer really representing with his or her data?" (Van Maanen, 1995, pp. 16–17)

Much of qualitative research entails observation as well as participation between the researcher and the researched. The power of the researcher resides along all points of the research process—from deciding on the research question(s) and the type of research method used to data analysis and interpretation of research findings. Some critics of traditional qualitative research analyses are concerned about representing the life stories of those researched, especially the lived experiences of those who are oppressed in terms of their race, gender, class, age, and so on (see Wolf, 1996). Emerson (2001) traces the breakdown of the "colonial" model of ethnography, toward a more "reflexive" turn, which breaks down the division between the researcher and the researched:

With the decline of colonialism, conditions that had been taken for granted became uncertain and problematic. Researchers had to obtain more direct approval of the people to be studied, without implicit or explicit reliance upon colonial power. . . . As access and the day-to-day process of fieldwork became more problematic, more dependent on actively establishing working relations with particular people, personal and relational self-consciousness inevitably increased. (Emerson, 2001, p. 23)

Ethnographic accounts have become more reflective of the power imbalances and issues of authority and representation in the analysis and interpretation of findings (see also Hesse-Biber & Leavy, 2004, pp. 409–425). Contemporary ethnography is turning toward a more "interpretative ethnography," one that acknowledges the existence of multiple realities. There is no one-to-one correspondence between the researcher's understanding and the experiences of "the other." Denzin notes: "There can never be a final, accurate representation of what was meant or said—only different textual representations of different experiences" (Denzin, 1997, p. 5 as cited in Emerson, 2001, p. 50). Postmodern and poststructural ethnographic perspectives in particular question the belief in the authority of the ethnographic gaze. These perspectives stress ethnographic accounts as no more than a tale told through a specific set of differences in terms of race, class, gender, and so on. As Denzin and Lincoln (2000) note:

Poststructuralists and postmodernists have contributed to the understanding that there is no clear window into the inner life of an individual. Any gaze is always filtered through the lenses of language, gender, social class, race and ethnicity. There are no objective observations, only observations socially situated in the worlds of—and between—the observer and the observed. (p. 19)

For some postmodernists, reality itself becomes only representation. Gubrium and Holstein (1997) note the following concerning the postmodern turn and its "crisis of representation":

Indeed, the challenge comes in crisis proportions, taking qualitative inquiry away from and beyond empirically grounded what and how questions. The crisis is about representation itself, with radical postmodernism completely displacing reality with representation. In this context, the how question shifts from the substance, process, and indigenous constitution of social life, to the representational devices used by society and the sociological to convey the image of objective (or subjective) reality. Postmodernist inquiry tends to veer away from how members of society interact to produce their lives and experience, turning more toward the representation practices used by those claiming the authority to offer "true" representations. (p. 76)

For some postmodernists like Jean Baudrillard (1981, 1988) reality, in fact, takes on a "hyperreal" quality. Reality becomes a set of images, not unlike what we are bombarded with on electronic media, such as television, or electronic simulated games. Time and space become jumbled, as well as our ideas about what constitutes a chronological ordering. Gubrium and Holstein (1997) note:

> Reality, or modern time and space, are "cranked up" to the point where the objects and order normally associated with the real no longer apply. As simulation supplants the actual, substantiality becomes a matter of images. Presence is thrown to the wind in literally mindless projects. Subjects with footing in the world disappear, and significances are so flattened that representation ceases to have any particular reference to things. Reality becomes a playful field of signs, signs of other signs and other signs of signs. (p. 78)

Not all ethnographers are in agreement with this point of view, and there are those, like Gubrium and Holstein (1997), who are representative of ethnographers who advocate taking a middle ground by retaining some version of reality while developing strategies to take into account the multiple perspectives onto the social world (see, for example, Gubrium & Holstein, 1997). They note:

> Not only are we reluctant to fully embrace the unbridled relativism and "self"-ish orientation of skeptical postmodernism, we don't want to give up on reality, so to speak. While we do not reject postmodernism out of hand, we do share . . . commitment to documenting the social world, to the possibility of empirically based description of everyday life for us, this is the enduring stuff of qualitative inquiry. In the wake of post modernism, the challenge lies in cultivating these objectives in light of new epistemological questions and analytical sensibilities. (Gubrium & Holstein, 1997, p. 99)

Such strategies included self-reflexivity on the part of the researcher—how our own biases enter into the research process, to begin to "decenter" the ethnographer in the ethnographic process of representation. Some researchers have in fact presented postmodern representations called "messy texts" (Marcus, 1994). These are artful ways of getting at the voices of the researched by a critical reflection on the nature of power within the research process. Patti Lather and Chris Smithies' book, *Troubling the Angels: Women Living with HIV/AIDS* (1997), provides a good example of this type of reflective writing style. Lather and Smithies interviewed 25 women living with HIV/AIDS from 1992 to 1997. They create a text that interweaves the voices of these women while at the same time partitioning off the authority of the researcher by dividing the text into layers. The top layer is the voices of their respondents, and the bottom layer consists of the researchers' own tales of conducting their research and their reflections on how they understand the lived experience of these women by also placing their stories in a wider cultural context. Lather (2000) notes:

> We wanted to create a "messy text" . . . while still honoring our charge of producing a book that would do the work the women wanted. . . . The book begins with two prefaces, the first introducing the book and the second the women, many of whom have written their own introductions. The heart of the book consists of a series of short chapters that narrate the interview data around topics on the day-to-day realities of living with the disease: relationships, efforts to make sense of the disease in their lives, death and dying issues, and the role of support groups. . . . Interspersed with these short data chapters are angel intertexts and illustrations. . . . Running across the bottom is a subtext commentary where Chris and I, as coresearchers, spin out our tales of doing the research. . . . Scattered throughout the book are some of the women's own writings . . . Finally, the book concludes with an epilogue that updates the reader on each of the women. (p. 286)

Denzin advocates what he terms a "seventh" moment in knowledge building that employs the methods of "performance ethnography." Performance ethnography uses a variety of data collection approaches to access the multitude of meanings contained within a setting. He stresses the importance of using all our senses—sight, sound, smell, and touch—in order to especially access the subjugated knowledge of those who have been oppressed (what he terms "getting at indigenous epistemologies"). Very often such an approach will cross disciplinary boundaries, borrowing techniques of data gathering from the arts (dance, music) and humanities (poetry and creative writing) (see Denzin, 1997; McCall, 2000).

CONCLUSION ●

The ethnographic method provides the researcher with an important window into understanding the social world from the vantage point of those residing in it. Ethnographies provide the reader with an in-depth under-standing of the goings on of those who inhabit a range of naturally occur-ring settings. Participant observation is a primary means of data collection, although other forms of data are also collected from the setting, such as doc-uments. Writing and analyzing field notes are important features of this method. Data analysis requires the researcher to be open to discovery, with data analysis and collection proceeding almost simultaneously. Interpretation of the data requires sensitivity on the part of the researcher to the variety of multiple meanings in the setting and an awareness of their own standpoint (in terms of their class, race, gender, etc.). While ethnographic methods are not good at making broad generalizations about a given social phenomenon, they provide an important context for understanding the results from large-scale research, such as surveys. Ethnographers take a range of approaches to social reality, depending on their specific discipline and theoretical bias. Some ethnographers may be more interested in social change than others (critical ethnography); others are more focused on studying populations that have been overlooked by traditional ethnography, such as women (feminist ethnography). What characterizes and underscores all of these approaches, however, is the emphasis on interpretation—getting at meaning from the perspective of those who are researched.

● GLOSSARY

Analysis Memos: Ideas that you write down to help you think through how you are going about your work, what something means.

"Analysis" Notes: These notes link *On-the-Fly Notes* and *Thick Descriptions*.

Anthropology: Research is conducted in foreign cultures in order to capture understanding of the "native" population—the customs, values, artifacts associated with a given group and its wider culture.

Codes: Ways to organize your data by categories or labels.

Complete Observer: The researcher's identity remains hidden; the researcher does not interact with those in the setting but instead makes observations of the setting by using such devises as hidden video cameras or by remaining invisible behind a one-way mirror or a screen to avoid detection.

Complete Participant: The researcher actively engages with members of the setting; however, the researcher's identity is not known to the participants in the setting.

Covert Research: The researcher does not reveal his/her identity, in order to "pass" as an authentic member of that setting.

Critical Ethnography: Research conducted from this perspective seeks to understand social life in order to change the way that those in power marginalize those with less power.

Dramaturgical Perspective: Developed by symbolic interactionist Erving Goffman (1967), this perspective is interested in the roles played to sustain everyday microinteractions. In essence a "show" is "put on" in order to sustain these types of interactions.

Ethnographic Research: Seeks an in-depth understanding of how individuals in different cultures and subcultures make sense of their lived reality. Ethnographers "go inside" the social worlds of the inhabitants of their research setting, "hanging out" and observing and recording the ongoing social life of its members by providing "thick descriptions" (Geertz, 1973) of the social context and the everyday goings on of the people who live in these worlds, spending a good amount of time engaging with the fine details of events, people, and activities within the setting.

Exiting Strategies: Plans that allow the researcher to leave the setting easily and without causing harm to the people in the setting.

Field: In ethnography this concept differs depending upon the type of research project you pursue. For an anthropologist studying a foreign culture like Malinowski, the field is a *cultural* setting. For Anderson, studying a local bar or local neighborhood, the "bar" or "neighborhood" becomes the field. In short, the field is the setting a researcher studies.

Field Notes: Written accounts of the researcher's everyday experiences in the field; which are written while in the field, on the fly, or shortly after leaving the field.

Gatekeepers: Formal gatekeepers grant you permission to enter the research site if formal permission is needed (also see *Informal Gatekeepers*).

Inductive Process: A process of discovering what the data you gather means.

Informal Gatekeepers: These are people who hold key positions in the setting and their influence on others in the setting determines your level of access. Informal gatekeepers have the power to give your presence a "heads up" or "heads down."

Informants: These are people in the setting who provide the researcher with critical information and tips.

Interpretive Perspective: Ethnographers often work from this theoretical tradition. This perspective developed as a direct challenge to positivist epistemology and its interpretation/application of objectivity. The interpretive epistemology is based on the interpretation of interactions and the social meaning that people assign to their interactions (Nielsen, 1990, p. 7). This perspective epistemologically believes that social meaning is created during interaction and by people's interpretations of interactions. The implication is that different social actors may in fact understand social reality differently, producing different meanings and analyses. Research of this kind involves the building of relationships between the researcher and research participants who are collaborators in the research process.

Observer-as-Participant: The researcher is required to reveal their identity in the setting, but the extent to which the researcher actively engages with the members of the setting is limited.

On-the-Fly: Notes that can consist of some key words or phrases to help you remember important events or ideas that occur while making your observations. These can be thought of as "jottings" that you elaborate on further when you leave the field.

Natural Settings: Places where individuals go about their daily lives, rather than a prefabricated place "set up" by the researcher at a specific site.

Participant-as-Observer: The researcher participates fully in the ongoing activities of the research setting, and the identity of the researcher is known to the members of the setting.

Positivist Perspective: The researcher seeks "the truth" that is waiting to be understood if only they remain objective, by not allowing their own attitudes and values to enter into the setting. The gathering of information is primarily a one-way street—with the researcher asking questions and those studied answering questions the researcher poses.

Proxemics: The study of how individuals use space.

Participant Observation: A primary research tool of ethnography and its practice; the researcher lives in or makes extensive visits to the setting they are studying, observing as well as participating in the activities of those they are researching.

Saturation Point: The point in the research where nothing new is found in the setting and the researcher may even lose their perspective if they stay in the setting any longer.

Theme: This is when codes start to come together and show a larger pattern in the data. Put differently, when certain pieces of the puzzle fit together, something that provides us with an idea of what the puzzle is and allows us to move forward toward our goal of completing the picture.

"Thick Descriptions": This term was coined by Clifford Geertz (1973) and refers to all the things that you can remember about exactly what took place in the setting. These are very detailed descriptions and rely on a researcher using his/her senses.

Triangulating Data: Look for several independent sources that might support an idea you have—for example, using documents/interviews in addition to your observations.

Urban Ethnography: Study of a neighborhood or city.

DISCUSSION QUESTIONS ●

1. Discuss the meaning of "ethnography" and when it is appropriate to use it as a method of social research.

2. What is the importance of adopting an interpretative (as opposed to positivist) model when conducting ethnographic fieldwork?

3. In ethnographic fieldwork, the researcher's understanding comes from the members of the social setting being researched. How can that fact, therefore, serve as an empowering experience for the researched (i.e., aid in social activism efforts)?

4. What is the importance of field notes in ethnographic fieldwork?

5. How does gaining entry into a specific social setting impact data collection?

6. How does your role in the social setting shape what types of data you will or will not be able to collect?

7. If you were interested in studying a religious cult, discuss the factors that would influence how you went about conducting your research project (i.e., discuss the considerations brought up in this chapter, as well as other considerations not brought up in this chapter). Most importantly, discuss the factors that are going to influence *why, where,* and *how* you conduct your research project.

8. When studying members of a certain social setting, a researcher may be introduced to unfamiliar rituals and customs (perhaps rituals/customs they do not agree with). Discuss how these factors would impact your research project.

9. Although it is important for the researcher to gain access to a social setting through a gatekeeper (of some sort), the authors warn that it is important that a researcher not be *too reliant* on one member of the setting. Why is that?

10. How do constraints on gaining access to private settings impact the extent to which you, as the researcher, can understand the members of the social setting you wish to study?

11. This chapter discussed the role that you, as a researcher, should have when carrying out your research process. Discuss the factors that influence what role/identity you should adopt when conducting your research. What role will you take in the setting? There is often a tension between wanting to get close to those in the setting while at the same time maintaining the role of researcher, which involves a degree of detachment. The important thing is to find a balance between the two and let the *circumstances* of your research project determine what role(s) you will play.

12. In this chapter, Emerson (2001) notes "fieldworkers cannot necessarily stand back and watch social interaction with absolutely no involvement with those engaged in that interaction. Nor can the fieldworker simply declare a detached position by fiat" (p. 17). Therefore, researchers should not completely detach themselves (nor completely immerse themselves) in the social setting. Do you agree with this statement? Why? Why not? (i.e., can you think of an instance where it would be beneficial for the researcher to completely immerse, or detach, her- or himself from the social setting in which they are studying?)

13. Discuss some of the options available to researchers as they attempt to gain access to more "private" settings.

● SUGGESTED WEBSITES

Participant Observation

http://www2.chass.ncsu.edu/garson/pa765/particip.htm

This website is an overview of a course offered at North Carolina State University. There is an extended bibliography and a link to a journal that has information on participant observation and other field studies.

http://uk.geocities.com/balihar_sanghera/qrmparticipantobservation.html

This website offers an in-depth look at participant observation by including information on the history of the practice, the researcher's role, how to take good field notes, and the analysis of the field notes.

NOTE ●

1. While I am neither dreadlocked nor tattooed, I am quite partial to big boots, so this drawing was not a complete piece of fiction.

REFERENCES ●

Addams, J. (1910). *Twenty years at Hull-House.* New York: Macmillan.

Anderson, E. (1996). Jelly's place. In C.D. Smith & W. Kornblum (Eds.), *The field: Readings on the field research experience* (2nd ed., pp. 12–20). Westport, CT: Praeger.

Anderson, E. (1976). *A place on the corner.* Chicago: University of Chicago Press.

Anderson, N. (1923). *The hobo.* Chicago: University of Chicago Press.

Baca Zinn, M. (2001). Insider field research in minority communities. In R. M. Emerson (Ed.), *Contemporary field research: Perspectives and formulations* (2nd ed., pp. 159–166). Prospect Heights, IL: Waveland Press.

Bailey, C. A. (1996). *A guide to field research.* Thousand Oaks, CA.: Pine Forge Press.

Baudrillard, J. (1988). *Cool memories.* New York: Verso.

Baudrillard, J. (1981). *For a critique of the political economy of the sign.* St. Louis, MO: Telos.

Booth, C. (1902). *Life and labour of the people of London.* London: Macmillan.

Cressey, P. G. (1932). *The taxi-dance hall.* Chicago: University of Chicago Press.

Daniels, A.K. (1967). The low-caste stranger in social research. In G. Sjoberg (Ed.), *Ethics, politics and social research* (pp. 267–296). Cambridge, MA: Schenkman.

Deegan, M. J. (2001). The Chicago school of ethnography. In P. Atkinson, A. Coffey, S. Delamont, J. Lofland, & L. Lofland (Eds.), *Handbook of ethnography* (pp. 11–25). Thousand Oaks, CA: Sage.

Denzin, N. K., & Lincoln, Y. S. (2000). The discipline and practice of qualitative research. In N. K. Denzin & Y. S. Lincoln (Eds.), *Handbook of qualitative research* (2nd ed., pp. 1–28). Thousand Oaks, CA: Sage.

Douglas, J. (1979). Living morality versus bureaucratic fiat. In C. B. Klockars & F. W. O'Connor (Eds.), *Deviance and decency* (pp. 13–33). Beverly Hills, CA: Sage.

Emerson, R. M. (Ed.) (2001). *Contemporary field research: Perspectives and formulations* (2nd ed.). Prospect Heights, IL: Waveland Press.

Emerson, R. M., & Pollner, M. (2001). Constructing participant/observation relations. In R. M. Emerson (Ed.), *Contemporary field research: Perspectives and formulations* (2nd ed., pp. 239–259). Prospect Heights, IL: Waveland Press.

Famradt, J. (1998). Studying up in educational anthropology. In K. Bennett deMarrais (Ed.), *Inside stories: Qualitative research reflection* (pp. 67–78). London: Lawrence Erlbaum.

Fishman, P. (1990). Interaction: The work women do. In J. McCarl Nielsen (Ed.), *Feminist research methods: Exemplary readings in the social sciences* (pp. 224–238). Boulder, CO: Westview.

Frazier, E. F. (1932). *The negro family in Chicago.* Chicago: University of Chicago Press.

Galanter, M. (1989). *Cults: Faith, healing, and coercion.* New York: Oxford University Press.

Geertz, C. (1973). *The interpretation of cultures.* New York: Basic Books.

Glaser, B. G., & Strauss, A. L. (1967). *The discovery of grounded theory: Strategies for qualitative research.* Chicago: Aldine.

Goffman, E. (1967). *Interaction ritual: Essays on face-to-face behavior.* Chicago: Aldine.

Goffman, E. (1961). *Asylums: Essays on the social situation of mental patients and other inmates.* Garden City, NY: Doubleday.

Gold, R. L. . (1958). Roles in sociological field observation. *Social Forces, 36,* 217–223.

Gubrium, J. F., & Holstein, J. A. (1997). *The new language of qualitative method.* New York: Oxford University Press.

Hammersley, M., & Atkinson, P. (1995). Documents. In *Ethnography: Principles in practice* (2nd ed., pp. 157–174). New York: Routledge.

Hesse-Biber, S., & Leavy, P. (2004). *Approaches to qualitative research: A reader on theory and practice.* New York: Oxford University Press.

Horowitz, R. (1986, January). Remaining an outsider: Membership as a threat to research rapport. *Urban Life, 14*(4), 409–430.

Hsiung, P. C. (1996). Between bosses and workers: The dilemma of a keen observer and a vocal feminist. In D. L. Wolf (Ed.), *Feminist dilemmas in fieldwork* (pp. 122–137). Boulder, CO: Westview.

Humphries, L. (1976). Methods: The sociologist as voyeur. In. P. Golden (Ed.), *The research experience* (pp. 100–114). Itasca, IL: F. E. Peacock.

Kaya, N., & Feyzan, E. (1999). Invasion of personal space under the condition of short-term crowding: A case study of an automatic teller machine. *Journal of Environmental Psychology, 19,* 183–189.

Kondo, D. K. (2001). How the problem of "crafting selves" emerged. In R. M. Emerson (Ed.), *Contemporary field research* (2nd ed., pp. 188–202). Prospect Heights, IL: Waveland.

Lather, P. (2000). Drawing the line at angels: Working the ruins of feminist ethnography. In E. A. St. Pierre & W. S. Pillow (Eds.), *Working the ruins: Feminist poststructural theory and methods in education* (pp. 284–311). New York: Routledge.

Lather, P., & Smithies, C. (1997). *Troubling the angels: Women living with HIV/AIDS.* Boulder, CO: Westview.

Lofland, J., & Lofland, L. (1984). *Analyzing social settings: A guide to qualitative observation and analysis* (2nd ed.). Belmont, CA: Wadsworth.

Malinonwski, B. (1922). *Argonauts of the Western Pacific.* Prospect Heights, IL: Waveland Press.

Marcus, G. (1994). What comes (just) after "post"? In N. Denzin & Y. Lincoln (Eds.), *Handbook of qualitative research* (pp. 563–574). Thousand Oaks, CA: Sage.

McCall, M. (2000). Performance ethnography: A brief history and some advice. In N. K. Denzin & Y. S. Lincoln (Eds.), *Handbook of qualitative research* (2nd ed.). (pp. 421–433). Thousand Oaks, CA: Sage.

McKinney, J. C. (1966). *Constructive typology and social theory.* New York: Appleton-Century-Crofts.

Myerhoff, B. (1978). *Number our days.* New York: Simon & Schuster.

Rollins, J. (1985). *Between women: Domestics and their employers.* Philadelphia: Temple University Press.

Sleeter, C. E. (1998). Activist or ethnographer? Researchers, teachers, and voice in ethnographies that critique. In K. Bennett deMarrais (Ed.), *Inside stories: Qualitative research reflections* (pp. 49–57). London: Lawrence Erlbaum.

Sleeter, C. E. (1992). *Keepers of the American Dream.* London: Falmer Press.

Smith, R. Q. (1998). Revisiting Juanita's Beauty Salon: An ethnographic study of an African-American beauty shop. In K. Bennett deMarrais (Ed.), *Inside stories: Qualitative research reflections* (pp. 79–85). London: Lawrence Erlbaum.

Sommer, R. (1969). *Personal space: The behavioral basis of design.* Englewood Cliffs, NJ: Prentice Hall.

Sullivan, P., & Elifson, K. (1996). In the field with snake handlers. In C. D. Smith & W. Kornblum (Eds.), *In the field: Readings on the field research experience* (2nd ed., pp. 33–38). Westport, CT: Praeger.

Thrasher, F. M. (1927). *The gang.* Chicago: University of Chicago Press.

Van Maanen, J. (1995). An end to innocence. The ethnography of ethnography. In J. Van Maanen (Ed.), *Representation in ethnography* (pp. 1–35). Thousand Oaks, CA: Sage.

Wax, R. (1971). *Doing fieldwork: Warnings and advice.* Chicago: University of Chicago Press.

Whyte, W. F. (1996). On the evolution of street corner society. In A. Laureau and F. Schultz (Eds.), *Journey through ethnography: Realistic accounts of fieldwork* (pp. 9–74). Boulder, CO.: Westview Press. [Originally published as an "appendix" in W. F. Whyte's second edition of *Street corner society* (University of Chicago Press, 1955).]

Whyte, W. F. (1943). *Street corner society: The social structure of an Italian slum.* Chicago: University of Chicago Press.

Williams, T. (1996). Exploring the cocaine culture. In C. D. Smith & W. Kornblum (Eds.), *In the field: Readings on the field research experience* (2nd ed., pp. 27–32). Westport, CT: Praeger.

Williams, T. (1989). *The cocaine kids.* New York: Addison-Wesley.

Wolf, D. L. (Ed.). (1996). *Feminist dilemmas in field work.* Boulder, CO: Westview.

CHAPTER 8

CONTENT ANALYSIS AND UNOBTRUSIVE METHODS

. . . social science research has to confront a dimension of human activity that cannot be contained in the consciousness of the isolated subject. In short, it has to look at something that lies beyond the world of atomistic individuals.

—Lindsay Prior (2004, p. 318)

Texts, then, are defined as being the semiotic manifestation of material social processes.

—R. Iedema (2001, p. 187)

Content analysis is one of very few research methods that can be employed qualitatively or quantitatively, opening up a wide array of methodological possibilities. Up until this point we have been

AUTHOR'S NOTE: Parts of this chapter are adapted from Hesse-Biber, S., & Leavy, P. (2004). Unobtrusive methods, visual research, and cultural studies. In S. Hesse-Biber & P. Leavy (Eds.), *Approaches to qualitative research: A reader on theory and practice.* New York: Oxford University Press.

reviewing qualitative methods that rely on obtaining data directly from people using interviewing and observational skills. But how can qualitative researchers use nonliving materials in order to study the social world? How can texts, in their varied forms, be used as the starting point to understanding social processes and generating theories about social life? What are the benefits of using nonliving data? Let's return to our body image example and examine how a researcher might use "texts" as a means of researching this topic.

We might be interested in studying body image issues within a hierarchically structured society—such as a patriarchal society. Focusing this topic more specifically, we might be interested in the relationship between the American popular culture and gendered body image issues prevalent within the United States. A literature review would reveal several things. First, adolescent and college-age females are the population most likely to suffer from eating disorders, disorderly eating, negative body image, and appearance-related low self-esteem. Second, this group is most visibly impacted by the cultural ideals of beauty constructed in the media in terms of their attitudes and behaviors. Third, exposure to and internalization of mass media impacts people's attitudes and is thus a part of the context through which they see themselves. Given this, we might decide to study girls and mass media. We would then construct a research question such as: What is the relationship between media images and female beauty ideals?

As we saw in earlier chapters, this kind of research question could be explored through a variety of interview methods. In that instance we would define the sample of girls we are interested in and ask them about their media consumption, their body image ideals and issues, and what they perceive as the relationship between popular culture and their own body image. One question might be: How do you feel when you see images of models and actresses? This kind of research design privileges the way individuals subjectively think about and feel toward their body in relation to their media consumption. The knowledge gained reflects the experiences of individuals. This is important but is merely one way a qualitative researcher can go about studying this topic. A researcher interested in how cultural forms are created and projected in a given society may use content analysis. For example, a qualitative researcher interested in how media images *themselves* reflect and construct a particular ideal of female beauty, instead of how women subjectively relate to such images, will find content analysis very useful. Let's return to our example and look at how content analysis can be employed.

A qualitative researcher might wish to study women's magazines in order to critically investigate the portrayal of women. Some guiding questions might include: What are the body sizes of women represented? What positions are women shown in? What text accompanies visual images? Differing from a researcher conducting in-depth interviews, in this project the researcher studies how body ideals are created and reflected by the mass media. The focus of inquiry here is on the *cultural forms* in which beauty ideals are distributed and the *cultural processes* that construct these ideals. When using this approach the point of departure for the research is no longer individuals who themselves live in a social context and have been "imprinted" by the media images that constitute part of the socialization process in their society. Critical scholars explain that individuals are "imprinted" by their culture's power-knowledge relations and researchers must use "texts" as their starting point in order to more accurately investigate social power (Taylor, 1987). Let's take an example. If a researcher were to approach you, present you with a variety of parents' magazines and ask you to interpret the images of boys versus girls, how would you go about performing the task? How would you respond to questions about activeness versus passiveness and pastels versus primary colors? Given that you live in the context where these images circulate and have thus been exposed to comparable images over an extended period of time, it is fair to assume that the very images you are now being asked to respond to are also mediating your perception of boys and girls, or masculinity and femininity. A qualitative researcher interested in going beyond the mediated vision of individuals whose vision is already filtered by societal norms may use the magazines themselves as the starting point for research. By deconstructing preexisting images of boys and girls in popular magazines, the researcher is interrogating the process by which the images came to be (and be normalized) and how they represent (or in some cases challenge) the prevailing paradigm. As you can see, depending on the research question and the researcher's goals, content analysis may be more appropriate than interviewing or another interactional method.

As the preceding parent's magazine example illustrates, content analysis can be used to study difference. Let's return to our body image women's magazine example, which focused solely on representations of females. Instead of only focusing on images of women, a researcher could also study gender *differences* in beauty ideals and body representations. For example, what are the differences in how male and female models and actors are portrayed? How do these mass-mediated images impact (reinforce and/or construct) cultural ideas about masculinity and femininity?

Malkin, Wornian, and Chrisler (1999) conducted a qualitative content analysis of 21 popular men's and women's magazine covers in order to examine gender differences regarding body image messages. They looked at a total of 69 women's magazine covers and 53 men's magazine covers. Their research showed that 78% of the women's magazine covers contained numerous messages regarding bodily appearance, while the men's magazine covers had no such messages. Additionally, 25% of the women's magazine covers contained conflicting messages regarding weight and nutrition. Perhaps most revealing, the placement of weight-related messages in women's magazines indicated that happiness was correlated with weight loss, which was not seen on any of the men's covers. For example, titles about losing weight were placed directly next to titles about improving the quality of one's life, creating the connotation that these two things are connected. Content analysis enables this kind of inquiry because it can be conducted holistically—looking at individual images but also their relation to other words and/or images. This provides a broader perspective on what we are seeing in any given textual data set. Finally, images of women appeared on the majority of both men's and women's magazines. The women on the covers of both kinds of magazines were very slim and met the cultural standards of the ideal female body. This has many social implications and raises sociological questions about the relationship between women and their bodies within American culture.

The messages sent out by the media regarding bodily appearance are quite different for women and men. A strong emphasis has been placed on the bodily appearance of women that equates a thin body to beauty, sexuality, and social status; less focus has been placed on the bodily appearance of men (Freedman, 1986). These gendered messages can clearly be seen in magazine articles and advertisements. . . . "Instead of simply reflecting the weight and shape ideals of our society, popular media may be, to some extent, imposing gender-related norms, which then lead to sex-related differences in the frequency of critical behaviors." (Anderson & DiDomenico, 1992, p. 286). (Malkin, Wornian, & Chrisler, 1999, p. 647)

As we can see, in this instance, textual analysis was very useful for contributing to our knowledge about gender differences within mass-mediated forms—in particular, gender differences in regard to body image and related phenomena. In addition to exposing and describing a cultural phenomenon,

Malkin, Wornian, and Chrisler also generated theory from their data about the implications of these gendered differences. Let's look at another example.

As content analysis offers many options, gender differences and body image can also be studied using data in other mediums. For example, a qualitative researcher could examine audiovisual material such as film or television in order to look at any number of things including representations of male and female body image and related interactions in particular genres of cinema or TV. Lauzen and Dozier (2002) conducted a content analysis of 104 television shows that aired during prime time in 1999–2000. They studied these shows in order to examine the number and types of appearance-based comments made by and to male and female characters. Additionally, they looked at whether or not the gender of the writers had any bearing on the amount and kinds of appearance comments made. Their findings suggest that female characters receive more appearance-based comments from both female and male characters and that the nature of these comments differs from the kinds of comments men received. They also found that the employment of female writers increased the overall number of appearance-driven comments made.

> The concern with appearance may reflect the centrality of appearance and beauty in the lives of all women, including writers. Writers bring their life experiences to the scripts they create. Women are socialized to place a premium on appearance, and so women write what they know, interweaving appearance as an important and even central aspect of the lives of both female and male characters. Somewhat paradoxically, although the presence of women writers has broken the stereotypically rigid code of all-male writing teams, it has also increased the frequency with which appearance comments are made overall and particularly about female characters. (Lauzen & Dozier, 2002, p. 8)

While we don't necessarily agree with the researchers' conclusions, as perhaps this phenomenon can be linked to increased pressure on women writers to acquiesce to normative gender ideals in a male-dominated terrain, this is a clear example of generating theory about gender difference out of audiovisual content analysis data.

Diana Rose is a researcher in the United Kingdom who used audiovisual content analysis to study representations of "madness" on British television. In the following Behind-the-Scenes, Rose talks about how she came to study this topic and where it has taken her.

Behind-the-Scenes With Diana Rose

I have been working in the field of mental health research for 12 years. Before this I conducted research on language and education and gender studies. There was a gap between the two types of research. This is because I have a diagnosis of bipolar affective disorder and for some time was too unwell to work. I lived on state welfare benefits and a small pension.

The first piece of research on mental health which I undertook was for my PhD for which I studied quite late in life (40 years old). The topic I chose was "Representations of Madness on British Television." I considered this a "safe" topic, one that would not require me to disclose my mental health problems. I was very aware of stigma. After a while I became unwell at the university and it all came out. Everybody knew where I was drawing my inspiration. I did not really mind—I had a political commitment. In the British media at the time there was much criticism of the policy of care in the community and I wished to expose how biased this was. I was not a disinterested scholar!

In the last year of my doctoral studies, I was offered a job at a mental health charity to do research. This was *because* of my experience of mental health problems—having a diagnosis was a qualification for the job (Rose, 2000). I decided to embrace this wholeheartedly, be upfront about my diagnosis and treatment and use my experience of treatments and services to inform my research practice.

This has led me to develop an "empowerment" epistemology. In terms of enlightenment thought, mental health service users (we don't like the term "patient") are in a similar position to that described for women by feminist epistemologists—only worse. Irrationality defines us according to psychiatrists and the public, we have no intellectual capacities—only out of control emotions and chaotic lives. There are still psychiatrists who believe that mental health service users are damaged in the "cultural" parts of their brains and so are closer to nature. An empowerment epistemology seeks to overturn these beliefs.

Just as the women's movement contributes to feminist scholarship, the user/survivor movement has contributed to my own thinking. I first became aware of this movement in the mid 1980s when I was not working. It was a consciousness-raising experience, just like feminism. I came to realise that the way I was being treated by the mental health system was unjust. Later, I theorised this in terms of the mental health system being a dominant discourse and practice, drawing on the work of Foucault.

What does this mean in terms of research practice? It leads to a participatory form of research. There are two ways this can happen. First, when other service users are participants in our research we are able to understand their perspectives as we have been there too—we share their experiences. From a methodological point of view, we are also very careful that we capture exactly what individuals and groups think—often going back several times to check on the contents of an interview or focus group. This is good qualitative research practice but it is also informed by a deep respect for our participants. This does not happen in mainstream mental health research.

The other form of participatory research is to involve service users as *researchers*. People with little or no research experience are trained to do research, alongside experienced researchers. They design interview schedules drawing on their own experience. Using these schedules, they conduct interviews with other service users. The general view is that when users interview other users, the situation is more open and relaxed and the information is different to what a professional would obtain.

My preferred method of analyzing data from qualitative projects is qualitative content analysis. This is more a methodological choice than a choice informed by my experience as a mental health service user. I do not believe it is possible to come to a set of data with no preconceptions. I do not believe this is ever possible. Having a coding frame, albeit informed by initial examination of the data, makes one's preconceptions explicit. In the research I do and the research I supervise, many of our coding categories are developed from our personal knowledge of distress, treatments and services.

Some would say that this constitutes bias. But I have yet to meet a professional researcher in the mental health field, which is mostly quantitative, who is not researching a topic that is close to his or her heart, where there is some personal investment.

User involvement in research is quite fashionable in the U.K. at the moment. I am now responsible for a unit of 5 researchers all of whom are or have been mental health service users. I am committed now to developing the ideas outlined here.

Now that we are getting a sense of how content analysis can be used, and used differently than other methods in relation to our body image example, let's look more closely at what exactly unobtrusive methods are, how they developed, and how they can be employed.

● UNOBTRUSIVE METHODS: QUALITATIVE AND QUANTITATIVE APPROACHES

Unobtrusive methods developed out of the assumption that we can learn about our society by investigating the material items produced within the culture. In other words, we can learn about social life, whether it be norms or values or socialization or social stratification, by looking at the things we produce which reflect macro social processes and our world view. The texts and objects that groups of humans produce are embedded with larger ideas those groups have, whether shared or contested. The other major methods of qualitative research rely on collecting data from individuals and groups through interactional and observational ways of knowing. Unobtrusive methods differ and use texts as the starting point of the research process. Specifically, unobtrusive research uses nonliving forms of data generally categorized as "texts" or "artifacts" (broadly conceived). There are two primary benefits to working with nonliving data forms: (1) the data are noninteractive, (2) the data exist independent of the research (Reinharz, 1992, pp. 147–148). Because the data are not influenced through researcher interaction, as with interviews, and they already exist in the world regardless of the research currently being done, the data are "naturalistic." This quality gives the data a unique level of authenticity which is carried through the research process. Researchers do not intrude into social life by observing or interviewing but rather examine existing noninteractive texts, and, thus, the research process is classified as unobtrusive. Many different kinds of texts and artifacts can be studied, including, but not limited to: historical documents, newspapers, magazines, photographs, books, diaries, literature, music, cinema, television, websites, and so forth.

While unobtrusive methods encompass a wide range of methodological possibilities, historically, *content analysis* has been the major method under this rubric. Content analysis traditionally referred to the examination of written texts. Originally this practice was quantitative in nature and researchers would count the occurrence of a particular thing they were interested in, such as gendered or racialized terms in a newspaper. These early researchers were considered "bean counters." Many researchers now don't think in terms of qualitative or quantitative when they think about content analysis— content analysis merges these categories and can be considered a hybrid. Content analysis can be conceptualized as an inherently mixed method of analysis, or a method that always contains the possibility of both qualitative and quantitative applications. Bauer (2000) refers to content analysis as a "hybrid technique" which has always, even when performed quantitatively, been an implicitly hybridized approach to inquiry. He explains as follows:

> While most classical content analyses culminate in numerical descriptions of some features of the text corpus, considerable thought is given to the "kinds," "qualities" and "distinctions" in the text before any quantification takes place. In this way, content analysis bridges statistical formalism and the qualitative analysis of the materials. In the quantity/quality divide in social research, content analysis is a hybrid technique that can mediate in this unproductive dispute over virtues and methods. (p. 132)

Regardless of the extent to which we think about content analysis as implicitly hybridized or a method with deductive and inductive capabilities, there is no doubt that with this method of inquiry social scientists have contributed to our overall body of knowledge in significant ways with statistical and descriptive power.

Historically, quantitative researchers, alone and in combination with qualitative practice, have demonstrated the importance of content analysis as a method of gaining "hard data" about macrophenomena. This kind of research has contributed significantly to social scientific knowledge and directly influenced social policy. In briefly reviewing the history of content analysis we will see how it can be an effective tool for promoting social change on a policy level.

Quantitative content analysis has been integral to creating our repository of social scientific knowledge, including that aimed at social justice. The strength of this method is that it enables researchers to examine patterns and themes within the objects produced in a given culture. Researchers can analyze preexisting data in order to expose and unravel macro processes. The quantitative practice of content analysis is important because researchers are able to present their findings on easily readable charts and tables, often in numerical form. The force of this form of data cannot be underestimated when trying to call attention to systemic practices of inequality and when attempting to change public policy. In terms of adding to our knowledge about social inequality, quantitative content analysis has been a standard method for analyzing the role of mass-produced texts in the socialization process. For example, Gooden and Gooden (2001) studied gender representation in 83 notable children's books that were published from 1995 to 1999. Their research showed that sex stereotyping is lower than in the 1970s;

however, sex stereotyping remains prevalent in children's literature. As children's books are a significant source of socialization, this research indicates more work must be done in terms of making children's books more gender neutral. In their present form, these stereotyped representations can negatively impact girls' self-esteem and self-identity. Moreover, these texts reinforce traditional gender roles and thereby may limit the behavioral choices boys and girls believe are available to them.

Merskin (1999) conducted a quantitative content analysis of teen magazines published from 1987 to 1997 in order to find out how advertisements represent feminine hygiene and menstruation in ways that "perpetuate" or "dispel" cultural myths. In particular, Merskin wanted to know the extent to which these advertisements present menstruation as "something to be feared as well as a hygienic crisis that encouraged guilt, diminished self-esteem" (p. 941). This research shows that old gendered myths that represent women's bodies as something dirty or unpleasant are alive and well in advertising, though, on the positive side, they are presented in more liberated ways. Nonetheless, advertisers have not redefined menstruation as a positive bodily process. Furthermore, Merskin's research revealed that white models are privileged in these advertisements and thus it appears women of other racial and ethnic backgrounds are not being marketed to. The strength of this study rests on the researcher's use of clear quantitative data.

Likewise, traditional content analysis has been used to help shape social policy by calling attention to systemic inequalities in need of change. For example, Thomas and Treiber (2000) conducted a quantitative content analysis of 1,709 advertisements taken from four magazines, two marketed to white consumers and two marketed to black consumers, in order to examine race, gender, and status stereotyping. Their research indicated that there are a few patterns of gender and racial stereotyping within image-based media. For example, the white subjects often appear to be of higher status than the black subjects, who are portrayed as of lower status. Thomas and Treiber conclude:

Racial and gender stereotypes endure as exaggerated, over-simplified images used to sell products. We have demonstrated that magazine advertisements differentially use these superficial images when targeting products to women, men, Blacks, and Whites. The use of stereotypical images in magazine advertising confirms to the readership that subordinate groups should remain in lower status. In this study, both gender and race were found to be strong underlying principles of organizing everyday experience. One of the tragic characteristics of media-generated stereotypes is their ability to generate self-fulfilling prophecies, although stereotypes in ads often provide an incorrect image of race and gender. (p. 370)

This research was enabled through quantitative content analysis. The use of clear statistical charts facilitated the researcher's generation of convincing theory regarding the social implications of socializing people via harmful stereotypes.

Wysocki and Harrison (1991) conducted a content analysis of periodicals in order to expose patterns of AIDS representation. This method allowed the researchers to investigate the way information about AIDS is transmitted to children and teenagers. Research of this kind is frequently used as a vehicle for changing social policy—the data created is used as "evidence" that public policy is ineffective and in this way social justice-oriented researchers can fight for the rights of those who may be marginalized, disenfranchised, or otherwise disadvantaged in the society. Even beyond exposing patterns and themes, unobtrusive methods can help researchers to *describe* and *explain* macro social processes.

Content analysis has historically been conducted quantitatively; however, now there is a rich tradition of qualitative content analysis as well as mixed approaches. The primary difference in these two broad applications is in research design. Quantitative approaches to content analysis are largely deductive and follow a *linear* model of research design. Qualitative approaches are mainly inductive and follow what we term a *spiral* model of research design.

Let's take the former first. When using a *linear design* the researcher has a preconceived set of steps to follow in a linear (vertical) path through each phase of the research process. A *spiral design,* employed by qualitative researchers, allows the investigator to, metaphorically, dive in and out of the data as he or she proceeds. In this model a researcher generates new understandings, with varied levels of specificity, during each phase of the project and uses this information to double back and gain more information. This forms a "spiraled" approach to knowledge building if one were to visualize the process. The flowchart on the following page depicts the phases of the research process in quantitative and qualitative studies— linear versus spiral models. Bear in mind that one need not follow these steps precisely as the chart represents a very general depiction of these two approaches, and any research design should be specifically suited to the goals of a particular project.

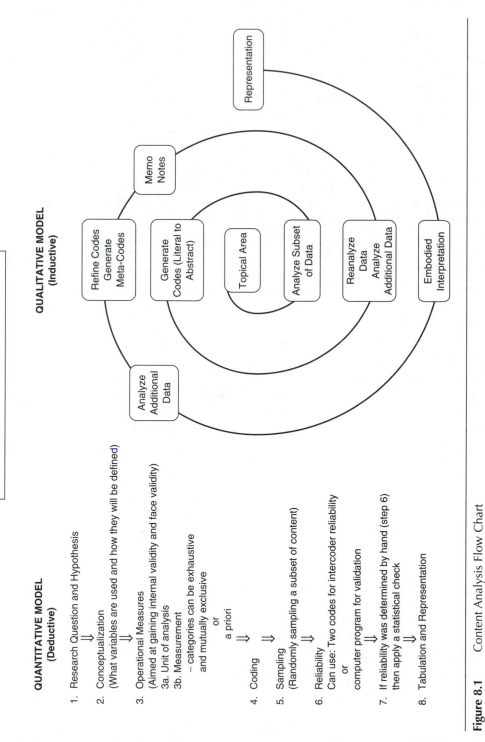

CONTENT ANALYSIS FLOW CHART

**QUANTITATIVE MODEL
(Deductive)**

1. Research Question and Hypothesis

2. Conceptualization
   (What variables are used and how they will be defined)

3. Operational Measures
   (Aimed at gaining internal validity and face validity)
   3a. Unit of analysis
   3b. Measurement
       – categories can be exhaustive
         and mutually exclusive
            or
         a priori

4. Coding

5. Sampling
   (Randomly sampling a subset of content)

6. Reliability
   Can use: Two codes for intercoder reliability
            or
   computer program for validation

7. If reliability was determined by hand (step 6)
   then apply a statistical check

8. Tabulation and Representation

**QUALITATIVE MODEL
(Inductive)**

Representation

Memo Notes

Refine Codes Generate Meta-Codes

Generate Codes (Literal to Abstract)

Topical Area

Analyze Subset of Data

Analyze Additional Data

Reanalyze Data Analyze Additional Data

Embodied Interpretation

Figure 8.1 Content Analysis Flow Chart

SOURCE: Adapted from Neuendorf, K. A. (2001). *The content analysis guidebook.* Thousand Oaks, CA: Sage.

In qualitative content analysis a researcher begins with a topical area which he or she starts to query from his or her embodied standpoint and epistemological position. Quickly into the process, the topic is also examined in relation to the research question. The researcher does not begin with preconceived codes but rather generates code categories directly from the data. These codes can range from very literal to abstract. As code categories emerge from the data the researcher doubles back to reexamine data applying the new code categories. Many researchers also engage in *memo writing* throughout this process as a way of interpreting and reflecting on the data as they go. This is why we refer to inductive approaches as a process of "diving in and out of the data." The resulting knowledge can be represented in numerous ways.

The wide-ranging ways in which unobtrusive methods can be employed to yield varied kinds of data with both descriptive and explanatory power distinguishes this set of research tools and their broad methodological configurations. During the past 3 decades qualitative researchers from diverse epistemological and theoretical positions have dramatically enlarged the conceptualization and use of unobtrusive methodologies. Increased attention to this set of practices is directly linked to the growth of cultural studies and the postmodern critique of social scientific knowledge construction.

QUALITATIVE TEXTUAL ANALYSIS, ● POSTMODERNISM, AND POSTSTRUCTURALISM

Traditionally, text analysis has been the most commonly used form of content analysis. Text analysis is when a researcher uses written texts as the primary form of data (although a researcher might combine textual and visual data or combine text analysis with another method). At the present time, the term *text* is used more broadly to encompass the range of mediums in which cultural texts appear. Over the past few decades new scholarly conceptions about the nature of social reality and the nature of social inquiry have led to increased use of elaboration of unobtrusive methods. In particular, the postmodern and poststructural critiques of research have influenced the practice of unobtrusive research by changing the theoretical perspective from which many researchers practice these methodologies.

In essence, postmodernism posits that there has been a shift from the modern era into the postmodern era, which Frederic Jameson (1984) defines as the "cultural logic of late capitalism" which constitutes a new pervasive form of social power. In this new era, there has been an implosion of media forms constituting what Jean Baudrillard refers to as a "hyperreality" in which "the real" and "the imaginary" have become blurred to an unprecedented level. In such a context, it becomes important to investigate the material aspects of culture such as texts (broadly defined) which, during production and dissemination, are embedded with historically specific power relations. But what do postmodern and critical scholars mean by studying the power imbued in objects?

Michel Foucault was at the forefront of influencing conceptions of power. Foucault (1978) theorized that power and knowledge are inextricably linked, creating a complex web of power–knowledge relations. In short, Foucault's work shows that all knowledge is contextually bound because it is produced within a field of shifting power relations. Scholars must interrogate cultural texts in order to reveal traces of the dominant worldview embedded within the them as well as the "silences" (what has been marginalized or left out of the text that in Avery Gordon's terms "haunts" that which is there). Specifically, researchers in this tradition examine the discursive practice embedded in the text, which means the specific ways that language is used within texts. Foucault proposed an archeological method of investigation to unravel how a text assumed its present form (Prior, 1997). This specific technique relies on tracing the text's process of production and distribution. Stuart Hall (1981) explains that it is within cultural texts that hegemony is enacted. Hall goes on to explain that popular texts also have an "oppositional" possibility, and within texts hegemony is also contested, resisted, and challenged. Texts do not simply mirror social reality but are also an integral component in shaping that reality (Hall, 1981) or "hyperreality." Prior (1997) asserts that we can "know the world through the representational orders contained within the text" (p. 67).

A similar critique of social scientific knowledge construction, which has influenced the way scholars think about social reality, is the development of poststructural thought. Jacques Derrida (1966) was at the forefront of this development. Derrida coined the term *deconstruction*, which is a method of conducting an internal critique of texts. In essence, a deconstructive approach to textual analysis aims at exposing what is concealed within or has been left out of a text (but, in Gordon's terms, "haunts" the text). Deconstruction is based on the notion that the meaning of words happens in relation to sameness and difference. In every text, some things are affirmed, such as truth, meaning, and authorship/authority; however, there is always an "other" that contrasts with that which is affirmed. This other, that which has been left out or concealed, appears absent from the text but is actually contained within the text as a different or deferred meaning.

Through the process of deconstruction, these different and deferred meanings are revealed. The aim of deconstruction is thus not to find "the truth" of the text but rather to displace assumptions within the text (such as the meaning, the truth, and authorship/authority). Luce Irigaray (1985) posits deconstruction as a way of "jamming the theoretical machinery" (p. 78). Ultimately this process shows that the meaning of a text is never single or fixed.

Since the postmodern and poststructural critique of knowledge construction, which has influenced the growth in cultural studies, many qualitative researchers who use textual analysis now do so in order to provide a critical (power-reflexive) analysis of the text in question. We have already discussed deconstruction, and while there are many other approaches researchers can take, we will discuss discourse analysis and semiological readings of texts.

Influenced by poststructuralism, ethnomethodology, and linguistics, discourse analysis is a strategy employed when one is concerned with the social meanings within language and discursive practices. In other words, discourse analysis is concerned with the process of communication. For Foucault, discourses are practices that are comprised of ideas, ideologies, and referents that systematically construct both the subjects and objects of which they speak. Thus, discourses are integral to the construction of social reality. Many qualitative researchers perform discourse analysis when studying texts in order to reveal the hidden ideas embedded within written language. Researchers can investigate how the dominant discourse is produced, how it is disseminated, what it excludes, how some knowledge becomes subjugated, and so forth. This kind of research is rooted in the postmodern and poststructural conceptualization that language reflects power. Moreover, the structure of society is embedded within language (and representational forms). A qualitative researcher conducting discourse analysis of texts can follow the "spiral model" of knowledge construction and dive in and out of the text in order to gain deeper insights into the ideology within the text and how language is being used to create social meanings.

Semiological readings of texts are another approach to analysis. Roland Barthes (1998) argues that semiological analyses of representations are a necessary part of social research. Semiological analyses examine the way meaning is constructed through a process of signification or connotation. Barthes created a tripartite system detailing how people, places, times, and events (the signified) are distilled into signifiers (concepts) that are then planted in a host of signs (representations) (Hesse-Biber & Leavy, 2004). From the point of view of a semiologist, this three-part process is the way in which cultural interpretive practices become naturalized—take on the appearance of fact when they are actually socially constructed.

Figure 8.2

Researchers can analyze the signs or representations produced within a society in order to deconstruct the process of meaning construction that created them. This process generally occurs in a contextualized way. By this we mean that in addition to analyzing isolated texts, researchers can analyze how meaning is constructed within a given text by the placement of words next to other words, or images next to other images, or images and words together. Meaning is not constructed out of one aspect of the text alone, but also in how the various components of the text sit in relation to each other (thereby creating different connotations or meanings). In short, semiological textual analyses center on revealing social processes of making meaning. Given that postmodernists conceptualize a "crisis in representation" brought about by the high-speed flow of images and texts within popular culture, this kind of research is becoming increasingly popular, particularly among those interested in media studies. Let's look at an example of semiological textual analysis.

If we are to create a semiological reading of the *Time* magazine cover on the previous page, what would it look like? Let's begin with the image: a pumpkin pie with an American flag stuck in it. This image is composed of two images (the pie and the flag) and creates a connotation between the two images through their placement. These images are the signs (representations), but what is signified with the fusing of these two images to create one image? What signifiers (concepts) have been implanted into this sign (the image)? The American flag contains the concept of patriotism and, thus, patriotism is being signified within the pumpkin pie. But this is only part of the story. To get a full read we have to consider the image in conjunction with the words. The caption next to this image was: "Thanksgiving 2001: Next week American families will set their tables, count their blessings and discover how their lives have changed—and how they haven't." Clearly this image, with the words, is meant to evoke patriotic feelings on the first Thanksgiving after September 11th. The words and image work together to create a particular connotation—the signified (9–11) is distilled into the signifier (the concept of patriotism) which is presented in the representation (the image of the flag in the pumpkin pie). A semiological approach to content analysis rejects the idea of naturalistic meaning in favor of examining how meaning is culturally constructed. Let's take the same image of the American flag in the pumpkin pie. Now let's pretend the image was created in 1991, 10 years earlier. What if *the same image* had the following words next to it?: Leading Native American Activist Questions the True Meaning of Thanksgiving.

The same image now takes on a very different meaning—it was constructed and presented to do so. Instead of overarching patriotism in the wake of 9–11, the image now evokes thoughtful contemplation about how the United States was founded, about genocide, about a more textured questioning of patriotism. The same image connotes a very different meaning.

Lindsay Prior is a Reader of Sociology at the University of Wales, Cardiff, and author of several books, including *Documents in Social Research: Production, Consumption and Exchange*. Prior has written extensively about what it means to use content analysis, to study nonliving forms of data, and the theoretical underpinnings of such investigation. He addresses these issues in the following Behind-the-Scenes.

Behind-the-Scenes With Lindsay Prior

I have always been fascinated by the ways in which the spaces within buildings are arranged, which is why I always include plans of hospitals or mortuaries or whatever in my studies (Prior, 1989; 1993). Elements of front stage and back stage, entrances and exits, areas where only women can enter or men can leave, rooms for children that restrict where they can and cannot learn or play or sleep—all these are of utmost significance. So, studying the arrangement of the material space in which people live and work is for me an essential precursor to any ethnographic study, and I always find it worthwhile to find an architect's plan of the key sites in which such ethnographic work is to be based. This is so even though a building will be used in ways undreamed of by its creators. Indeed, the similarities and differences that can be noted between the ways in which a site is used and the intentions of its designer can often highlight fundamental changes in the ways in which people see things over time. Hospital plans, for example, certainly illustrate major shifts in the ways in which "disease" and sickness have been conceptualised over the decades, and this can be noted in the smallest detail—such as the positioning of windows in a hospital ward.

Although people think with things as well as words, it is also important to note that humans arrange things in words as well as in space and time—which leads us to a second great source of social scientific data: documents. I always find it something of a puzzle as to why, when people consider social scientific research, they almost always rule out a study of documentation in favour of interpersonal interviews. Perhaps it is something to do with those aforementioned anthropologists who worked in societies where written documentation was negligible or non-existent. I don't know. Nevertheless, almost every study of the contemporary social world will involve documentation of some kind. In my own work the documentation that has most concerned me are the notes and descriptions made by health professionals of the people they care for. In other words the kinds of things that doctors and nurses write about when they encounter "patients"—including dead patients. How, for example, do doctors explain death in official terms? We know that they have to write on a death certificate, but how do they know what to put on that certificate? And what kind of things can they *not* put on that certificate? Questions such as these normally lead one into an investigation of other types of documentation—generative documents such as are represented in nosologies or classifications of disease. Nosologies and other "big" classificatory schemes are invaluable for a number of reasons. First of all they change at regular intervals, so one can actually track thinking in progress. The Diagnostic and Statistical Manual of Mental Disorders (DSM)—a publication of the American Psychiatric Association—for example, documents the ways in which psychiatric disorders have been theorized between 1952 and the present day. Second, these big documents constitute the frame in which people at street or health centre level have to operate. If a disorder is not in the DSM then it can't be diagnosed, it can't be billed for, it can't be treated—and disorders come and go in the DSM with interesting consequences. In the same way there exists an international list (classification) of diseases and conditions that people can die from—if a condition isn't on the list then people can't die of it. You will be glad to hear, perhaps, that old age and poverty are not on the list.

The issue for me, then, is how people represent and arrange worlds in documents, and how such documentation is subsequently used in social interaction. I am especially keen to note how people use and make sense of the *rules* that are contained in documents (Prior, 1989). As I have explained elsewhere (Prior, 2003), the notion of use and circulation of documents can form an entire theme for research in itself—and all this without recourse to a single interview. However, even when one is right there in the midst of human interaction, there is no necessary call on behalf of the researcher for intrusive acts of questioning. Instead, one can often get what one wants from judiciously recording the "naturally occurring" data that arises from routine activities—as for example in studies of medical decision-making (Wood, Prior, & Gray, 2003).

In Belfast, the city where I undertook a large part of my work on death and psychiatric illness there was a phrase that was in common use during the 1970s and 80s. Viz. "Whatever you say, say nothing" (in Belfast, of course, the "nothing" is pronounced more like "nathn"). The advice to say nothing was advice to be wary of declaring details about oneself. Advice not to declare too much about one's identity, or of one's views on matters political or religious, or an opinion on anything at all that might be sucked into the whirlpool of sectarian strife that formed the backdrop to everyday life in the city. In the context of this book, such a keenness to say "nothing" can also stand as a reminder to the social researcher that asking people questions does not always get answers—or at least, true and reliable answers. More importantly, it serves as a reminder that even should people remain determined to say nothing, there is a whole world of data just laying around and about, waiting for the keen eyed and systematic observer to collect.

References:

Prior, L. (1989). *The social organization of death. Medical discourse and social practices in Belfast.* London and New York: Macmillan and St. Martin's Press.

Prior, L. (1993). *The social organization of mental illness.* London: Sage.

Prior, L. (2003). *Using documents in social research.* London: Sage.

Wood, F., Prior., L., & Gray, J. (2003). Making decisions in a cancer genetics clinic. *Health Risk and Society, 5*(2), 185–198.

● VISUAL RESEARCH: PHOTOGRAPHS, IMAGES, AND INTERACTIVE VISUAL RESEARCH

Qualitative researchers can use visual representations as the starting point of social scientific inquiry. We have already discussed the use of media images, such as magazine covers or advertisements, but the media is merely one source of visual imagery. In addition to media-produced images, researchers can study photographs. Broken down further, the researcher can use pre-existing photographs or photographs constructed for the purpose of research (taken by the researcher herself or someone hired by the researcher). In this section we will discuss these varied forms of visual research and how a researcher must conceptualize images in relation to their epistemological framework in order to holistically construct a cohesive research project.

When working with photographs and other visual images you must consider how you, broadly speaking, conceptualize the images you are working with. Prosser and Schwartz (1998) explain that photographs can be conceptualized in two different ways: (1) as "visual records" and (2) as "visual diaries." This distinction is important and is intimately linked to your epistemological position. If you choose to conceive of photographs as visual records then you imbue them with a sense of authority. It is like the saying "a picture is worth a thousand words." In other words, a "record" is a representation of some aspect of social reality—it is an aspect of social reality that has been captured. If you decide to conceptualize photographs as visual diaries then you are implying that photography is a medium which is utilized by embodied actors who *take* the pictures and *view* them from particular perspectives. Under this conceptualization, the researcher uses photographs much like memo notes which are marked by the researcher's position within the project. This is a way of infusing reflexivity into the research process.

Neither of these approaches is necessarily right or even better, but again will be influenced by epistemological and theoretical commitments. For example, a researcher working from a postpositivist frame who is studying images of the terrorist attacks of September 11th might conceive of photographs as visual records for the sake of that particular research project. In doing so, he or she is able to conceptualize the photographs as material records of one of the darkest days in world history. The photographs can be used as "memory enhancers" under this frame (Hesse-Biber & Leavy, 2004, p. 312). Typically, researchers working from critical perspectives such as feminism and postmodernism are more likely to view photographs as visual diaries influenced by their point of production and the context of viewing. For example, a postmodern researcher interested in studying how meanings about

September 11th were constructed in American newspapers might conceive of newspaper images as visual diaries. In this situation, the researcher would examine the social power embedded in the photos, the connotations created through the placement of photos both on each page and in the newspaper as a whole, and the standpoint of the researcher him-/herself viewing the photos. By situating the images in these ways, the researcher can begin to disentangle how ideas about September 11th were constructed, disseminated, and consumed in ways that created a baseline collective memory of the event.

Instead of using preexisting photographs, researchers can also adopt the role of photographer and take photographs that will then serve as data. Researchers interested in studying social change might act as photographers in order to document and then interpret varied forms of social change. This could be done, for example, to study changes surrounding the urbanization of a particular area or to study how social and economic change impacts a residential environment, community center, or, work site.

> If you are interested in exploring or revealing the precise nature of change, then photographs taken at regular intervals from exactly the same place can be revelatory. Changes in urban neighbourhoods, landscapes or the contents of a room; the condition of a tree, a wall or human body "before" and "after" a significant change; all these, when properly attested and witnessed, and logged for time, place and circumstance, can have powerful evidential or persuasive value. (Loizos, 2000, p. 96)

Likewise, historical research can be conducted by combining preexisting photographs with those taken by the researcher in order to document and analyze change.

Reflexivity becomes critical when using a traditionally unobtrusive method in this way. First, this is one of the rare instances in which the research is not unobtrusive but is *interactive.* The researcher impacts social reality by being present and taking photographs. In addition to changing that aspect of visual research from noninteractive to interactive, the data is produced directly from the vantage point of the researcher. Consider Paul Byer's (1964) assertion that "cameras don't take pictures [people do]." This is always true, however, when the researcher is the one taking the photos. The practice of reflexivity, examining and disclosing one's position within the process, becomes critical. Let's return to the example of studying 9–11 photo images. Let's say that you wanted to study the 9–11 recovery process immediately following the event and/or the search for survivors. One way to do this would be to go to Ground Zero and the Pentagon site and take photographs, which then serve as your data. You may even conceive of your photographs as visual field notes. There are other methods of using content analysis in interactive ways, such as computer-driven content analysis, which we will discuss in a later section of this chapter. For now, let's return to studying preexisting visual images.

Researchers can also combine qualitative and quantitative approaches to visual analysis in order to explore social issues such as inequality in representation. This can be done by applying a range of theoretical perspectives and creating the opportunity for many methodological approaches. Pedersen (2002) was interested in newspaper photographic coverage of female and male high school athletics. Conceptualizing the mass media and sports as two of the "most prominent and hegemonic social institutions" (p. 304), Pederson wanted to compare male and female sports coverage in order to examine to what degree hegemonic masculinity is projected in newspaper sports coverage. Pederson studied 827 photographs taken from 602 randomly selected newspapers and examined the amount and type of photographs given to cover male and female athletics. This study employed a descriptive analysis of the photos in order to ascertain information, such as whether the photos were still or action shots, which is very important in the study of gender and media representation. Ultimately Pederson found that there is inequity in sports coverage across gender lines and argues that photographic coverage reaffirms hegemonic masculinity. Using unobtrusive methods allowed Pederson to ask and answer a social scientific question regarding social inequality that would otherwise be inaccessible.

This is a clear example of how mass media images can be used as the starting point for research. But once you decide what you want to study and what data you will use, research design becomes critical to the practice of visual studies. The primary issue regarding research design centers on analysis. Let's say you have decided to study mass-mediated images of female beauty and you have selected a sample of fashion magazines. What will be the unit of analysis? Typically, individual images or ads would serve as your unit of analysis. But how do you code this data? There are many strategies qualitative researchers can employ for coding visual data. As we saw in the Pederson example, codes such as "still" and "action shot" can be employed. Likewise, researchers can code for gender, race, and other social attributes. This process can occur from a grounded theory approach where code categories emerge from analysis or, alternatively, preconceived code categories can be employed.

The following is an exercise aimed at familiarizing you with the process of conducting visual content analysis, although it can also be modified for audiovisual analysis. This exercise can be adapted to suit particular skill sets or can be adapted as a part of exploratory or preliminary research protocol.

————————))))————————

Exercise on Coding Advertisements

We suggest that you work in pairs in order to add a dimension of reliability to the research process. In pairs, code 10 advertisements (any number of sampling strategies can be employed). Both scholars should agree on the primary figure(s) in the advertisement and then independently code the following characteristics: sex of the primary figure, basis for credibility, setting, category of product, and the arguments given on behalf of the product. Below are details of the coding categories which are adapted from McArthur and Resko (1975). This exercise can be adapted and conducted in groups or by individuals.

Primary Figure: Primary figures are the individuals who play a major role in the advertisement, as denoted by prominent visual exposure. If there are more than two adults present, choose those that appear central (where the looker's eye is drawn). If it unclear which two figures are most central, you can pick primary figures of each sex or racial group represented. If there are only two adult figures present, both should be coded.

Basis for Credibility: When determining who the primary figure is you must consider how to justify your decision. The basis for credibility of the primary figure usually falls under three main categories: (1) product user, (2) authority, and (3) other. The primary figure is a product user when he or she is depicted as the primary user of the product or service being advertised. The primary figure is an authority when he or she is depicted as having the information about the product being advertised. The primary figure is other if he or she is being persuaded by another central figure to use the product, that is, if the primary figure is represented as a potential consumer.

Role: Primary figures should be coded according to the major roles in which they are shown, such as teacher, worker, parent, spouse, child, and so forth.

Setting: Primary figures should be coded according to their location, such as home, work, store, outdoors, vacation setting, school, concert, etc.

Type of Product: The category the product best fits into should be coded (such as beauty products, food products, home products, automotive products, technology-based products, etc.).

Persuasion Arguments (some may be more relevant to audiovisual advertisements, so adapt accordingly): The argument made on behalf of the product should be coded. The argument made may be based on factual or scientific evidence aimed at encouraging consumers to use the product for its "proven" benefits or superiority. The argument may also be based on opinions consisting of personal testimonies that encourage consumers to use the product. In some cases there aren't any arguments on behalf of the product and the advertisement doesn't make any truth claims about the quality of the product. In this case the primary figure is simply displaying the product or creating an atmosphere around the product.

In lieu of the above more in-depth exercise, try analyzing the following magazine ads taken from an array of magazines aimed at different demographics. Try analyzing them using the exercise above. Then try analyzing them from different theoretical perspectives. Try a deconstructionist approach. Then read the texts from a semiological

Figure 8.3

perspective—what connotations are created in the representation by implanting distilled concepts (such as beauty) in the signs? How would a feminist interpret these ads? By applying different "lenses" to these ads, do you *read* them differently?

————————))) ————————

Figure 8.4

Figure 8.5

● AUDIOVISUAL ANALYSIS: WORKING WITH "MULTIPLE FIELDS"

Many scholars across the disciplines use audiovisual material as their data. If a researcher is interested in studying cinema or television they can content analyze audiovisual footage. Though it can be researched as another narrative form, audiovisual data is unique and thus requires a particular set of considerations. What makes audiovisual data distinct from the kinds of texts we have been discussing is that it has *multiple components*, including visual, sound, and dialogue. Rose (2000) refers to audiovisual material as a "multiple field," because of its distinct but interrelated components. Furthermore, the data is *moving*.

During research design with audiovisual data certain considerations arise. Sampling issues are relatively consistent when performing content analysis with any kind of material. What to sample, how much to sample, and the extent to which sampling is randomized are all things to consider. For example, let's say we are interested in studying television news coverage of the terrorist attacks of September 11th. We have to decide which networks we will sample from. Then we must decide what to sample. We could use all coverage in a certain time frame, such as 2 weeks. Or, we could use coverage between certain hours of the day for a selected number of days. We could also select certain news programs, and they would be our data. Beyond sampling issues, we would have to decide what the unit of analysis is and what the coding procedure will be. The coding process is one of the most important decisions when working with moving data.

As discussed in Chapters 1 and 2, as a part of research design researchers create a research question, which is linked to their research purpose. In the case of audiovisual content analysis, researchers also construct a definition of the kind of representation they are looking for. After creating an operational definition, researchers must determine the unit of analysis and coding scheme, all of which is complicated by the multidimensional nature of audiovisual data. Let's look at an example.

Ramasubramanian and Oliver (2003) wanted to study the portrayal of sexual violence in Hindi films. They chose this topic because rates of male sexual violence against women are higher in male-dominated countries, including India. The public sexual harassment of women, referred to as "eve-teasing," is prevalent in urban India. A literature review also revealed two important factors: (1) there is a relationship between media sexual violence and real-world aggression and "rape myths," which culturally legitimate the sexual violation of women, and (2) prior research on Hindi films showed that violence and sexuality were often intertwined, and sexual violence was normalized and even portrayed as "expected" in romantic relationships. So, Ramasubramanian and Oliver decided to analyze the content of Hindi films regarding violence and sexuality and thus analyzed the films' portrayals of sexuality. They first developed a definition of the kind of representation they were looking for. Films were watched in their entirety for the presence of sexual scenes. They defined a sexual scene as "one in which two or more characters were involved in activities such as having sex, kissing, petting, initiating or suggesting sexual contact, displaying nudity, engaging in sexual talk, bathing in an erotic way, wearing provocative or revealing clothing, or shown as a sexual object of gaze" (2003, p. 330).

After constructing an operational definition of the kind of scene they were looking for, the next step was to determine the unit of analysis. Their units of analysis were characters and scenes. Characters who spoke and were present in sexual scenes were coded. The coding method here was to code for gender and type of character role. Then, characteristics of the characters were coded only after the film was viewed in its entirety. A scene was defined as a "continuous action in one place such as a single situation or a unit of dialogue in the film" (2003, p. 330). Sexual scenes were further broken down into (1) mutually consenting scenes and (2) sexually violent scenes. The coding method of scenes consisted of a list of variables considered relevant to the topic. These codes included: gender, character role, presence of sexual violence, severity of sexual violence (moderate to severe including harassment to rape), primary perpetrators/victims, and fun/seriousness of scene. Their findings show that a significant number of sexual scenes in Hindi films consist of sexual violence regardless of the audience the film is aimed at (including those rated for children less than 12 years old). Additionally, females are almost exclusively the victims of male violence. Most disturbing, the way in which the sexual violence is portrayed normalizes it. It is not just "bad guys" who commit sexual violence but also those who are portrayed as hero figures. Sexual violence is shown as a marker of masculinity.

While we have reviewed how this particular project created a definition of the kinds of representations under investigation and then determined the unit of analysis and constructed a coding scheme, there are other ways to determine the unit of analysis and coding strategy.

While the method of using scene change is common among film and television program analyzers, the change of camera shot is another option. Additionally, one could demarcate units based on a time-fragmented system. This might be appropriate in our example of studying 9–11 news coverage. The unit of analysis could be every 5 minutes of coverage for example. The specific kind of audiovisual data being used (i.e. films, news, etc.) in conjunction with the research goals help determine an appropriate unit of analysis.

In terms of coding, several strategies can be employed depending on the degree to which the study will be deductive or inductive. It is helpful to thing of inductive and deductive approaches as existing on a continuum rather than as an either/or decision. Coding categories, such as those used in the study of Hindi films, can be constructed prior to data analysis. In this deductive approach, the researcher already has a set of codes that he or she is looking for. When this kind of strategy is used, it is helpful to have other scholars participate in the construction of the code list. Additionally, validity and reliability can be enhanced by having multiple coders examine the same data, which is what occurred in the study of Hindi films, where two coders coded the data set and verbally discussed discrepancies until there was a consensus. If you employ a preset code list, we suggest adding a category such as "other" or "miscellaneous" in the event that there is additional pertinent information in the data that you hadn't considered before data analysis. The usefulness of this extra code is dependent on the research goals. This includes the extent to which you want to be able to replicate the study and achieve generalizability. Researchers can also blend deductive and inductive strategies. For example, a researcher can determine some codes in advance of analysis and then, as analysis is underway, the codes can be modified. This might include the removal of codes no longer deemed appropriate, the renaming of codes based on the language of the data under investigation, and the adding of codes to categorize information not previously known to be there, or any combination of the aforementioned.

On the inductive side of the continuum researchers can create code categories as they analyze and interpret the data. This can be done using a grounded theory approach or the similar spiral model of diving in and out of the data that we have explained. In this instance, the code categories develop directly out of the data. So, the researcher analyzes a portion of the data and constructs code categories based on what was in the data, often using the language of the text itself as code categories. With some categories in place, the researcher goes back through the data, and another portion of the data, to see if the code categories "hold up," and adds more as the data warrant. The researcher may begin with very specific literal codes and through the process develop large code categories, or "meta-codes," under which the subcodes will be placed. Conversely, but perhaps less frequently, you could begin with broad-based meta-code categories, and as you cycle back through the data, code categories could be refined and new, more specific categories added.

The strategy of coding, particularly with the complexity of working with a multiple field, will be dependent on the research goals and theoretical framing of the topic. The methodological and epistemological components of the project should fit as tightly together as possible.

There is one final issue that must be considered during the coding, analysis, interpretation, and representation phases: *translation*. All qualitative research produces an abundance of data, such as the thick descriptions common in ethnography and the hundreds or thousands of pages of transcripts produced in the various methods of interview. These data then go through a process of reduction whereby large amounts of data are reduced so that the data can tell a story or explain some aspect of social life. Audiovisual content analysis also requires a process of reduction. For example, the researcher doesn't actually reproduce all of the television shows or films studied in their entirety—one wouldn't need research to simply present this material as it already is. The key difference between reducing audiovisual data and other forms of qualitative data is that an additional process of *translation* occurs as we move from one medium to another (Rose, 2000). In the other examples discussed, the original data are in textual form; so is the resulting knowledge. In the case of audiovisual data we are moving from moving pictures, sound, and words to words alone. So in addition to reducing or simplifying the large amounts of data studied, we are also translating it, as if into another language. Researchers should be cognizant of this at they consider how to best interpret and represent their data. This is another reason why disclosing coding strategies is so important.

● COMPUTER-DRIVEN CONTENT ANALYSIS: IS IT UNOBTRUSIVE AND HOW CAN IT BE PERFORMED ETHICALLY?

A recent development in content analysis has been the use of computer-driven data. Similar to audiovisual data, this kind of data may appear in the form of a multiple field (though this is not always the case). Computer-driven data is very unique and raises its own set of issues as it simultaneously pushes the practice of qualitative research in new directions while raising long-standing questions about ethics.

First, computer-driven content analysis can be unobtrusive, but it isn't necessarily unobtrusive. And even when the practice is not obtrusive, particular ethical concerns not present with other forms of text analysis may arise. Frequently, computer-directed data is data obtained from Internet websites, message boards, and chat rooms. Let's look at websites and message boards first.

Websites and message boards (where people can post messages available to anyone who enters the site) are two forms of computer-driven data. Websites may be multiple fields containing graphics and words and should be coded accordingly. Message boards are typically text-based. If we are interested in going to a message board to study people's responses to the Martha Stewart verdict and sentencing we can simply go to a site and print its content. This textual data can then be analyzed using the variety of perspectives discussed in this book. This kind of research is unobtrusive and the information placed on website message boards is placed there freely by people who know that it can be looked at and used by anyone who wishes too. Let's look at an example of using this kind of data.

Harmon and Boeringer (1997) were interested in exploring sexual content on the Internet. Web-based forms of pornography are relatively new, and so they decided to conduct content analysis as a means of conducting exploratory research. After a preliminary review of Internet websites, they decided to collect 200 "postings" from a website with explicit sexual content. Postings refer to information (comments and so forth) placed on the site. They decided four postings were "unusable," and so they ended up with a sample of 196 postings collected over a 2-week period. Using a line-by-line method of analysis with codes developed directly out of the text, they assigned each line of text a code such as "pedophilia" and other "fetishes." When they completed the coding process they were stunned by the presence of "nonconsensual" expressions, which dominated the postings. The research process and findings were so troubling that one of the researchers sought a professional "debriefing" from a university counselor—showing that researchers using content analysis are susceptible to some of the emotional challenges field researchers and other qualitative researchers face. For example, a content analyst studying representations of tragic events such as September 11th may experience emotional and psychological difficulties traditionally attributed to the practice of interactive methods such as ethnography. Researchers should bear this in mind as they select research topics.

The Harmon and Boeringer study is an excellent example of using qualitative content analysis as a method of developing data in a new field. The computerized form of the data is actually a part of what is being studied. This is a method of using computer-driven data in a way that is congruent with the principles of unobtrusive research. However, there are other forms of computer-driven data that blur these lines, raising a host of new ethical considerations.

Qualitative researchers can study ongoing interaction using chat rooms as the location of social data. What is interesting about chat room data is that even though it is "dialogue" to the extent that multiple people are typing in their responses in a fluid manner, it is not the same as face-to-face talk. People write differently (including more slowly) than they normally speak. Likewise, the people in the chat room cannot see each other and have a new kind of technologically created anonymity. Typically, you really don't know who you are speaking to in a chat room (from their gender to their age, etc.). Researchers who use chat room discussion as data can do so in two ways: as an observer or as a participant (much like in ethnography). Let's look at the former first.

A researcher can observe chat room discussions and perform discourse analysis (Mann & Stewart, 2000). The chat room data appear as line-by-line text, although the data occur in the form of mediated conversation. In this kind of research, the researchers assumes the role of "voyeur" to interaction (Mann & Stewart, 2000). The researcher can conceal his or her presence and the dialogue would be occurring regardless of the research, thus maintaining the principles of unobtrusive research. However, this kind of voyeuristic research does raise ethical issues. What are the implications of sitting in on a conversation for the purpose of research? Is it fair to the people participating in the chat room discussion for a researcher to use that information without obtaining informed consent? Is it possible to obtain informed consent in a chat room situation when people enter and exit the chat room routinely? Likewise, since chat room participants can assume false identities, how does a researcher know whether or not there are minors present? These are some of the issues one must consider when thinking about this kind of research.

Researchers can also choose to disclose their identities and, thus, to some extent participate in the chat room discussion. On the flip side, researchers can participate in the chat room discussion, and this becomes a part of the text they use as data, without disclosing their identity. In this instance the research is no longer unobtrusive, as the researcher directly impacts the development of the data. This raises considerations regarding ethics, confidentiality, disclosure, and researcher/effect, all which must be carefully considered.

As Web-based technology increases, computer-driven data in even more forms will likely emerge. The extent to which newer data can be studied unobtrusively and ethically is something that remains to be seen. With that said, following the basic principles of ethical research, as discussed in Chapter 2, will help qualitative researchers forge through these new terrains, asking and answering a host of social scientific questions.

● CONCLUSION

We hope this chapter has introduced you to some of the many ways that qualitative researchers can investigate texts as the starting point of research or as a part of a multimethod design. The primary advantage of working with non-living data is that it allows us to go beyond the subject perceptions of individuals, which, while very important, are not the only point of departure for knowledge building. By interrogating texts from a variety of epistemological and theoretical positions social scientists continue to ask new research questions and offer new insights about social reality.

● GLOSSARY

Content Analysis: Systematically analyzing texts.

Interactive Research: When the researcher impacts social reality by being present (e.g., by taking pictures), and thus the data are produced directly from the vantage point of the researcher.

Linear Model: A method of research design in which the researcher has a preconceived set of steps which follows a vertical path through each phase of the research process.

Memo Writing: Used by a researcher engaged in the spiral model of research design as a way of interpreting and reflecting on the data as they go.

Spiral Model: A method of research design that allows the investigator to, metaphorically, dive in and out of the data as she or he proceeds. In this model a researcher generates new understandings, with varied levels of specificity, during each phase of the project and uses this information to double back and gain more information.

Translation: This is the process where large amounts of textual data are reduced into codes. In the case of visual or audiovisual analysis, translation refers to the process of putting data in one medium (visual or moving images) into words, as if translating the data from one language into another.

DISCUSSION QUESTIONS ●

1. How has the growth in cultural studies and postmodernism impacted the use of content analysis? What are the congruencies between these theoretical traditions and this particular method, particularly in terms of the nature of knowledge and its construction?

2. What is unique about working with nonliving data? How does this impact the research questions and resulting knowledge?

3. What does it mean to say that content analysis is a "hybrid technique"? How can qualitative and quantitative approaches to content analysis be combined? What benefits does this have?

4. Explain the difference between linear (quantitative) and spiral (qualitative) approaches to content analysis.

5. What are the specific issues that arise when using visual and audiovisual data? Explain the process of "translation" that occurs. What are different strategies for dealing with this kind of data?

6. Discuss emergent practices in unobtrusive methods. What ethical issues are raised by these new approaches?

● SUGGESTED WEBSITES

Cultural Studies Central

http://www.culturalstudies.net/

This website allows for interactive learning. You can participate in online discussions. This site offers links to cultural Web projects as well as other related links. We think this website provides a lot of options to the viewer.

Cultural Studies Study Group

http://members.tripod.com/~warlight/

This website appears to be privately owned but offers discussions, articles, and links to various types of culture studies, including youth, media, and popular culture.

The Critical and Cultural Studies Division of NCA

http://www.vcsun.org/CCS/

This website appears to be appropriate and useful for people looking for information on cultural studies. This organization publishes newsletters and holds conventions and conferences related to the field. The site includes related links.

Cognitive Cultural Studies

http://cogweb.ucla.edu/

This website is from UCLA and offers the viewer conference dates, forums, and papers related to the field. It also has an extended bibliography, including links to more information.

REFERENCES ●

Barthes, R. (1998). Myth today. In S. Sontag (Ed.), *A Barthes reader* (pp. 93–149). New York: Hill and Wang.

Bauer, M. (2000). Classical content analysis: A review. In M. Bauer & G. Gaskell (Eds.), *Qualitative researching with text, image and sound* (pp. 131–151). London: Sage.

Byers, P. (1964). Still photography in the systematic recording and analysis of behavioural data. *Human Organization, 23,* 78–84.

Derrida, J. (1966). The decentering event and social thought. In A. Bass (Trans.), *Writing the difference* (pp. 278–282). Chicago: University of Chicago Press.

Foucault, M. (1978). *The history of sexuality: An introduction, volume 1.* New York: Vintage Books.

Gooden, A. M., & Gooden, M. A. (2001). Gender representation in notable children's picture books: 1995–1999. *Sex Roles: A Journal of Research, 13,* 89.

Hall, S. (1981). Notes on deconstructing "the Popular." In J. Storey (Ed.), *Cultural studies & the study of popular culture.* Athens: University of Georgia Press.

Harmon, D., & Boeringer, S. B. (1997). A content analysis of Internet-accessible written pornographic depictions. *Electronic Journal of Sociology, 3*(1). Retrieved from http://www.sociology.org/content/v01003,001/boeringer.html

Hesse-Biber, S., & Leavy, P. (2004). (Eds.). *Approaches to qualitative research: A reader on theory and practice.* New York: Oxford University Press.

Iedema, R. (2001). Analysing film and television: A social semiotic account of *Hospital: An Unhealthy Business.* In T. van Leeuwen & C. Jewitt (Eds.), *Handbook of visual analysis* (pp. 183–204). London: Sage.

Irigaray, L. (1985). The power of discourse and the subordination of the feminine. In C. Porter & C. Burke (Trans.), *This sex which is not one* (pp. 68–85). Ithaca, NY: Cornell University Press.

Jameson, F. (1984). Postmodernism, or, the cultural logic of late capitalism. *New Left Review, 146,* 59–92.

Lauzen, M. M., & Dozier, D. M. (2002). You look mahvelous: An examination of gender and appearance comments in the 1999–2000 prime-time season. *Sex Roles: A Journal of Research, 9,* 429–438.

Loizos, P. (2000). Video, film and photographs as research documents. In M. W. Bauer & G. Gaskell (Eds.), *Qualitative researching with text, image, and sound* (pp. 93–107). London: Sage.

Malkin, A. R., Wornian, K., & Chrisler, J. C. (1999). Women and weight: Gendered messages on magazine covers. *Sex Roles: A Journal of Research, 40*(7–8), 647–656.

Mann, C., & Stewart, F. (2000). Chapter 4: Introducing online methods. In *Internet communication and qualitative research: A handbook for researching online* (pp. 65–98). London: Sage.

McArthur, L. Z., & Resko, B. G. (1975). The portrayal of men and women in American television commercials. *The Journal of Social Psychology, 97,* 209–220.

Merskin, D. (1999). Adolescence, advertising, and the ideology of menstruation. *Sex Roles: A Journal of Research, 40*(11), 941–957.

Pedersen, P. M. (2002). Examining equity in newspaper photographs. *International Review for the Sociology of Sport, 37*(3–4), 303–318.

Prior, L. (2004). Following in Foucault's footsteps: Text and context in qualitative research. In S. Hesse-Biber & P. Leavy (Eds.), *Approaches to qualitative research: A reader on theory and practice* (pp. 317–333). New York: Oxford University Press.

Prior, L. (1997). Following in Foucault's footsteps: Text and context in qualitative research. In D. Silverman (Ed.), *Qualitative research: Theory, method and practice* (pp. 63–79).

Prosser, J., & Schwartz, D. (1998). Photographs within the sociological research process. In J. Prosser (Ed.), *Image-based research: A sourcebook for qualitative researchers* (pp. 115–130). London: Falmer Press.

Ramasubramanian, S., & Oliver, M. B. (2003). Portrayals of sexual violence in popular Hindi films, 1997–99. *Sex Roles: A Journal of Research, 10,* 327–336.

Reinharz, S. (1992). *Feminist methods in social research.* New York: Oxford University Press.

Rose, D. (2000). Analysis of moving images. In M. W. Bauer & G. Gaskell (Eds.), *Qualitative researching with text, image and sound* (pp. 246–262). London: Sage.

Taylor, C. (1987). Interpretation and the sciences of man. In P. Rabinow & M. W. Sullivan (Eds.), *Interpretive social sciences. A second look* (pp. 33–81). London: University of California Press.

Thomas, M. E., & Treiber, L. A. (2000). Race, gender, and status: A content analysis of print advertisements in four popular magazines. *Sociological Spectrum, 20,* 357–371.

Wysocki, D. S., & Harrison, R. (1991). AIDS and the media: A look at how periodicals influence children and teenagers in their knowledge of AIDS. *Health Education Journal, 22,* 20–23.

CHAPTER 9

MIXED METHODS RESEARCH

The following excerpt is an account from a BBC news reporter on the efforts of one Thai village to rebuild their community in the aftermath of one of the worst natural disasters to strike South Asia.

At first glance, the small island community of Khlang Prasang might count itself lucky.

Like much of Thailand's west coast it was hit by the devastating Asian tsunami, yet no one in the 400-strong community died.

But the tsunami changed the lives of far more people than those now mourning loved ones. Away from the famous resorts and tourist beaches, hundreds of small communities like Khlang Prasang now face a long, difficult challenge to rebuild.

Before the disaster, the people of Khlang Prasang had two sources of income—fishing and tourism.

Now they are struggling to make money from either.

"We're afraid we're going to get forgotten, and all the aid is going to go to Phi Phi island and other areas where the destruction is greater," said Donjit Hafah. . . .

Two weeks on from the tsunami, the people of Khlang Prasang are still suffering from the trauma of their experience.

"I still can't sleep. I keep thinking another tsunami is going to come. The waves and the tides are still not normal and I'm very scared," said Samari Koonlong.

> "Last night I was just sitting watching the waves," Maad Oonbutr said. "I thought about the children who ran towards the sea when the tsunami came, and how near they were to drowning. . . ." (McGowan, 2005)

A massive tsunami struck South Asia on December 26th, 2004. It was one of the largest natural disasters in recorded history. In its wake, private and public relief efforts were launched from all parts of the globe to aid the survivors and to help rebuild much needed infrastructures. Newspaper reports warn of the severe psychological posttrauma among the survivors. One CNN report warns of posttraumatic effects from the tsunami, especially on its young survivors.

> "The psychological effects are immense," explains Dr. Michael Wasserman, a pediatrician with the Ochsner Clinic Foundation in New Orleans, Louisiana. "Children understand sameness. And for reasons out of everybody's control you've yanked that away. You've devastated their world." (CNN, 2005)

It is unclear how survivors are coping with the aftermath of this devastating event. While media reports give anecdotal information, much more is needed to assist with relief efforts. Social scientists can provide funding and relief agencies with a fuller understanding of the economic and personal scope of this tragedy at the village and national level, as well as ascertaining the lived experiences of those whose lives have been dramatically impacted by the disaster. The following research questions will provide some important data toward that effort.

- How many people died as a direct result of this disaster? What villages were affected? What is the extent of property damage? Who are the survivors (in terms of their demographics, such as age, sex, class, etc.)?
- How are survivors managing their lives on a day-to-day basis? What are their lived experiences? What are their specific needs and concerns?

● MIXED-METHODS RESEARCH

A mixed-methods research approach might be a good starting point for beginning our inquiry. Mixed methods is a research design for data collection and/or analysis. The term usually refers to the use of *both* qualitative and quantitative methods in *one* study or *sequentially* in two or more studies.

An important logic behind the application of this design is that "the whole is greater than the sum of its parts" (Greene & Caracelli, 1997b, p. 13). Greene and Caracelli (1997b) note that having a "conversation" between different methods and the paradigms that they represent promotes "more comprehensive, insightful and logical results than either paradigm [interpretivist or postpositivist] could obtain alone" (p. 10; see also Greene, Benjamin, & Goodyear, 2001). Tashakkori and Teddlie's new *Handbook of Mixed-Methods* refers to mixed methods research designs as the "third methodological movement" (2003, p. x). It requires that the researcher, who is usually trained in only one method or who has more experience in one method over the other, to reach out across their methods comfort zone, to think outside their normal everyday methods routines. In this sense, the practice of mixing methods may even upend the researcher's ongoing philosophical, methodological, and methods practices.

The combination of two different methods can create a *synergistic* research project whereby one method enables the other to be more effective, and, together both methods provide a fuller understanding of the research problem (Greene & Caracelli, 1997a; see Sieber, 1973, for an early example of the synergy in mixing the methods of "fieldwork" and "survey research"). Mixed methods designs can also help to get at "subjugated knowledge" and give voice to those whose viewpoints may be left out of the research process with the goal of presenting "a plurality of interests, voices and perspectives" (Greene & Caracelli, 1997b, p. 14). Combining methods can often assist the researcher in tackling highly complex problems that involve several layers of understanding that may also require different levels of analytical techniques.

The selection of a particular research method is tightly linked to the research problem. Some methods are more effective in getting at certain types of questions and specific dimensions of a research question. *Qualitative methods* are useful at getting at the "lived experiences" of the individual, by asking such questions as: "To what extent is psychological trauma experienced longterm by tsunami survivors?" Qualitative collection methods require an analytical design that often deals with the analysis of textual data for meaning and are NOT particularly useful for getting at the "overall picture." Quantitative methods, such as surveys, answer questions such as: "How many?" and "How often?" Quantitative methods allow the researcher to test hypotheses and draw out generalizations from the data. As we will discuss later, the use of a mixed method is also subject to some "practical constraints" (Brannen, 1992, p. 17) dealing with the cost of doing this research, the training of the researcher, as well as the type of funding available for doing this type of research design.

In deciding on our research design for our tsunami study, we would begin with our specific research question(s): "How many people died as a direct result of this disaster? What villages were affected? What is the extent of the damage? Who are the survivors (in terms of their demographics (age, sex, class, etc.)?" This set of questions is asking for some numerical data—"How many?" "How widespread?" A quantitative method such as a *demographic survey* of the social and economic aspects of the population as well as a comparison of these demographic figures with the latest national and regional census and population data will provide a context within which to assess the extent of the devastation at the village and national level. This method provides the researcher with an "overall picture" within which to place survivors' lived experiences. The next set of questions asks: "How are people within affected areas managing their lives on a day to day basis?" "What is their lived experience?" In order to address this set of questions, you might begin with an *exploratory study* of a sample of villages affected by the disaster. These questions are getting at issues of *interpretation*. You will want to listen to the narratives of those who have experienced the disaster firsthand—their attitudes, feelings, and concerns. You might consider a range of interpretative methods such as intensive interviews, or focus groups, as well as participant observations gathered from a cross-section of individuals from key villages destroyed by the tsunami. These data collection techniques allow for a fuller understanding of the effect of the disaster on individuals' lives, including the extent to which people are able to cope with loss of relatives and friends as well as the economic loss and destruction of their property and livelihood. This type of method allows the researcher to listen in-depth to the specific needs and concerns of survivors and capture nuances in their stories of survival and their issues and concerns, both short term and long term. In essence, we are employing a mixed-methods design by gathering both qualitative and quantitative data to answer our research questions. Let's look more in-depth about why and how we should proceed with this type of design.

- Why use mixed-methods design?

Greene, Caracelli, and Graham (1989) discuss five specific reasons why researchers might want to utilize a mixed-methods approach. The first and perhaps most common reason is *triangulation*. This strategy involves using more than one method to study the same research question. The researcher is looking for a "convergence" of research findings to enhance the credibility of the research findings. As an aside, it is important to note that while we are using the term triangulation in this context to mean using *different methods* (methods triangulation), it has also come to mean using different theoretical perspectives (theoretical triangulation), as well as different data sources using the same method as well as different methods (data triangulation; see Denzin, 1978). In the case of the tsunami project, we might opt to administer a "paper-and-pencil" quantitative psychological test in order to ascertain the well-being of those we interview, together with conducting a more extensive in-depth interview. The psychological, more quantitative, scales would serve as a validity check on the in-depth psychological findings gathered from our intensive interviews. A second reason for employing a mixed-methods design is that of *complementarity*, whereby the researcher seeks to gain a fuller understanding of the research problem and/or to clarify a given research result. Mixed methods are employed in the service of *assisting* the researcher's total understanding of the research problem. An example of this might be when a researcher uses a qualitative study of the tsunami disaster to ascertain the lived experiences and in-depth feelings of disaster survivors, while the quantitative component involves utilizing a survey research study to assess how villagers impacted by the event perceive the effectiveness of relief efforts and their overall attitudes and values regarding social policies undertaken to help with reconstruction of their villages. A third factor is that of *"development,"* whereby "results from one method help develop or inform the other method" (Greene et al., 1989, p. 259). In the tsunami example study, the researcher will be able to use the findings from the exploratory qualitative study to develop a survey questionnaire for the quantitative study. Another reason cited for using mixed methods is that of *"initiation,"* whereby a given research study's findings raise questions or contain contradictions that require clarification. A new study is then initiated to add new insights to the understanding of the phenomenon under investigation (Greene et al., 1989, p. 260). In the case of the tsunami disaster study example, it may turn out that there are contradictory qualitative findings concerning how men and women view natural disasters, and attitudes towards coping post-disaster may differ by gender and national origin. Such divergent findings may lead in fact to a more nuanced interpretation of research results by gender and nationality. In fact, such findings may serve to launch a whole new investigation, which leads us to a fifth reason for doing mixed methods research, *"expansion."* Expansion is initiated to "extend the breadth and range of the study" (Greene et al., 1989, p. 259). The researcher may want to compare gender differences in coping across different types of disasters. So, for example, a researcher might decide to expand the study to include interviews with survivors of the 9/11 terrorist attack, with the intent of examining similarities and differences in coping mechanisms by gender and nationality and type of disaster. Here the goal is not to increase the validity of one's study but to broaden the study to encompass a broader range of purposes.

● PARADIGM WARS?

Research questions are rooted in both a qualitative and quantitative understanding of the nature of the social world (Lincoln & Guba, 2000). The mixing of methods also involves the *mixing of philosophical paradigms*. A paradigm is a way of knowing; it is our window into the social world. A mixed-methods design mixes qualitative and quantitative philosophical assumptions, especially as these pertain to issues concerning the nature of the individual and society and the problem of "objectivity versus subjectivity." A researcher's philosophical position often impacts their decisions *concerning how to use a mixed method, if and when to use it, and for what reasons.* Quantitative methods are often rooted in a positivistic paradigm that makes certain assumptions regarding the nature of the social world—that there is a singular social reality "out there" waiting to be found out by having the researcher remain objective, not allowing feelings, values, and attitudes to enter into the research process (see Tashakkori & Teddlie, 1998, for a fuller discussion of these issues). A qualitative method draws up an interpretive paradigm where there are multiple truths regarding the social world—knowledge gathering is always partial, and the researcher is encouraged to be on the same plane as the researched in an effort to promote a co-construction of meaning. A die-hard positivist/postpositivist might find it difficult to mix methods that involve crossing over into a qualitative research approach.

Those researchers who find it difficult or impossible to cross these philosophical and methods boundaries are known as "purists" who see these two methods as independent and unmixable philosophically. Those known as "pragmatists" often embrace a mixed-methods design if it will enhance their understanding of their research problem with little regard for the philosophical underpinnings of either research perspective. Tashakkori and Teddlie (1998) note that pragmatists:

> . . . consider the research question to be more important than either the method or the worldview that is supposed to underlie the method. Most good researchers prefer addressing their research questions with any methodological tool available, using the pragmatist credo of "what works." (p. 21)

There is often a tendency to depict these differences in terms of "paradigm wars" (see Tashakkori & Teddlie, 1998, 2003), yet many researchers find themselves straddling these two poles, not seeing these positions as a dichotomy but as lying along a "purist/pragmatic" continuum with areas of compatibility between the two perspectives. Guba (1985) noted early on the incompatibility of these two paradigms. He notes: ". . . we are dealing with an either-or proposition, in which one must pledge allegiance to one paradigm or the other" (Guba, 1985, p. 80 as cited in Byman, 1988, pp. 107–108). For example, some researchers may use both methods, but keep them as separate studies (see especially Morse, 2003). Others may advocate using both but *favoring* one philosophical perspective over the other when it comes to interpretation of their research findings. One can, in fact, envision a set of *paradigmatic standpoints* coming into play when a researcher is using a mixed-methods approach to social research. A researchers' paradigmatic viewpoint may even shift over the course of any given research project. If I were a positivist by training, yet open to multiple methods, I might start out with a mixed-methods design and be open to qualitative procedures, yet favor my quantitative findings over the qualitative if they are contradictory. Or, as a pragmatic positivist, I might be open to moving in the direction of multiple interpretations in my mixed methods data, looking for a more nuanced interpretation of my quantitative results. In essence, I "give up a little positivism" to gain more in-depth, grounded understanding of my data. The change in any one researcher's point of view may often be incremental and not dramatic, but over time, a definite subtle revolution in thinking and the practice of social research on the part of this researcher will be evident. The change may take place at different stages in the research process (problem construction/data gathering/data analysis/data interpretation) as well.

MIXED-METHODS RESEARCH DESIGNS ●

David Morgan (1998) provides some practical strategies for designing a mixed methods study. He suggests *four mixed-methods research designs* based on the sequencing (time ordering) as well as relative importance (priority) of each method. In designing your project, several decisions need to be made in setting up the particular mixed-methods design. You can do this by asking yourself the following two questions:

- What is the primary research method and what is the secondary (complementary) method?
- What method will come first and which second?

Morgan (1998) notes that how a researcher answers these two questions provides four possible mixed-methods research designs. However, it is

Table 9.1 Combining Qualitative and Quantitative

Design 1.	qual followed by QUANT*
Design 2.	quant followed by QUAL
Design 3.	QUANT followed by qual
Design 4.	QUAL followed by quant

SOURCE: Adapted from David Morgan (1998).

NOTE: All lower case means secondary method and all upper case denotes primary method.

important to note that there are a multitude of other mixed-methods designs that combine qualitative and quantitative methods using different criteria. Some mixed-methods designs combine methods concurrently, that is, at the same time; but maintain the primary/secondary distinction (see Creswell, 2003). Morgan's (1998) distinction only considers sequential (time ordering) studies—one after the other. Yet other mixed-methods researchers conduct their studies concurrently (at the same time) often placing both methods on an equal footing without distinguishing between a primary and a secondary method (Creswell, Fetters, & Ivankova, 2004, 2003, 1999). Still others talk about issues of one method (qualitative or quantitative) being nested or "embedded" in the other, with the nested method being given a lower priority. The nested method may even answer a different research question, yet both methods are used to analyze the data (Creswell et al., 2003, p. 229). There is also the possibility of mixing two qualitative and two quantitative studies. Teddlie and Tashakkori (2003) refer to this type of design as "multiple method" designs.

We present David Morgan's (1998) typology for mixing methods with the above caveats in mind. We can see from Table 9.1 the four research design possibilities.

● MIXED-METHODS DESIGNS WITH EXAMPLES

The first design (qual———QUANT) involves conducting the qualitative component of the research project first, but keeping it secondary (designated by lower-case letters) to the the project's goals. The quantitative method is primary (all upper-case letters), but administered as a follow-up to the qualitative study. Using a qualitative design before a quantitative one provides the researcher who is unfamiliar with a given topic the opportunity to generate specific ideas/hypotheses that they might address more specifically in the quantitative part of the project. An illustrative example of this form of mixed methods study design comes from a research project conducted by Kutner, Steiner, Corbett, Jahnigen, & Barton (1999) on terminally ill patients.

The researchers were interested in understanding the lived experiences of those who are terminally ill. At this stage of illness, "care" often means taking into account more of the patient's mind, body, and spiritual needs with less and less emphasis on medical interventions. It is important to understand the lived experiences of the terminally ill and to convey such needs directly to those who provide care to them, especially their doctors. The researchers also wanted to be able to generalize the results of their study to the wider terminally ill population.

The research design starts out with a qualitative exploratory interview study (qual) of 22 terminally ill patients utilizing open-ended interviews with the idea of understanding the concerns of the terminally ill. The qualitative information gathered enables the researchers to create a set of closed- and open-ended questions and scales based not on hypothetical "scenarios" but directly on the experiences of the termainlly ill populaton. In other words, the survey component of the study (QUANT) was "grounded" in the direct experiences of the terminally ill population. The quantitative study was the primary study and consisted of a structured survey of 56 terminally ill patients. The goal of the survey was to assess how patient characteristics were related to the gap between patient and physician expectations for terminal care. What the researchers found was that doctors and patients can often have different values concerning what it means to have a terminal illness. While doctors concentrate on the "medical" aspects of the illness, patient needs concerning social and personal issues often get short shrift and outweigh medically related issues. In fact, what the qualitative data shows is that the terminally ill hold valuable information concering what specific care and interventions they need in order to feel empowered in their daily lives, but doctors do not often elicit this valuable information.

In the second design—quant followed by QUAL—the quantitative study is used secondarily (quant) with the qualitative study being primary (QUAL). In this case, the quantitative study is used to *identify specific populations or issues* that need to be further explored indepth. An example of this type of research comes from a study done on general practicioners' (GPs) attitudes toward discussing the issue of smoking with their patients. The authors wanted to identify a pool of general practictioners who held a range of different attitudes. The quantitative study (quant), based on a short attitudinal survey of 327 GPs, helped the researchers identify a diverse attitudinal pool of respondents they could do follow-up qualitative interviews with, ensuring an in-depth understanding of smoking concerns across different types of GPs (Coleman, Williams, & Wilson, 1996).

The third design QUANT followed by qual, notes Morgan (1998), is designed to have the quantitative study be the primary mode of inquiry with the qualitative study second. This type of design is often used when there is a need to provide clarification/elaboration of research results from quantitative findings. The qualitative study assists in understanding such things as negative results and what are called "outliers" (findings that do not appear to fit the overall hypothesis or theoretical pespective). In essence qualitative data can be used to supplement quantitative data to help the quantitative researcher "salvage" their data by understanding "erroneous results" in his or her survey data (Weinholtz, Kacer, & Rocklin, 1995). An example of this design comes from a reseach project on the integration of immigrant families into Swedish society (Bjeren, 2004). The primary data for this study are based on two social surveys (QUANT) whose purpose was to gather demographic information on immigrant and native-born Swedes from available data (a previous large-scale study on the welfare of immigrants) and a large-scale quantitative survey of 3,408 adults (native and foreign born) concerning their work and family lives. The researchers wanted to compare the economic and social conditions of Polish and Turkish young adult immigrants with those of their native-born counterparts. The qualitative study (qual) was employed as a secondary method in order to clarify some of the issues of "family dynamics" and community relationships among Turkish and Polish immigrants. A convenience sample of interviews, as well as formal and informal observations with young immigrants and some of their parents, was also conducted. The authors note the qualitative study

> . . . points to inconsistencies, areas that should be given more attention and possible consequences of the non-response to the social surveys. In the other direction, analysis of survey data have indicated that some of the conclusions drawn from the intensive studies seem to have limited validity, maybe reflecting the restriction under which those studies were made or more profound issues around differences between the self-images people present and what they actually do. (Bjeren, 2004, p. 6)

An important finding that the survey data appeared to lack was an understanding of the importance of religion in the lives of immigrants. The authors note that Sweden is a secular society that does not place much emphasis on "religious sentiments which are likely to be regarded as throwbacks to distant times" (Bjeren, 2004, p. 7). It is interesting to note here that the quantitative study was conducted by demographers while the qualitative study was done by anthropologists. This raises the question of the training required to engage in a mixed-methods design, and in fact a mixed-methods approach also requires interdisciplinary engagement. This may also raise issues of communication between researchers who do not share the same philosophical and methods perspectives.

In the fourth research design—QUAL followed by a quant study—the qualitative research study (QUAL) is primarily followed up with a smaller quantitative study (quant). The quantitative study is used to test results on different populations in order to ascertain whether or not the qualitative findings "transfer" to other populations (Morgan, 1998, p. 370). Gioia and Thomas's (1996) multimethods study is interested in how academic administrators identify the important issues that impact universities undergoing "strategic change." It is an example of the fourth and final mixed-methods design that we take up in this chapter. The researchers use a qualitative method—a single case study of one university's management team—in order to get at the lived experiences of high-level administrators in higher education. The qualitative case study enables the researchers to identify "image" and "identity" as two key themes that are particularly important in helping administrators sort out what strategic changes universities will require as they continue to undergo dramatic organizational changes. In the minds of administrators, fostering a desired university image was very much related to how their insitutions were going to be envisioned in the future. These two factors were also important in understanding how top officials labeled university concerns as either strategic (those that would move the university forward) or "political" (often viewed as internal and promoting the "status quo"). The qualitative findings were phrased in terms of a set of propositions concerning the relationships beween identity, image, and interpretations (strategic versus political). These propositions were then tested out in a quantitative survey of a sample of 611 high-level college administrators drawn from 372 colleges and universities across the United States. In this mixed-methods research design, the qualitative data becomes a critical element in understanding the research problem, and the quantitative study serves to assist the researchers in "testing out" the findings from the qualitative study in order to generalize its results to a wider population of university administrators. In general, the survey findings supported the importance of the relationship between image and identity held by key administrators, and they can become an important lens through which administrators make interpretations about what the key concerns are that they should be tending to in a climate of dramatic change.

● PROBLEMS AND PROSPECTS OF MIXED-METHODS DESIGNS

A range of concerns have arisen regarding the practice of mixing methods. Some researchers are not clear about what to do when findings from each method are not in agreement with each other or the qualitative study gets short shrift. Brannen (1992, p. 27) suggests that even in studies where the qualitative component is primary, there may be a tendency for the quantitative findings to overpower the qualitative. She (1992) cites a study conducted on home workers (Cragg & Dawson, 1981) and notes that the qualitative component of this study was not praised for its theoretical insights, but for the size of the qualitative sample!

There are economic costs incurred in doing this type of research, given the amount of time and energy needed to complete any project. There is the added issue of whether or not individual researchers can acquire the range of skills needed to mix methods (Brannen, 1992, p. 20). Zeller (1993) notes that " . . . most researchers have a research method loyalty. Researchers are comfortable operating in their own area of methodological expertise; they are vulnerable operating outside that area" (p. 110). In fact some of these studies may be conducted by two different research teams who may or may not integrate their research findings. The consumers of this type of research may also not be knowledgable about both methods, and therefore it is important for the researcher to take the time to introduce concepts that may be foreign to individuals not versed in a particular paradigm. Given that these studies straddle two different paradigms and methods there is the added concern that such research will fall through the cracks of academic journals, many of which may be hostile to the mixing of methods (Brannen, 1992).

● FUTURE DIRECTIONS FOR MIXED-METHODS RESEARCH

With the advent of computer-assisted qualitative data analysis software, known as CAQDAS, (see Fielding & Lee, 1998; and Hesse-Biber & Maietta, 2005) new directions in analysis have blurred the boundaries between qualitative and quantitative methods. It is now possible for a researcher to take their qualitative data, such as interview material, which is textual data and create "variables" from this data, a process known as "quantizing" data. Computer-assisted software for qualitative analysis programs assists the researcher in creating "variable" data based on qualitative material (codes) and in exporting this information for statistical analysis. Some qualitative software programs also permit the researcher to import quantitative data, for example, data gathered from a survey, directly into their computer software programs, thereby allowing the researcher to simultaneously work with both a qualitative and a quantitative database. As qualitative data analysis programs continue to advance toward quantizing, there are new software techniques that allow the researcher to generate and test their theories on qualitative material. Some programs employ artificial intelligence—knowledge-based expert systems. HyperRESEARCH's "hypothesis tester" provides for the creation of "if/then" propositions or hypotheses. HyperRESEARCH supports the use of "production rules" to help researchers generate and create relationships between coded text segments and to formulate and test hypotheses about the nature of these relationships (Hesse-Biber & DuPuis, 1995). ETHNO (Heise, 1991; Heise & Lewis, 1988) is a software program that performs an "event structure analysis" that examines the timing of specific events and analyzes the logical temporal sequence of relationships between events, based on causal narratives within data.

THE PROCESS OF QUANTIZING: QUAL (CODES) BECOMES QUANT (VARIABLES). AN EXAMPLE

Qualitative data ("codes") are "labels" given to segments of textual data, from text that has been transcribed from an interview or other narrative data (magazines, newspapers, etc.), that can be transformed into numbers. Previously qualitative material becomes quantitative ("variable") data that allows for the application of statistical analytical techniques. This is a technique that is known as "quantizing" (Miles & Huberman, 1994, were the first researchers to use this term; see also Sandelowski, 2000, p. 253). The application example of this technique comes from Hesse-Biber and Carter's (2004) analysis of 55 young women two years postcollege who were interviewed about their eating patterns and body image concerns (see Hesse-Biber, 1996). The authors are interested in exploring this data in order to understand the following question:

- Is there a relationship between critical remarks from family and friends and the development of eating-disordered symptoms among young women?

The qualitative data reveal that, while some families and peers are supportive of young women's weight and body image, some are quite critical. The following is an excerpt from several of the interviews conducted by

Hesse-Biber (1996, as cited in Hesse-Biber & Carter, 2004). In this first excerpt, we can note how Joanna's mother is supportive of her body image:

> **Joanna:** My mother, all she wants is that I'm happy. I can weigh 500 pounds as long as I'm happy. Her focus was always on my health, not so much with my appearance. So her comments were more towards always that positive support. Very rarely do I remember her giving like negative comments about how I looked. It was mostly encouraging. My mother would stay stuff like "You have a beautiful face, you have beautiful hands." She'd focus on individual qualities about me.

On the other hand, Joan and Becky relay stories about how critical their families are concerning their weight and body image.

> **Joan:** My brothers and sisters would go around and make pig noises. . . . My dad would say, "You need to lose weight." And I'd try and I'd be successful.

> **Becky:** My brothers would mention to my mother, and she would say, "Rob thinks you are getting fat," and then she'd say, "Maybe you should stop eating so much." He [father] commented a lot. Never bad. Always good. He'd say, "You look good, you lost weight." He was always commenting on pretty young girls. So I knew it was important to him that I look good too. I wanted him to see that I could be as pretty as all the girls he was commenting on. I wanted him to be proud of me for that, and I knew he was.

With 55 interviews, however, it quickly becomes difficult for these researchers to establish clear relationships among the data. In fact, using qualitative analysis to answer a quantitative question became difficult as the numbers of interviews increased. As we mentioned earlier, qualitative data is good at getting at experience, but this question is about causality: "Is there a relationship between X (critical) and Y (eating disorders)?" In this question "critical" becomes the independent variable (cause) and "eating disorders" becomes the dependent variable (effect).

The *quantizing process* allows us to look at the qualitative data more quantitatively by transforming our qualitative data (codes) to quantitative data (variables). Let's see how this process works.

PROCESS OF LINKING QUALITATIVE ● AND QUANTITATIVE: QUANTIZING (QUAL TO QUANT)

Step One: Coding the Text

To aid in identifying the key patterns in these 55 interviews, Hesse-Biber and Carter (2004) coded them with a qualitative data analysis software package HyperRESEARCH (Hesse-Biber, Dupuis, & Kinder, 1991). For example, Joan's comment concerning her family, "My dad would say, 'You need to lose weight'" was given the qualitative code "Parents-or-peers-or-siblings critical" (PPSC) (see the analysis of data in Chapter 10, for a more detailed description of the qualitative coding process). A similar coding procedure was carried out to create codes for "eating disorders" and so on.

Step Two: Converting Codes Into Variables (qual to quant)

Qualitative codes were then transformed into quantitative variables. The researchers note that 16 of the interviews reported that a parent, peer, or sibling was critical of their eating habits and bodies and were assigned the PPSC code. A computer software program for qualitative analysis then transformed the "variable" PPSC by giving these 16 interviews the value of "yes" and the other 39 a value of "no." The same type of procedure was done to obtain variables such as "eating disorders" (EATDIS) and values of "yes" and "no" (see Hesse-Biber & Carter, 2004, p. 89, for a more detailed account).

Step 3. Exporting Quantized Codes Into a Statistical Software Package for Quantitative Analysis (Quantizing Analysis)

These quantized codes (now transformed into variables) were exported to a statistical package in order to obtain quantitative summaries of key relationships identified in the research question. We can see some of the results of this process in Table 9.2.

Specifically, Table 9.2 shows a strong relationship between PPSC and reported eating disorder symptoms such as bulimia and anorexia (EATDIS). In fact the authors went on to elaborate on this relationship by looking at other quantized variables they theorized might be related to this finding and to further validate this finding by looking for other factors that might weaken or strengthen the relationship between criticism and the development of eating disorder symptoms. Interestingly, the researchers found that when a parent is overweight and is critical of their daughter's body, the parent's words have less power than if the parent is not overweight.

Table 9.2   The Relationship Between Having an Eating Disorder (EATDIS) and Growing Up With Parents, Peers, or Siblings Being "Critical" of One's Body and Eating Habits (PPSC)

		(PPSC)	
		No	Yes
	Yes	12.8	56.3
		(5)	(9)
EATDIS			
	No	87.2	43.8
		(34)	(7)
		100%	100%
		(39)	(16) N = 55

Table from Hesse-Biber & Carter, 2004, p. 89.

The quantizing process enabled the researchers to fully articulate the conditions under which the original relationship between criticism and eating disorders becomes stronger (when mother is not overweight) or weaker (when mother is overweight). The authors note:

> interaction between PPSC and having an overweight parent (or not) in determining the likelihood of an interviewee developing an eating disorder. More specifically, we find that PPSC only really matters in the context of a family where the parents are *not* overweight. In sum, having a critical parent who is at the same time overweight seems to have little impact on a daughter developing an eating disorder, whereas a daughter with parents who are both "thinnish" and *critical* has a strong likelihood of developing bulimia or anorexia. (Hesse-Biber & Carter, 2004, p. 89)

● USING QUANTITATIVE VARIABLES TO DIRECTLY ENHANCE QUALITATIVE ANALYSIS: QUALITIZING DATA (QUANT TO QUAL)

How can the researcher use quantitative information directly in the qualitative analysis of his or her data? This is the situation of directly incorporating insights from quantitative data into a qualitative analysis. The term *qualitizing* is used to refer to the process of transforming quantitative data into qualitative data (see Tashakkori & Teddlie, 1998, who first coined this term; see also Sandelowski, 2000, pp. 253–254). Qualitizing quantitative data serves to enhance the researcher's understanding of the quantitative data by placing it in a qualitative context, creating a hybrid analysis. The quantitative data also provides researchers with a set of variables with which to sort their qualitative data into quantitative categories to enhance the generalizability of their findings. A researcher who qualitizes their data may want to enhance their understanding of quantitative variables by nesting these variables in a qualitative context. Hesse-Biber's (1996) study on women's body image and eating disorders contained both qualitative and quantitative data. She conducted intensive interviews with a sample of women 2 years postcollege and followed up this interview by having her respondents fill out a self-administered questionnaire regarding women's attitudes toward eating as well as a range of quantitative eating-disorder scales. The interviews and questionnaires were matched for each respondent in her study. She created an "eating typology" based on the quantitative data. The qualitative data from the intensive interviews provided a more detailed "grounding" of the meaning of the eating typology Hesse-Biber created. In addition, the quantitative typology provided her with quantitative categories with which to differentiate her qualitative sample and enhance the generalizability of her findings regarding women's eating patterns. Hesse-Biber used insights from the quantitative study to make inferences about the qualitative data.

Steps in the Qualtizing Process

Step 1. Data Collection. How will you collect your quantitative data? Alongside the Qualitative data (in the same study, Time 1)? Different Studies (Time 1 and 2)? Which will you collect first? Should you collect each type of data overtime (longitudinal mixed methods design, Time 1, Time 2, Time 3 and so on)? Hesse-Biber (1996) collects both types of data in the same study by conducting in-depth interviews on college women's eating atittudes (QUAL) as well as administering a structured questionnaire on eating attitudes (QUANT) she gives them right after the in-depth interview.

Hesse-Biber (1996) considers both types of data to be primary (QUAL and QUANT). Her analysis design is based on her research problem. However, this is but one of the many ways you might combine qualitative and quantitative data and raises the issue of how to integrate both types of data into your analysis plan. Questions of integration go to the heart of what it means to qualtize your quantitative data.

Step 2. Determine type and level of integration of quantitative data. "Qualtizing" involves bringing quantitative variables in interaction with qualitative data and is usually done when the researcher wants to triangulate on their data or clarify particular concepts in their study by asking the folowing questions:

- Do you want to use quantitative data to inform your qualitative data?
- Do you want to use qualitative data to inform your quantitative data?

These two questions make for different ways of "qualtizing." The first question has to do with using quantitative variables within a qualitative study to inform/provide a more in-depth understanding about the meaning of qualitative codes. Let's go back to Hesse-Biber's study (1996) . She brings in respondents' test scores on the Eating Attitudes Test (EAT) and the Eating Disorders Inventory (EDI) to create a quantitative dichotomous variable called Eating Disorders (ED) that has two categories "yes" and "no." She wants to understand the extent to which this quantitative variable corresponds to a similar measure she derived from her qualitative data on eating disorders, an inductive category titled EATDIS (eating disorders). Where is there agreement? (Triangulation on this concept) Disagreement? (this may help her to clarify the meaning of her qualitative code, EATDIS). The purpose is to help inform the meaning of her qualitative codes.

The second question involves the "meaning" of a quantitative variable in a context. What does it mean for a respondent to score high and the ED variable? We might use the ED variable to sort respondents by a number of qualitative body image codes in order to get a more in-depth understanding the context in which individuals talk about their eating issues by ED categories. By contextualizing our quantitative variable we are able to obtain more clarity of meaning at the micro and macro levels.

One of the important advantages of using a mixed-data *analysis design* is that it enables the researcher to see complex relationships in his or her qualitative data. The ability to quantify the qualitative data and incorporate quantitative data into qualitative analysis provides a different analytical window into finding patterns within qualitative data and coming up with precise numbers to manipulate with statistical techniques. It also provides a context within which to understand quantitatively derived variables. Use of these quantizing/ qualitizing techniques for transforming and analyzing data, however, creates a range of issues that stem from crossing the boundary between quantitative and qualitative *analytical* realms.

There are conceptual issues (epistemological/methodological concerns) as well as more practical issues (such as how to choose an appropriate statistical analysis for qualitative variables and how to interpret research results) to consider as the researcher applies these new techniques. Transforming qualitative codes and treating them as "variables" violates some important measurement assumptions regarding how quantitative variables are gathered (e.g., statistical issues regarding random sampling) especially when the research data digresses from standardized question formats, as is the case with open-ended interviews and much other qualitative research. For example, in the eating disorder study cited above, Hesse-Biber and Carter (2004) note that while many interviewees discussed how their parents, peers, and siblings were critical of the their bodies—and the researchers transformed this "code" into a "variable" called PPSC—not all interviewees were asked about this issue in a standardized way, as would be done in a quantitative survey. Nor did the interviewer strive to bring up this particular issue in every single interview. Thus, measurement error is a real concern for anyone following the path that we are suggesting in this chapter.

There are counter points of view to these criticisms. First, many would argue that interviewees tend to bring up those issues most salient in their lives—and thus the research need not be overly concerned about not having directed every interviewee's attention to every particular "code" (Hesse-Biber & Carter, 2004). There is also the added concern about how to analyze this type of data. Should standard statistical procedures be employed, such as obtaining statistical measures of the association between two variables, like chi square, or other more complex statistical procedures, like log-linear analysis?

Each of these issues needs to be addressed by going back to the basic goals of the mixed methods research project as well as the self-reflexivity of the researcher concerning their epistemological stance. What is a limitation for one researcher is an opportunity for another, depending on researcher goals and epistemological standpoints. A positivist might cringe at the idea of turning codes into variables and would definitely view this as a major violation of positivist measurement standards. On the other hand, a qualitative researcher who had also received quantitative training might be open to positivistic analyses, using quantized variables as an important *heuristic device* that reveals potential relationships that can be explored more fully in more refined studies taken from both qualitative and quantitative approaches. In fact, such an analysis could enhance the positivistic scientific underpinnings of the research by repeating studies, and in repeated study ensure that the "codes" the researcher found most important in the previous study were introduced to all interviewees. In addition, by quantizing variables from our qualitative study, we are pinpointing important codes that can be, for example, recast as fixed-choice survey items or incorporated into qualitative studies using more directed and focused interviewing.

Quantizing or qualitizing should be considered "a means of making available techniques which add power and sensitivity to individual judgment when one attempts to detect and describe patterning in a set of observations" (see Weinstein & Tamur, 1978, as quoted in Miles and Huberman, 1994, p. 41).

● CONCLUSION

Mixed-methods designs hold a great deal of promise for the researcher who wants to tackle complex issues that reside at multiple levels—the individual as well as the societal. It can enhance the type of information gathered and can serve to increase the validity of both qualitative and quantitative projects. There is the idea that by using both approaches the researcher can bring out the best in both methods (increasing the validity of a given study through triangulation, for example), while offsetting the weaknesses of the other. The idea, as we have noted earlier, is that "The whole is greater than the sum of its parts." However, having said this, there are a range of caveats from the conceptual to the practical that one must consider when using mixed methods designs. Mixed methods blur the line between research paradigms, and it is unclear how concerned researchers should be about this. There are those "pragmatists" who advocate for whatever methods work, sometimes with little regard for issues of epistemology and methodology, while others, known as "purists," see such boundary crossings as violating the very foundations of scientific thought. Many others take positions between these views on what we see as a continuum of opinions on this matter.

Mixed methods is not a panacea; a magic elixir that one pours onto a research project to make it work. Mixed methods are techniques for getting at knowledge building. More is not necessarily better; the sum may not be greater than its parts. In fact, in our Behind the Scenes interview(see below), Janice Morse, a leading qualitative researcher, warns about embracing mixed methods as a substitute for sharp conceptual thinking and insightful analyses. She raises again the important issues we addressed earlier in this chapter that have to do with the cost of carrying out a mixed methods project and the training required to do so. How well versed can any given researcher be in both methods? Can more harm than good be done when researchers are not adequately trained in both methods? In addition, Morse raises issues stemming from the expectations of funding agencies and the pressure some researchers may feel to do a mixed methods design at the behest of the funding agency, independent of the research problem (see also Brannen, 1992, p. 20)! Perhaps the right word cited by Morse in her interview is "fiddlesticks" to those who feel that any one method contains THE answers to research problems. What Morse is unequivocal about is the importance of not losing sight of the contribution qualitative methods continue to make, in their *pure* form, to our understanding the nature of the social reality (see also Morse, 1996). Keeping vigilant on the essence of this insight is what is needed to avoid losing our way in the quest for knowledge building.

Behind-the-Scenes With Janice Morse

Behind the Scenes With Janice Morse, a leader in qualitative research in North America. She founded the International Institute for Qualitative Methodology at the University of Alberta, Canada, in 1998 (http://www.ualberta.ca/~iiqm/). We present only a small excerpt of the entire interview which was conducted (by Mexican sociologist César Cisneros) in two parts, in January and May, 2004:

Mixed Methods and "Theoretical Drive"

Cisneros: In what ways do you see multimethods evolving? How will qualitative researchers deal with such diversity?

Morse: I think it is going to get into a terrible mess but it will sort itself out in the end.

Cisneros: What kind of "terrible mess" are you talking about?

Morse: I think people lack analytic skills to handle both qualitative and quantitative data. I don't think there has been enough work done on theory development, I think that not enough people even want to do theoretical development and are content with their descriptions. I think the pressure to do mixed methods, in order to get funding, overwhelms or overrides the goals of qualitative inquiry. I think the funding agencies say they fund qualitative inquiry, meaning that they really do fund mixed methods. This still places qualitative inquiry in an inferior position.

Cisneros: What are the empirical implications of using mixed methods? I mean, facing the complexity of the actual world every one of us for sure will be more in need of mixed and multiple methods.

Morse: I do not think we all have to give in to these pressures. I feel I use multimethods if it is required in the design, not simply to please funding agencies.

Cisneros: Because we need this kind of multimethod research to produce knowledge?

Morse: Nonsense. Fiddlesticks. Basic knowledge also comes from doing qualitative research alone.

Cisneros: But qualitative research needs multimethods?

Morse: No, it does not need multimethods; the funding agencies need multi-methods and some questions need multimethods.

● GLOSSARY

Complementarity: A reason for employing a mixed-methods design is that of *complementarity* whereby the researcher seeks to gain a fuller understanding of the research problem and/or to clarify a given research result.

Concurrent: This is when methods are used at the same time but maintain the primary/secondary distinction.

Data Triangulation: Different data sources using the same method as well as different methods.

Development: This is when "results from one method help to develop or inform the other method."

Equal Footing: This is when both methods are placed on an *equal footing* without distinguishing between primary and secondary method.

Expansion: Expansion is initiated to "extend the breadth and range of the study" and may be why mixed methods are employed.

Heuristic Device: A qualitative researcher who has also received quantitative training might be open to positivistic analyses, using quantized variables as an important *heuristic device* that reveals potential relationships that can be explored more fully in more refined studies taken from both qualitative and quantitative approaches.

Initiation: One reason for using mixed methods is *initiation,* whereby a given research study's findings raise questions or contain contradictions that require clarification.

Methods Triangulation: The use of multiple (different) methods.

Mixing of Philosophical Paradigms: A mixed methods design mixes qualitative and quantitative philosophical assumptions, especially as these pertain to issues concerning the nature of the individual and society, the problem of "objectivity versus subjectivity."

Nested: This is when one method (qualitative or quantitative) is *nested* or "embedded" in the other, with the nested method being given a lower priority. The nested method may even answer a different research question, yet both methods are used to analyze the data.

Paradigmatic Standpoints: A researcher's paradigmatic viewpoint may even shift over the course of any given research project.

Quantizing Process: The *quantizing process* allows us to look at the qualitative data more quantitatively by transforming our qualitative data (codes) into quantitative data (variables).

Sequential (Time-Ordering) Studies: This is when studies occur back-to-back.

Synergistic: The combination of two different methods can create a *synergistic* research project whereby one method enables the other to be more effective and, together, both methods provide a fuller understanding of the research problem (Greene & Caracelli, 1997; see Sieber, 1973, for an early example of the synergy mixing the methods of "fieldwork" and "survey research").

Triangulation: This strategy involves using more than one method to study the same research question. The researcher is looking for a "convergence" of research findings to enhance the credibility of the research findings.

Theoretical Triangulation: This has come to mean using different theoretical perspectives in one study.

DISCUSSION QUESTIONS ●

1. What are some of the reasons why a researcher might employ a mixed-method approach?

2. How do methods "speak to each other"?

SUGGESTED WEBSITES ●

Glossary of Mixed-Methods Terms/Concepts

http://www.fiu.edu/~bridges/glossary.htm

This website is a resource for terms and concepts related to mixed methods research. The terms found on this site are adopted from Tashakkori and Teddlie's *Handbook of Mixed Methods in Social and Behavioural Research* (2003).

Research Design and Mixed Method Approach: A Hands-On Experience

http://www.socialresearchmethods.net/tutorial/Sydenstricker/bolsa.html

This site is helpful for seeing mixed methods put to actual use in a study.

Employing Multiple Methods

http://writing.colostate.edu/references/research/observe/pop4b.cfm

This website offers a writing guide to using multiple methods.

● REFERENCES

CNN. (2005, 10 January). *Treating children's emotional wounds.* Retrieved from http://www.cnn.com/2005/WORLD/asiapcf/01/05/tsunami.children.cope/

Bjeren, G. (2004, November 25–27). *Combining social survey and ethnography integration research: An example.* Paper presented at the 2nd conference of the EAPS Working Group on International Migration in Europe, Rome, Italy.

Brannen, J. (1992). Combining qualitative and quantitative approaches: An overview. In J. Brannen (Ed.), *Mixing methods: Qualitative and quantitative research* (pp. 3–36). Aldershot, UK: Avebury Press.

Byman, A. (1988). *Quantity and quality in social research.* London: Unwin and Hyman.

Cisneros-Puebla, C. A. (2004, September). "Let's do more theoretical work . . .": Janice Morse in conversation with César A. Cisneros-Puebla [96 paragraphs]. *Forum Qualitative Sozial-forschung/Forum: Qualitative Social Research* [On-line Journal], *5*(3), Art. 33. Available at: http://www.qualitative-research.net/fqs-texte/3–04/04-3-33-e.htm

Coleman, T., Williams, M., & Wilson, A. (1996). Sampling for qualitative research using quantitative methods: Measuring GP's attitudes towards discussing smoking with patients. *Family Practice, 13,* 526–530.

Cragg, A., & Dawson, T. (1981, May). Qualitative research among homeworkers. Research Paper No. 21. London: Department of Employment.

Creswell, J. W. (2003). *Research design: Qualitative and quantitative approaches* (2nd ed.). Thousand Oaks, CA: Sage.

Creswell, J. W. (1999). Mixed-method research: Introduction and application. In G. J. Cizek (Ed.), *Handbook of educational policy* (pp. 455–472). San Diego, CA: Academic Press.

Creswell, J. W., Fetters, M. D., & Ivankova, N. V. (2004, January/February). Designing a mixed methods study in primary care. *Annals of Family Medicine, 2*(1), 7–12.

Denzin, N. K. (1978). *The research act: A theoretical introduction to sociological methods.* New York: McGraw-Hill.

Fielding, N. G., & Lee, R. M. (1998). *Computer analysis and qualitative research.* London: Sage.

Gioia, D. A., & Thomas, J. B. (1996). Identity, image, and issue interpretation: Sensemaking during strategic change in academia. *Administrative Science Quarterly, 41,* 370–403.

Greene, J. C., Benjamin, L., & Goodyear, L. (2001). The merits of mixing methods in evaluation. *Evaluation, 7*(1), 25–44.

Greene, J. C., & Caracelli, V. J. (Eds.). (1997a). *Advances in mixed-method evaluation: The challenges and benefits of integrating diverse paradigms (New Directions for Evaluation # 74).* San Francisco: Jossey-Bass.

Greene, J. C., & Caracelli, V. J. (1997b). Defining and describing the paradigm issues in mixed-method evaluation. In J. C. Greene & V. J. Caracelli (Eds.), *Advances in mixed-method evaluation: The challenges and benefits of integrating diverse paradigms (New Directions for Evaluation #74)* (pp. 5–17). San Francisco: Jossey-Bass.

Greene, J. C., Caracelli, V. J., & Graham, W. F. (1989). Toward a conceptual framework for mixed-method evaluation designs. *Educational Evaluation and Policy Analysis, 11,* 255–274.

Guba, E. G. (1985). The context of emergent paradigm research. In Y. S. Lincoln (Ed.), *Organizational theory and inquiry* (pp. 79–104). Newbury Park, CA: Sage.

Guba, E. G., & Lincoln, Y. S. (1994). Competing paradigms in qualitative research. In N. K. Denzin & Y. S. Lincoln (Eds.), *Handbook of qualitative research* (pp. 105–117). Thousand Oaks, CA: Sage.

Heise, D. (1991). Event structure analysis: A qualitative model of quantitative research. In N. Fielding & R. Lee (Eds.), *Using computers in qualitative research* (pp. 136–163). London: Sage.

Heise, D., & Lewis, E. (1988). *Introduction to ETHNO.* Raleigh, NC: National Collegiate Software Clearinghouse.

Hesse-Biber, S. (1996). *Am I thin enough yet? The cult of thinness and the commercialization of identity.* New York: Oxford University Press.

Hesse-Biber, S., & Carter, G. L. (2004). Linking qualitative and quantitative analysis: The example of family socialization and eating disorders. In G. L. Carter (Ed.), *Empirical approaches to sociology: A collection of classic and contemporary readings* (4th ed., pp. 83–97). Boston: Pearson/Allyn & Bacon.

Hesse-Biber, S., & Dupuis, P. (1995). Hypothesis testing automation for computer-aided qualitative data analysis. In U. Kelle (Ed.), *Computer-aided qualitative data analysis: Theory, methods and practice.* London: Sage.

Hesse-Biber, S., Dupuis, P., & Kinder, T. S. (1991). HyperRESEARCH: A computer program for the analysis of qualitative data with an emphasis on hypothesis testing and multimedia analysis. *Qualitative Sociology, 14*(4), 289–306.

Hesse-Biber, S., & Maietta, R. C. (2005). *When methods meets technology: A critical examination of qualitative software evolution.* Thousand Oaks, CA: Sage.

Johnson, B., & Christensen, L. (2000). *Educational research: Quantitative and qualitative approaches.* Boston: Allyn and Bacon.

Kutner, J. S., Steiner, J. F., Corbett, K. K., Jahnigen, D. W., & Barton, P. L. (1999). Information needs in terminal illness. *Social Science & Medicine, 48,* 1341–1352.

Li, S., Marquart, J. M., & Zercher, C. (2000). Conceptual issues and analytic strategies in mixed-method studies of preschool inclusion. *Journal of Early Intervention, 23,* 116–132.

Lincoln, Y. S., & Guba, E. G. (2000). Paradigmatic controversies, contradictions, and emerging confluences. In N. K. Denzin & Y. S. Lincoln (Eds.), *Handbook of qualitative research* (2nd ed., pp. 163–188). Thousand Oaks, CA: Sage.

Lincoln, Y. S., & Guba, E. G. (1985). *Naturalistic inquiry.* Beverly Hills, CA: Sage.

McGowan, K. (2005, 10 January). Thai village struggles to rebuild. *CNN.* Retrieved from *http://news.bbc.co.uk/go/pr/fr/-/1/hi/world/asia-pacific/4160753.stm*

Miles, M. B., & Huberman, A. M. (1994). *Qualitative data analysis* (2nd ed.) Thousand Oaks, CA: Sage.

Morgan, D. (1998). Practical strategies for combining qualitative and quantitative methods: Applications to health research. *Qualitative Health Research, 8,* 362–376.

Morse, J. (2003). Principles of mixed methods and multimethod research design. In A. Tashakkori & C. Teddlie (Eds.), *Handbook of mixed methods in social and behavioral research* (pp. 189–208). Thousand Oaks, CA: Sage.

Morse, J. (1996). Is qualitative research complete? *Qualitative Health Research, 6,* 3–5.

Sandelowski, M. (2000). Combining qualitative and quantitative sampling, data collection and analysis techniques in mixed-methods studies. *Research in Nursing and Health, 23,* 246–255.

Sieber, S. D. (1973). The integration of field work and survey methods. *American Journal of Sociology, 78*(6), 1335–1359.

Tashakkori, A., & Teddlie. C. (Eds.). (2003). *Handbook of mixed methods in social and behavioral research.* Thousand Oaks, CA: Sage.

Tashakkori, A., & Teddlie, C. (1998). *Mixed methodology: Combining qualitative and quantitative approaches.* Thousand Oaks, CA: Sage.

Teddlie, C., & Tashakkori, A. (2003). Major issues and controversies in the use of mixed methods in the social and behavioral sciences. In A. Tashakkori and C. Teddlie (Eds.), *Handbook of mixed methods in social and behavioral research* (pp. 3–50). Thousand Oaks, CA: Sage.

Weinholtz, D., Kacer, B., & Rocklin, T. (1995). Salvaging qualitative research with qualitative data. *Qualitative Health Research, 5,* 388–397.

Weinstein, E. A., & Tamur, J. M. (1978). Meanings, purposes, and structural resources in social interaction. In J. G. Manis & B. N. Meltzer (Eds.), *Symbolic interaction* (3rd. ed., pp. 138–140). Boston: Allyn & Bacon.

Zeller, R. A. (1993). Combining qualitative and quantitative techniques to develop culturally sensitive measures. In D. G. Ostrow & R. C. Kessler (Eds.), *Methodological issues in AIDS behavioral research* (pp. 95–116). New York: Plenum Press.

PART III

ANALYSIS AND REPRESENTATION

CHAPTER 10

ANALYSIS AND INTERPRETATION OF QUALITATIVE DATA

I n the following passage, ethnographer Michael Agar distinguishes between analysis and interpretation:

> In ethnography . . . you learn something ("collect some data"), then you try to make sense out of it ("analysis"), then you go back and see if the interpretation makes sense in light of new experience ("collect more data"), then you refine your interpretation ("more analysis"), and so on. The process is dialectic, not linear. (1980, p. 9)

The process of turning your observations into what Harry Wolcott terms "intelligible accounts" (1994, p. 1) calls forth reflection on how you might answer the following questions (Hesse-Biber & Leavy, 2004, p. 409).

AUTHOR'S NOTE: Parts of this chapter are adapted from "Analysis, Interpretation, and the Writing of Qualitative Data" in Sharlene Nagy Hesse-Biber and Patricia Leavy (Eds.). (2004). *Approaches to qualitative research: A reader on theory and practice.* New York, Oxford University Press.

- How do you know if you focused on the major themes contained in your interview material or ethnographic fieldwork account?
- Do the categories of analysis you gathered make sense?
- What type of analysis should you proceed with?
- Should you conduct a descriptive study or venture beyond descriptive findings with your own interpretation?
- How much interpretation?

● STEPS IN QUALITATIVE DATA ANALYSIS AND INTERPRETATION

While we are providing you with some "steps" to consider as you proceed with your analysis, you should not get the idea that qualitative analysis proceeds in a cookbook fashion. There is no one right way to go about analysis. C. Wright Mills noted early on that qualitative analysis is after all "intellectual craftsmanship" (Mills, 1959, cited in Tesch, 1990, p. 96). As Renata Tesch (1990) notes, "qualitative analysis can and should be done artfully, even 'playfully,' but it also requires a great amount of methodological knowledge and intellectual competence" (p. 97). Norman K. Denzin (2000) posits that there is an "art of interpretation.":

> This may also be described as moving from the field to the text to the reader. The practice of this art allows the field-worker-as-bricoleur . . . to translate what has been learned into a body of textual work that communicates these understandings to the reader. (p. 313)

With these caveats in mind, we break down data analysis and interpretation as a series of steps, beginning with data preparation (Step 1).

Step 1: Data Preparation Phase

It is important to think about *what* data you are going to analyze and whether or not these data are going to provide you with an understanding of your research question. If you are conducting interviews or focus groups, for example, you might want to make a transcript of your data. You will probably need to enter and store these data into a database of some type. You can print out copies of what you have entered in your database and carefully begin to read through and perhaps correct any data entry errors.

Transcribing Your Data

The transcription process is not passive. How we collect our data is crucial to analysis and interpretation. If you are conducting an interview or focus group, for example, several key issues arise in terms of how you will collect this data:

- Will you videotape or audiotape your interview session or what?
- Will you transcribe the entire data session? Will you only summarize key passages or quotes? Will you select only those passages you perceive to be key research issues, or what?
- Will you transcribe all types of data you collect (all verbal data including laughter, pauses, emotions such as sadness or anger, as well as non-verbal data such as hand gestures, etc.)?
- Who will transcribe your data?
- What transcription format will you use? How will you represent a respondent's voice, nonverbal information, and so on.

How a researcher answers these questions is often dictated by his or her research question as well as the type of theoretical framework he or she holds regarding the interview as a process of meaning making. A positivist might in fact dispense with some of these questions, opting to view the transcription process as a simple translation from the "oral" to the "written" language; something that can be done by almost anyone who can listen to the tape and has good typing skills, for example. What is transcribed is regarded as "the truth," and each transcription is considered to contain a one-to-one correspondence between what is said orally and the printed word.

Those with a more interpretative viewpoint might not view the transcription process as so transparent (see Mishler, 1991). In fact they would stress the importance of the researcher's point of view and the researcher's influence on the transcription process itself. Those researchers with a more discourse analytic or linguistic theoretical framework will be especially aware of the lack of transparency in the translation process by noting the importance of multiple levels of meaning within the transcription process that includes such things as pauses and the way in which something is said as well as the nonverbal cues given off by a respondent.

Feminist researchers such as Marjorie Devault (2004) are especially aware of the importance of listening to the data when transcribing interviews especially from those groups whose everyday lives are rendered "invisible" by the dominant society. Devault notes the significance of listening to those moments in the interview where the interviewee is tentative or says "you know what I mean?" She suggests that these are the very moments where the researcher is able to unearth hidden meanings of interviewees whose lives and language are often overshadowed by the dominant discourse. She suggests the following wisdom she has garnered in conducting interviews with women regarding the daily activities they perform in their homes, especially the work they perform in feeding their families:

> . . . the words available often do not fit, women learn to "translate" when they talk about their experiences. As they do so, part of their lives "disappears" because they are not included in the language of the account. In order to "recover" these parts of women's lives, researchers must develop methods for listening around and beyond words. I use the term "listening" . . . in a broad sense, to refer to what we do while interviewing, but also to the hours we spend later listening to tapes or studying transcripts, and even more broadly, to the ways we work at interpreting respondents' accounts. . . . As the interviews progressed, I became increasingly fascinated with some characteristic features of my respondents' talk. They spoke very concretely, about the mundane details of everyday life, but they often said things in ways that seemed oddly incomplete . . . they assumed certain kinds of knowledge on my part ("like, you know, the Thursday section of the newspaper," an implicit reference to the fact that many U.S. newspapers include recipes and features on food and diet in their Thursday editions). . . . I began to pay more and more attention to the ways things were said. (Devault 2004, pp. 233–234).

Devault notes tentative words, like "you know?" might in fact be discarded in transcribing one's data, but in fact are the very moments where "standard" vocabulary is inadequate, and where a respondent tries to speak from experience and finds language wanting (p. 235). Devault comments that her own transcripts of interviews with women regarding the work they do to feed their families were " . . . filled with notations of women saying, 'you know?', in sentences like 'I'm more careful about feeding her, you know, kind of a breakfast.' This seems an incidental feature of their speech, but perhaps the phrase is not so empty as it seems. In fact, I did know what she meant. I did not use these phrases systematically in my analyses, but I think now that I could have. Studying these transcripts now, I see that these words often occur in places where they are consequential for the joint production of our talk in the interviews. In many instances, 'you know' seems to mean something like "Ok, this next bit is going to be a little tricky. I can't say it quite right, but help me out a little; meet me halfway and you'll understand what I mean" (p. 235).

Transcribing research data is interactive and engages the reader in the process of deep listening, analysis, and interpretation. Transcription is not a passive act, but instead provides the researcher with a valuable opporturnity to actively engage with his or her research material right from the beginning of data collection. It also ensures that early on, the researcher is aware of his or her own impact on the data gathering process and he or she has an oppor-tunity to connect with this data in a grounded manner that provides for the possibilitiy of enhancing the trustworthiness and validity of his or her data gathering techniques.

At this point, if you have not already done so, you might want to orga-nize your field notes and interviews in chronological order by *date, time,* and *place.* Be sure to number your text pages. You might also consider if you want to use a computer software program to assist with the analysis because some programs may require that you input your data in a certain manner, such as in paragraph form; others don't require you to do this.

Steps 2 and 3: Data Exploration
Phase and Data Reduction Phase

These two phases work hand-in-hand. In the exploration phase you read your textual and/or visual or audio data and *think about it.* In the process of thinking about it, you might begin to mark up your text by highlighting what you feel is important. You might write down these ideas in the form of a memo. We want to emphasize the importance of *description* during this phase. You might begin by summarizing what data you have collected thus far. Write down (memo) any ideas that come to you as you are reading your notes, interviews, etc. What things fit together? What is problematic? You might think about using some visual aids—like diagrams—to help you think about ideas. What are the most telling quotes in your data? Summarize these and also give some examples of what you mean. All of these "first run through the data techniques" are engaged in by researchers who want to get a closer picture of their data in order to build theory and to potentially draw out some findings.

You might also begin to *code* your data. The "coding" process can start as soon as you begin to collect some data. Don't wait for all your data to be collected! A little bit of data collection and data analysis can reveal some

Data Collection

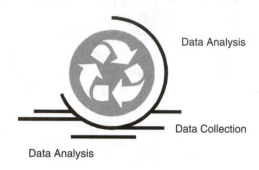

Data Analysis

Data Collection

Data Analysis

Figure 10.1   Diagram of the "Iterative" Process in the Analysis of Data

important patterns, as we shall see in the excerpt of an interview with black adolescent female concerning body image issues. Data collection and data analysis are iterative processes—the two work interactively.

● CODING AND ANALYZING: A GROUNDED THEORY APPROACH

The process of coding and analysis we describe below is modeled after a grounded theory approach to the analysis of qualitative data. Kathy Charmaz's work with grounded theory provides us with one important strategy for extracting meaning from qualitative data (Charmaz, 2004). Grounded theory is a form of analysis developed initially by Glaser and Strauss (1967). This analysis perspective starts from an engagement with the data and ends with a theory that is generated or grounded in the data. Charmaz distills the ideas of grounded theory into a concise set of step-by-step analysis instructions. She takes the reader through the process of collecting data, analyzing, and writing memos. All of these parts of the analysis work interactively. As one collects the data, one is analyzing the data. One begins the process, says Charmaz, by doing "open coding." This consists of literally reading *line by line*. One begins with carefully coding each line, sentence, and paragraph. Charmaz (2004) suggests that you might ask the following questions during this process to assist with your coding:

- "What is going on?"
- "What are people doing?"

- "What is the person saying?
- "What do these actions and statements take for granted?"
- "How do structure and context serve to support, maintain, impede, or change these actions and statements?" (Charmaz, 2004, p. 507)

As the process continues the researcher may begin to see more developed codes—focused codes especially through the process of writing memos.

MEMO WRITING ●

By writing memos one can raise a code to the level of a *category*. The idea of a grounded theory approach is to read carefully through the data and to uncover the major categories and concepts and ultimately the properties of these categories and their interrelationships. Memo writing is an integral part of the grounded theory process and assists the researcher in elaborating on their ideas regarding their data and code categories. Ideally, memo writing takes place at all points within the analysis process. Reading through and sorting memos can also aid the researcher in integrating his or her ideas and may even serve to bring up new ideas and relationships within the data.

The grounded theory approach represents only one of many analysis strategies (such as narrative analysis or discourse analysis) one might employ to analyze qualitative data. There is no right or wrong way to synthesize data, and often the researcher jumps back and forth between collection analysis and writing. We have also suggested some specific analysis strategies at the end of each research method we present in our book. However, a grounded theory approach is a widely utilized analytical technique that spans several research method approaches, from the analysis of interviews and field observations to the analysis of unobtrusive data.

Coding is a central part of a grounded theory approach and involves extracting meaning from nonnumerical data such as text and multimedia such as audio and video. If we were to describe how the coding process was actually done, for example, with text materials such as interviews, it would sound something like this: Coding usually consists of identifying "chunks" or "segments" in your textual data (in this case your interview) and giving each of these a label (code). Coding is the analysis strategy many qualitative researchers employ in order to help them locate key themes, patterns, ideas, and concepts that may exist within their data. Analyzing qualitative data presents a distinct challenge for the qualitative researcher. Perhaps the best way to approach this topic is to say that there are a multitude of different forms of analysis with many different goals, depending on the stated research question.

Example of the Coding Process

Let's return to our guiding example of body image.

Hesse-Biber (1996) collected interviews and participant observations from research on how black American teens view their body image (Hesse-Biber, Howling, Leavy, & Lovejoy, 2004). She did not have any specific "hypothesis" she wanted to test out on the data, but instead, she was interested in discovering the following:

- How do adolescent black American girls view their body image?

She spent many hours observing and interviewing black American teenagers at a variety of local community centers in an inner city in the Northeast. She obtained hours of interviews and observations with black American teens and recorded field note observations of the goings on at each of the community centers for several years. Data collection and data analysis should proceed together—as soon you begin to gather the first bit of data from the field, it is important to begin to make sense out it. In conducting such a study, you might begin the process of analysis by *reading over* and becoming familiar with the data that is collected after each visit to the Center. As you read these data you might be interested in *marking up* or *highlighting* anything you think is relevant to your understanding of how black American women perceive their identity and body image. The marking up of the text in effect is to locate those *segments* that you believe are important. You might then apply a name or *code* to each of these segments. Some *segments of text* may contain more than one code. Your coding procedure is *open ended* and "holistic." Your goal is to gain insight and understanding. You do not have a predefined set of coding categories. Your analysis procedure would be primarily *inductive* and would require an immersion of yourself in the text until themes, concepts, or dimensions of concepts arise from the data. You would especially look for the common ways or patterns of behavior whereby individuals come to terms with their body image and identity.

- How do you code data?

When we talk about analysis you may get the feeling that the discussion is progressing in terms that are somewhat technical and procedural, and you are right. Analysis usually begins with looking for *descriptive codes* within one's data, eventually hoping to generate a set of key *concepts* (categories) which are much more analytical concerning black American girls' body image and identity.

Excerpt of an Interview with an African American Teenager with Some Initial codes (see Hesse-Biber, et al., 2004).

Excerpt:	Initial Code:
I don't think that the ideal woman has to	Ideal woman
look like anything personally. I think the ideal woman . . .	Importance of personality
has personality and character, its how you act.	
My looks don't bother me, it's just my personality.	Physical appearance is secondary
My personality. I wanna have a good personality	Importance of personality
and have people like me, if they don't like me for	Importance of personality
my personality, or just because of my looks, then	
they must be missing out on something.	Missing out on noticing personality
Um, when you have it [self-esteem]	Self-esteem
so much that you don't care what people	Don't care what others say
think about you. I man, I flaunt my self-esteem, ...	Flaunting myself
not like 'Oh yeah, dahdadada,' I just sit up real	Sits straight
straight and that shows self-esteem right there.	
I'm a woman, I'll wear stuff to school that's	
like . . . wacked.	Wears what she wants
I have earrings that are about this big, and that	Wears big earrings
shows my self-esteem, I don't care what you say	Doesn't care what others say
about them . . . Oh well, that's what I think,	
I don't care, I don't fit in anywhere anyway,	
I'm my own self so why can't I act like that, ...	Internal self-assessment: own person
why can't I dress like that?	Internal self-assessment: wears what she wants
. . . .	

As you can see from the above example of coding, some codes listed above are *literal* codes—these words also appear within the text and are usually descriptive codes. Others listed in the code list are more *interpretative* (e.g., "*internal self-assessment*"). These codes are not tied as tightly to the text itself but they begin to rely on the researcher's insights for drawing out interpretation. This type of coding relies on more *focused coding*. A focused coding procedure allows for the building and clarifying of concepts. In focused coding a researcher examines all the data in a category, compares each piece of data with every other piece, and finally builds a clear working definition of each concept, which is then named. The name becomes the code (Charmaz, 1983, p. 117). Focused coding requires that a researcher develop a set of *analytical categories* rather than just labeling data in a topical fashion. Modifying code categories becomes important in order to develop more abstract code categories in order to generate theoretical constructs. So, for instance, in the above example, we do identify the category *"internal self-assessment"* but we can also see some additional codes that might help us clarify the meaning of this concept from the respondent's perspective:

Going From Initial Codes to More Focused Codes

Initial Code (literal code)	evolves into	Analytical (more focused) Code
don't care what others say	. . . .	internal self-assessment: ignores external
flaunting self	. . . .	supercharged identity: belief in abilities
sitting straight	. . . .	supercharged identity: being proud
wears what she wants	. . . .	internal self-assessment: ignores external
wears big earrings	. . . .	internal self-assessment: ignores external

---

As your coding progresses you will have an opportunity to expand on the varied ways in which respondents talk about "internal self-assessment" as a process. To get from the more literal to the conceptual level of analysis, you might mark up what you see as the different and similar ways the respondent talks about the idea of "internal self-assessment." In fact, you might begin to memo about this idea (see the memo on internal self-assessment below). As more and more interviews are analyzed and you continue to memo about what is going on in your data, you may come up with several *analytical dimensions* or subcodes to the concept of "internal self-assessment" (such as the subcode entitled "ignores external").

By memoing on the idea of "internal self-assessment" the researcher is encouraged to theorize about the meaning of this concept and the ways in which it may be related to other factors. In fact, "internal self-assessment" was found to be related to the code categories "cultural pressures to be thin," and "racism." The researchers who conducted this study (see Hesse-Biber et al., 2004) found that black American girls often protect themselves from the cultural pressures of white Western norms of beauty by adopting a stance of "internal self-assessment." The process of "internal self-assessment" was found to be an early coping strategy young children learn within their communities to cope with racial discrimination from the wider society (Hesse-Biber et al., 2004). Let's go "behind the scenes" and look at a memo that was written for this project.

Memo on Internal Self-Assessment

"An interesting and significant pattern of responses emerged in the interviews that we captured with the code "internal self-assessment." This code category describes an orientation in which the self assesses itself according to a set of internal standards rather than by the (external) judgments of others. Typically this type of response emerged in relation to questions about whether the respondent was worried about her weight or appearance or felt pressured to look or act a certain way by peers or the media. Typically, respondents answered this kind of question with an assertion that they didn't care about what others thought about them (**Ignores External**), or that they were only concerned about how good they feel about themselves (**Listens to Internal**), or some combination of the two (**Ignores External Listens Internal**)—for instance: "I don't care what others say, as long as I look good to myself, it doesn't matter what people say"). Nineteen respondents made statements which could be characterized as demonstrating the orientation of *Internal Self-Assessment*.

Often these kinds of statements included the assertion that the respondent loved or felt good about themselves the way they were and that they were not willing to change in order to please others. Some respondents said they learned this attitude from their mother/parents. One respondent said she had learned it from Bill Cosby, her role model: "I watched this show where he told his daughter that she shouldn't worry about what boys say to her. She should just worry about what she thinks about herself."

Significantly, this strategy or attitude protects these girls from the judgments of others and may make them less susceptible to white Western norms of beauty and the propensity to lose themselves in their efforts

(Continued)

(Continued)

to please and attract men. In fact, several respondents said that they did not feel pressured to please men (re: skin color, body size, and other aspects of appearance) because it is more important in their view to feel good about themselves. It is unclear from the interviews to what extent this strategy is based on a kind of defensive denial or on genuine self-acceptance and maturity. This attitude may be a coping strategy developed in the black community in response to racism and societal devaluation. For instance, when asked what it means for her to be a black female, one girl said that it meant "to be strong with what I'm doing and you know I can't really worry about what other people think." This strategy may also develop in response to often fierce teasing by peers that many of these girls describe (see "Influence of peers regarding appearance and weight"). Several subcodes were arrived at for further reflection on the overall meaning of the concept of internal self-assessment:

Subcodes for Internal Self-Assessment

Internal Self-Assessment: Ignores External—Respondent indicates that she doesn't care or is not worried about others' judgments about her. Not willing to change in order to please others.

Internal Self-Assessment: Listens to Internal—Respondent indicates that what matters to her is how she feels about herself or what's on the inside. Often the respondent asserts that the important thing is that she likes/loves/feels good about herself.

Internal Self-Assessment: Ignores External Listens Internal—Respondent indicates that she doesn't care what others think of her because she feels good about herself, or it only matters what she thinks about herself" (Meg Lovejoy) (see Hesse-Biber et al., 2004).

Coding and Memoing: A Dynamic Process

The qualitative coding process consists of cycles of coding, memoing, and coding, as we can observe in Figure 10.2.

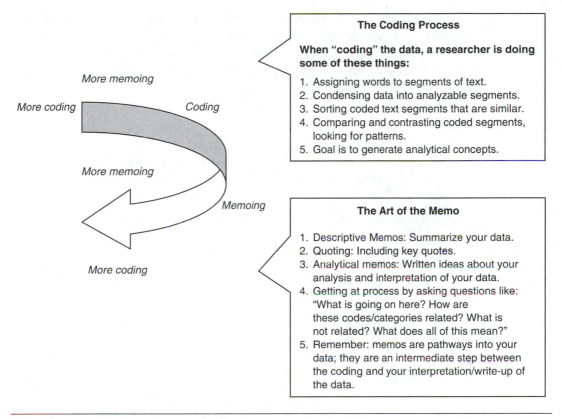

The Coding Process

When "coding" the data, a researcher is doing some of these things:

1. Assigning words to segments of text.
2. Condensing data into analyzable segments.
3. Sorting coded text segments that are similar.
4. Comparing and contrasting coded segments, looking for patterns.
5. Goal is to generate analytical concepts.

The Art of the Memo

1. Descriptive Memos: Summarize your data.
2. Quoting: Including key quotes.
3. Analytical memos: Written ideas about your analysis and interpretation of your data.
4. Getting at process by asking questions like: "What is going on here? How are these codes/categories related? What is not related? What does all of this mean?"
5. Remember: memos are pathways into your data; they are an intermediate step between the coding and your interpretation/write-up of the data.

Figure 10.2   Coding and Memoing: A Dynamic Process

Step 4: Interpretation

It is important to note that analysis and interpretation are not necessarily two distinct phases in the qualitative research process, as we have seen in the case of grounded theory analysis. The process is much more fluid, as the researcher often engages simultaneously in the process of data collection, data analysis, and interpretation of research findings. Memo writing as we have see in grounded theory is an important link between analysis and interpretation. With early observations in the field or with the first interviews conducted, early memo writing will allow the researcher to look at what ideas seem plausible and which ones ought to be revised. David Karp notes the following concerning early memo writing:

Especially at the beginning you will hear people say things that you just hadn't thought about. Look carefully for major directions that it just had not occurred to you to take. The pace of short memo writing ought to be especially great toward the beginning of your work. I would advocate the "idea" or "concept" memos that introduce an emerging idea. Such memos typically run 2 to 3 pages. (Karp, personal communication, September)

Karp (personal communication) notes that after pondering the ideas in the memos and coding the interviews—when you think you have been able to "*grab onto a theme*"—it is time to begin what he terms a "data memo."

By this I mean a memo that integrates the theme with data and any available literature that fits. By a data memo I mean something that begins to look like a paper. In a data memo always array more data on a point than you would actually use in a research paper. If you make a broad point and feel that you have 10 good pieces of data that fit that point, lay them all out for inspection and later use. Also, make sure to lay out the words of people who do NOT FIT THE PATTERN. (Karp, personal communication, September 2004)

Working with qualitative data, whether that data is collected from fieldwork observations or intensive interviewing, the task of the researcher is one of involvement with the data at an intimate level—it means gathering data from individuals or groups of individuals. As we transition from problems with data collection and coding of the data to issues of interpretation and writing up research results, other questions begin to emerge concerning the interpretation of qualitative data. At the heart of this questioning are issues of power and control over the interpretation process.

As we mention in many chapters, some qualitative researchers follow a "scientific" model of research, using patterned research procedures along the lines of the natural sciences and following the tenets of positivism. Under this framework it is imperative that the researcher be "objective," that is, not allow his or her values to enter into the research process. In this model of research the scientist remains "objective" in order to gain a "true" understanding of reality. It is as if "reality" or the "true" picture will emerge if only the researcher is true to the scientific tenet of "objectivity."

Much of qualitative research, however, deals with observation and interviewing, and these are methods which require constant interaction between the researcher and the researched. The researcher can impact the research process at multiple points along the research path—from the choice of research project/problem to the type of research design to the analysis and interpretation of findings. There are important *power dynamics* within the interviewer/interviewee relationship which can affect the interpretation of research results, a topic covered heavily in our discussion of oral history interviews. In the chapter on in-depth interviewing we noted that certain social attributes of researcher and researched can impact issues of power and authority in the research process. We also saw in the chapter on ethnography how these attributes can guide one's entire research project—from gaining access to the setting, to the social relations in the setting, to how one exits the setting.

We now turn to another important way in which the researcher's social attributes can impact the research by looking at issues of interpretation. One of the central issues to be examined in this discussion of the interpretation of findings is the extent to which power differences between the researcher and researched impact the research findings and the researcher's assessment of what they mean (the interpretation process).

- What power does the researcher have in determining whose voice will be heard in the interpretation of research findings?

This question is of central importance in the work of Katherine Borland (1991). She explores the range of interpretive conflicts in the oral narrative she conducts with her grandmother, Beatrice Hanson. She asks her grandmother to relay the story about a trip to the Bangor, Maine, Fair Grounds in which she accompanies her father to the racetrack, an event which happened over 42 years ago. Borland is interested in understanding the different levels of "meaning making" which take place in the telling and interpretation of oral narratives. She recognizes that there are multiple levels of interpreting narratives. A "first-level narrative story"—that is, the story her grandmother tells her—conveys the particular way her grandmother constitutes the meaning of the event. There is, however, a second level of meaning to the narrative. This is the meaning the researcher constructs—it is the meaning of narrative which is filtered through the personal experience and expertise of the researcher. Borland interprets her grandmother's story, but as she listens to the narrative, she reshapes it by filtering her grandmother's story through her own inward personal life experiences and outward experiences—keeping in mind the expectations of her scholarly peers, to whom, she notes, "we must display a degree of scholarly competence" (Borland, 1991, p. 73). Borland uses a gender-specific theoretical

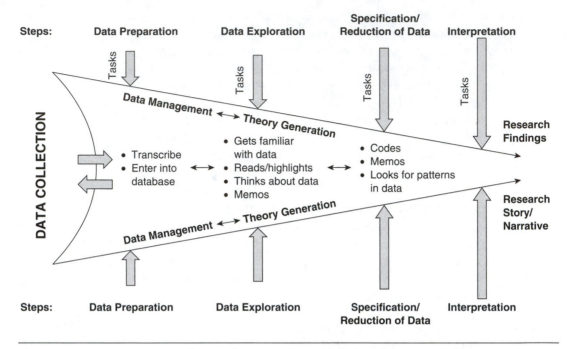

Figure 10.3   Steps in Data Analysis and Interpretation: A Visual Model

lens to interpret her grandmother's story as a feminist account. How-ever, her grandmother does not agree with "her" interpretation. In dealing with these issues of authority or ownership of the narrative, Borland raises issues about who has the authority to interpret narrative accounts. For Borland the answer lies in a type of delicate balancing act. Borland shows her interpretation to her grandmother, and the process of exchanging ideas and interpretations begins. It is clear that no story should remain "unmediated." In other words, the storyteller's viewpoint ought to be pre-sent within the interpretation. While not all conflicts can be resolved, it is important that the researcher be challenged by the narrator's point of view. It is the exchange of points of view that might provide new ways of understanding our data.

Figure 10.3 sums up what we talked about concerning the "four" phases of the data analysis and interpretation process. We can observe that as we move from one step to another we begin to reduce and collapse our data. Coding helps to reduce our data and memoing assists with thinking about how to organize our data into meaningful categories and patterns.

Validity and Reliability of Interpretation

Now that you have interpreted your qualitative data, how do you know your interpretation is valid and reliable? When thinking about the validity of the research findings, you can put your interpretations against competing knowledge claims and see how your findings stand up. You should also provide strong arguments for any knowledge claims you draw from your data. Ask yourself:

- What factors make the research findings resonate for you?

Beyond this, we suggest following Kvale's (1996) three-part model for judging the validity of qualitative data: validity as craftsmanship, communicative validity, and pragmatic validity. These dimensions of validity were discussed in detail in Chapter 2, but at this point in the research we suggest the following steps/questions (derived from Kvale):

- Are you telling a convincing story?
- Try theorizing from your data interpretations.
- Have you reached your findings with integrity—have you checked your procedures?
- Look for negative cases.
- Make your interpretations available for discussion (agreement and debate) among "legitimate knowers" (others in the social scientific community).
- How do your findings impact those who participated in the research, and how do your findings impact the wider social context in which the research occurred?

Once you have gone through this list of checks, and the research findings resonate with you, validity has been appropriately considered. As we saw in Chapter 2, reliability is different in qualitative research compared with quantitative research, which is more easily replicated. With this in mind, in terms of reliability, ask yourself the following:

- Is there "internal consistency" (Neuman, 2003)? Does the data add up?

If your data makes sense, if your method was suited to your question and your procedures were implemented systematically, you can proceed from the interpretive phase to writing up your findings.

● COMPUTER-ASSISTED SOFTWARE FOR QUALITATIVE DATA ANALYSIS

As researchers collect many pages of text, they may want to use a computerized software program to analyze their data. However, important analysis and interpretation issues may arise when using such an analysis tool (Hesse-Biber & Leavy, 2004, p. 410):

- Should a researcher employ a computer software program at all? After all, isn't analysis more of an art form?
- Will the software program interfere with the creative process of analysis?
- Will using a computer software program make the researcher more distant from their data?

As researchers begin the process of turning their research data into a finished product, they may find that their analysis is more complex and overwhelmed by the mounds of research data consisting of unanalyzed textual data that may often number in the thousands of pages of text. Miles and Huberman note:

> A chronic problem of qualitative research is that it is done chiefly with words, not with numbers. Words are fatter than numbers and usually have multiple meanings. This makes them harder to move around and work with. Worse still, most words are meaningless unless you look backward or forward to *other* words. . . . Numbers, by contrast, are usually less ambiguous and may be processed with more economy. . . . Small wonder, then, that most researchers prefer working with numbers alone, or getting the words they collect translated into numbers as quickly as possible. . . . [However] converting words into numbers, then tossing away the words gets a researcher into all kinds of mischief. . . . Focusing solely on numbers shifts our attention from substance to arithmetic, and thereby throws out the whole notion of qualitativeness; one would have done better to have started with numbers in the first place. (1984, p. 546)

A researcher's analysis can be enhanced by the use of computer software packages. As Fielding and Lee (1998) note, the work of researchers over the past 2 decades is being transformed by computerized software programs. Software programs can be categorized into two main types. The first consists of *"generic software"* that was not specifically designed for qualitative research. There are three types of software in this category. "Word processors" assist the researcher with the typing and organizing of field notes and interviews as well as developing an organizing scheme for these data. "Text retrievers" can also quickly sort through a range of data to find a specific pattern or "string" of characters in the data to enable the researcher to identify themes or topics within a large body of data. The last type of generic software is "textbase" managers. These are large database systems that allow for the retrieval of semistructured information, which is entered into "records" and "fields."

A second type of software is that specifically designed for qualitative data analysis. These packages fall into four types: (1) "code and retrieve programs," (2) "code-based theory-building programs," (3) conceptual network-building programs, and (4) "textual mapping software." "Code and retrieve programs" allow codes to be assigned to particular segments of text and make for easy retrieval of code categories using sophisticated "Boolean search functions" (i.e., using "and," "or," and "not" to filter your data). Code-based theory-building programs allow the researcher to analyze the systematic relationships among the data, the codes, and code categories. Some programs provide a rule-based systems approach which allows for the testing of hypotheses in the data, while others allow for a visual representation of the data. Conceptual network-building and textual mapping software programs allow researchers to draw links between code categories in their data, and they see this as an "add-on" feature to their code-based theory building programs. Miles and Huberman note the following uses of computer-assisted software in analyzing qualitative data.

Uses of Computer Software in Qualitative Studies

Making notes in the field

Writing up or transcribing field notes

Editing: correcting, extending, or revising field notes

Coding: attaching keywords or tags to segments of text to permit later retrieval

Storage: keeping text in an organized database

Search and retrieval: locating relevant segments of text and making them available for inspection

Data "linking": connecting relevant data segments to each other, forming categories, clusters, or networks of information

Memoing: writing reflective commentaries on some aspect of the data as a basis for deeper analysis

Content analysis: counting frequencies, sequence, or locations of words and phrases

Data display: placing selected or reduced data in a condensed, organized format, such as a matrix or network, for inspection

Conclusion-drawing and verification: aiding the analyst to interpret displayed data and to test or confirm findings

Theory building: developing systematic, conceptually coherent explanations of findings; testing hypotheses

Graphic mapping: creating diagrams that depict findings or theories

Preparing interim and final reports

SOURCE: Miles & Huberman (1984, p. 44)

Fielding and Lee (1998) note that the field of qualitative software development has grown over time, and there is a growing and extensive national and international community of software users. The growing usage of computer software programs as tools in qualitative analysis raises a number of methodological and theoretical concerns regarding data analysis and interpretation of qualitative data. Sharlene Hesse-Biber (1995) discusses five fears that critics frequently express in discussing the use of computer software. The first of these fears is that computer programs will separate the qualitative researcher from the creative process. Hesse-Biber notes that some analysts liken the experience of doing qualitative work to "artistic work"—just as the artist prefers a brush or pencil and paper, so too do some qualitative researchers. The use of computer technology is seen as incompatible with art. There is a strong fear that the use of computer programs will turn the researcher into an "unthinking and unfeeling human being." Another fear Hesse-Biber discusses is that the line between quantitative and qualitative analysis will be blurred by imposing the logic of survey research onto qualitative research and by sacrificing in-depth analysis for a larger sample. These concerns stem from the fact that computer software programs now permit the easy coding and retrieval of large numbers of documents. The volume of data now collected for some qualitative studies is comparable to quantitative research, and there is the fear that qualitative research will be reduced to quantitative research. Additional issues discussed include the fear that computer usage may dictate the definition of a particular field of study. Computer software program structures often set requirements for how a research project should proceed. This raises concerns among some critics that computer software programs will determine the types of questions asked and specific data analysis plans. Another concern is that researchers will now have to be more accountable for their analysis. Computer programs for analyzing qualitative data require the researcher to be more explicit in the procedures and analytical processes they went through to produce their data and their interpretations. Asking qualitative researchers to be more explicit about their method and holding their interpretations accountable to tests of validity and reliability will raise some controversies: Should there be strict tests of validity and reliability for qualitative data? Hesse-Biber also discusses the fear of the loss of confidentiality through the use of multimedia data.

What computer software programs are out there and which one should I choose?

Hesse-Biber and Crofts (forthcoming) suggest the following set of reflective questions to consider when you are choosing a qualitative software program. This checklist is partly derived from the wisdom of Renata Tesch (1990), Eben Weitzman and Matthew Miles (1995) John Weitzman (2000) and John Creswell and Ray Maietta's (2003) work on computer software usage and the evaluation of specific computer software programs.

The perspective taken by Hesse-Biber and Crofts is grounded in a user's perspective. It would be important for the user to prioritize which questions are most relevant for their research agendas.

1. "What type of computer system do you prefer to work on or feel most comfortable working on? Does the program support your operating system? Do you need to upgrade your system or perhaps purchase a new computer to meet the requirements of a specific program? Do you like the look and feel of a program's interface? What excites you about this program at a visceral level?"

2. "Does the look and feel of the program resonate with your own research style? What is your analysis style? How do you plan to conduct your analysis, and how might computers fit into that style? How might each program enhance (or detract from) your analysis? In what sense? For example, do you plan on coding most of your data—what type of coding do you want to do? How do you prefer your data be retrieved and how important is it to you to be able to look at the full context from which the data was taken? Are

you a visual person? Do you like to see relationships and concepts selected in some type of diagram or network? Do you anticipate quantifying any of your data?"

3. "What research project or set of projects do you anticipate using a computer software program? For example, what type of data does your project consist of—textual, multimedia?"

4. "How do you want a computer program to assist you? What tasks do you want to mechanize? What specific tasks do you want computerized? You may not want all the features espoused by these programs. What are my expectations of what the program will be able to assist you in doing? Are your expectations realistic?"

5. "What resources are available to you? Which programs can my computer support? Which programs can I afford? What resources (time, personnel, material) necessary for learning how to use this program are available to you?"

6. "What are my preconceptions about these programs? How have other users' opinions, product marketing, or other sources of information about qualitative data analysis software programs influenced your preferences? Are your assumptions about programs accurate? What more would you like to learn about particular programs?"

7. "What of the above questions/concerns are most important to you? How would you rank-order what are your most important factors in considering a software purchase? What questions have been left out?" (Hesse-Biber & Crofts, forthcoming)

Reflecting on these types of user concerns *before* attempting to select a qualitative data analysis program puts users in the position to critically evaluate *for themselves* how each program might integrate into their unique research programs. By trying out free demonstration versions and reading through each program's features, as well as looking at examples of how one's colleagues use these programs, the user can get a feel for how each of these programs may be of use to them. Going through this checklist serves to enhance user empowerment and program accountability. It is important to also note that there is no technological tool, regardless of its features, that can independently "perform" your analysis (Hesse-Biber & Crofts, forthcoming).

Computers hold out the promise of revolutionizing the way researchers conduct their analysis, but they also hold out a set of caveats for the qualitative analyst. The researcher who uses these programs should assess their strengths and weaknesses as well as the implications of using computer software programs to analyze qualitative data. We recommend that you try these programs when appropriate and see how they work for you. A useful website for downloading free demonstration copies of commercial and freeware products is known as CAQDAS (Computer-Assisted Qualitative Data Analysis Software) and is available at http://caqdas.soc.surrey.ac.uk/. This Website contains invaluable information on how to select software packages, workshop information on software demonstrations, and a variety of resources for learning more about using computer-assisted qualitative software.

INTERPRETATION AND WRITING UP OF QUALITATIVE DATA: REALIST AND NONREALIST TALES ●

- How can a researcher represent those he or she studies?

Carol Bailey (1996) contrasts two modes of writing up a research project; one is a "realist tale" and the other a "nonrealist tale." In the writing of a "realist" tale, the author is working within a *traditional writing genre* that often takes the form of a scholarly publication for a journal, a research paper/report, or a book-length monograph. The presentation of respondents' voices is assumed to be a "true" reflection of their point of view. The researcher dispenses a realistic tale as the disembodied voice of authority. The writing approach is "formal" and follows the norms of conventional writing one may see in a standard book on writing up research results. What we are addressing is a writing "paradigm" whose very epistemological foundations assume that there is "truth" out there waiting to be captured by the researcher. Bailey explains the "realist tale" writing style in a bit more detail:

> First, the members in the setting are written about, but any details about the author are absent from the body of the text. The text is written as if anyone who was there would have experienced the same thing, so characteristics of the author, even his or her presence are irrelevant to the tale. Second, realist tales contain concrete details of what is done, how often, in what order, and by whom. The goal is not to document everything that occurred, but rather to identify the typical activities and patterns of behavior in the setting. Third, realist tales present the members' points of view. The author includes quotations, interpretations by members,

summaries of informal interviews, and members' accounts and interpretations of events. Finally realist tales include interpretations of the setting. The field research is written as if the meaning of the setting is now understood from the perspectives of the members of the setting. (Bailey, 1996, p. 106)

The postmodern turn in writing goes against the "positivist" model of research writing and strives to push on the boundaries of what is considered "real" and "unreal," often leaving researchers to struggle with exactly how to write up their research findings. This perspective argues that a researcher's power and authority are ever present within the research process and impact how a tale is framed. There is, in effect, a "crisis of representation" launched by postmodern researchers that has in effect changed the very ways that some researchers chose to represent their research findings. The post-modern turn in writing sees all research results as mediated through the researcher's personal values, style, and ethical perspective (Shapiro, 1985–1986 in Richardson, 1995, p. 199). Richardson (1995) talks about several writing styles that strive to take into account the power dynamics in the researcher/researched relationship in order for the voices of the respondents to be heard and to create space for a multitude of tales to be told, each of which is considered, at best, to provide only a partial understanding of the nature of the social world under investigation. An important goal of this type of writing is to especially allow for the voices of those who are subjugated to be heard and to also provide space for the researcher to reflect on their own role within the research process. Several nontraditional genres of writing style have come out of reflections on the postmodern turn. Laurel Richardson (1995, p. 200) sees a narrative form of writing as a particularly useful mode of "reasoning and representation." The narrative form "reflect[s] the universal human experience of time and link[s] the past, present, and future" (Richardson, 1995, p. 218). A narrative form makes "individuals, cultures, societies, and historical epochs comprehensible as wholes" as it allows people to see themselves as part of a larger system (Richardson, 1995, p. 200). In this way, the narrative fosters dialogue; it "reveal[s] personal problems as public issues, to make possible collective identity and collective solutions" (Richardson, 1995, p. 216). Norman Denzin suggests that a new "moment" of writing is emerging in the postmodern era. Researchers are turning their ethnographic findings into various "performative" styles, borrowing from the arts and the humanities to create a writing genre not unlike that of a theater performance (Denzin, 2000).

Experimental writing and traditional writing are not dichotomous choices. A researcher may decide to move to an experimental model in some parts of their research while retaining a more traditional model in other aspects of their writing. We can think of the analysis, interpretation, and writing up of research as an iterative process. Moving from a traditional to an experimental model can take place at different points during the research process. Switching to a more experimental model of research may require time to retool one's research and writing skills. Some researchers working within a more experimental genre may have to contend with some publishers of journals and monographs who do not embrace this form of scholarship (even though many experimental works are published by mainstream journals and publishing houses). And the student who is writing a paper in a course or writing a dissertation thesis may find that his or her professor or thesis adviser is wedded to a more standard writing style (see Bailey, 1996, p. 108).

The postmodern turn toward writing has, overall, encouraged many researchers, even those who embrace a standard writing format, to write with a more *reflexive* style. A reflexive writing style asks questions such as: How will I represent myself in the research process? To what extent have my own biases, values, and points of view entered into my selection of the questions I ask? The data I collect and analyze? What I see and what I don't see? How much of my own voice is represented? In what sense have I not let others speak for themselves? To write reflectively means to have a good sense of your own positionality onto the research you are conducting.

Whatever method of writing you choose, it is important to bear in mind that you are a storyteller charged with telling the story of another. You need to find a way to make sense of large amounts of qualitative data in a way that is congruent to the data you have collected and helped create. Let's join David Karp for a final Behind-the-Scenes.

Behind-the-Scenes With David Karp

What you might now imagine is, a big, thick folder that looks like this [shows a folder with several hundreds of pages]. I'm writing now about obligations, so I'm writing a chapter on obligations. This is a folder that has all the data from my current work on obligations. Well, I would produce such a thing. And I would then spend maybe a month sitting and reading these pages. And if I opened this up, you would see that I scribble on every page almost, making comments. Because what I'm trying to do is have a dialogue with this material. I'm trying to envelop myself in this material. I'm trying to live with it, to be with it, you know, for maybe a month. I mean, the insistent question as I'm scribbling in what are now several hundred pages of material is, "What kind of story can I tell from this data? What are the uniformities that I'm seeing in this material?"

(Continued)

(Continued)

You see, everything we write is, in fact, a story we are telling. We are trying to tell a compelling story, but it must be a story that is disciplined by your data. I mean, you just can't tell *any* story. And the reason that I'm spending a month reading all this stuff and having this dialogue, in effect, with the data, is to try to see my way to what are the underlying forms, the underlying dimensions, of an interesting story, a truthful story, that I can tell about the experience of having depression.

I do things like I create a book index. After I've read this whole thing, making marginal notations, I literally create the equivalent of a book index. So, I might have 25–30 categories and the pages where I find the data for each one of them. What you're trying to do throughout this whole thing is to gain clarity, continue to gain clarity, on what's there. And at some point you stop and say, "This is what I think is a reasonable story that is consistent with this data, a story to tell about the experience of living with depression." I then create a kind of scenario, a vision, an outline of where the chapter might go. Finally, then, I begin to do the writing.

That's another whole thing, because you learn through the process of writing. You might have a scenario about how this thing is going to go, but once you get into the writing and actually begin to use the data to tell the story, you see that maybe the story is going to be slightly different, or it doesn't quite work the way you first thought about it. And I really believe what Howie Becker says in his book on writing: that writing is not the process of putting down what you think; it's the process of *telling* you what you think. So, for me, the actual act of writing tells me what I have to write. You see, what I'm trying to do is to give a picture of qualitative work where you have to continually get as close as you possibly can to the data on the issues that you think are important. It begins with the construction of an interview guide; then you make voluminous notations on the very first interview that you do, and so on. Even transcribing the interviews. I transcribed all these interviews. I have mixed feelings about that. But there is some real value to transcribing them yourself. It's another way to get close.

The key to all of this is to stay close, you know? Which means writing memos all the time. It means writing one-sentence memos. Sometimes you think you've got an idea and it means writing five pages, sometimes a paragraph, sometimes doing a broader assessment—"What do I have here now?" Let me write a memo about some of the themes. The great strength of qualitative analysis, I think, is that the processes of data collection and data analysis go on simultaneously. And if you don't constantly make efforts to analyze the stuff, right from the git-go. . . . If you just collect your data and wait till the end to do the analysis, you are abusing the great strength of this method. And so even with all of that close work, you still get to the point where you have to create the data books—at least that's how I do it—and work intensively with them. By the time you get to that point, you really know what's in these interviews.

CONCLUSION ●

As we end this chapter, we provide you with a checklist you might consult as you begin to undertake your research project. This list of questions is not exhaustive but is meant to highlight some of the important factors you might consider in undertaking your own evaluation of your research project as a whole.

This is the Evaluation Checklist of questions you might ask yourself as you put the finishing touches on your research project. You can think of these as a set of guidelines for evaluation of your research project.

- **Overall Research Question**

Ask: Is my research question clearly stated? Is the question too broad? Too narrow?

- **Issues of Credibility**

Ask: Why should anyone "buy" your story? Trust your story? What are some criteria for assessing the validity of your research study? Do participants recognize their own experiences in your analysis and interpretation of the data? Why or why not? Do you provide an "audit trail" of your work? Can the reader follow the analytical steps you provide as evidence of credibility?

- **Significance of Your Work**

Ask: What is the significance of your research? How is your research linked to other research studies? How can your research by applied to your own discipline and other disciplines? What are some social policy implications of your research project?

- **Data Collection**

Ask: Does the data fit the research question?

- **Method**

Ask: Is the method (describe the method/s you are employing to answer your research question) compatible with the purpose (research question)? How thoroughly and well are your data collection strategies described?

- **Sample**

How were respondents chosen? Are these respondents a valid choice for this research?

- **Ethics**

Ask: How are human subjects issues dealt with?

- **Analysis**

Ask: How did you arrive at your specific findings? Are specific analysis strategies talked about? Have you done what you said you would do? Are data analysis approaches compatible with your research question?

- **Interpretation**

Ask: Can readers get a sense (gestalt) of the meaning of your data from your written findings? Are your research findings placed in context of the literature on the topic?

Ask: Does the evidence fit my data? Are the data congruent with my research question?

- **Conclusions/Recommendations**

Ask: Do conclusions reflect your research findings? Do you provide some recommendations for future research? Do you share what you perceive to be some of the limitations of your research?

Qualitative data analysis and interpretation proceed as an iterative—back and forth—process, keeping in mind the metaphor we suggested in Chapter 7 of putting together the pieces of a puzzle, and the spiral metaphor discussed in the last chapter. A little bit of data can go a long way in gathering meaning and one should not be tempted to gather too much data while failing to reflect on the data bit by bit. What is required is a creative spirit and a set of analytical and interpretative skills. Coding and memoing are two powerful techniques you might employ in the process of understanding and interpreting your data. You may encounter false starts as well as moments of discovery and generation of theoretical insight into the analysis and interpretation of your data. This type of work is not for the "fainthearted." It often requires an attention to detail and perseverance in the face of chaos, as well as a knack for tolerating ambiguity. The writing up of your research also requires that you, the researcher, be reflective of your own positionality—the set of social and economic attributes you bring to bear in analyzing and interpreting your data. It is a journey well worth taking, for the journey leads to our understanding and capturing the lived reality of those we research.

Analytical Categories: Focused coding requires that a researcher develop a set of analytical categories rather than just labeling data in a topical fashion.

Analytical Codes: Analytical codes are not tied as tightly to the text itself, but begin to rely on the researcher's insights for drawing out interpretation.

Analytical Dimensions: As more and more interviews are analyzed you may come up with several analytical dimensions to a given concept.

Coding: Coding usually consists of identifying "chunks" or "segments" in your textual data and giving each of these a label (code). Coding is the analysis strategy many qualitative researchers employ in order to help them locate key themes, patterns, ideas, and concepts that may exist within their data.

Descriptive Codes: Analysis usually begins with looking for descriptive codes within one's data, eventually hoping to generate a set of key *concepts* (categories) which are much more analytical.

Focused Coding: A "focused" coding procedure allows for the building and clarifying of concepts. In focused coding a researcher examines all the data in a category, compares each piece of data with every other piece, and finally builds a clear working definition of each concept, which is then named.

Literal Codes: These words also appear within the text itself and are used as codes. They are usually descriptive codes.

Power Dynamics: There are important power dynamics within the interviewer/interviewee relationship which can affect the interpretation of research results. In Chapter 4 on in-depth interviewing we noted that certain social attributes between researcher and researched can impact issues of power and authority in the research process.

DISCUSSION QUESTIONS ●

1. Discuss the pros and cons of using computerized analysis tools.

2. How can coding best be used when analyzing data; are there any drawbacks to using coding; is there such a thing as too many codes—can this become problematic?

3. What accord does the researcher owe the researched during the analysis phase—should the researched have a say in how they are represented?

4. How does the relationship between researcher/researched affect the interpretation process?

5. Explain grounded theory approaches to data analysis. How is this process inductive?

6. What is the relationship between analysis, interpretation, and writing?

7. How can a qualitative researcher check the validity of his or her findings?

● SUGGESTED WEBSITES

Computer-Assisted Qualitative Data Analysis Software

http://caqdas.soc.surrey.ac.uk/training.htm

This website offers workshops and trainings sessions (as well as general information) about using computer-assisted analysis programs to analyze qualitative data. This is a great website for those interested in exploring computer-assisted analysis.

● REFERENCES

Agar, M. (1980). *The professional stranger: An informal introduction to ethnography.* New York: Academic Press.

Bailey, C. A. (1996). *A guide to field research.* Thousand Oaks, CA: Pine Forge Press.

Borland, K. (1991). That's not what I said!: Interpretive conflict in oral narrative research. In S. Berger Gluck & D. Patai (Eds.), *Women's worlds: The feminist practice of oral history.* New York: Routledge.

Charmaz, K. (1983). The grounded theory method: An explication and interpretation. In R. M. Emerson (Ed.), *Contemporary field research: A collection of readings* (pp. 109–126). Prospect Heights, IL: Waveland Press.

Charmaz, K. (2004). Grounded theory. In S. Hesse-Biber & P. Leavy (Eds.), *Approaches to qualitative research: A reader on theory and practice* (pp. 496–521). New York: Oxford University Press.

Creswell, J. W., & Maietta, R. C. (2003). Qualitative research. In D. C. Miller & N. J. Salkind (Eds.), *Handbook of design & social measurement.* Thousand Oaks, CA: Sage.

Denzin, N., (2000). The practices and politics of interpretation. In N. Denzin & Y. Lincoln (Eds.), *Handbook of qualitative research.* Thousand Oaks, CA: Sage.

Devault, M. (2004). Talking and listening from women's standpoint: Feminist strategies for interviewing and analysis. In S. Hesse-Biber & M. Yaiser (Eds.), *Feminist perspectives on social research.* New York: Oxford University Press.

Fielding, N., & Lee, R. (1998). Introduction: Computer analysis and qualitative research. In *Computer Analysis and Qualitative Research.* London: Sage.

Glaser, B. G., & Strauss, A. L. (1967). *The discovery of grounded theory: Strategies for qualitative research.* Chicago: Aldine.

Harrington, W. (Ed.). (1997). A writer's essay: Seeking the extraordinary in the ordinary. In *Intimate journalism* (pp. xvii-xlvi). Thousand Oaks, CA: Sage.

Hesse-Biber, S. (1996). *Am I thin enough yet? The cult of thinness and the commercialization of identity.* New York: Oxford University Press.

Hesse-Biber, S. (1995). Unleashing Frankenstein's monster: The use of computers in qualitative research. *Studies in Qualitative Methodology* (Volume 5). Westport, CT: JAI Press.

Hesse-Biber, S., & Crofts, C. (forthcoming). Computer-aided software for qualitative data analysis: An historical overview and contemporary perspectives. In S. N. Hesse-Biber & R. Maietta (Eds.), *When methods meets technology.* Thousand Oaks, CA: Sage.

Hesse-Biber, S. N., Howling, S. A., Leavy, P., & Lovejoy, M. (2004). Racial identity and the development of body image issues among African American adolescent girls. *The Qualitative Report, 9*(1), 49–79.

Hesse-Biber, S. N., & Leavy, P. (Eds.). (2004). *Approaches to qualitative research: A reader on theory and practice.* New York: Oxford University Press.

Kvale, S. (1996). *InterViews: An introduction to qualitative research interviewing.* Thousand Oaks, CA: Sage.

Miles, M. B., & Huberman, A. M. (1984). *Qualitative data analysis: An expanded sourcebook* (2nd ed.). Thousand Oaks, CA: Sage.

Miles, M. B., & Weitzman, E. A. (1996). The state of qualitative data analysis software: What do we need? *Current Sociology, 44, 3*(2), 206–224.

Mills, C. W. (1959). *The sociological imagination.* New York: Oxford University Press.

Mishler, E. G. (1991). Representing discourse: The rhetoric of transcription. *Journal of Narrative and Life History, (1),* 255–280.

Neuman, L. (2003). Social research methods: Qualitative and quantitative approaches (3rd ed.). Boston: Allyn & Bacon.

Quinn Patton, M. (2002). *Qualitative research & evaluation methods* (3rd ed.). London: Sage.

Richardson, L. (1998). Writing: A method of inquiry. In N. Denzin & Y. Lincoln (Eds.), *Collecting and interpreting qualitative materials* (pp. 345–371). Thousand Oaks, CA: Sage.

Richardson, L. (1995). Narrative and sociology. In J. Van Maanen (Ed.), *Representation in ethnography* (pp. 198–221). Thousand Oaks, CA: Sage.

Robson, C. (2002). *Real world research* (2nd ed.). Oxford: Blackwell.

Shapiro, M. (1985–1986). Metaphor in the philosophy of the social sciences. *Cultural Critique, 2,* 191–194.

Tesch, R. (1990). *Qualitative research: Analysis types and software tools.* London: Falmer Press.

Weitzman, E. A. (2000). Software and qualitative research. In N. Denzin & Y. S. Lincoln (Eds.), *Handbook of qualitative research* (2nd ed., pp. 803–820). Thousand Oaks, CA: Sage.

Weitzman, E., & Miles, M. (1995). *Computer programs for qualitative data analysis: A software sourcebook.* London: Sage.

Wolcott, H. (2001). *Writing up qualitative research* (2nd ed.). Thousand Oaks, CA: Sage.

Wolcott, H. (1994). *Transforming qualitative data: Description, analysis and interpretation.* Thousand Oaks, CA: Sage.

CHAPTER 11

THE RESEARCH NEXUS

*Staying Centered
and Building Knowledge*

Qualitative research is unique in content, focus, and form. We began this book by explaining that qualitative research is a *holistic process* that explicitly integrates epistemology, theory, and method in order to develop unique approaches to the study of the social world. The relationship between epistemology, theory, and method can be thought of as a "nexus"—the research nexus. As explained, by a holistic process we mean that, from topic selection to final representation, research involves a series of interrelated choices that all influence one another. A prime consideration is the research nexus and how the theoretical and epistemological positions brought to bear on the research process deeply impact the knowledge-building process, including the selection and use of appropriate research tools or methods. By conceptualizing research as a holistic process we are able to attend to a range of factors that influence the knowledge-building process, including:

- Our own topical interests
- Assumptions about what can be known and who can be a knower

- Ethical considerations
- The kinds of research questions we want to ask and to whom
- The kind of data we want to produce
- The tools available for gathering the data
- Practical considerations such as time, money, career, physical safety, and emotional well-being

Methods are but one part of the research endeavor. The research question and method should always work well together and have a "tight fit." From the vast range of options available to qualitative researchers, from perspectives to methods to representational forms, the qualitative research process truly requires creativity and is accordingly often viewed as a craft. Through the metaphors of dancing with data and spiral approaches to research we have illustrated the process by which qualitative researchers build knowledge and generate theory through a process of getting to know the data, jumping in and out of the data, and often engaging in inductive and reflexive practice. Perhaps now we should return to the example that opened this book.

QUALITATIVE APPROACHES TO THE STUDY OF AN EPIDEMIC: CREATING VITAL KNOWLEDGE

Imagine an epidemic is sweeping the globe, but this epidemic is like none ever seen before. The disease causing this epidemic has devastating physical consequences, and, unlike many other diseases, it includes a period often referred to as "living dying." Sadly, there is no cure for this debilitating illness, and the mortality rate is increasing to such an extent that some populations are losing significant numbers of people. Without a cure, the outlook is bleak. But well beyond the devastating transmission and mortality rates of the disease is what really makes it unlike others, the social meanings and stigma attached to infection, which vary across cultures. Beyond the social repercussions of illness is a series of educational, health, and economic realities not associated with epidemics such as cancer that accompany this often long-term illness. Moreover, as can be the case with cancer, even family structures are altered by this disease, as roles are reversed when young people are the ones getting sick, and seniors and sometimes children must care for the dying. And this is just the tip of the iceberg. And of course we all know that we don't have to "imagine" such an epidemic, we have one: HIV/AIDS, from which no group is immune. But from the point of view of research, imagine how limited our knowledge would be if we relied solely on quantitative methods of building knowledge about this disease.

Quantitative research could tell us rates of infection and transmission, the populations most likely to engage in sexual and drug-taking "risk behavior," and even the kinds of risk behaviors different segments of the populations are most likely to engage in. We actually don't have to imagine how limited our HIV/AIDS knowledge would be if we relied solely on quantitative research, we did so for more than a decade, and as a result we got answers to important questions. Quantitative research helped answer research questions such as who is most at risk for infection, what risk behaviors do people participate in, and what people are most likely to engage in particular risk behaviors? However, despite this important information, quantitative research cannot provide answers to questions like why do some people engage in sexual risk behavior, how does social context, environment, and education impact people's sexuality, how does sexual identity help shape sexual behavior, what is the experience of being tested positive, what is the experience of living with HIV/AIDS, how is sexuality shaped by a positive diagnosis, what is the experience of HIV social stigma, what is the experience of caring for a loved one with HIV/AIDS, including any restructuring of the family, role reversal, financial strain, and so on? These are just some of the questions that cannot be addressed through quantitative means, but that qualitative researchers in various fields, including sociology, psychology, anthropology, healthcare, education, and gender studies, are asking and answering. The knowledge that is coming from these multidisciplinary efforts is adding tremendously to our knowledge about HIV/AIDS and how we can create effective prevention, services, intervention, and social reform. Let's take a look at some of the research produced by qualitative researchers across disciplines in order to get a better picture of how significantly qualitative research contributes to our knowledge. In particular, let's look at how qualitative researchers have been able to "get at" understanding sexual risk taking and the experience of caregiving in ways that otherwise remain invisible.

Daniel Wight and Patrick West (1999) conducted a study to compare the effectiveness of survey research versus in-depth interviews in a study of heterosexual males' sexual behavior and understanding. As medical sociologists Wight and West were concerned with how we can best gather information about sexual behavior in light of the AIDS epidemic. Their study included 58 heterosexual males in Glasgow. At one end of a year the men were surveyed and at the following end of the year they participated in qualitative interviews. Wight and West concluded that the in-depth interview data provided greater validity than the survey research. Their finding illustrates two important points.

First, on a substantive level there is a great deal we can learn about important subjects such as human sexuality and risk behavior from qualitative methods. This information also provides a level of depth and description that is vital to expanding our knowledge base. Second, the issue of validity makes us think back to issues we talked about in Chapters 1 and 2. While quantitative research conducted on the basis of positivism is frequently used as a marker of "scientific" work and has been used as the model when creating definitions of validity, in fact, there is now a great deal of research that indicates that well-conducted qualitative research can yield more valid results than quantitative counterparts.

Qualitative researchers across the disciplines are using in-depth interview as their primary method of inquiry in generating knowledge about HIV/AIDS. Mark Davis (2002) conducted an important study merging health and education research. His study aimed at understanding the rationality narratives of gay men who engage in sexual risk behavior. As such, he conducted in-depth interviews with 16 homosexual men, some of whom were HIV-positive and some of whom were HIV-negative. The interviews "explored the ways HIV risk and social context were interpreted" (Davis, 2002, p. 287). This kind of research is integral to our understanding of sexuality and risk and how to help protect people from infection.

In order to create effective prevention education, intervention programs, and cultural health messages that resonate with at-risk persons, it is vital that we understand people's decision-making process. This makes qualitative research essential. While quantitative research can tell us what groups are most likely to engage in particular sexual behaviors, these methods do not tell us why. Quantitative methods of knowledge building simply cannot answer the most pressing social questions of our time, not alone, questions such as: Why do people continue to engage in dangerous sexual behavior? What is motivating them? What pressures do they face? How do people interpret and negotiate the contexts in which they make sexual decisions? As we have tried to demonstrate throughout this text, qualitative research is not simply an augment to quantitative research but rather can help us ask and answer a range of research questions, adding immeasurably to our overall repository of knowledge on any given subject.

When thinking about the history of HIV/AIDS research, it becomes clear why our knowledge base was so limited: most research was conducted in the biomedical community and little was initially done by social scientists. One key thing that anthropological, psychological, and sociological research has contributed to our understanding of this issue and how to create effective prevention programs is that communication between sexual partners is a critical component of sexual risk practices. Put simply, most education programs have always been based on the assumption that sexual partners are two rational-acting individuals who speak freely and openly about their issues, concerns, and so forth. However, there is little research to show that this is actually the case. For example, gender roles impact people's communication in intimate relationships in many different ways and may hinder such "open and rational" communication, the kind we imagine when creating prevention programs. Qualitative researchers across the social sciences, health, and education have added tremendously to our understanding of the context in which people communicate with intimate partners and make personal decisions. This knowledge could not have been gained without the use of qualitative methods. Moreover, researchers from across the disciplines have examined how groups that are particularly vulnerable think about sexuality and what their behaviors are.

In this vein, a multidisciplinary team of researchers, including people in sociology, psychology, and health, came together to study the relationship between gender roles and HIV vulnerability in Roma ("Gypsy") men and women in Bulgaria and Hungary. This group is the largest ethnic minority in Central and Eastern Europe and also a group that has demonstrated high risk sexual behavior. However, until Kelly et al. (2004) decided to use in-depth interviews to study this group, little was known about the cultural and social context in which sexuality was practiced. After conducting 42 in-depth interviews, the researchers had unearthed a great deal of knowledge about sexual norms within this group. For example, male infidelity is commonplace, whereas women are sexually active only with their husbands. This kind of information—and more so the "thick descriptions" of how men and women think and feel about these norms, how they negotiate them, and so on—is vital to the development of effective educational programs aimed at this vulnerable population. Moreover, this study is a perfect example of how qualitative methods cross disciplinary boundaries and allow multi- and interdisciplinary research questions to be asked.

Qualitative research can also add important new insights to older research questions formerly only addressed with quantitative means. For a long time research indicated that men who have sex with men (particularly high-risk sex) and people who use drugs (particularly with needles) are at risk for HIV transmission. But what about men who have sex with men and use drugs? In this case, rates of disease transmission have been attributed to sexual practices; however, the relationship between sexual practices and drug use has not been properly investigated (Clatts & Sotheran, 2000, p. 169).

In order to understand the complex relationship between, and nature of, risk-taking practices among men who are engaged in both homosexual sex and drug use, Clatts and Sotheran (2000) conducted ethnographic public health research with this population. This group is particularly difficult to get at for intervention purposes because little is known about who they are and where they are located (2000, p. 171). Clatts and Sotheran's primary method was participant observation so that they could gain firsthand knowledge about the practices and beliefs of this group, their behaviors, and the rationales for their behaviors. The use of participant observation as a way to understand risk behaviors was integral to "disentangling" the varied factors that contribute to STD vulnerability. This research purpose, and desired population, provides a clear example of when qualitative methods are needed to fill a gap in current knowledge. Ethnography was the method that could best address this research problem.

> Ethnography is not a single method, but rather a set of methodological tools oriented to studying social phenomena in the natural environments in which they are situated, and interacting with research subjects in their own languages and environments. At a general theoretical level, this "naturalistic" research tradition differs from experimental paradigms employed in laboratory and clinical research, for example, which assume, all relevant environmental effects are "known" and can be held constant so that the deductively derived effects or theoretical interest can be "isolated." In contrast, ethnography "problemitizes" the effects of physical and social environment and thus places methodological emphasis on observing a research population in its natural environment. This methodological orientation derives from the assumption that behavioral phenomena are connected in complex ways that can always be reduced to a simple set of relationships amenable to experimental isolation. (Clatts & Sotheran, 2000, p. 170)

It is clear from this comparison of quantitative experiments and qualitative ethnography that qualitative research is necessary for the study of many social phenomena. Ethnography was pivotal in constructing meaningful knowledge in the case of this interdisciplinary research project—what are the practices, thoughts, feelings, and rationales guiding drug use among men who also engage in homosexual sex and what is the relationship between these practices in terms of HIV vulnerability?

The ethnographic research conducted by Clatts and Sotheran provided a great deal of important and previously unknown information about this population. The kind of information they gathered also speaks to the strength of qualitative research. For example, their ethnographic research allowed them to make important distinctions in general categories of behavior popularly thought of as one single category of behavior. Clatts and Sotheran conclude their study by explaining how important descriptive qualitative data is when thinking about creating successful prevention, services, and intervention aimed at particular populations (2000, p. 178).

While qualitative research has helped us learn new information about populations hit hard by this epidemic, qualitative research has also been vital to creating knowledge about the unseen population affected by AIDS, namely, caregivers. This disease is very particular in that it impacts both personal relationships and social institutions in profound ways. Included in the personal and social impact of AIDS is the set of social and cultural meanings attached to the disease—it is a disease with a social component, a stigma attached to the illness that from a social science perspective is as much a problem as the disease itself. This epidemic also presents a unique caregiving situation. While the ill are always in need of care with any long-term illness, this disease and its social and physical peculiarities, presents a unique caregiving circumstance that we need to explore.

For starters, given the age range of those most frequently suffering from the disease, the caregiving relationship often presents a role reversal. In the case of AIDS it is often the elderly parents or young children of an afflicted person who take on the caregiver role (D'Cruz, 2004, p. 414). Additionally, it is arguable that caring for people with AIDS is more stressful than caring for those with other diseases because (1) there is a prolonged "living dying" period, (2) the disease targets mainly young adults who are economically productive and sexually active, and (3) because of the cultural meanings associated with the disease (the stigmatizing nature of the illness) (D'Cruz, 2004, p. 414). Given the uniqueness of caring for a person with this disease and the number of disciplines concerned with the disease and its social, institutional, and interpersonal impact, it is surprising that so little has been done to empirically investigate this aspect of the disease.

Premilla D'Cruz (2004), who works in organizational behavior with a background in the social sciences, decided to conduct a qualitative research project on the family experience of caregiving for those with HIV/AIDS in India, where AIDS is reaching epidemic proportions (D'Cruz, 2004, p. 414). D'Cruz conducted in-depth interviews (in multiple sessions) and ethnographic observations with 19 family members who were giving or receiving care. D'Cruz recruited her subjects through purposive sampling, discussed in Chapter 2. The importance of ethics in the research process really came to bear in direct ways on D'Cruz's research, given the social stigma attached to AIDS and the issues of medical confidentiality and privacy she encountered as she recruited participants. By following her own ethical guidelines, using informed consent and building rapport, she was able to successfully carry out this challenging project. D'Cruz employed a phenomenological approach because she was interested in understanding "experience" and subjective meanings and interpretations. When interviews were conducted within the home she also recorded ethnographic observations in order to understand the "situational context" in which care occurred (D'Cruz, 2004, p. 415). By combining in-depth interview, observations, and a phenomenological approach, D'Cruz ended up with a great deal of qualitative data that she coded thematically after engaging in a process of immersion, as we suggest in Chapter 10. The result is a much greater understanding of the process of taking care of a person with HIV/AIDS and the various ways people experience the role of caregiver given the social context of the disease. This research can be used to continue to develop important research projects on this and related subjects.

● CONCLUSION: QUALITATIVE PERSPECTIVES ON KNOWLEDGE BUILDING

What we can see from the example of HIV/AIDS research is that qualitative research is an important approach to knowledge building. This is a prime example of how researchers across the disciplines, including anthropology, psychology, sociology, healthcare, and education, have all found ways to use qualitative approaches to knowledge construction in order to shed light on various invisible aspects of the AIDS crisis. These approaches have allowed researchers to access subjugated knowledge from marginalized groups both inside the United States and abroad and to conduct their research from multiple epistemological and theoretical perspectives in order to suit their purposes. A comparison between quantitative research and qualitative research shows that without qualitative research there is much we would not understand about this, or any, social phenomenon.

This book has focused on the qualitative approach to knowledge building or, the qualitative interpretive paradigm. Specifically, we have examined the relationship between epistemology, theory, methodology, and method—the research nexus—in the knowledge-building process. What we have learned throughout the book, and that is further evidenced by our closing example of HIV/AIDS research across the disciplines, is that qualitative approaches to knowledge building are an important part of creating new knowledge, expanding or contesting old knowledge, and accounting for perspectives that had previously been invisible. Beyond the causal explanations that typically characterize quantitative research, qualitative research yields descriptive, exploratory, and explanatory data and is often used to generate theory.

This book has focused on both traditional qualitative methods and mixed-methods research designs that combine both qualitative and quantitative research paradigms. The field of qualitative methods is ever changing as new theoretical perspectives such as the turn toward postmodernism as well as large-scale trends toward an increasingly globalized and digitized society challenge researchers to ask new questions that traditional research methods may not adequately address. Methods are not fixed entities, as we have noted; they are "flexible and fluid." There are newly *emergent qualitative methods* under construction that are interspersed throughout the disciplines, and we do touch on a few of these in our book. We call these methods "emergent" because they are new methods or hybrids of tried-and-true qualitative techniques. Imagine how some of these methods might continue to contribute to our knowledge about HIV/AIDS and other important social issues. For example, in our forthcoming book *Emergent Methods in Social Research: Theories, Methods and Methodologies* (Sage), we talk about a method called "daily diary research" created by Hyers, Swim, and Mallett (2005).

Under this method research participants keep a diary in which they record their thoughts, feelings, experiences, and observations about a given topic. Imagine how this method could contribute to our understanding of caring for a child or parent dying of AIDS or the experience of living with an HIV-positive person and dealing with daily discrimination. This is just one of many emergent qualitative methods that will continue to expand our knowledge base. These methods continue to develop in order to address the concerns, questions, and issues brought to light by new theoretical and epistemological positions. In this way, qualitative research is a holistic process not only in practice but also in development, where methods are created in order to operate with new theories.

REFERENCES ●

Clatts, M., & Sotheran, J. (2000). Challenges in research on drug and sexual risk practices of men who have sex with men: Applications of ethnography in HIV epidemiology and prevention. *AIDS and Behavior, 4*(2), 169–180.

Davis, M. (2002). HIV prevention rationalities and serostatus in the risk narratives of gay men. *Sexualities, 5*(3), 281–299.

D'Cruz, P. (2004). The family context of care in HIV/AIDS: A study from Mumbai, India. *The Qualitative Report, 9*(3), 413–434.

Hyers, L. L., Swim, J. K. & Mallett, R. M. (forthcoming). The personal is political: Using daily diaries to examine everyday gender-related experiences. In S. N Hesse-Biber & P. Leavy (Eds.): *Emergent methods in social research*. Sage.

Kelly, J. A., Amirkhanian, Y. A, Kabakchieva, E., Csepe, P., Seal, D. W., Antonova, R., et al. (2004). Gender roles and HIV sexual risk vulnerability of Roma (Gypsies) men and women in Bulgaria and Hungary: An ethnographic study. *AIDS Care, 16*(2), 231–246.

Wight, D., & West, P. (1999). Poor recall, misunderstandings and embarrassment: Interpreting discrepancies in young men's reported heterosexual behavior. *Culture, Health & Sexuality, 1*(1), 55–78.

INDEX

ABOUT THE AUTHORS

Sharlene Hesse-Biber is Professor of Sociology at Boston College in Chestnut Hill, Massachusetts. She has published widely on the impact of sociocultural factors on women's body image, including her book *Am I Thin Enough Yet? The Cult of Thinness and the Commercialization of Identity* (1996), which was selected as one of *Choice* magazine's best academic books for 1996. She is coeditor of *Feminist Approaches to Theory and Methodology: An Interdisciplinary Reader* (1999) and *Approaches to Qualitative Research: A Reader on Theory and Practice* (2004). She is coauthor of *A Feminist Research Primer* and coeditor of *Emergent Methods in Social Research* (both forthcoming from Sage). She is the editor of *The Handbook of Feminist Research* (forthcoming from Sage) and a co-developer of *HyperResearch,* a computer-assisted software program for the analysis of qualitative data (from reesearchware,com).

Patricia Leavy is Assistant Professor of Sociology and Criminology at Stonehill College in Easton, Massachusetts. She is also Director of the Gender Studies Program at Stonehill College. She has published in the areas of feminist and critical theory, collective memory, popular culture, and qualitative and feminist research methods. She is coauthor of *A Feminist Research Primer* and coeditor of Emergent Methods in Social Research (both forthcoming from Sage).

BEHIND-THE-SCENES AUTHORS

Carol Bailey is an Associate Professor in Sociology and the Women's Study Program at Virginia Polytechnic Institute and State University. Her interests lie in the areas of deviant behavior and gender.

Carolyn Ellis is a Professor of Communication and Sociology in the Department of Communication at the University of South Florida. She and Arthur Bochner coedited *Ethnographically Speaking: Autoethnography, Literature, and Aesthetics* (2002) and the AltaMira book series *Ethnographic Alternatives.* She is the author of *Final Negotiations: A Story of Love, Loss, and Chronic Illness* (1995). Her current interests include talking about illness and pain and aging well.

Dana Jack received her Ed.D. from Harvard in 1985 and a Master's in Social Work from the University of Washington in 1972. She has worked in psychological counseling. She is the author of *Behind the Mask: Destruction and Creativity in Women's Aggression* (1999) and *Silencing the Self* (1993). She is also the coauthor of *Moral Visions and Professional Decisions: The Changing Values of Women and Men Lawyers* (1989) with Rand Jack. She has also written extensively in the area of research methodology and gender.

David Karp received his Ph.D. from New York University in 1971. He is the author of *The Burden of Sympathy* (2002), *Speaking of Sadness: Depression, Disconnection, and the Meanings of Illness* (1997), *Being Urban: A Sociology of City Life* (1994), *Sociology in Everyday Life* (1993), *Experiencing the Life Cycle: A Social Psychology of Aging* (1993), and *Research Craft: An Introduction to Social Research Methods* (1992). He is currently a Professor of Sociology at Boston College.

Sarah Maddison received her Ph.D. in Government and International Relations from the University of Sydney in 2004. She is the coauthor of *Activism Speaks: Practical Knowledge and Creative Tension in the Life of Social Movements* (forthcoming) with Sean Scalmer. Her interests lie in the fields of social movement theory, gender, and public policy. She is currently a Lecturer in Australian Politics and Public Policy at the School of Politics and International Relations at the University of New South Wales.

Lindsay Prior is a Reader in Sociology at the University of Wales, Cardiff. He recently served as Director of the Research Programme in Risk and Health at the University of Wales College of Medicine (1999–2002). He is the author of *Documents in Social Research: Production, Consumption and Exchange* (2002). Previous publications include *The Social Organisation of Mental Illness* (1993) and *The Social Organisation of Death* (1989). He is currently working on a number of projects relating to health issues. The latter include studies of risk assessment in genetics, the prescription of antidepressants in primary care, lay attitudes to flu vaccination, lay assessments of traumatic brain injury, lay perspectives on chronic fatigue syndrome, and how caretakers recognize symptoms of Alzheimer's in people with Down's syndrome.

Diana Rose is senior researcher at the User-Focused Monitoring Team at the Sainsbury Centre for Mental Health in London. She received her Ph.D. from London University and has written extensively on qualitative research methods, sociolinguistics, television, and mental health.

Julia Johnson Rothenberg is Professor of Education at the Sage Colleges in the United States. Her primary areas of teaching and researching are the study and practice of teacher preparation, particularly for multicultural education, inclusion practices, and diverse student populations. In addition to her work in the United States, Dr. Rothenberg has taught at the University of Capetown, South Africa, and the University of Lesotho in the Kingdom of Lesotho. She has been a guest of the Netherlands Institute for Advanced Study in the Netherlands, where she worked with faculty at the Rijksuniversiteit Leiden on issues in multicultural education.

Barrie Thorne is Professor of Sociology and Women's Studies at the University of California, Berkeley, where she has also directed the Center for Working Families. She previously taught at the University of Southern California and at Michigan State University. She is the author of *Gender Play: Girls and Boys in School* (1993). She is the coeditor of *Feminist Sociology: Life Histories of a Movement* (1997), *Rethinking the Family: Some Feminist Questions* (1992), and *Language, Gender and Society* (1983). She is currently working on an ethnography of childhood in a mixed-income, ethnically diverse area of Oakland, California.